South Street
A Maritime History of
NEW YORK

By RICHARD C. McKAY

AUTHOR OF "SOME FAMOUS
SAILING SHIPS AND THEIR BUILDER"

HASKELL HOUSE PUBLISHERS Ltd.
Publishers of Scarce Scholarly Books
NEW YORK, N. Y. 10012
1971

First Published 1934

HASKELL HOUSE PUBLISHERS LTD.
Publishers of Scarce Scholarly Books
280 LAFAYETTE STREET
NEW YORK, N. Y. 10012

Library of Congress Catalog Card Number: 76-160128

Standard Book Number 8383-1280-2

Printed in the United States of America

ACKNOWLEDGMENTS

IN preparing this history of New York's shipping I have been aided by the following writings: "An English Visitor in New York," by John Lambert; "Biography of Noah Brown, Ship-Builder" (given to me by a member of the family); "A History of the American Privateers and Letters of Marque During Our War with England," by George Coggeshall; "The Picture of New York," printed for and published by A. L. Goodrich and Company; "The Old Merchants of New York," by Walter Barrett, Clerk; "Incidents in the Life of Jacob Barker," author unknown; "Minutes to A. A. Low, Records of the Chamber of Commerce, January 9, 1893"; a brief sketch of "The Chamber of Commerce of the State of New York," by L. Elsa Loeber; "Treatise on Marine Architecture," by John W. Griffiths; "John Taylor" and "John Johnson," both by Mrs. Emily J. de Forest; "Clipper Ship Era," by Captain Arthur H. Clark; "Greyhounds of the Sea," by Carl C. Cutler; "A Memorial to Captain Charles H. Marshall," by William Allen Butler, and "The Diary of Philip Hone," from which I have been kindly granted permission to quote by the New York Historical Society, who also gave me access to their files of old New York newspapers.

RICHARD C. MCKAY.

Contents

PART ONE

Pre-Constitution Period

1783–1789

PAGE

THE DAWN OF AMERICAN COMMERCE UPON NEW YORK'S EAST RIVER WATERFRONT, WHEN WE DEPENDED UPON SMALL BRITISH "COCK-BOATS" FOR INTERNATIONAL COMMERCE — ARISING FROM THE WRECK OF THE REVOLUTIONARY WAR, THE FIRST AMERICAN VESSEL SAILS FROM NEW YORK TO GREAT BRITAIN—FRENCH LINE OF PACKETS—BEGINNING OF THE CHINA TRADE, AND TWO PIONEER VENTURES THEREIN—HOW ENGLAND'S NAVIGATION LAWS, PREVENTING OUR TRADING WITH THE WEST INDIES AFTER THE WAR, WORKED MOST INJURIOUSLY TO HER HOME INTERESTS—NEW YORK'S AFTER-WAR RECOVERY   3

PART TWO

After the Constitution and Until the Close of the Eighteenth Century

1789–1799

BENEFICIAL EFFECT TO AMERICAN SHIPPING OF LEGISLATION BY THE FIRST UNITED STATES CONGRESS IN 1789—OUR FOREIGN TRADE EXTENDED TO SEAS NEVER BEFORE VISITED BY AMERICAN SHIPS—A FRANCO-BRITISH NAVAL COMBAT OFF SANDY HOOK TREATED AS A GALA AFFAIR—LAUNCH AT ACKERLEY'S SHIPYARD, A GREAT SOCIAL EVENT—DEVELOPMENT OF SHIP-

	PAGE
BUILDING AT NEW YORK—MATERIAL USED FILLING-IN SOUTH STREET CLAIMED CAUSE OF MUCH SICKNESS—CITY FATHERS GENEROUSLY GRANT FUND "TOWARD SUBSISTING" IMMIGRANTS—FIRST VESSEL TO CARRY STARS AND STRIPES AROUND THE WORLD—ANECDOTAL ACCOUNT OF A VOYAGE FROM BRISTOL TO NEW YORK IN 1797—REMINISCENT OF A DISTINGUISHED GROUP OF MERCHANTS AT THE FAMOUS BELVEDERE CLUB—OUR SHIPS CONTINUE BRINGING IN SLAVES, "INDENTURE MEN"—AN HONOR ROLL OF NEW YORK MERCHANTS AT THE CLOSE OF THE EIGHTEENTH CENTURY	15

PART THREE

New York Shipping and Commerce From the Beginning of the Nineteenth Century Until Congress Declares War Against Great Britain

1800–1812

SOME FAMOUS OLD SHIPBUILDERS AND SHIPYARDS ALONG THE EAST RIVER—THEIR ACTIVITY MEANT MUCH FOR NEW YORK'S COMMERCE—HENRY ECKFORD AND HIS GREAT WORK—CHRISTIAN BERGH, MASTER-SHIPBUILDER—SHIPYARD MECHANICS INDITE A MEMORIAL TO THE UNITED STATES SENATE AND HOUSE OF REPRESENTATIVES—JACOB BARKER'S CAREER—NOAH TALCOTT, MERCHANT—NEW YORK MERCHANTS' PROTEST TO PRESIDENT JEFFERSON AGAINST BRITISH ATTACKS UPON AMERICAN VESSELS—JEFFERSON'S "LONG EMBARGO"—JOHN JACOB ASTOR MANAGES TO SEND HIS SHIP *BEAVER* TO CHINA—BIOGRAPHICAL SKETCH OF JOHN JACOB ASTOR—AN ENGLISH VISITOR'S INTERESTING DESCRIPTION OF THE CITY'S SHIPPING, BEFORE AND AFTER THE EMBARGO OF 1807-8—NOTES ON AFRICAN SLAVE TRADE—PROHIBITED AFTER JANUARY FIRST, 1808, BY ACT OF CONGRESS—THE *PHOENIX*, THE FIRST STEAM VESSEL TO NAVIGATE THE OCEAN—HISTORY OF MARINE INSURANCE—JEFFERSON'S AND MADISON'S ATTITUDE TOWARD THE GROWTH OF THE AMERICAN MERCHANT MARINE—SHORT RELIEF AFFORDED BY NON-INTERCOURSE ACT—ERIE CANAL PROJECT VIRTUALLY STARTED IN 1811—BRITISH AGGRESSIONS CONTINUE, SO, FINALLY, WAR IS DECLARED!	35

Contents

PART FOUR

How New York's Merchants, Ship-Builders and Her Shipping Interests Contributed to the Defense of Our Country During the Second War for Independence

1812–1815

NEW YORK IN 1812—ITS DEFENSELESS CONDITION—SHIPBUILDERS, "THE TRUE VICTORS OF THE BATTLES UPON OUR GREAT LAKES"—GOVERNOR DANIEL D. TOMPKINS, THE GREAT WAR GOVERNOR—MAYOR DE WITT CLINTON—COMMODORE ISAAC CHAUNCEY ARRANGES FOR CREATING A FLEET, ETC., ON GREAT LAKES—MEETS NEW YORK'S FOUR LEADING SHIPBUILDERS AT COLONEL RUTGERS' MANSION—HENRY ECKFORD GOES TO SACKETT'S HARBOR AND BUILDS CHAUNCEY'S FLEET — DEPARTURE ON FULTON'S STEAMBOAT *PARAGON*—ECKFORD AND HIS MEN ENTER UPON A WONDERFUL SHIPBUILDING CONTEST—NOAH BROWN IS CALLED—SETS OUT FOR LAKE ERIE WITH A BAND OF MECHANICS FROM NEW YORK'S EAST SIDE SHIPYARDS TO BUILD COMMODORE PERRY'S WARSHIPS—PROGRESS OF EVENTS IN NOAH BROWN'S BIOGRAPHY—POEM "NOAH BROWN"—NEW YORK GOES A-PRIVATEERING—BRIEF HISTORY OF PRIVATEERING—NAPOLEON ADMITS AMERICAN PRIVATEERS IN FRENCH PORTS—HARRYING FLEETS OF PRIVATEERS DID MUCH TO BRING THE WAR TO AN END—SUFFERING OF NEW YORK MERCHANTS FROM DEPREDATIONS BEFORE THE WAR—SOME NOTED NEW YORK PRIVATEERS AND THEIR ACHIEVEMENTS—TRADE CONDITIONS DURING WAR AND EMBARGOES—EXCITEMENT CAUSED BY GLAD TIDINGS OF PEACE.................................... 65

PART FIVE

A Period of Invention, Prosperity and Progress

1815–1829

AMERICAN COMMERCE SPRINGS INTO LIFE WITH THE ADVENT OF PEACE—AGAIN THE SHIPYARDS ARE BUSY AND SOUTH STREET BECOMES A BUSY HIVE OF INDUS-

TRY—MARCH THIRD, 1815, CONGRESS PASSES A LAW TO OBTAIN RECIPROCITY IN FOREIGN TRADE—VIGOROUS STRENGTH IS INFUSED IN EVERY DEPARTMENT OF OUR COMMERCE—PROGRESS AND COSMOPOLITANISM OF THE NEW YORK MERCHANT—EAST INDIA MERCHANTS —SOME HISTORY ABOUT N. L. AND G. GRISWOLD— MURRAY, MUMFORD AND BOWEN, MURRAY AND MUMFORD AND GORDON S. MUMFORD—TALBOT, OLYPHANT AND COMPANY—ANENT SUPERCARGOES—INTERESTING CAREER OF THOMAS H. SMITH AND SONS, THE GREATEST TEA MERCHANTS IN THE UNITED STATES—HOW A SOUTH STREET MERCHANT COULD BE A "PLAY BOY"—THE "FIRE CLUB" AND WHEN THEY WERE "STUMPED"—BIOGRAPHICAL SKETCHES OF JONATHAN GOODHUE, PELATIAH PERIT, AND THE HOUSE OF GOODHUE AND COMPANY—ANOTHER "EAST INDIA FIRM," HOYT AND TOM—A SCOTTISH MERCHANT OF GLASGOW AND NEW YORK, JOHN TAYLOR—ARCHIBALD GRACIE AND HIS WONDERFUL CAREER—GRACIE'S PETITION TO CONGRESS—G. G. AND S. HOWLAND—FIRM CHANGED TO HOWLAND AND ASPINWALL—MINTURN AND CHAMPLIN, WHO CARRIED ON THE LARGEST CHINA BUSINESS IN NEW YORK—LOSS OF THEIR SHIPS AND CARGOES ABROAD CAUSES FAILURE—AFTERWARDS, JOHN T. CHAMPLIN ORGANIZES THE FARMERS LOAN AND TRUST COMPANY, NEW YORK—LIFE STORY OF ECCENTRIC PRESERVED FISH—FORMATION OF THE FIRM, FISH AND GRINNELL—POST AND RUSSELL, JOHN W. RUSSELL, MERCHANTS AND SHIPOWNERS—THE LARGEST NEW YORK MERCHANT IN IRISH TRADE, WILLIAM NEILSON—ORGANIZES NEILSON AND SON— FATHER AND SON ENTER INSURANCE BUSINESS, SERVING IN VARIOUS OFFICIAL CAPACITIES—JOHN PATRICK; SHEDDEN, PATRICK AND COMPANY; B. AYMAR AND COMPANY—INTERESTING ACCOUNTS ABOUT "BEN" AYMAR—A FEW FACTS RELATING TO YANKEES CAPTURING BUSINESS IN NEW YORK—WHEN THE BATTERY WAS A FASHIONABLE PROMENADE; STATE STREET AND AROUND BOWLING GREEN WAS THE "SEAT OF FASHION"—WHEN NEW YORK'S WATERFRONT ELICITED ADMIRATION FOR ITS NATURAL ATTRACTIONS—STATE STREET THE IDEAL PLACE IN NEW YORK FOR A RESIDENCE—WHEN THE "PEEP O'DAY BOYS" LOOKED FOR THEIR SHIPS COMING INTO PORT FROM THE BATTERY —THE SIGNAL STAFFS AT THE BATTERY TO ANNOUNCE ARRIVAL OF SHIPS—THE OLD MERCHANT TAKES AN

List of Illustrations

House Flags	*Frontispiece*

FACING PAGE

The First Vessel to make the Direct Voyage from the United States to China, Sloop *Experiment*, 85 tons, Coming into Her Wharf at New York—1786	8
Hoisting Elephants on Shipboard	18
Facsimile of Custom House Entry Made by John Aspinwall	18
Henry Eckford	40
Sunday Morning in the Office of the "Courier and Enquirer"	54
Coffee House Slip and New York Coffee House	54
Preserved Fish	116
Moses H. Grinnell	116
Black Ball Packetship *Montezuma*	130
South Street, New York City—View in 1828 with Packet Ship *Leeds* at Her Pier	150
South Street about the Year 1831, with Warehouses, etc., at Dover Street	160
"Mr. Boyd Finally Met Mr. Paulding"	168
David Brown	176
Jacob Bell	176
Jacob A. Westervelt	176
View of the Great Conflagration of December 16th and 17th, 1835, from Coenties Slip	186
Edward Knight Collins	200
The Signal Gun of Distress on the *Arctic*	200
The *Victoria*, New York-London Packet, Entering New York Harbor	232
Stevedores Unloading a Ship on South Street	250
Scene Showing "Landing from an Emigrant Ship"—1853	254
Preaching in the Open Air—Along the New York Docks	246
Rainbow—Pioneer New York Built Clipper—1845-1848	258

I

THE DAWN OF AMERICAN COMMERCE UPON NEW YORK'S EAST RIVER WATERFRONT, WHEN WE DEPENDED UPON SMALL BRITISH "COCK-BOATS" FOR INTERNATIONAL COMMERCE—ARISING FROM THE WRECK OF THE REVOLUTIONARY WAR, THE FIRST AMERICAN VESSEL SAILS FROM NEW YORK TO GREAT BRITAIN—FRENCH LINE OF PACKETS—BEGINNING OF THE CHINA TRADE, AND TWO PIONEER VENTURES THEREIN—HOW ENGLAND'S NAVIGATION LAWS, PREVENTING OUR TRADING WITH THE WEST INDIES AFTER THE WAR, WORKED MOST INJURIOUSLY TO HER HOME INTERESTS—NEW YORK'S AFTER-WAR RECOVERY.

IN THE present enlightened state of the world, and the powerful influence which commerce exercises over everything connected with national politics and human affairs, it is interesting and instructive to trace the course of American commerce from its first dawning, as it were, to its achievement of brightness and splendor upon New York's leading commercial thoroughfare or "Street of Ships," South Street, when it developed from a newly-filled-in shore into an extensive line of wharves crowded with sailing vessels from the four corners of the earth.

At the time President Washington lived and signed documents in a colonial mansion on Franklin Square, New York depended upon small English vessels, brigs of less than 200 tons burthen, for much of its international communication, passenger and mail service, as well as import and export trade with England, the Maritime Provinces of Canada and other English colonies. Not inaptly called "Coffin Brigs," because so many of them had succumbed beneath the wintry waves of the North Atlantic, it seems incredible that they continued to ply their trade for almost twenty-five years after American Independence had been declared!

In connection with the issue of "sea letters" for the *Empress of China*, we find a letter recorded in the *Journal of Congress* (1784) which is interesting because of its pompous phraseology. Those for whom the documents were intended are addressed as follows:

"Most serene, most puissant, puissant, high illustrious, noble, honorable, venerable, wise and prudent emperors, kings, republics, princes, dukes, earls, barons, lords, burgomasters, counsellors, as also judges, officers, justiciaries, and regents of all the good cities and places, whether ecclesiastical or secular, who shall see these patents or hear them read." How gratifying that the form of address for international communication is now much simpler.

When Supercargo Shaw arrived at Whampoa, the Chinese nicknamed him and all Americans after him "New People," in contradistinction to the British. With a cargo, mostly tea, also a quantity of silks, muslin and nankeens and chinaware, the *Empress* set sail for home, on December twenty-sixth, by way of the Cape of Good Hope. She brought over three services of table china, marked in Canton with the insignia of the Cincinnati; one of these, more elaborately decorated than the others, Major Shaw presented to General Washington, and one to General Knox. It is said that the third is still in the possession of his descendants.

The successful establishment of a direct trade with the far-distant Chinese empire, gave fresh impulse and energy to American industry, and other New York vessels soon followed the *Empress of China's* lead.

In 1786, aboard the ship *Hope*, James Magee master, Major Shaw sailed a second time from New York, holding the honorary title of United States Consul at Canton, to establish the first American commercial house in China. He had rented a godown and hoisted his flag beside the ensigns of the great trading nations of Europe, when the *Empress of China* arrived on her second voyage, and not long afterward, the ship *Grand Turk*, of Salem, one of enterprising King Derby's fleet. So rapidly did the commerce he opened increase, that, in 1789, there were fifteen American vessels at Canton—a greater number than from any other nation, except Great Britain.

Pre-Constitution Period

Nearly all the prominent merchants who figure in the newspaper advertisements of the day, were located in the vicinity of the Old City Dock. (The region between the present Coenties Slip and Whitehall Street, is about the site of this wharf, the first built on Manhattan.) Old City Dock was the cornerstone of the commerce of our metropolis, the progenitor of our miles of wharves. That famous monopoly, The West India Company, built it, and its quaint, round-bottomed, high-pooped Dutch ships were the first vessels there. They gathered the grain, pelts, lumber, potash and medicinal herbs that then formed New Netherlands' exports, or landed the hardware, groceries, household goods, brick, "cow calves" and "ewe milk sheep" and other peculiar Dutch imports. As late as 1702, this dock formed almost the sole wharfage of the city, and seventy-four vessels, pinks, galleys, snows, a few brigs and ships, were moored to it during the year, two-thirds of them from the West Indies and Southern provinces. The town then contained 5,250 inhabitants, living in 750 dwellings, so that the wharf was ample for their needs.

New York's recovery after the Revolution was amazing. Within five years the population had reached 30,000, and her commerce was fast returning to its former figure. While South Street, in certain places was constructed before the War, work was now pursued diligently, filling in the East River to afford deep-water wharfage for the larger ships needed for the long Far Eastern voyages. As the land was extended into the river, various merchants, as the riparian owners, became possessed of lots on Water Street. On the further filling-in of the riverfront, houses were added on Front Street; and on its final extension to South Street, say in 1802 to 1809, some merchants put up warehouses there on an improved plan, which for a long time served as models.

The second venture to China sailed from New York in 1785, when a few of her merchants pooled their resources in order to send a little Albany sloop, of only eighty-five and one-half tons, to Canton, her principal owner being Elias Nexsen, who, it is claimed, was the first Collector of the Port of New York under the Continental Congress. She was well-named *Experiment*. It is said that she took 1,000 pounds of ginseng along, valued at 5,000 dollars, and 40,000 dollars' worth of Spanish "pillar" dollars, and about seventy-five dollars' worth of furs—all to be exchanged for tea, silks, nankeens, and the bright willow-ware to be the favorite breakfast china of generations of Americans. This crowded the sloop, and her master, Captain Stewart Dean, was allowed 100 pounds additional perquisites for the use of his cabin—cheap when compared to what, in later years, American clipper ship commanders received for letting "dead Chinamen in pine boxes" usurp their cabins, en route from San Francisco to Hong Kong or some other Chinese port.

Upon her appearance in Chinese waters, the *Experiment* was so small, she was regarded as the tender of some larger vessel and was asked—"Where is the large ship?" To which query came the astounding reply, "We are the great ship." It was, indeed, a matter of much surprise to the Chinese and the European residents at Canton that such a small vessel, from so remote a country as the United States, should visit that port. So tiny was this little craft that no insurance could be effected for her long and hazardous voyage. Furthermore, it must be borne in mind that whatever trading New York enjoyed with the Far East had been through the British East India Company, and Captain Dean had to use one of their old charts and sailing directions "To and From and In the Indian Ocean."

Again, there were pirates to be reckoned with, murderous, blood-thirsty Chinese and Malayans, whose swift proas swarmed in the Malay Archipelago and adjacent waters, to cope against which the *Experiment* mounted six carriage guns, and carried plenty of muskets, boarding-pikes and cutlasses. Evidently the owners appreciated the hazards of this voyage, when they issued these instructions to the commander of their vessel: "When you reach the Straights (Straits) of Sunda, it is recommended to you to keep yourself always on your guard against the natives of Java and the other Islands, and to endeavor to get through the Straights (Straits) and to your destined port as soon as you can."

Her crew is variously estimated, from seven to twenty men and boys—all records agree there were "two boys." But from an original source, we learn that, in addition to Stewart

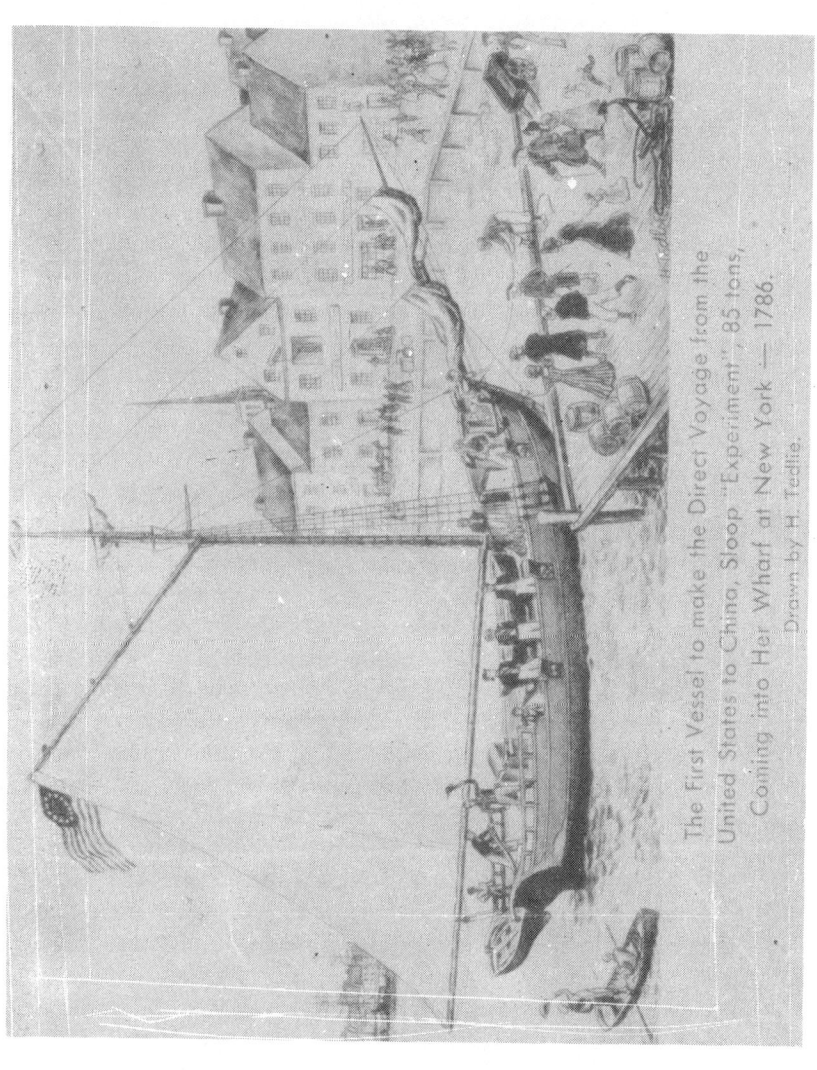

The First Vessel to make the Direct Voyage from the United States to China, Sloop "Experiment", 85 tons, Coming into Her Wharf at New York — 1786.

Drawn by H. Tedlie.

Pre-Constitution Period 9

Dean, master; John Whetten,* 1st mate, who afterwards commanded some of the finest ships out of New York, owned by John Jacob Astor and other prominent merchants of that city; and Isaac Seaman, 2d mate; she was manned by five seamen, whose names are given, and "two boys," one of whom was a negro, attractively named "Prince." In this, the early period of our Far-Eastern commerce, the most amazing records of youthful energy and invention are to be found. Boys went to sea at thirteen, landed upon the quarter-deck at seventeen and often in the captain's berth at nineteen. Vessels of two or three hundred tons' burden were sent out to circumnavigate the globe, under young shipmasters who had never crossed the Atlantic.

The *Experiment* was the first vessel to make the direct voyage from the United States to China. Her master being unacquainted with the customs regulations at Canton, did not know that "cumshaw" duty was as large on a sloop of eighty-five tons as on a ship registering 500 tons. This and other excessive charges exacted by the Chinese, used up all the profits of the voyage. In looking through the *Experiment's* papers, now at the New York Historical Society, in New York, the writer came across this, which lists Stewart Dean's disbursements: "Paid for Measurements and Presents at Canton, $3,166.00." Verily, your Cantonese officials, of high and low degree, merchants of the "Hong" class and others; in fact, every Chinaman with whom these mariner-merchants came in contact, practiced the gentle art of graft as scientifically as any of our present-day "one-way pocket" politicians, bank presidents and others.

During the Revolutionary War Captain Dean commanded a private armed vessel, called the *Enterprise*, which captured the first British government cruiser that was taken by the Americans after the Declaration of Independence; so that when the *Experiment* warped alongside the wharf in New York, her commander and his crew were in full uniform, and the scene, which was witnessed by an admiring throng, was enlivened by "martial music and the boatswain's whistle, with all the pomp

---
* John Whetten was the ninth President of the Marine Society of the Port of New York and also, the first Governor of Sailors' Snug Harbor.

and circumstance of war." The gallant ex-privateersman had things done in regular man-of-war fashion.

As Britain's colonies we could trade freely with the British possessions in America, and the West Indies, exchanging lumber, corn, fish, and other provisions, together with horses and cattle, for sugar, molasses, coffee and rum; but immediately upon the conclusion of the war the people of the new nation were put on the same footing as other foreign countries, and under the operations of the British navigation laws were, in common with them, excluded from nearly all participation in an extensive and flourishing part of their former maritime commerce. And, as illustrating the then temper of the times and the illiberal spirit that then pervaded the counsels of nations, it may be mentioned that this policy was persevered in by Great Britain, even after it was proved in repeated instances to work most injuriously to her own home interests, and to have occasioned great suffering upon her West Indian colonies. Thus, between 1780 and 1787, no less than 15,000 slaves were known to have perished from starvation in the British West Indies, by reason of inability, through the operation of the British navigation laws, to obtain the requisite supplies of food from us at a period when the home grown portion of their substance had been destroyed by successive hurricanes.

It is asserted by some authorities, that the exclusion of American vessels from trade in the West Indies, had the beneficial effect of our mariners going on long voyages they would never have risked, and drove our ships and our sailors to the uttermost parts of the world.

How few Americans realize that from the signing of the Treaty of Versailles, in 1783, we had no President or formal head of government until 1789, when George Washington stood at the helm of the ship of state. During those six years, although business revived slowly, the mercantile interests of the city were discussed with vigor and various were the methods proposed for encouraging trade. It must have been galling to the patriotic New Yorker, when looking through the shipping notices of his *Daily Advertiser,* even as late as the spring of 1789, to see—"*For Liverpool,* the ship *Paragon,* a new British vessel, with a Mediterranean pass; or "*For Charter to*

Jamaica, ship *Nelly,* with an undeniable British register." In another part of the same newspaper, he would find: *"For Cork*—the ship *Bonny Lass,* a British bottom, with a Mediterranean pass."

But a new era was soon to dawn, so we will whip the tale along!

PART II
AFTER THE CONSTITUTION AND UNTIL THE CLOSE OF THE EIGHTEENTH CENTURY

1789—1799

II

BENEFICIAL EFFECT TO AMERICAN SHIPPING OF LEGISLATION BY THE FIRST UNITED STATES CONGRESS IN 1789—OUR FOREIGN TRADE EXTENDED TO SEAS NEVER BEFORE VISITED BY AMERICAN SHIPS—A FRANCO-BRITISH NAVAL COMBAT OFF SANDY HOOK TREATED AS A GALA AFFAIR—LAUNCH AT ACKERLEY'S SHIPYARD, A GREAT SOCIAL EVENT—DEVELOPMENT OF SHIPBUILDING AT NEW YORK—MATERIAL USED FILLING-IN SOUTH STREET CLAIMED CAUSE OF MUCH SICKNESS—CITY FATHERS GENEROUSLY GRANT FUNDS "TOWARD SUBSISTING" IMMIGRANTS—FIRST VESSEL TO CARRY STARS AND STRIPES AROUND THE WORLD—ANECDOTAL ACCOUNT OF A VOYAGE FROM BRISTOL TO NEW YORK IN 1797—REMINISCENT OF A DISTINGUISHED GROUP OF MERCHANTS AT THE FAMOUS BELVEDERE CLUB—OUR SHIPS CONTINUE BRINGING IN SLAVES, "INDENTURE MEN"—AN HONOR ROLL OF NEW YORK MERCHANTS AT THE CLOSE OF THE EIGHTEENTH CENTURY.

THE Fathers of our Republic, all of them from seaboard states, and many of them acquainted with the shipping business, by legislation, sound in economy and wise in patriotism, gave the American Merchant Marine an impetus that was no less than magical! The first real legislation of the First Congress of the United States, when they met at New York in 1789, was to encourage shipping, and they passed laws strongly protective of shipbuilding, and went so far as to practically exclude foreign tonnage from our domestic trade. The Americanism of their action has never been exceeded in the legislative history of this country, and the attendant growth of our merchant fleet, from December thirty-first, 1789, when we had 123,893 tons of shipping in deep-water commerce, which seven years later had increased to 576,733 tons, is without parallel in the annals of commerce. These congressional acts induced many of the aliens in our commerce and navigation to become citizens, and the policy adopted resulted in our ship-owning and shipbuilding trades acquiring a large share of capital, enterprise and skill from foreign countries.

Previously American ships had been compelled to go into the few fields of employment open to them; soon our foreign trade not only returned to the channels in which, to some extent, it had flowed before the war, but it began to extend itself to seas never before visited by American vessels. Not only were the ports of Western Europe resorted to by a daily increasing number of our ships, but those of the Baltic and the Mediterranean were now, for the first time, visited by our countrymen; and, not content with this, American merchants turned their thoughts to China, to the Indian Archipelago, to the northwestern coast of North America, and the islands of the Pacific, several of which were discovered by our navigators; for, it must be borne in mind, the United States had bred a purple-blooded, iron-corpuscled tribe of sea goers who recognized no peers on salt water—and who admittedly had none! The courage and self-reliance with which these enterprises were undertaken, almost surpass belief.

A little digression, leading up to a Franco-British naval combat off Sandy Hook, when New York was visibly disturbed by the irregularities of the French Revolution, may now interest our readers, especially the dyed-in-the-wool New Yorker who continues to crave excitement, as did, evidently, his Knickerbocker forebears. Let us visualize conditions as they were late in the summer of 1793. Here are the scenes: The Liberty Cap, the Red Cockade, the song of the Camarole, the rencontre of the French frigate *L'Ambuscade* with the *Boston*, British, and the commotion arising from Jay's treaty. Jealousy of Britain, affection for France, was now the prevailing impulse, and the business of the day was often interrupted by tumultuous noises in the streets. Groups of sailors might be collected on the docks and at the shipping along the East River waterfront, ready to embark on a voyage of plunder or in the peaceful pursuit of commercial gain; merchants and traders in detached bodies might be seen discussing the hazards of commerce, but the fraternity of the two nations was the great theme.

At the foot of Maiden Lane and South Street lay the frigate that brought Citizen Gênet to our shores, *L'Ambuscade*, with liberty-caps conspicuously decorating her head, her foremast, and her stern; and from her masts floated white burgees, with words that echoed the egoistic proclamation of the French National Convention. Captain Dennis of the U. S. Revenue vessel *Vigilant*, arriving in port, stated that Captain George W. Courtenay of the *Boston*, off Sandy Hook, challenges Captain Bompard of the *L'Ambuscade* to single combat. The challenge was accepted by the French commander, but, not receiving an answer, he sallied forth to meet the issue. Nine vessels were chartered by different parties to see the action; and, from all accounts, this naval duel, which occurred August third, 1793, had as eager a crowd of excursionists watching it as ever saw an international yacht race sailed over the same waters. Bets had run high as to the results of the encounter, for, evidently it was looked upon as a gala affair, and there was much popular excitement and bustle.

A severe action ensued, the *Boston* was much damaged, and Captain Courtenay killed. When the French frigate returned to the city after the engagement, the delight of the multitude gathered to meet it burst forth in cries as wild as ever resounded through Paris under the bloody ministers of misrule. "When the wounded were landed," an English traveler recites, "nothing but commiseration resounded through the streets, while the ladies tore their chemises to bind up their wounds!"

Besides the acts of protection, the chief events affecting our commercial and nautical advancement during the period under consideration were these: the continued war between England and France; a British order in Council, November sixth, 1793, forbidding commerce with the French colonies; an embargo for thirty days on all ships bound to foreign ports, which was extended to May twenty-fifth, because of the perils to which American commerce was exposed; the Algerine piracy of our vessels; and the raising of tariff duties.

Shipbuilding at the port of New York dates back to a very early period. As far back as 1614, oaks that had sheltered bears where Wall Street "bulls" now contend with financial bruins, were fashioned into a trim-built vessel, named the *Onrust* or *Restless*. Such was the beginning of the vast merchant marine of the city of New York; and, strange to relate, about where this little ship was constructed, forty-five Broadway, the solons of our Shipping Board now (1934) hold sway.

The development of shipbuilding in the colonial period was of a very uncertain character, mainly for the reason that our commerce carried on with foreign countries was with vessels owned abroad. It was not until after the treaty of peace with Great Britain that there are any records of shipbuilding in New York City. Among the first that we find thus recorded is the "beautiful ship *Favorite*, intended for the London trade, and owned by John Franklin & Co. of this city." Her launching, at Samuel Ackerley's shipyard, foot of Market Street and what is now South Street, was performed in the presence of a vast assemblage of people, and it must have been a social event, too, for among them were numbered the principal belles and beaux of our metropolis. She sailed for London, November twentieth, 1786, about five weeks after being launched, with her owner, John Franklin, and another New York merchant, William Rowlett, as passengers; and, judging from the frequency of their advertising importations from England afterwards, they certainly established profitable connections there.

That there were very limited facilities for shipbuilding at New York at this time is seen by the fact that not until 1788 was another good sized vessel launched, the *America*, of 561 tons, built for account of Messrs. Gouverneur and Kemble. This vessel, by the way, brought from Bengal the first elephant ever seen in America. It is said that this animal behaved remarkably well during the passage, "accommodating himself to his straitened quarters and hard fare with a patient philosophy worthy of general imitation." He was accompanied by a native Bengali, who made a tour of the United States with him. Hoisting an elephant on shipboard and lowering him into the hold being rather hazardous work, we are appending an illustration, showing how they were securely slung and raised by a windlass.

At the time of the enactment of the helpful legislation of 1789, only seventeen per cent of our imports and thirty per cent of our exports were being carried in vessels of the United

Hoisting Elephants on Shipboard.
From an old print in the author's possession.

DISTRICT OF THE CITY OF NEW-YORK.

I *John Aspinwall* do solemnly *swear* that the Entry, now delivered by me to the Collector of this District, contains, to the best of my Knowledge and Belief, a true Account of all the Goods, Wares, and Merchandize imported by me, or consigned to me, in the *Ship Sea Mars John Kennedy* Master, from the Port of *Liverpool* And that the said Entry also contains a true Account of the Net Prime Cost thereof; and that the Invoice and Bill of Lading, herewith produced, are the true and genuine ones by me received, of the said Goods, Wares, and Merchandize. And if I shall hereafter discover any other, or greater Quantity of Merchandize than is contained in the Entry aforesaid, I will forthwith make due Report of the same to the said Collector. And I further *swear* that all Matters whatsoever, in the said Entry expressed, are, to the best of my Knowledge and Belief, just and true. —So help me God.

Sworn this *15th* Day of *October 1794*

John Aspinwall

John Aspinwall, who signed the above Custom House entry upon his ship "Fort Mary," was one of New York's prominent merchants in 1794, a member of the firm of Gilbert & John Aspinwall, and he often brought in and shipped out cargoes aboard his own ships, in his own name, as did his partner. His sons, William H. and John Lloyd Aspinwall, with Gardner G. and Samuel S. Howland, organized the famous South Street shipping house of Howland & Aspinwall.

Fac-simile of Custom House Entry Made by John Aspinwall.

States; and, a few years later, we were holding our own, being on more than a fifty-fifty basis, which, in 1811, ran up to ninety per cent for imports and eighty per cent for exports carried in American bottoms. While shipping was increasing gradually, it must be remembered that New York had virtually no vessels for sea-borne commerce at the close of the Revolution. In the last decade of the eighteenth century, Philadelphia was considered to be the one city in the United States having the best talent for designing and constructing sea-going vessels, as it was the center of the most progress in the arts and sciences in the country. But in a few years New York City made such rapid strides in the industrial line that the shipbuilding industry of Philadelphia was no longer in the lead. After 1800, New York forged so rapidly ahead, that, at the close of 1809, she could boast a registered tonnage more than double that of her former rival. By this time also, the average size of ships engaged in foreign and coastwise trade, too, had greatly increased and their quality improved.

During the period of which we write, practically all of South America remained closed to American ships. It was difficult, but not impossible, for them to obtain access to ports under British control in the West Indies, South Africa and elsewhere. While they were cut off from the large islands in the Far East under the dominion of the Dutch, they were no worse off than the traders of other nations, but, as Carl C. Cutter writes in that marine authority, "Greyhounds of the Sea," "the facts are essential to an understanding of the general conditions under which the commerce of the United States developed."

By this time, July, 1796, South Street had been filled in (in the neighborhood of "the Whitehall,") but the material used contained filth, and this, it is believed, caused the sickness which then prevailed in the lower sections or First Ward of the City. In consequence, the Common Council passed four ordinances for filling up sunken lots on South Street.

A little later, a ship arriving with 450 Irish immigrants, the Common Council grants 800 dollars "towards subsisting the said passengers during time of their quarantine." This happened under the régime of Richard Varick, who, when Mayor, always distributed cookies on New Year's Day, and was famed as a generous host. His dinners and entertainments were unsurpassed. Among the City Fathers were Robert Lenox, Nicholas Bayard, Cornelius C. Roosevelt, Jotham Post and Mangle Minthorne.

In the year 1797, there sailed from New York a little ship-of-war of about ninety tons, named the *Betsey*, in command of Captain Edmund Fanning, and she was the first vessel to carry the Stars and Stripes around the world. The voyage, lasting two years, was a commercial success.

This anecdotal account of a voyage from Bristol to New York, in the year 1797, by a passenger, John Davis, who embarked on board the snow, *Two Brothers*, of 200 tons, conveys an idea of life on shipboard, as well as hardships and oddities then encountered in a passage across the Atlantic:

"For my passage, which was in the steerage, I paid seven guineas to the merchant who chartered the vessel, and my mess cost me only three pounds more. Out of this money, besides provisions, we purchased a stove, which, during the voyage, was a treasure. It not only fortified us against the cold, but we cooked our victuals upon it.

"We had scarcely been out a week when a sea broke over the quarter, washed a hencoop from its lashings, and drowned nearly three dozen of fowls. But it is an ill wind that blows nobody any good. The sailors made the fowls into a huge 'sea pye' of three decks, which they called 'the United States Man-of-War,' and fed on it eagerly. These sons of the ocean were humorous beings, but none of them in archness surpassed the cabin-boy, who often called the watch in the following manner:

> 'Starbaulins stout
> You must turn out
> And sleep no more in sin;
> For if you do,
> I'll cut your cue,
> And let Larbaulins in.

Hoa! The watch ahoy! Come, bear a hand up there, you Tory dogs!'

"The 'Two Brothers' was a miserable sailing tub, and her passage a most tedious one. Head winds constantly prevailed, and scarcely a week elapsed without our lying to more than once. To scud her was impracticable, as she would not steer 'small,' and several times the Captain thought she was going to founder. Her cargo, which consisted of millstones and old iron, made her strain so with rolling, that incessant pumping could hardly keep her free. She had only one suit of sails; not a single extra spar, and her cordage was old. If a sail was split by the wind there was no other alternative but to mend it; and when, after being out six weeks, we had sprung our foretop mast, we were compelled to reef it.

"Arriving at the 'parched spot,' very properly called Sandy Hook, we found only one habitation, which was a tavern. The landlord, who had much the appearance of a waterman, received us very coolly. 'You can get nothing here, gentleman,' said mine host. 'Our cow eat some damaged coffee that was landed from a wreck about a week ago, and died a few hours after. We are very hard put to it.' 'What, old Boy,' cried our Captain, 'have you no grub at all in the house?' 'No! O, be joyful!' 'No grog;—not a toothful of music? Come, my Noble, we want to splice the main brace!'

"'Why Captain,' replied the landlord, 'we have no fresh grub in the house; but you can have some nice bacon and eggs fryed, with grog to the mast. Gentlemen, will you walk in?!' 'Hurrah!' cried the Captain. 'Stretch along the eating halyards. Hail Columbia!'"

Then Davis continues his narration:

"The pleasantries of the Captain enlivened our breakfast, which was prolonged nearly till noon; nor do I think we should have risen then from table, had not the mate, who was left in charge of the snow, like a good seaman, hove short, and loosened his sails in readiness to avail himself of the breeze which had sprung up in our favor. The Captain thereupon clamored for the bill, and finished his last bowl of grog with the favorite toast of 'Here's to the wind that blows, the ship that goes, and the lass that loves a sailor.'

"We made good progress to the town (New York) and our vessel was soon moored to one of the wharves along the East River."

In the spring of 1798, the City of New York was greatly excited by the prospect of war with France. Its commerce had suffered much by the depredations of French cruisers and the mercantile classes were greatly exasperated.

On June thirteenth, 1798, Congress suspends all commercial intercourse with France. Great preparations for war! A subscription paper is circulated among New York merchants, and considerable sums of money are readily subscribed, which are intended to be applied to the purchase, arming and equipping of several vessels, to cruise on our coasts for the protection of commerce. This war with France, as foolish in its origin and aim as it was brief in duration could not be made to help the fortunes of the Federalists, to which party the majority of our merchants belonged. But, on September thirtieth, 1800, representatives of France and United States sign at Paris a convention by which peaceful relations are restored.

We are reminiscent of the year 1797. There was a high tone prevailing at that time, which is now nowhere to be seen, and New Yorkers had not succeeded to the worship of Mammon, which characterizes this age. Pleasure and business were joined together in the gatherings of the solid men of old New York. The hour of meeting was generally at six o'clock, and the debates, very often long-winded arguments, were held over long tables, where bread and cheese, beer punch, pipes and tobacco, and not infrequently the potent Madeira of the period or West India Rum were provided. This latter drink was the invariable choice of the master or other officer of the merchant's ship, who, while in port, would be included in the gathering, because at that time shipmasters and supercargoes often owned a share in the vessel and were also the business managers; they not only paid the running expenses of the ship, but bought and sold the cargoes, under instructions from the owners if they were possible to be had, otherwise they acted upon their own responsibility. The profit of the owner depended to a considerable degree on the shrewdness and honesty of both these men, who were the merchant's trusted representatives, for he could not be both on land and at sea.

A group of gentlemen, principally of the then powerful mercantile class, are seated around a table in the club and ballroom of the Belvedere, an exclusive club and tavern, too, distinguished at that time as New York's most fashionable resort.

Until Close of Eighteenth Century

The Belvedere Club was an organization founded by thirty-two of the city's prominent citizens, merchants for the most part, actively engaged in promoting the commercial welfare, not only of the young and growing metropolis, but of the country at large. In those good old days and on to 1812, the principal merchants would go out a few miles into what was then the country, to dine every Saturday, at Hardenbrook's, a place of public resort on the East River, about where Twenty-fifth Street is now; or to the Belvedere, situated on the top of a high hill, where now dwells the heterogeneous population of the East Side block bounded by Monroe, Cherry, Clinton and Montgomery Streets. The name Belvedere was appropriate to the site. To the southward stretched the scattered houses of the young city, and the beautiful bay, with its strictly rural shores; to the westward lay in full view the Hudson River with the Jersey heights beyond; to the northward were smiling farms and orchards, while beside Belvedere Hill flowed the East River, with Brooklyn village beyond, unconscious of its future absorption by greedy New York.

It was a distinguished group that gathered here, late one Saturday afternoon, in the Belvedere Club room, and the family names of these gentlemen can still be found in the directory or "Who's Who" of today, so mention of some of them may be interesting.

At the head was Joseph Gouverneur and his partner, Robert Kemble, comprising the mercantile firm of Gouverneur and Kemble; Charles McEvers, another merchant, junior partner in LeRoy, Bayard and McEvers, who, some years later, became one of the founders of the New York Stock Exchange; Samuel Corp and John Shaw, whose firm, Corp, Ellis and Shaw, commanded a considerable portion of the import and export trade between Great Britain and her former American colonies; also Gulian Ludlow, who, with his uncle, Daniel Ludlow, formed the wealthy mercantile banking house of Daniel Ludlow and Company. Then there was General Nicholas Fish of Revolutionary fame, who, although a lawyer by profession, was now engaged in promoting New York City's pioneer banking, as well as her commercial interests, whilst stepping into her political arena and the exclusive social circle then prevalent; Josiah

Ogden Hoffman, the first in a line of great lawyers; James McVickar, of the European importing house of J. McVickar, Stewart and Company; James Constable of a family eminent in commerce; Thomas White, who had a country seat where now the dry goods district is found and whose rural roadway became a street bearing his name; and Augustus Van Horne, of Knickerbocker mercantile fame. Below them was stretched New York's shipping along the East River, on South Street or what afterwards became that thoroughfare, in which all of them were more or less interested, for her business interests were then confined to a small, select coterie, of which the gentlemen named represented a very important part.

American shipping had grown, so that at the close of 1799 we could boast of the possession of 657,142 tons in the foreign trade. It must be borne in mind that our early maritime ventures were carried on chiefly with vessels owned and operated by enterprising merchants, in New York, Boston, Baltimore and Charleston, the leading seaports of the United States during this period. Americans were then able to purchase foreign built vessels, and both members of the house of Gouverneur and Kemble were expatiating upon the merits of a ship, named *Orion*, that had been "built in Blackwall, London River; completely repaired in Bombay, was newly spiked and bolted with copper," which they then had up for sale. With a carrying capacity of 1300 tons, she was undoubtedly the largest and finest merchant vessel in the United States, and she mounted forty-four guns, with a battery of thirty, and was otherwise completely armed. Described as "a remarkably fast sailer," we have no doubt Gouverneur and Kemble soon found a buyer.

Let us glance over some of the New York newspapers of the time, and see what certain members of the Belvedere Club were doing to promote the commercial progress of the port of New York:

LeRoy, Bayard and McEvers, of which firm Charles McEvers was junior partner, offered a wide variety of merchandise, representing importations from various parts of the world, as only they can offer for sale. From his elegant point of vantage, on Belvedere Hill, Mr. McEvers can see his brig *Harriott*, at Jones' wharf, about where Wall now runs into

South Street, which, among her cargo, had landed fifty pipes of Teneriffe wine of a superior quality, some of which, no doubt, found its way into the possession of "Mine Host" John Avery, tavern keeper of Belvedere House.

Then there was the cargo of the good ship *Mary*, just arrived from Canton and then discharging from Delafield's wharf, at the extreme lower end of South Street and the first dock along the East River waterfront, in which vessel several members of this group of merchants were interested.

Gulian Ludlow, whose firm had recently gone in for New Orleans cotton, might be speculating upon a foreign market for that staple, because we had not then "arrived" as a manufacturing nation. Or Gouverneur, for instance, might be telling of advices he had just received from his French correspondents, as to how the fortunes of Napoleon Bonaparte were progressing, for in those days, and for years afterward, the great topic of conversation was Bonaparte. While John Shaw, who was decidedly pro-British and had, in the War of Independence, "lived within the lines," as the phrase described those loyal to King George, expressed the hope that Napoleon's downfall would soon be accomplished.

Still another merchant member, Henry Sadler, not present on this occasion at the Belvedere, advertised extensively, and offered: "Out of the ship *Union* from Amsterdam, pipes Gin, Linseed Oil, chests of Glassware assorted, 300 pieces Harlem stripes, 100 German—do—;" also "Jamaica Rum and Sugar," and in another advertisement, "400 pieces Russia sheeting, Green Coffee by the hogshead and case, Gin in pipes, as well as Brandy, Madeira," etc.

The storage of merchandise in "a new fireproof store," owned by another Belvederean, was quite an innovation in those days when New York suffered from a frequency of fires. An inadequate water supply and inferior methods and apparatus, prevented the noble band of volunteer firemen, generally working with willing and frequently anxious citizens, from extinguishing these conflagrations without great loss to life and property. The Coffee House Slip Fire, of December ninth, 1796, was still fresh in the minds of New York merchants. It began in the store of Robinson and Hartshorne on Murray

Wharf, now the eastern end of Wall Street, and spread to Maiden Lane, burning all the buildings below Front Street from Cruger's Wharf to the Fly Market. Half a dozen other fires were reported during the next few days, and New York was thrown into great excitement by a rumor that the negroes had again conspired to destroy the city. The Common Council offered five hundred dollars' reward for the arrest and conviction of the incendiaries, and urged all good citizens to form themselves into companies "to consist of such numbers as shall be necessary for the purpose of keeping a watch for the safety of the city." This was done in a few wards, and the precautions, if any were needed, proved effective. No more fires occurred, and the excitement soon subsided, but the mercantile community, whose stores and warehouses, as well as ships lying in the East River, not to mention their own homes, suffered such great losses from these conflagrations that the construction of fireproof buildings readily received their most serious consideration.

In view of these circumstances, is it not interesting and instructive to learn that some years after these events yet before we had learned to more properly control conflagrations, with our first "paid" firemen, and were way beyond preventing them, as we are to some extent today, fire insurance in Japan was simple and effective. No paid-up capital. The "company" consisted of the Mikado, who issued one general "policy," which he called an "edict." The chief condition of the policy was, that every person whose house caught fire "shall have his head cut off." The losses, from all accounts, were very light.

Conditional servitude, under "indentures" or covenants, had from the first existed in Virginia. Later, and as time changed, and we shouted "freedom" till the heights of the Alleghenies reverberated with the echo, both New England and what is now classified as the Middle Atlantic States, had "white slaves," as well as "negroes." Even after we had won our "War *of* Independence," which any close student of American history will agree is wrongly named, "indentured" men or white slaves were brought into New York, as well as other ports along our Atlantic seaboard. Previous and some time after the period of which we are writing, advertisements were placed in the local newspapers offering a reward for the apprehension of an "indenturer" who had run away. This cannot be regarded as strange when one considers the situation in those times of a person without means, but it was a strong and favorable argument, used effectively by the Southern planter and others below the Mason-Dixon line, just previous to the War of Secession. And gloss it over as one will, the condition of the black man (Southern slave) was heaven itself compared with that of the Yankee laborer, even in the year 1800.

We've culled this from the New York *Minerva and Evening Advertiser* of February fourth, 1797:

"*120 German Redemptioners*, Just arrived per the ship 'Criterion,' Captain Johnson, from Amsterdam, among which are men of various occupations," and so forth.

And, shortly below, in the same newspaper, is:

"*40 German Redemptioners*, Just arrived in the ship 'Minerva,' Captain Crowingshield, from Hamburg, consisting of carpenters, joiners, blacksmiths and bricklayers, &c. Their times to be disposed of. For further particulars, inquire of the Captain on board, at the foot of Dey Street, North River,—or Edward Goold & Son."

Some of these redemptioners came, as did other laborers, indentured for their passage money only, but the "veritable serfdom" of so many others has never been recorded in history —and never will!

Less than a hundred years ago the great majority of immigrants were very poor—so poor, indeed, that they could not prepay their passage. Accepting advances, they were bonded to the shipowners, who derived enormous profits from the sale of their bodies into temporary slavery. Charles Reade has given a vivid description of the emigrant traffic at this period in his delightful story of "The Wandering Heir." Whenever a vessel arrived at Philadelphia or New York, the steerage passengers were sold at public auction to the highest bidder. The country people either came themselves to purchase, or sent agents. Parents sold their children, that they might remain free themselves, and families were scattered never to be reunited. Old people and widows did not sell well, while healthy parents with healthy children and youths of both sexes always found a ready market. When one or both parents died on the voyage, the expenses of the whole family were summed up, and charged to the survivor or survivors. Adults had to serve from three to six years, and children until they became of age. Runaways had to serve one week for each day, one month for each week, and six months for each month of their absence. Technically, the emigrants were called "indented servants" but in effect they were slaves.

The last sales of immigrants took place in Philadelphia during the years 1818 and 1819. The American government then interfered with the traffic, and encouraged the emigration of a superior class of people.

Nature seems to have predestined the site of New York as the site of a commercial center. No other locality in the world possesses such ocean gates or so extended and yet compact a waterfront. And her merchants for several decades during the past century and a half, have formed her aristocracy. There was scarcely a family in New York, at the close of the eighteenth century, which in at least one of its branches was not engaged or financially interested in commerce. On the long and honorable list of merchants are to be found the Schuylers, Baches, Murrays, Franklins, Clarksons, Beekmans, Setons, Van Zandts, Van Hornes, Ludlows, Waltons, Gouverneurs, Schermerhorns, DePeysters, Lows, and Remsens.

High on New York's roll of merchants is the name of Broome, Platt and Company, who were among the first to go into the India trade after our Revolutionary War. Canton, China, it must be remembered, was an open market, accessible to all nations. So soon as we became a nation, American ships were dispatched thither from New York, and Broome, Platt and Company were early in the field. In 1791 we imported from China direct 2,601,852 pounds of tea. This altered the tea trade very much. That year old English houses imported 416,625 pounds of tea from London; but a comparison of prices in New York on November fifth, 1791, and in London on the same day, was proof that tea could never be imported save from China direct. Soon after there was an end of all China trade except on American vessels; and we got our porcelain, nankeens, silks, and all other Chinese commodities direct. A worthy treasurer and also a president of the Chamber of Commerce was John Broome, of this East Indian trading firm. He became Lieutenant Governor of the State and after him was named Broome Street and Broome County. Even when Lieutenant Governor he lived in democratic fashion in the upper stories of the house wherein he transacted his business, on Hanover Square.

Perhaps the largest merchants in New York for years after the British left that city, was the house of Shedden, Patrick and Company, 206 Water Street, who did an immense business, importing goods from the West Indies, owning ships, trading to Saint Petersburg, in Russia. They imported Manchester goods; they sold silks, Jamaica spirits of seventeen—brand (long extinct and maybe never to be resurrected after our many years of Prohibition), and puncheons of Grenada rum, and so forth, and this house bought an immense quantity of American produce to ship to the West Indian Islands. Their ship *Minerva*, whenever she came into port from Newcastle, not only brought them coal, but large lots of window glass, flint glassware, and cream-colored and brown earthenware. They kept all sorts of "iron mongery," as it was called then, meaning nails, brads, tacks, carpenter and broad axes, hoes and other tools. They were also in the China trade, and sold largely of teas. Sending off vessels every month to the James River, they were enabled to ship large quantities of tobacco to European ports.

A major general in the Revolution, who afterwards became a prosperous merchant, was Ebenezer Stevens. No one can form an idea of the extent of business done by him, for he had ships and brigs innumerable, and did business with all parts of the world. At Stevens' Wharf, near Peck Slip, one would often find warped alongside the well known Stevens' brigantine *Prudence*, commanded by old Captain Dingley. She was in the Antigua trade, and regularly carried out American produce, returning with her two hundred puncheons of Antigua rum. His sloop *Juno* in the Bordeaux trade, brought him cargoes of brandy and fruit from that famous port of France, and he had sloops trading to Lisbon and other ports. From a biographical sketch of Ebenezer Stevens, we note—"he had but few rivals"; of course, in a commercial way, and judging from his attractive advertisement, offering "Rum, Wines &c." he would positively have "few" today:

"50 hhds. high proof N.E.Rum; 3 pipes and 14 hhds. choice picked London Particular Madeira Wine, 10 years old, now landing at Stevens' Wharf, and for sale from $3. to $5. per gallon." [This was stiff for 1795.]

Then comes:

"Puncheons of Jamaica Rum, high proof and good flavor; pipes of Old Port, casks of Claret; pipes high 4th proof Brandy, do. Cognac."

Later on, this article reads:

"Talk about the advance of civilization, Christianity, sciences, &c. It may be, but there has been no advance in good liquors and wines, except in price. Those were pure, good, and, of course healthy. How is it now? You cannot get such liquors or wines as are alluded to in that advertisement at any price. The liquors are made out of pure spirits—Kerosene, and flavored with Creosote—so that the moment you drink a little too deep, you feel as if you had taken poison, and find your nervous system shattered."

And this was an expression of opinion before the Civil War.

The firm of Ebenezer Stevens' Sons, slightly changed, continued down—father and son—about eighty years. It is an honor to have such old firms. There are too few such now in New York.

Merchants of a former generation felt a just pride in being connected with the great house of LeRoy, Bayard and Company. People in these days cannot comprehend the feeling. There are so many large firms (most of them incorporated) and corporations, that we cannot now even imagine the profound respect inspired by LeRoy and Bayard, founded by Herman LeRoy, whose daughter married Daniel Webster, and William Bayard one of the city's most influential men, socially, politically and in a business way. It was to the latter's home, in what is now Greenwich Village that Alexander Hamilton was taken after being mortally wounded by Burr. Its partners changed to LeRoy, Bayard and Company, then LeRoy, Bayard and McEvers, and lastly to LeRoy, Bayard and Company, but it rolled on many years and was one of the most remarkable commercial houses in this or any other American city. They traded to all parts of the world for more than thirty-five years. In 1826, an event occurred that made the name of LeRoy, Bayard and Company ring through the whole world. This was the Greek Frigates' scandal, about which so many accounts have been given out; it is difficult at this late date to get at all the true facts. The firm failed in 1827, but there was no LeRoy connected with it then.

It would be a very difficult matter to find a name more famed in mercantile annals of this city than that of Aspinwall. Old John Aspinwall, father of Gilbert and John Aspinwall, a famous firm of merchants, from 1790 to 1812, when the two brothers dissolved partnership, was a sea captain who commanded vessels out of this port long before the Revolutionary War. He was also in mercantile business and dabbled in real estate. Gilbert and John Aspinwall were heavy importers as well as wholesale jobbers of dry goods and other merchandise, as all importers in early New York had to be, for even the importer could not sell over a case of goods at a time, and more frequently had to sell by the piece. They also did a large general commission business, received consignments of goods from foreign ports, were large purchasers of domestic produce for foreign account, and the old house shipped abroad largely on their own account. They owned ships; Gilbert owned the ship *Aristomes,* about 350 tons burthen, trading direct to Saint Petersburg, and it is said they sold Russian goods to the extent of one hundred thousand dollars a year. John also owned vessels. One of his ships, *Port Mary,* sailed between New York and Liverpool for some years, establishing connections in England that were continued many years after by Howland and Aspinwall, of which firm this John Aspinwall's sons were partners. Another of his vessels was the brig *Blooming Rose.* In the war, she went into the French business, and cleared twenty thousand dollars in one trip. In 1812, the two brothers dissolved partnership, but the name of Aspinwall was carried to greater commercial fame by the next generation during the packet and clipper, also early steamship periods, in connection with the Panama Railroad and the founding of Aspinwall, now Colon, Panama.

If one searches through the advertising columns of the journals of the day, he will find the name of Murray and Mumford, who did an enormous business with both the East and West Indies, their store and counting house being upon Crane Wharf; of Henry A. and John G. Coster, who had strong connections in old Dutch cities, traded with their own ships and sent out supercargoes to all parts of the world, and did a heavy importing business with the West Indies; of Archibald Gracie, shipowner and merchant, a Scotchman who came over as supercargo before the Revolution and became one of New York's merchant princes; of John B. Desdoity, one of many Frenchmen who came to New York following the French Revolution and created a large business; of Joel and Jotham Post, who imported drugs and medicines; of Minturn and Champlin, which continued to be a great house even after the War of 1812; of Isaac Hicks, a Quaker located at Crane Wharf, dealing largely in whale oil, spermaceti, smoked herrings, spermaceti candles, soap, ivory, etc.; of John and Francis Atkinson, who did a heavy importing business with England; of Joseph Lyon, who imported coal from Liverpool, also earthenware, canvas, and a few hogsheads of "Irish glew"; of Joaquim Monteiro, a Portuguese merchant, who came here in 1796 and commenced business, continuing for many years swindling operations which netted him a huge fortune; finally he transferred to Havana, Cuba, to escape his creditors; but, alas, we digress from the "virtues" of our old time merchants!

A mercantile encyclopedia would be necessary to catalogue the names and virtues of all the old famous merchants of New York. Furthermore, as the opportunities offered by the professions, law, medicine and sundry, were limited in a city of less than 65,000 inhabitants, for most young men the choice of a mercantile career was then inevitable, and many of them, within the next decade or two, brought New York into preëminence.

On the thirty-first of December, 1799, the day appointed by the citizens of New York to pay the most solemn funeral honors to the Memory of their beloved Chief and Fellow Citizen, General George Washington, every kind of business ceased and the flags were at half mast on all shipping in the harbor.

PART III

NEW YORK SHIPPING AND COMMERCE FROM THE BEGINNING OF NINETEENTH CENTURY UNTIL CONGRESS DECLARES WAR AGAINST GREAT BRITAIN

1800—1812

III

SOME FAMOUS OLD SHIPBUILDERS AND SHIPYARDS ALONG THE EAST RIVER—THEIR ACTIVITY MEANT MUCH FOR NEW YORK'S COMMERCE—HENRY ECKFORD AND HIS GREAT WORK—CHRISTIAN BERGH, MASTER-SHIPBUILDER—SHIPYARD MECHANICS INDITE A MEMORIAL TO THE UNITED STATES SENATE AND HOUSE OF REPRESENTATIVES—JACOB BARKER'S CAREER—NOAH TALCOTT, MERCHANT—NEW YORK MERCHANTS' PROTEST TO PRESIDENT JEFFERSON AGAINST BRITISH ATTACKS UPON AMERICAN VESSELS—JEFFERSON'S "LONG EMBARGO"—JOHN JACOB ASTOR MANAGES TO SEND HIS SHIP *BEAVER* TO CHINA—BIOGRAPHICAL SKETCH OF JOHN JACOB ASTOR—AN ENGLISH VISITOR'S INTERESTING DESCRIPTION OF THE CITY'S SHIPPING, BEFORE AND AFTER THE EMBARGO OF 1807-8—NOTES ON AFRICAN SLAVE TRADE—PROHIBITED AFTER JANUARY FIRST, 1808, BY ACT OF CONGRESS—THE *PHOENIX*, THE FIRST STEAM VESSEL TO NAVIGATE THE OCEAN—HISTORY OF MARINE INSURANCE — JEFFERSON'S AND MADISON'S ATTITUDE TOWARD THE GROWTH OF THE AMERICAN MERCHANT MARINE—SHORT RELIEF AFFORDED BY NON-INTERCOURSE ACT—ERIE CANAL PROJECT VIRTUALLY STARTED IN 1811—BRITISH AGGRESSIONS CONTINUE, SO, FINALLY, WAR IS DECLARED!

EACH period of our national history has had its peculiarly profitable industry, and before the Revolution *shipbuilding* was the one which took first rank with us. During the war, however, it was nearly suspended. *English cruisers* hovered near our coasts and captured and destroyed large numbers of vessels. Few vessels, except privateers intended especially for preying upon English merchantmen, were fitted out at any American port. For the time being, privateering was profitable, and quite a few New York merchants engaged in it and recouped losses sustained in the ordinary channels of business.

The recognition of *American Independence* by Great Britain, found New York, like her sister cities, destitute of commerce and of its legitimate fruits. None, however, were so completely divested of the last relic of commercial prosperity as New York. Her shipbuilders had exchanged the ax for the musket, and her merchants had valorously taken up arms in her defense. Those who survived the conflict were, with few exceptions, impoverished. Commencing with what scanty means they then possessed, by dint of enterprise, industry and an indomitable perseverance, their efforts were crowned with success, and before the eighteenth century was about to wind up a period of memorable events, commerce revived, the foreign shipping trade was again opened and New York shipbuilders found themselves abundantly employed.

The history of commercial transactions generally are full of interest, but an especial importance is attached to the history of shipbuilding in the Empire City, for it may be said to stand without a parallel. The earliest New York shipbuilder, now known, was Thomas Cheeseman; but his operations were restricted to the then limited demands of commerce, and what particular vessels he ever did build is not known. His son, Forman Cheeseman, was also a shipbuilder, and was burnt out some time in the latter part of his life, when all the books and family records were destroyed. This was doubly unfortunate, as the real history of their operations would undoubtedly have constituted an important part of the history of shipbuilding in this city.

Forman Cheeseman was one of the few naval architects and shipbuilders in the city, at the opening of the nineteenth century, who had a reputation of a high order for designing and construction, beyond their own locality. He commenced building vessels in his yard which was located near the foot of Rutgers Street prior to 1800, but in that year Congress authorized the building of the frigate *President*, which was placed on the stocks by Mr. Cheeseman. The important events connected with this vessel are engraven on the national mind, and form a page in our naval history.

The vessels of our Revolutionary Navy were entirely disposed of in 1785, and, when our difficulties with France and the Barbary powers became acute, the citizens of a number of cities along the seaboard built, on public subscription, vessels which they presented to the United States Navy. Among them was the frigate *New York*, the construction of which was begun by Messrs. Peck and Carpenter, and completed by the last-named member of that firm, Stephen Carpenter. She was an excellent specimen of marine architecture, which the loyal merchants and business men of New York contributed to their country's need, while those of Philadelphia presented the ill-fated frigate *Philadelphia*.

"Another auxiliary to our infant Navy was added this morning," states the New York *Commercial Advertiser*, April twenty-fourth, 1800, "by the launch of the beautiful frigate 'New York,' pierced for thirty-eight guns. She moved from the lower shipyard into her destined element a few minutes past ten o'clock, amidst the loud acclamations of thousands of citizens. On her entering the water, Federal salutes were fired from the 'Aspacia' Indiaman and the 'Governor Jay' cutter, which lay in the stream brilliantly decorated with the colors of different nations.

"She is the voluntary production of the Merchants of the City of New York, from which she takes her name; and her construction, workmanship, &c., reflects much credit upon Mr. Stephen Carpenter, the master-builder. Captain Robinson is appointed to her command."

After building the *President*, Forman Cheeseman laid the keel of the *Braganza*, of about 300 tons. He then joined Charles Brownne, with whom he built several vessels fine for that day, such as the *Silenus* of 400 tons, the *Triton* of 340, and the *Illinois* of 396 tons. Mr. Cheeseman then retired, and Mr. Brownne continued the business on his own account.

When Charles Brownne opened his yard on what was called "Manhattan Island," which remained prominently identified with shipbuilding activities for some years, that place was on the outskirts of New York City, very few dwellings being then around Corlaer's Hook on the east side of the city. This property was part of the James DeLancey estate, that was forfeited to the people of New York State by DeLancey's loyalty to the British cause during the War of the Revolution, and sold by the Commissioners of Forfeitures. This "Manhattan Island" has a local as well as a national historical interest, from the fact that it was there Robert Fulton's *Clermont,* the first successful steamboat in the world, was built in 1807, and where the first steam war vessel in any navy, *Fulton the First,* or *Demologos,* was constructed in 1814, for the United States Navy, by Adam and Noah Brown. All of Robert Fulton's steamboats were built by Charles Brownne up to the time of Fulton's death; and after that, for a time, the steamboats of the North River Steamboat Company were built here by Adam and Noah Brown and Henry Eckford.

Charles Brownne, in 1810, moved his yard to the corner of Water and Montgomery streets, and remained there until 1822. Fortune did not favor him in his later days, and when he died, in September 1831, the property he had occupied on Manhattan Island, was found to have been purchased by Adam and Noah Brown, who occupied most of it after his removal; Henry Eckford also occupying a small portion of it. This "Manhattan Island" was an oasis of solid ground, several acres in area, close by the river shore. On three sides of it were salt meadows or marshes, and on its eastern border flowed the waters of the East River. Being almost completely isolated from the shore of the Island of Manhattan, it was called an "island," and for the sake of distinction had been known from early times as "Manhattan Island." With the progress of the city, the salt marshes were filled in, the shore line was advanced into the river, and "Manhattan Island" disappeared from the map of New York City.

As business increased, the number of shipyards also increased, and the year 1800 was the beginning of a shipbuilding era in New York. For, although no exact and definite account can be given of particular transactions in that line of business, at any time previous, it is well known that until then the operations of building were confined to only a few individuals; that no vessels of any considerable size or importance had then been built by any one, and that the launching of a craft of almost any description was an occasional, and therefore, a rare and extraordinary event. Even to a much later date it was a prevailing impression that orders for the construction of ships could not be so well supplied here as in other cities of the Union; and Philadelphia was awarded the palm over all others, in constructing large and seaworthy vessels.

After the Cheesemans and their contemporaries, Messrs. Samuel Ackerley, William Valleau, Carpenter and White, Thomas Vail, William Vincent and George James, came Henry Eckford, Adam and Noah Brown, Christian Bergh, and soon afterward, Jabez Williams, Jacob A. Westervelt, Isaac Webb, Stephen Smith, John Allen and others of their stamp, who formed the rank and file, established themselves in several firms, and conducted their operations with so much skill, industry and fidelity, as very soon to secure to New York a name and fame as a shipbuilding center among the nations of the earth.

It may be stated here that a new era in the modeling of vessels on this side of the Atlantic began soon after the opening of the nineteenth century; to this we are indebted very largely for the success of the War of 1812, and for the great activity of our commercial marine. Almost simultaneously, a group of master-builders appeared, whose united talents and efforts brought about a revolution in the principles of ship construction. We think it no overstatement to say that to no one are we more indebted for this result than to Henry Eckford. Fashioned after his models, our vessels gradually dispensed with their large and low stern frames, the details of their rigging underwent changes, and in the important particulars of stability, speed and capacity, they soon surpassed their rivals.

Henry Eckford was a Scotsman who came to New York in 1796, found employment readily in the shipyards, and after a few years established himself in the business of shipbuilding, in connection with Captain Edward Beebe, and began building vessels at their yard near the foot of Jefferson Street. The *Samuel Elam*, of 350 tons, was among the first that he built, which was originally called the *Sportsman*, and had a figurehead, representing a man on horseback. This caused her bowsprit to steeve very high, in order to clear the man's head. Vessels were generally built in those days with large figureheads and large quarter galleries, both of which features were extremely disadvantageous in heavy weather when running off before the wind or scudding, as they were subject to being caught by the seas, and Eckford ever afterwards discriminated against large figureheads and quarter galleries. It is said that, from the master of each ship, he gained information enabling him to improve on the construction of the next, and thus his successive ships became models and his shipyard took rank as the best in America.

Among other ships he built the *Beaver* for John Jacob Astor, who was then creating his trading empire, which was to extend to the Pacific Coast and envisioned the globe. Her register was 427 tons, while she carried 1,100 tons of cargo. So well built was she that after forty years' service her liveoak frame was used in the construction of a larger vessel for the same owner.

It was the War of 1812 that established Eckford's reputation. At this time the shipyards here were not very busy, and Mr. Eckford was employed by the Government in the construction of war vessels at Sackett's Harbor, on Lake Ontario, and here the world witnessed with astonishment a fleet of brigs, sloops of war, frigates and ships of the line, constructed within an incredibly short space of time. At the present day, we can scarcely appreciate the difficulties and discouragements under which operations on so extended a scale had to be conducted. The country was comparatively wild and uninhabited, the winters long and severe, provisions and men, with the ironwork, tools, rigging and sails, had to be transported from the sea coast, hundreds of miles distant; the timber was still waving in the forest, and, to crown the whole, the funds provided by the Government were in such bad repute, that, to obtain current funds therefrom, Mr. Eckford was obliged to give his personal guarantee. When peace was declared, he had on the stocks a vessel, to carry one hundred and two guns, which it was calculated would have been in the water in twenty-seven days more.

Then he was made superintendent of the Brooklyn Navy Yard, and there built the *Ohio*. On first coming into the yard to assume the duties and responsibilities of his office, he observed a pair of horses in the smith's shop, which belonged

Henry Eckford.
From a painting in the possession of the Long Island Historical Society

to the Commodore, and had been sent there for the purpose of being shod. He ordered them to be taken away immediately, adding, "that the shops were there for the vessels, and not for the Commodore's horses." The first steam vessel built for ocean service was the *Robert Fulton*, which Mr. Eckford constructed at New York, in 1819; and she proved a success. He built frigates for Brazil, Colombia, Peru and Chili, constructed vessels of war for various European powers, and his reputation was so worldwide that he received a commission from the Turkish Government as naval constructor at Constantinople.

He accepted the offer and his departure was the occasion for one of the strangest demonstrations ever witnessed in New York. Eckford combed his organization for the best mechanics, offering them the extraordinary high wages of two dollars a day from the day of their departure from New York. Most of them were men of large families which had been reared in this city. As the date of departure approached, there were some misgivings, and the prospect of long separation from family and friends for "life in a heathen country" was too overpowering for some of the mechanics. Groups of wailing women and children assembled at the pier on the day the party set sail, and there were many who openly expressed their fears that the undertaking would end in disaster. In a measure these fears were realized, for in less than a year after their arrival at the Turkish capital Eckford died. No wonder there was consternation when the news reached New York many weeks later.

It was Henry Eckford's chief object to have New York shipbuilders excel all others, and he would not withhold any means when he could find a suitable opportunity for encouraging his men, especially the apprentices, with extra pay and rewards. To so great an extent did he follow this practice, that it is said Mr. Isaac Webb, the father of William H. and Eckford Webb, who learned his trade with Mr. Eckford, was in possession of 1,000 dollars, when his term of apprenticeship expired, in addition to his stipendiary dues. Such acts of generosity and friendship, on the part of the master towards his apprentices, imbued them with a spirit of emulation as well as gratitude; and they would not only labor more assiduously, but they would strive to improve their labors, as their munificent patron and teacher had encouraged them to do.

Christian Bergh began shipbuilding in 1804 with the ship *North America*, 400 tons, owned by Minturn and Champlin, who employed her in the European trade, chiefly with Russia and Great Britain. The following year he launched the brig *Gypsey*, a very sharp vessel for those days, carrying several per cent less than her tonnage, belonging to General Ebenezer Stevens. This vessel seemed unfortunate, for, afterwards, when rigged into a schooner, she went to France, was chased by the English blockading squadron, and in a heavy squall was lost, with all hands. The ship *Galloway*, about 350 tons, considered by "scientific men" to have been the handsomest modeled ship ever built in this country, up to 1807, was next launched from his yard. She was owned by three prominent New York merchants, Robert Lenox, James Lenox and William Maitland, and duly entered the India trade. About 1808-09, the Government seriously turned its attention toward the Great Lakes, and Mr. Bergh, with Henry Eckford, constructed the brig *Oneida*, at Oswego, N. Y., for service on Lake Ontario, which was the only war vessel we had there when hostilities commenced in 1812 and for some time afterward.

With the large demand for ships during the early part of the Packet period, Christian Bergh, who had been on the Lakes during the War of 1812-14, soon began active operations at his new and larger yard, situated near where South Street meets Corlaer's Hook,—continuing there until he retired, in 1837.

The celebrated New York diarist, Philip Hone, records, among the deaths during June 1843:

"Friday June 23d.

"Died this day Christian Bergh, aged 81 years, the oldest ship carpenter in the City, the father of that great system of Naval Architecture, which has rendered the City of New York famous throughout the world. Christian Bergh," continued Hone, "was the first to raise the Character of Yankee packet Ships to a height which as yet has been unapproached by any foreign nation."

Thomas Vail, in 1802, contemplated retiring from business, gave a sub-contract to Adam and Noah Brown, who completed it and took the yard, at the foot of Montgomery Street and what is now near the extreme end of South Street. They built several vessels during the next ten years, in the meantime locating on "Manhattan Island," for the latter part of this time was a comparatively lively period in shipbuilding at New York, some of the vessels launched being as large as 450 tons each. During this period there were other builders who were very actively engaged in the construction of vessels for our merchant marine, but none were more so, or had so extensive a plant as A. and N. Brown.

At a session of Congress, early in the year 1803, it was evidently proposed to cede the rights and trade the benefits of our prosperous marine, to give up its protection by discriminative duties and turn it out to free trade, as the following "Memorial of Sundry Mechanics of the City of New York," under date of January twenty-seventh, 1803, addressed to the U. S. Senate and House of Representatives, would seem to indicate:—

"To the Honorable Senate and House of Representatives of the United States.

"The Memorial of the Mechanics of the City of New York and others concerned in the building or equipment of vessels, respectfully shows:

"That your Memorialists cannot observe, without much anxiety, that it is now proposed to Congress to repeal all discriminating duties between this country and Great Britain, so as to admit the vessels of that nation, and in the end the vessels of all foreign nations, to enter our ports on equal terms with our own. As it is certain, in the judgment of your Memorialists, that foreigners can build their vessels cheaper, equip them cheaper, and navigate them cheaper than we do; the consequence must be that they can afford to enter, and will enter our ports and take the carrying trade from our merchants, by underbidding them for freight. Our carrying trade being thus shifted from our own to foreign countries, the necessary effect will be to produce a very material, if not a total stagnation in our shipbuilding; and that numerous class of mechanics who are concerned in either building or equipping of vessels, must cease to find that employment in their own country which they have hitherto done. They therefore pray that the proposed repeal may not take place.

"New York, 18th January, 1803."

This Memorial was signed by 174 well known citizens and prominent firms of New York, all actively engaged in promoting shipbuilding or its kindred trades.

So much pressure being brought to bear against this meditated repeal of discriminating and countervailing duties, a motion to discharge the Committee of the Whole, in Congress, from all further consideration of it, was duly carried without division, and thus ended an abortive effort to serve British shipping and mercantile interests. American merchants and their vessels having control of the import carrying, through the operation of our discriminating duty system, they could not be forced out of export carrying, though cargoes would have to be taken at lower rates, and so they were. To meet the new conditions, we built our vessels larger, improved their models, and gave the hulls such proportions that they could sail safely with less ballast than any others on the ocean.

During these early days of the young Republic, New York's masters of the future were men of business, and probably to Robert Fulton and De Witt Clinton, with their industrial friends and helpers, that city then owed her position in the nation and the world, more than to men of science or letters, scholars or statesmen. Even her great statesmen had much business sagacity in their composition; and surely Hamilton was as much of a financier and soldier as a jurist; as for Chancellor Livingston, he earned as much honor by his encouragement of Fulton as by his law and statesmanship.

That eventful span of time from 1800 to the "Long Embargo" of 1807-08, thence to the commencement of the War of 1812, was the golden dawn of a coterie of Yankee traders who did much for the commercial prosperity and growth of New York, also benefiting New England, especially their home town or own state, for they were ideal native sons. They were as clannish as their most formidable business rivals, the Quaker merchants who preceded them in New York's channels of trade, and they often supplanted them, after long striving and energetic labor, not unmingled with Yankee audacity and shrewdness. Perhaps, the most powerful outstanding figure among these sons of New England, who achieved fame and fortune in New York during this period, was Jacob Barker.

Soon after he arrived in New York, about 1797 a "green boy from Nantucket," Jacob Barker entered the counting-house of that fine old Quaker merchant, Isaac Hicks, who did an extensive commission business at fourteen Crane Wharf (South Street). His initial barter trade, on his own account, was confined to a twenty-dollar gold watch "bid in" at one of the street auctions, or *vendues* which were so tempting to a youngster fresh from the country.

He was sent to Messrs. James and Samuel Watson, a large commission house on Front Street, by his employer, Mr. Hicks, for a note, in payment for sperm candles sold them. The old shipping merchants when young men and serving as clerks, were allowed by their employers to make small business ventures of their own, and the Messrs. Watson proposed to the youngster a sale of ship bread, saying his fellow clerks often purchased it and then supplied the bread to ships on which Mr. Hicks had consignments. As young Barker possessed no money, and had no liver oil which seems to have often been used as a medium of exchange, so the story goes, they took the watch as payment for the ship bread.

To find a market for this bread, was the young speculator's next object. Being sent to collect a note for codfish sold Thomas Knox, a merchant of Wall Street, upon careful inquiry Barker learned that he had an order for three hundred barrels of ship bread. He received ten barrels for the watch, but knowing that the Messrs. Watson had a consignment of ship bread from Virginia, a conditional bargain was made and he sold the two lots to Mr. Knox, making a profit of 125 dollars on the transaction.

Young Barker and the other clerks of Isaac Hicks followed up their speculations to such an extent that Mr. Hicks found it expedient to restrict them, allotting to his brother, Samuel Hicks, the traffic in liver oil, and to young Barker the traffic in lime.

Once, as he was ascending the stairs in full view of a lot of soap which had been long on hand, he remarked, "Jacob, why does thee not sell that soap?" The reply was, "for the want of an applicant." "I will purchase it at eight cents if thee will give me four months' credit and allow me to send it as an adventure to Havana." Mr. Hicks replied in his rapid manner,—"Take it, take it, I am tired of the sight of it."

The soap was shipped by a fast schooner, commanded by Daniel Waterman (a native of Nantucket), about sailing for Havana at the time when the British were capturing and sending into New Providence all vessels in that trade. Captain Waterman returned safely in six weeks, bringing back fifty cents a pound in *specie* for the soap, which was brought to the office. Jacob was engaged in counting it, when Mr. Hicks, coming in from breakfast, remarked, "What's all this?" The reply was, "Money for the soap, and I am now ready to pay for it, although not due for more than two months." Mr. Hicks appeared pleased with the young man's success, and passed on.

Jacob Barker commenced business as a merchant on his own account in 1801, and while so engaged he received from his London correspondents a consignment for Robert Fulton,— the first steam engine ever in successful operation for propelling vessels, made by Messrs. Boulton and Watts, of Birmingham, England, celebrated for constructing steam machinery. It remained in Mr. Barker's store on South Street many months before Mr. Fulton could raise the funds to pay for it, when the engine was placed on the *Clermont*, afterward rebuilt and called *North River*. Little did he then think the discovery of the immortal Fulton would, in less than half a century, regulate the commerce of the whole world, become so powerful an auxiliary in all war measures, save time and shorten space to such a degree that to be deprived of its use would be universally considered a calamity of the first magnitude.

Long a vigorous figure in New York's mercantile, shipping and banking circles, Jacob Barker stood prominently among the rich men of the growing metropolis. He subscribed 100,000 dollars towards the Federal loan of 1813-14 to finance our "Second War of Independence," and he never flinched when called upon to render his country any possible aid. He succeeded Nathaniel Prime, as the most potent individual of a Wall Street, which was then in its financial infancy. Mr. Barker's notes were Wall Street's currency, even when he was losing heavily, for despite that, there were many who were confident he would make another fortune and honor them. An old history tells us that so interested was Jacob in his affairs, that he would not go home to dinner. He challenged David Rogers to a duel because he forged ahead of him in starting a bank. He owned many ships, and saved pilotage on them when they left New York harbor by steering them out himself. (A practice which is now being pursued, inimicably of course, in the year 1934, by the Standard Oil Company and other important ship owning interests—by making their captains "rate" for port licenses and pilot their own vessels in and out of New York and other ports along the Atlantic coast, on the Gulf, and so forth.)

All in all, Jacob Barker was one of the most versatile individuals of his age. Associated, in fact prominently identified, with a New York looming largely as a most fertile field for commercial endeavor, this "Nantucket Trader," generously contributed of his energy and time, as well as money, towards the success of innumerable projects that redounded to the benefit of his adopted city; until, after the North River Insurance Company scandal, when he and that other man of sterling worth, Henry Eckford, were unjustly accused of fraud. Disgusted but not discouraged, at an age when most men would have succumbed, Jacob Barker went to New Orleans—started life anew, and again met with success, not only as merchant but as a lawyer or "advocate of lost causes!"

When making a personal address, in court at New Orleans, while reciting the checkered history of his life, he proudly referred to his unrivaled enterprise as a merchant of New York, closing with the statement: "that the canvas of his ships had whitened every sea, and that the Star-Spangled Banner of this country had floated from the mastheads of his ships in every clime."

How very soon a smart young son of New England could

get into a large business in the olden time, is evidenced by the wonderful mercantile career of Noah Talcott. Whenever the good ship *Joseph* arrived from London, she had a valuable invoice for Noah Talcott. The schooner *Peggy* traded between New York and Martinique, and belonged to Mr. Talcott. The schooner *Ann Margaret* also was owned by him. He was largely in the Holland trade. The schooner *Robert Martha* was owned by him. We presume that Noah Talcott, on his arrival from "down east" went through the usual lengthy clerkship with one of our large commercial houses. In 1798 he formed a partnership—the firm was Talcott and Ellis, and their place of business was upon Stevens' Wharf; later they moved their store to Murray's Wharf. Two years after he located at Sixty-four South Street, and had his residence on Bowery Hill.

In 1810 there was no merchant in New York doing as large a business as Noah Talcott. In the Havre trade he had the brig *Eliza*, Captain Gray, carrying freight and passengers. He also owned the brigs *Waymouth* and *Rambler*, which continuously carried into port white and brown sugar, and the coffee that a former generation of New Yorkers was beginning to appreciate after decades of tea as a beverage, morning, noon and night, as well as other times during the day, as exemplified by the "Diary of Elizabeth deHart Bleecker," covering a few years previous to the time about which we are writing. While one merchant was doing this enormous business, it must be remembered that the domestic exports of all the states, for 1810, was not quite sixty-seven millions of dollars.

When at Sixty-four South Street, Noah took his brother David into partnership, under the firm name of N. and D. Talcott, and they kept together until 1819. He was alone again until 1825, when he took into partnership a Mr. Lyman, and the firm became Talcott and Lyman, continuing until 1827. During the years 1826 and 1827 the operations of this house in cotton alone were enormous, but not particularly fortunate. The consequence was a dissolution, and Mr. Talcott went into business again upon his own account, until he died.

On December twenty-sixth, 1805, there was a general meeting of merchants at the Tontine Coffee House, and they

From Beginning of Nineteenth Century

addressed a Memorial to President Jefferson and Congress, stating the ruinous consequence to the United States' commerce following acceptance of certain newly defined British principles, and complaining of piratical attacks upon American vessels in the West Indies and even on our own coasts. The peace of Amiens (March twenty-seventh, 1802) lasted but fourteen months; war conditions again put the British marine to disadvantage, but the ministry took care that neutrality should not again assist American shipping. Great Britain speedily made up her mind to aggressive conduct, as a ready and effective means of handicapping our commercial rivalry. The search of our ships for seamen, that had previously been so damaging, was offensively renewed. She had already contracted liabilities for millions of dollars for spoliations of our commerce, but seemed anxious to run still further into our debt, could she but vitally impair our shipping power. But for our tariff and tonnage discriminations she would have succeeded. All these actions provoked the War of 1812, and the messages of our Presidents contain authentic records of the way in which that war was brought about.

While the foreign commerce of our new Republic was flourishing, the new born Republic of France had yielded to the despotism of Napoleon, who was then at the height of his military power in Europe. France and England were engaged in a long conflict, and the weary sailors of England's great navy were deserting to American ships. Hence England insisted on her right to search American ships plying the ocean with their heavy cargoes, which she desired to have carried in British bottoms. The old question of "freedom of the seas" sprang into discussions of the hour. Since the United States had no navy sufficiently strong to protect her rights on the high seas, President Jefferson issued his famous Embargo on American shipping, forbidding, by Act of Congress, December twenty-second, 1807, all American ships to leave our ports. This Embargo was a terrible blow to American shipping.

It was at a time when the Embargo of Mr. Jefferson was in full blast. Not an oyster boat was allowed to go outside of Sandy Hook. Every merchant did the best he knew how, under the circumstances. Fancy the astonishment of the shipowners of this city, who had ships lying in the docks rotting and idle, when they took up the *Commercial Advertiser* of August thirteenth, 1808, and read:

"Yesterday the ship 'Beaver,' Captain Galloway, sailed for China."

There were at that time 80,000 people in this city, and, of course, every one knew that the *Beaver* was owned by John Jacob Astor. Though vivid and daring commercial imagination was common to all the leading China merchants, their visions were prosaic compared with Astor's gaudy dreams and dashing and brilliant execution.

There was trouble among the merchants and shipowners, when it became known that the ship of Mr. Astor had actually gone to sea on a long India voyage. Why should he be favored, and no one else? Finally it was ascertained that John Jacob was too smart for ordinary merchants. He had obtained a special permission from the President of the United States for his ship *Beaver*, navigated by thirty seamen, to proceed on a voyage to Canton, for the ostensible object of carrying home to China "A Great Mandarin of China." Story after story went the rounds of South Street or wherever shipping merchants congregated, each more fabulous than the other. One of them, to which some credence was given, related how John Jacob Astor had picked up a vagrant Chinaman in the Park, only a common Chinese dock laborer or coolie who had been smuggled out of China. But Astor determined to treat his "Mandarin" handsomely, fitted him out in silks, and so forth, regardless of expense. After that it was easy for that indomitable individual to create him a Chinese official "of one of the nine grades entitled to wear a button on his hat." Then he secured the Presidential permit, and sent his ship to sea before other merchants smelt the mice.

It is not likely that a Secretary of State in the time of Jefferson could have had his hands greased. At any rate, it is well known that Mr. Secretary of State Madison was a great friend of Astor's, for he furnished him with copies and letters and the names of his mercantile calumniators. It was a hard case. Whatever may have been the motives of the President, in granting the permission, there was no doubt that it was a clever dodge on the part of Mr. Astor.

It was also known that Mr. Astor had offered a month before to make contracts with other merchants to bring home goods from Canton, or freight; and there was not a shadow of doubt that his object, as owner of the ship *Beaver*, was to make a Chinese voyage at a time when all other merchants were restrained by the embargo.

Almost before the *Beaver* was outside Sandy Hook, the press caught on to the joke. Then the old *Commercial Advertiser* came out and pitched into Mr. Astor. It said editorially, in reference to the strange permission of President Jefferson:

"The time of granting this permit for the 'Beaver' to sail is remarkable. It is when a general embargo is imposed on all commerce with our nearest neighbors; when the exchange of domestic produce with Canada, New Brunswick and the Floridas is interdicted by an armed force; when the intercourse of our citizens in our own bays, rivers and harbors in small boats incapable of a sea voyage, is subject to the most vigorous control of the Custom House; nay, more—this permission has gone into effect, when on account of some new, or unknown political necessity, all other permissions which have not been carried into effect, are rescinded. The ship 'Beaver' is one of the most valuable, the number of men exposed to peril the greatest in any merchant's service, and the voyage not to the West Indies, but to the antipodes.

"Let us observe the progress of this affair; if the trade is safe, and can be prosecuted consistently with the public interests, let all who are willing engage in it, otherwise let all be restrained. Let there be an embargo or no embargo; but let us not countenance partial dispensation from the operation of genial laws."

Next day old John Jacob, greatly aroused, addressed the following letter:

"To the Editor of the *Commercial Advertiser*—

"I observed in your paper of the 13th instant, an article inviting public attention to a transaction (as you state it, of a most extraordinary character) relative to the ship 'Beaver,' and the Mandarin. If whoever wrote that article will give me his name, and if he is not prejudiced against any act of the administration, nor influenced from envy arising from jealousy, he shall receive a statement of facts relative to the transaction in question, which will relieve him from the anxiety under which he appears to labor for the honor of the Government, and the reputation of all concerned. He shall be convinced that the Government has not been surprised by misrepresentations in granting permission, and that the reputation of those concerned cannot be in the slightest degree affected.

"By giving the above a place in your paper, you will oblige, sir,

"Your humble servant,
"JOHN JACOB ASTOR

New York, August 15th, 1808."

Of course nothing happened. Mr. Astor never made any explanation, and the journals of the day did not spare him, but he was realizing gold, and he knew it. When the *Beaver* returned to New York, she added more than one hundred and fifty thousands dollars to his rapidly accumulating fortune.

John Jacob Astor's ordinary operations in the fur trade in connection with the American Company, and his foreign trade, went on with uniformly increasing success. While this trade, however, must be considered the leading pursuit of his life, as it was the foundation of his fortune, he early gave his attention to another line of operations, and it would be difficult to say whether the greater part of his immense fortune was derived from his mercantile dealings or his investments in real estate, up to the time of his retiring from active participation in the former. His foresight early anticipated the rapid growth and future greatness of the city of New York. He early began, and systematically followed up the policy of investing largely, not only in the inhabited parts of the city, where immediate income could be realized, but in unoccupied lots, or acres rather, of fields out of town, which he saw, in anticipation, covered by the spreading city. Many others have invested in the same manner, upon like calculation; few so systematically as he. A glance at the rapid growth of the city, even at that early day, might make the most prudent venturesome. The population of the city of New York was:

In

1773	21,876
1786	23,614
1790	33,031
1800	60,489
1805	75,770
1815	83,530
1816	100,619
1825	166,086
1845	371,223

These figures cover the whole period of Mr. Astor's active life. They might prove, to one of less insight than he, that there was something in the very dust beneath his feet more precious than ermine and sable. He was not, however, merely prudent; he had the means and spirit to enter into operations covering long periods, and to wait patiently the result of years. He was under no necessity of mortgaging one property for the purchase of another, under no temptation to dangerously expand. Thus he was enabled to make investments which it has been said, no doubt with literal truth, centupled on his hands.

Mr. Astor continued in active business fifty years, and during that long period he hardly made a mistake or misstep through defect of his own judgment. Sagacity, strength, activity, rapidity of action, industry, punctuality, integrity—such was the extraordinary combination of the qualities of a great merchant which met in him. He had an iron memory. He could recall the minute details of a transaction in Canada, ten years before. He rose early, and until fifty-five years of age was at his office before seven o'clock. He was a great horseman, and in the constant habit of riding out for pleasure and exercise. In the strength of his general grasp of a great subject, he did not allow himself to be too much disturbed by the consideration of details. His mind worked so actively that he soon got through the business of a day, and could leave his office earlier than many busier men who did less. Troubled and annoyed by petty trials, he was calm and self-possessed under great ones. "Keep quiet, keep cool," was the constant and familiar admonition from his lips. When the great trials came, his spirit rose with the emergency, and he was equal to the honor.

It was the rare felicity of Mr. Astor's most fortunate life, that he lived to a good old age to enjoy his extraordinary success. Many a man toils with all his might through the best years of his life for fortune, looking forward to the reasonable enjoyment of it in old age, qualified for the enjoyment of it by keeping his mind clear and his body free from disease, and not, like the fool in Scripture, bent merely upon taking his ease; yet like him, in the moment of fruition, he gets his summons to surrender all.

John Lambert an English visitor in New York, late during the years 1807 and 1808, gives the following interesting description of the city's shipping before and after President Jefferson's "Long Embargo";

"The waterside is lined with shipping which lie along the wharfs or in the small docks called slips, of which there are upwards of twelve towards the East River, besides numerous piers. The wharfs are large and commodious, and the warehouses, which are nearly all new buildings, are lofty and substantial. The merchants, ship-brokers &c. have their offices in front on the ground floor of these warehouses. These ranges of buildings and wharfs extend from the Grand Battery, on both sides of the town, up the Hudson and East Rivers, and encompass the houses with shipping, whose forest of masts gives a stranger a lively idea of the immense trade which this city carries on with every part of the globe. New York appears to him the Tyre of the New World.

"When I arrived at New York, in November, the port was filled with shipping and the wharfs were crowded with commodities of every description. Bales of cotton, wool and merchandise; barrels of pot-ash, rice, flour, and salt provisions; hogsheads of sugar, chests of tea, puncheons of rum, and pipes of wine; boxes, cases, packs and packages of all sizes and denominations, were strewed upon the wharfs and landing-places, or upon the docks of the shipping. All was noise and bustle. The carters were driving in every direction; and the sailors and labourers upon the wharfs, and on board the vessels, were moving their ponderous burthens from place to place. The merchants and their clerks were busily engaged in their counting-houses, or upon the piers. The Tontine Coffee House was filled with underwriters, brokers, merchants, traders and politicians,

Sunday Morning in the Office of the "Courier and Enquirer".

Coffee House Slip and New York Coffee House.

From Beginning of Nineteenth Century

selling, purchasing, trafficking, or insuring; some reading, others eagerly inquiring the news. The steps and balcony of the Coffee House were crowded with people bidding, or listening to the several auctioneers, who had elevated themselves upon a hogshead of sugar, a puncheon of rum, or a bale of cotton. The Coffee House Slip and the corners of Pearl and Wall Streets, were jammed-up with carts, drays and wheel-barrows; horses and men were huddled promiscuously together, leaving little or no room for passengers to pass. Such was the appearance of this part of the town when I arrived. Everything was in motion; all was life, bustle and activity. The people were scampering in all directions to trade with each other, and to ship off their purchases for the European, Asian, African and West Indian markets. Every thought, word, look and action of the multitude seemed to be absorbed by commerce, the welkin rang with its busy hum, and all were eager in the pursuit of its riches.

"But on my return to New York, the following April (1808) what a contrast was presented to my view! and how shall I describe the melancholy dejection that was painted upon the countenances of the people, who seemed to have taken leave of all their former gaiety and cheerfulness? The Coffee House Slip, the wharfs and quays along South Street, presented no longer the bustle and activity that had prevailed there five months before. The port indeed was full of shipping; but they were dismantled and laid up. Their decks were cleared, their hatches fastened down, and scarcely a sailor was to be found on board. Not a box, bale, cask, barrel or package was to be seen upon the wharfs. Many of the counting-houses were shut up, or advertised to be let; and the few solitary merchants, clerks, porters, and labourers that were to be seen, were walking about with their hands in their pockets. Instead of sixty or a hundred carts, that used to stand in the street for hire, scarcely a dozen appeared, and they were unemployed; a few coasting sloops and schooners, which were clearing out for some of the ports in the United States, were all that remained of that immense business which was carried on a few months before. The Coffee House was almost empty. In fact, everything presented a melancholy appearance. The streets near the waterside were almost deserted, the grass had begun to grow upon the wharfs, and the minds of the people were tortured by the vague and idle rumors that were set afloat upon the arrival of every letter from England or from the seat of government."

The commerce of New York, before the Embargo, was in a high state of prosperity and progressive improvement. New York merchants traded with almost every port of the world. The amount of tonnage belonging to that port in 1806 was 183,671 tons. And the number of vessels in the harbor December twenty-fifth, 1807, *when the embargo took place,* was 537. The money collected for the National Treasury on imports and tonnage, for several years amounted to one-fourth of the whole country's revenue. In 1806 this amounted to six million, five hundred thousand dollars. In the year 1808, the whole of this immense sum had vanished!

On January fifth, 1808,—there were lying in New York harbor, a total of 666 vessels. A few days previously, there had been meetings of seamen thrown out of employment by the Embargo, handbills were circulated, and popular feeling was generated in their favor. Temporary work being provided them by Captain (afterward Commodore) Isaac Chauncey, at the then new Brooklyn Navy Yard, a threatened disturbance was averted.

In common with other unpopular laws, the Embargo Act was a source of considerable lawlessness. Your true American was as disdainful of a law which incommoded him in 1807, as he would be in 1934, and we will state here that the Embargo had a considerable effect upon amusements and rendered the city gloomy.

The African slave trade, which was a source of no little revenue to certain shipping interests, at New York as well as in some of our Southern ports, was prohibited by Act of Congress after January first, 1808. The United States Government declared it piracy, warning the people that the death penalty would be inflicted on every American citizen found guilty of buying the natives of Africa and selling them as slaves to other countries. These just laws and strenuous efforts to abolish the trade were seconded by England and France, who soon after united with the government of the United States to furnish a considerable naval force, which was, for many years, stationed on the African coast and among the islands of the West Indies, to intercept and capture the slavers, and to punish those detected in this nefarious commerce.

Every exertion was then made by them to induce Spain and Portugal to join in the same compact. The excuse of the Spaniards and Portuguese was that their colonies were poor and required replenishing; consequently, the flags of these two nations were used for slave trade purposes for several years; in fine, until they found they were becoming degraded in the eyes of Europe and the United States, when they at length relinquished it, and only united with the before named Powers to abolish it.

All those concerned in the slave trade contended to the world that purchasing and transporting the natives of Africa, to Brazil, the West Indies and other southern climates, was humane and benevolent, as well as of vast advantage to the civilized portion of mankind; that, if they were not bought and removed from their shores, they would, as prisoners, be all put to death; that they were cannibals, and only fit for slaves. This plausible and specious reasoning on the part of these selfish, inhuman traders, was palmed upon the world, and believed by a large and credulous portion of those who had no means of confuting these false statements.

Considered from an historical standpoint the United States occupies a most prominent position in the department of steam navigation, in which it led all other countries.

The great possibilities for steam traffic in navigating our rivers, lakes, and sounds was an incentive which prompted the greatest exertions in developing steam vessels. The success which attended these efforts led Americans to venture the inauguration in 1819 of trans-Atlantic steam travel. While this experiment, undertaken largely for speculative purposes, did not prove remunerative, it, nevertheless, blazed the way for more successful ventures a few years later when the construction of steam vessels and their employment on the ocean were better understood.

The early efforts of American inventors to attain success in building steamboats were conducted under the most discouraging influences, conditions which would have prevented a continuation of labor on the part of men having less inspiration and determination. When we recall that there was not a properly organized machine shop in the United States at the time when many of the early steamboats were built and engined, we cannot but marvel at the results secured. While it is true that Fulton's *Clermont* was equipped with engines made in England, it is equally true that the craft devised before her time by Fitch, Rumsey, and Stevens had their engines built in America, and that the *Phoenix,* built by Stevens shortly after the *Clermont* was afloat, was fitted with a boiler and engine of domestic manufacture—a triumph of American skill and invention which it is difficult at this time to properly appreciate.

The story of Robert Fulton's *Clermont* and her maiden trip to Albany has been told and retold, yet the small amount of information which has been handed down to us of the *Phoenix,* the second steam vessel in the United States, is very surprising, when we take into consideration that she was built just opposite New York City, and but a few weeks after the completion of the *Clermont.* As she was debarred from navigating the waters of the Hudson by the monopoly given to Fulton by the Legislature of the State of New York, the *Phoenix* was sent by sea to Philadelphia and, therefore, she really was the first steamboat that navigated the ocean.

When the word was passed along the New York waterfront that Colonel John Stevens, of Hoboken, was to send this little steamboat on an ocean voyage, it was received with cold disbelief and even open sneers. Some of the habitués, sitting on the docks, said, as they spat derisively into the river, that they "would as soon volunteer for an expedition to the moon as go on that cruise in a little 'steam kettle.'" The Colonel's son, Robert L. Stevens, who had superintended the construction of the *Phoenix,* readily volunteered as captain and engineer, to take her around to Philadelphia by sea. What older men might call the folly of risking an unseaworthy craft was to him the beckoning of adventure, as well as the practical test of an experiment. It is due to the log he kept that we have any record today of the first coastwise navigation by steam power. The *Phoenix,* on the appointed morning, June tenth, 1809, left New York, and she reached Philadelphia on June twenty-third, various stops being made en route, for stores and supplies, also when "they concluded rash to encounter the great swell abroad," and so forth.

Marine Insurance was the first form in which insurance appeared in New York City, just as it was the first and only form of insurance developed by the men of the ancient world who went "down to the sea in ships." The first marine insurance company organized in New York after the War was the United Insurance Co., founded in 1795, or early in 1796, and chartered March twentieth, 1798, with a capital of five hundred thousand dollars. The first company that confined itself wholly to sea risks was The Marine Insurance Company, which commenced business November nineteenth, 1801, with a capital of two hundred and fifty thousand dollars.

The origin of insurance has occasioned much doubt among the writers upon mercantile history. Indeed, it is involved in so much obscurity, that, after all the researches which have been made, any very satisfactory solution of this doubt cannot be promised. One truth, however, is clear: that wherever commerce extended its influence, insurance must have soon followed as a necessary attendant, it being impossible to carry on any very extensive trade without it, especially in time of war. Some writers have ascribed the origin of this contract to Claudius Cæsar, the fifth Roman emperor. Other responsible authorities have given the honor of it to the Rhodians, thus laying a foundation for the idea that the law of insurance had obtained a place in most of the ancient codes of jurisprudence. The minute consideration of this question through those remote times would be attended with little satisfaction; the mind, perhaps, is more gratified to know, from authentic history, that it was introduced into England by the active and industrious Lombards, who went there in the thirteenth century; and that, whatever might have been its imperfect infant state, about the end of the fifteenth century, many considerable regulations were made at Barcelona, in Spain, respecting marine insurance.

In Colonial days, the American merchant traders obtained insurance on their cargoes from London underwriters in Lombard Street where the Italians had left their name. In the same manner that the great business of Lloyd's originated in the gathering of shippers at Thomas Lloyd's Tavern, so in old New York the first insurance office was in the Tontine Coffee House. It was to this rendezvous that a man whose fortunes were tossing on the sea in quaint sailing vessels came, in the latter part of the eighteenth century, to ask some citizen to underwrite them personally. At that time insurance hazards were underwritten at any rate acceptable to the two men making the contract. These early marine policies always stated that they were "as good and binding as if made in Lombard Street." The ancestors of the shipping firms that built up the American Merchant Marine in the first half of the nineteenth century were accustomed to seek insurance on their seaworthy ships against "the perils of the sea," and "Violence at the hand of man." By "perils of the sea," was meant all disasters due to the elements. "Violence at the hand of man" included attacks by pirates and men-of-war; the barratry of master and mariners, and "arrest, restraint and detainment of all Kings," which meant embargoes, a weapon of war employed by the European powers in their dynastic and economic rivalries.

It is an interesting phase of our records of discovery that the Latin countries not only assembled the machinery and personnel of America's discovery but to one of them must be ascribed the credit of introducing the *polizza* or policy of insurance developed by Italian mariners of the thirteenth century.

While marine insurance is the oldest known protection against loss by unforeseen and unpreventable disasters, it is claimed that "Bottomry Bonds" were the earliest form of insurance, although, strictly speaking, not insurance at all but loans made to finance a voyage or to insure its continuation if the ship was in distress, physically or financially. The ship was used as security on such loans, which were payable when the voyage was completed. "Respondentia Bonds" were similar bonds with the cargo as security. Today, both of these forms are practically obsolete.

A hundred and more years ago, merchant sailing vessels were a large factor in the wealth of the young nation, and were well worthy of government protection. All the capital that was available was turned into ships and outfits, for the richest prizes to be had in those days were to be won in the ocean carrying trade. Jefferson, reflecting the view of the agricultural interests which formed the mass of his party, looked with disapproval on the growth and activity of the American Merchant Marine and foreign commerce. The rapid increase in the size and wealth of cities on the seaboard also gave him concern. Madison, who succeeded him, largely shared these views, and, as a consequence of this attitude on the part of their administrations, the sailors and vessels of the United States were subjected to greater indignities during the decade preceding the War of 1812 than the shipping of any nation had ever suffered. It suffered severely from seizures and confiscations for which there was no redress, being ground ruthlessly between the upper and the nether millstones of British commercial avarice and Napoleon's greed for war funds.

Some relief came to New York's harassed shipping interests in 1809, when Madison succeeded Jefferson as President, through the substitution of the Non-intercourse law, forbidding trade with Great Britain and France, for the embargo which had utterly failed of its purpose. This relief was short lived, however, for, of the entire fleet of American ships which in the first year of Madison's administration set sail to continental ports, very few returned.

The embargo and consequent prostration of commerce, together with the substitution of the Non-intercourse Act, and the general belief that the country was rapidly drifting into another war with its ancient enemy, created an intense desire for the opening of a water route from the Hudson to the Lakes.

About 1810, the remarkable topography of New York State became a favorite topic of conversation, and the practicability of the canal a fixed fact in the minds of many influential citizens, and in that year a commission was appointed "to explore the whole route for inland navigation, from the Hudson River to Lake Ontario, and to Lake Erie." Their report, drawn by Gouverneur Morris, who acted as president of the board, was published in 1811, and DeWitt Clinton immediately introduced a bill into the Legislature, which became a law. While the project was thought no less interesting to the nation than to the State in which it was to be executed, it met with little favor at Washington. But from the time of these movements in 1811 until the conclusion of the war, little appears to have been done towards carrying the scheme into effect. The State was obliged to employ its funds on objects properly belonging to the general government, and the commissioners met with great opposition from those who would not believe that the hand of man could effect such a stupendous work.

British aggressions continued, despite the ominous note of a deeper and wider feeling of popular resentment which appeared in several measures adopted by Congress. The seizure of American ships, the rifling of American commerce and the impressment of our seamen continued with unabated insolence and with unrestricted violation of all law, common, maritime and international. The vacillation and fear heretofore inspired by the overwhelming size and power of Great Britain's naval and military forces were giving way to a wrath which made war inevitable, let the consequences be what they might; and at no time in our history was the United States in so poor a condition to fight. And, as we carefully scrutinize events, our conclusion is: A strong war spirit was manifested, and the people of the lusty young Republic decided that Great Britain must be chastised; so, in June, 1812, War was declared!

PART IV

HOW NEW YORK'S MERCHANTS, SHIP-BUILDERS AND HER SHIPPING INTERESTS CONTRIBUTED TO THE DEFENSE OF OUR COUNTRY DURING THE SECOND WAR FOR INDEPENDENCE

1812—1815

IV

NEW YORK IN 1812—ITS DEFENSELESS CONDITION—SHIPBUILDERS, "THE TRUE VICTORS OF THE BATTLES UPON OUR GREAT LAKES"—GOVERNOR DANIEL D. TOMPKINS, THE GREAT WAR GOVERNOR—MAYOR DE WITT CLINTON—COMMODORE ISAAC CHAUNCEY ARRANGES FOR CREATING A FLEET, ETC., ON GREAT LAKES—MEETS NEW YORK'S FOUR LEADING SHIPBUILDERS AT COLONEL RUTGERS' MANSION—HENRY ECKFORD GOES TO SACKETT'S HARBOR AND BUILDS CHAUNCEY'S FLEET—DEPARTURE ON FULTON'S STEAMBOAT *PARAGON*—ECKFORD AND HIS MEN ENTER UPON A WONDERFUL SHIPBUILDING CONTEST—NOAH BROWN IS CALLED—SETS OUT FOR LAKE ERIE WITH A BAND OF MECHANICS FROM NEW YORK'S EAST SIDE SHIPYARDS TO BUILD COMMODORE PERRY'S WARSHIPS—PROGRESS OF EVENTS IN NOAH BROWN'S BIOGRAPHY—POEM "NOAH BROWN"—NEW YORK GOES A-PRIVATEERING—BRIEF HISTORY OF PRIVATEERING—NAPOLEON ADMITS AMERICAN PRIVATEERS IN FRENCH PORTS—HARRYING FLEETS OF PRIVATEERS DID MUCH TO BRING THE WAR TO AN END—SUFFERING OF NEW YORK MERCHANTS FROM DEPREDATIONS BEFORE THE WAR—SOME NOTED NEW YORK PRIVATEERS AND THEIR ACHIEVEMENTS—TRADE CONDITIONS DURING WAR AND EMBARGOES—EXCITEMENT CAUSED BY GLAD TIDINGS OF PEACE.

LET us try to visualize conditions as they were in New York City, one hundred and twenty-two years ago. The principal occupation of its inhabitants was commerce by shipping, so it was most seriously disturbed by the war restrictions imposed on its commerce, foreign and domestic. New York's registered tonnage in 1812 was 268,548, nearly double that of any other port in the United States, and equal to Boston and Philadelphia together, the latter being next largest city; in 1800 it was larger than New York. Although Philadelphia had a population nearly as large and her manufactories were more extensive, the city of New York was the greatest commercial emporium of the Nation.

Unprepared as the whole country was for war, the defenselessness of New York at the time was an important adverse factor, well known to the enemy. What was to prevent Great Britain from sending her ships through the Narrows or Long Island Sound, and taking possession of the city? DeWitt Clinton was Mayor, and he so fully realized its exposed position that he drew up and presented to the Corporation a report on the means necessary to fortify the city—one of the most important documents to which his name is allied. This report, it is claimed, opened the eyes of Governor Daniel D. Tompkins to the weakened condition of New York's defenses and he gallantly came to the rescue. Governor Tompkins had assumed command of the State's troops; and no history of the second war with Great Britain can be complete without showing the superb services rendered to the American cause by the State of New York and its great War Governor, Daniel D. Tompkins.

When New York was thus pitifully defenseless, an appeal for protection was made to the National Authorities; the same reply came back that was returned a half century afterwards, when the *Merrimac* was expected to sail from Hampton Roads and bombard that city: "You must take care of yourself. The government can do nothing for you."

It was a calamity to the City that she was not ready earlier; for New York was blockaded closely throughout this war, which was far from popular with her merchants. Yet they ought to have seen that the war was most necessary to their commercial well being; for the frigates of Britain had for a dozen years of nominal peace kept the city under a more or less severe blockade in the exercise of the odious right of search. They kept a strict watch over all outgoing and incoming vessels, hovering off the coast like hawks, and cruising in the lower bay, firing on coasters and merchantmen to bring them to.

Shipbuilding was dull in the harbor of New York during the War of 1812, and the art was kept alive by the construction of privateers from time to time. How two of New York's

Defense During Second War of Independence 67

most notable builders, Henry Eckford and Noah Brown, found employment on our northern lakes, where they built the vessels that won the battles of Lake Erie and Lake Champlain, as well as Commodore Chauncey's wonderful fleet on Lake Ontario, which did much to prevent an invasion of this country from Canada during the greater part of the war, is now told; and it might be claimed for these master shipbuilders and their men that they were *"The True Victors of the Battles upon our Great Lakes."*

Early in September, 1812, when New York's present City Hall was new and we were at war with England for the second time, a neat equipage was drawn up in front of the broad stone steps that led up to the low-pillared entrance, alongside of which walked, with measured steps, a spruce looking young midshipman, keenly watchful, while awaiting its occupants. DeWitt Clinton, then Mayor of New York, was perhaps the most remarkable man that the State of New York has ever produced. Next to the President of the United States, the Mayor of New York City had at his disposal greater power and more patronage than any other public official in the country.

Coming down the stone stairway, inside City Hall, a double stair, which sweeping upward within the rotunda, is a marvelous achievement of grace and beauty, were two men deeply absorbed in conversation with DeWitt Clinton. They were the cynosure of all who happened to be there that lovely September afternoon. One whose strong, well-knit figure and active movements betokened a man in the thirties at the climax of his powers, was quickly recognized as Daniel D. Tompkins, the great war Governor of the State of New York. The third member of this illustrious group, whose new and brilliant uniform proclaimed him a commodore of the United States Navy, was Isaac Chauncey, who had just been appointed to chief command on the Lakes.

The Empire State and her most important city, situated at the point where its land and the sea meet, receiving little or no support from a great portion of the country, nobly fought the Nation's battles at sea and on land, but more prominently upon those inland waters, the control of which was a great requisite in carrying on the war. Furthermore, before the war had continued a year, the fact was demonstrated that Governor Tompkins was the most conspicuous, as he certainly was the strongest character which the crisis had brought forth. He occupied more offices at one time than any other man in the history of the government. Daniel D. Tompkins was not only Chief Executive and commander of all the forces of the State, but paymaster, quartermaster, commissary, commander of the Third United States Military District and general disbursing agent for the State of New York and for the United States during the three years of the war.

Commodore Chauncey entered upon his duties with great energy. At the time of his appointment, he was at the head of the Navy Yard in Brooklyn; and the time that intervened between the date of his orders and that of his departure to the Lakes station, he employed well, in organizing and despatching the means for creating the necessary force. A fleet of frigates, brigs, sloops of war and other vessels had to be built, and the work of transforming merchant vessels into warships carried on. All this had to be done in a newly-settled country where nothing could be supplied but timber; everything else had to be obtained from far distant places, reached only after considerable difficulty and hardship, and all within an incredibly short space of time. And, how could war vessels be launched upon waters controlled by the enemy?

Realizing that one of the first men whose assistance and coöperation he should secure was Governor Daniel D. Tompkins, Commodore Chauncey had obtained many interviews with him in New York before leaving to assume his duties at Sackett's Harbor, where his headquarters were to be. The policy of the National Government in those days was to drop all responsibility upon the States themselves, thus one can appreciate why Chauncey, supreme in command of naval operations on the Lakes, conferred with the Governor of the State of New York, who was also Commander-in-chief of its military forces. Later, events proved the wisdom of their concerted action, for New York having supported the war from the outset, felt the full brunt of England's wrath from first to last.

After parting with Mayor Clinton, Governor Tompkins and Commodore Chauncey now entered the carriage, beside

Defense During Second War of Independence

which the young naval subaltern, previously referred to, stood at attention. Leaving the open spaces of the pretty little park which at that time encircled City Hall, they soon reached the palatial home of Colonel Henry Rutgers, the well-beloved citizen of the East Side, where met all the leaders of the day.

Here they were joined by four men, who seemed to be upon most friendly terms with their host and Commodore Chauncey, also Colonel Marinus Willett, who lived close by and was of the party. To Governor Tompkins these men were introduced as Henry Eckford, Christian Bergh, Adam and Noah Brown. He knew them at once as the foremost shipbuilders of New York, who served also as superintendents of construction at the Brooklyn Navy Yard.

New York's shipbuilding colony was located along the East River, between Catherine Street and Corlaer's Hook and between Corlaer's Hook and Stanton Street. From the declaration of war, June eighteenth, 1812, until long after the treaty of peace, the greatest activity prevailed here, where a few years afterward, the superior construction of packet ships gave way to clipper ship building, and then began the greatest period of activity which the port of New York had ever seen.

But, we are running ahead of our shipbuilding period, for at this time the builders along the East River were mostly engaged in turning out a notable squadron of privateers that performed eminent services for the nation, acting also as a powerful auxiliary to the American Navy. Brigs and schooners, long, deep, and sharp on the floors, sitting low in the water, and sailing with a drag, built in defiance of the rules and prejudices of the age, and so fleet that one of these "sea devils" was seldom overtaken by the best frigates Great Britain could produce. Before the close of 1814, the exploits of our privateers had inspired the British with terror, and the mercantile classes were clamoring for peace.

Commodore Chauncey now showed how admirably he was fitted for the important post to which he had been appointed. He soon concluded arrangements with Mr. Eckford to go at once, with some forty ship carpenters, to Sackett's Harbor, which was the main naval and military depot along the lake frontier. It was "flint and steel" when these two master minds —naval commander and ship constructor—struck together.

At the present day, we can scarcely appreciate the difficulties and discouragements under which these operations had to be conducted. The country was so comparatively wild and uninhabited that it made traveling very difficult; moreover, fear of sudden attacks by the British with their Indian and Canadian allies, also the dreaded "lake sickness," deterred some of the mechanics from volunteering. Christian Bergh and Henry Eckford had built the brig of war *Oneida* at Oswego about four years previously, so a number of their men were conversant with conditions on the Lakes. Between these two master shipbuilders there existed for many years a Damon and Pythias friendship, which was only terminated by Henry Eckford's death.

The great New York shipyard of the period 1812-15 was that of Adam and Noah Brown, located at the foot of Stanton Street, on the East River. With that foresight and resource which so seldom deserts your real master mariner, Chauncey now arranged to secure the services of the Brown brothers. Rumors were rife that a fleet would soon be launched on Lake Erie, where there was no American naval force to contend for the supremacy of that body of water.

The merchants of New York, who had large interests at stake on the ocean, fitted out many fast sailing privateers within a few months after war was declared. Most of these vessels were launched from, or were then upon the stocks at the Brown and Bergh shipyards, in conscquence of which Christian Bergh and Adam Brown were obliged to remain in New York. They willingly agreed, however, to recruit mechanics for Chauncey's shipbuilding operations on the Lakes. Mr. Bergh, in conjunction with other East River shipbuilders, furnished Henry Eckford, during the entire period of the war, with hundreds of skilled workmen, while Adam Brown secured for his brother gang after gang of shipwrights for Erie's primitive shipyard. It was due to the skill and the strenuous efforts of Noah Brown and his men that the ships composing the American fleets on Lake Erie, and later on Lake Champlain were ever completed and rushed to victory! Thomas Macdonough won a higher fame than any other commander of the war, although Com-

Defense During Second War of Independence 71

modore Perry's name is more widely known. Every school boy reads about them, if of no other naval heroes; but the earnest student of American history can run through the entire gamut of histories on this war, and "mention" only will be found concerning Noah Brown and some brief references relating to Henry Eckford. Without the skill and industry of these two master builders of ships and their faithful followers, the British fleets on Lakes Ontario, Erie and Champlain, would have captured or destroyed every American vessel on those waters, besides enabling the British land forces, with their Canadian and Indian allies, to invade the United States.

At five o'clock on the afternoon of the day following the meeting at Colonel Rutgers' home, Henry Eckford with forty ship carpenters, men carefully selected from his own and other East River shipyards, were gathered on the steamboat dock, at the foot of Cortlandt Street, waiting to embark for Albany on the Hudson River steamboat *Paragon*.

Steamboats, which had become a reality six years before, owing to the inventive genius of Robert Fulton, attained a speed of from five to nine miles an hour, and covered the distance of about 150 miles, from New York to Albany, with numerous landings on the way, in about thirty-six hours. Passengers—seldom freight—were conveyed on what were termed "elegant conveniences" of which, early in September, 1812, there were three, built in the order named: the *North River* (formerly Fulton's *Clermont* increased in size and much improved); *Car of Neptune,* and the *Paragon*. It should be borne in mind that the main factor which contributed to progress, at this interesting period in New York's history was the steamboat. Although it was in the evolution stage, it did not take long to establish a claim for punctuality. And with the steamboat's continued improvement, transportation upon our inland waters began to assume an entirely new phase.

What was happening while the *Paragon* lay at her wharf? A change in tide had set in strongly and the Hudson looked "real choppy," its surface covered by white caps far as the eye could reach, so the gallant little steamboat was heeling to the force of the wind, as she strained and strained on hawsers, fore and aft. The trip from New York to Albany required from twelve to fifteen loads of pine wood; some of this fuel had not yet been received—hence the delay.*

Christian Bergh came down to see his friend and fellow shipbuilder, Eckford, depart for the Northern wilderness, upon an undertaking hazardous in the extreme, the difficulties and dangers of which he fully realized. Bergh's tall, commanding figure (he stood six feet, six in his stockings), his wide-flowing frock coat, blue trousers, and white neckcloth which no collar ever creased, made him a conspicuous figure in the group where he stood, alongside of Governor Daniel D. Tompkins, who was returning to his multitudinous duties at Albany, as commander of the military forces upon our Northern frontier, as well as Chief Executive of the State of New York.

Suddenly the little steam packet's bell clanged loudly, the engineer pulled open the throttle, the paddles bit into the water, and, trailing smoke and steam, the *Paragon* slowly wended her way up the Hudson. That river was then thronged with a multitude of sloops, packets and freighting boats, sailing craft by which the whole of the traffic between New York City and the interior of the State was transacted. There was an intense feeling against Fulton and his steamboats on the part of the river boatmen, many of whom foresaw what was to be the end—that they would be driven from the river by the steamboats. Their hostility was practical, too, and sometimes put him to a good deal of trouble and expense, as sloops constantly got in the way, and even ran against his boats bodily, hoping to smash the paddle wheels. One of these dastardly assaults was now made against the *Paragon*, but frustrated through the vigilance of her commander, Captain W. J. Wiswall, who skillfully bore away from the oncoming sloop, to the immense delight and admiration of his passengers, gathered on deck "to see the smash." There was an exchange of "verbal compliments," for the crews of these North River sloops were masters of profanity, but in the shipyard workers from "Manhattan Island" they met their match; and, after some swaying and swinging,

---

* "Steamboats on the North River first performed their trips with wood. Lackawanna coal was afterward introduced, by which the expense of fuel was reduced from $150 a trip to $30. This was the commencement of a new era in steamboating, hardly less important than the original application of steam to boats."—Valentine's Manual, 1852.

Defense During Second War of Independence

the steam-driven craft, with machinery clanking, soon left the slow moving sailer far in her wake.

Governor Tompkins shortly after arriving at Albany, despatched a confidential letter to General Stephen Van Rensselaer, who was charged with the duty of defending the frontier from invasion, from which we have extracted the following paragraph:

"The Government has at length been awakened to its duty with respect to the command of the Lakes. The most unbounded authority has been given to Cap'n Chauncey for that purpose and he will be with you soon. Forty ship-carpenters came up with me in the last steamboat and have gone on westward."

The *Paragon* reached Albany on Saturday, September sixth, 1812; but it was not until the following Monday that Henry Eckford and his faithful assistant Henry Eagle succeeded in arranging for transportation. Between the Hudson and the shore of Ontario, a distance of about two hundred miles, there existed no other means of communication than were offered by the ordinary highways and a few roads hewn through the wilderness, also a tedious water transportation, with portages en route.

As their services were much wanted and an attack upon Sackett's Harbor, by water, was apprehended by General Jacob Brown, who was charged with the defense of the frontier, Henry Eckford and his men proceeded to Rome from Albany, thence, by land, to their destination. They were soon unpacking their outfits, to enter upon a wonderful shipbuilding contest.

While, in the earlier stages of the three-year struggle between Great Britain and the United States, the vessels that fought the fresh water fights were often cockleshells of fore-and-aft rig—cutters, sloops and schooners, which had been converted from the peaceful pursuits of lake commerce to the purposes of war. Before the war closed, Ontario floated frigates more powerful than any on the ocean, and boasted line-of-battle ships rivaling Nelson's *Victory*, which enabled Commodore Chauncey to successfully keep Sir James Yeo and the British fleet at bay until hostilities ceased.

From New York's East Side shipyards, located near where South Street now terminates at Corlaer's Hook, on a bleak, cold day in February, 1813, another band of skilled mechanics, this time under the leadership of Noah Brown, master shipbuilder, set out for the then almost unknown forest fastness surrounding the shores of Lake Erie.

"Times were troubled, they all agree,
Foes were scourging the inland sea,
Rumors, panics and daily scares
Steeped the patriot soul in cares;
Fear was rampant and hope was down—
Then they rallied and sent for Brown.

This is the message the rider bore:
'Boats are needed on Erie's shore.'
What did the builder do or say?
Saddled his nag and rode away;
Loping, fording to Erie town—
'How many boats?' quoth Noah Brown."

(Extract from poem "Noah Brown," by W. R. Rose, in *Cleveland Plain Dealer*, September eighth, 1913.)

It is more than a century and one score years since Oliver Hazard Perry overcame the British on Lake Erie. Historians have recounted how that battle was fought and won upon America's inland sea; but, barring an occasional "mention" very little has ever been told us about the men, who, building and equipping the warships, also converting mercantile into war craft, made this historical event possible. Although these shipwrights, carpenters and other mechanics may be classed as "civilian adjuncts," each man's post of duty was as dangerous, as responsible, as well as more prolonged and arduous, as that of any men on board a ship of the conquering fleet. They paid their toll in sickness (especially from the Lake fever) and many died in the midst of their labor. In addition there was the horrible menace of a blood-thirsty Indian foe, lurking near by, waiting opportunity to kill and destroy. This certainly warrants that a rightful comparison with the dangers and hardships of the sailors and other combatants in the Battle of Lake Erie be granted them.

Defense During Second War of Independence 75

The eminent services rendered by Noah Brown and his men furnishes one of the finest illustrations in American history of the mutual dependence and coöperation of two great factors in civilization, the fighting (military) and the laboring (mechanical) man.

What should have been amply recorded as a glorious part of our naval history is known only to the earnest delver in historical facts. Yes, and a thought to hold is this: in that far distant hour of stress, it was private shipbuilders who built and kept our battle fleets afloat on the northern lakes.

Let us turn from printed history and follow the progress of events in the manuscript pages of one who played an important part—Noah Brown, master builder of ships. In his autobiography he states:

"In the spring of 1813 was called on by the Government to go and build Perry's fleet.

"I started from New York on the 14th day of February, and with a small gang arrived in ten days at the town of Erie, on Lake Erie. The weather was then very stormy and the snow very deep.

"I with my handful of men, made but little progress till some time in March, when I received some men from New York. We made all haste possible in getting timber and framing the three gunboats and two brigs, and I wrote to my brother for more hands. They arrived the last of April. Then we began to drive business with considerable speed, and the navy agent of Philadelphia sent on men, and they began to arrive on the beginning of May. We then became strong for hands and drove the work. In all there had collected about two hundred men, and then we were short of iron, oakum and pitch; but there was a British schooner off in the ice. We proceeded to her and got out about twenty barrels of pork and a quantity of rigging and cables. We made oakum of them, and burned the schooner and got her iron. It helped us with the gun-boats, and I rode all around to the neighboring towns and bought of all the merchants every bar of iron I could find.

"The government was to send iron, pitch and oakum, but the roads were so bad that I had almost finished the fleet before any arrived at Erie.

"I found great difficulty in procuring provision for my

men, but with great exertion I succeeded in sending men back into the country and then had to give a high price to procure it.

"My men several times raised and declared they would work no longer if they could not have better fare: I satisfied them by giving them liberty to go and buy all the cattle and other provisions they could find. Several were gone four or five days, and when they came back their report satisfied them all, so I had very little trouble afterwards. I did all that man could do to procure the best the country afforded. We, all this time, were driving the vessels as fast as possible. It appeared that every man was engaged as if he was on a strife—the enemy often appeared before our harbor and several times came to an anchor within three miles of us.

"Our men drew arms and volunteered to protect the shipyard, but the enemy did not venture to land, and we were as willing they should not land as they; so we had no use for our arms. We had completed our vessels by the middle of June, as follows: Three gunboats armed and fitted for use; two brigs and one sharp schooner for a dispatch vessel and to look out, as she could outsail anything that was in the English fleet. All the above vessels were built by me, and furnished with all materials, and we did not receive any funds from government till March 1814, when Commodore Chauncey came to New York and signed our bills.

"I returned in July to New York, and left my foreman, Sidney Wright, with sixteen men, to keep all the fleet and boats in order. The whole work that was done under my direction at Erie from the last of February to the middle of June was as follows:

Brig Lawrence	492.60/95
Brig Niagara	492.60/95
Schooner Porcupine	60.00
Schooner Scorpion	60.00
Schooner (Evidently the "Tigress")..	60.00
Schooner Ariel	75.00
Whole tonnage of the above vessels...	1,239.20
(This total copied from original ms.)	95

And now Perry is in difficult straits, because he cannot get his brigs across the sandbar at the mouth of Erie harbor, and

Defense During Second War of Independence

the British commander, Barclay, maintains a close blockade until August second, when he disappears to the westward. To get the *Lawrence* and *Niagara* over the shallow and into Lake Erie, required that they should be lifted at least four feet. Noah Brown had planned to effect this by the use of long decked scows or camels. These camels, an invention of Mr. Brown, were about ninety feet long, forty feet wide, and six feet hold. They had four holes cut through their bottoms, and plugs fitted to them.

After the guns and stores of the *Lawrence* had been taken ashore, the camels were placed one on each side of the vessel, the plugs taken out and filled with water. Long heavy timbers were then shoved athwart the vessel through her ports, and strongly lashed to her deck frame, and large ring-bolts in her side. Blocking was then placed under the ends of the timbers on the camels, and wedged up. The holes were then plugged up, and the pumps set to work, and as the water was discharged, the vessel was lifted. Owing to continued easterly winds, causing the water to lower, the process of sinking the camels had to be repeated, before the *Lawrence* floated. Thus, after a most laborious task of night and day work, she was floated over, and towed to anchorage. Some of the smaller vessels were then taken over with but little difficulty.

Next day the same plan was pursued with the *Niagara*, mightiest of all the warships Erie Harbor sheltered, and which was to turn the tide of victory in that great battle, September tenth, 1813.

Perry now had his squadron all safely in the lake:

> "There they huddled with lines to shore;
> Cleared for cannon, and sail and store;
> 'Lawrence,' 'Niagara,' 'Porcupine,' too;
> 'Scorpion,' 'Ariel,' stout and true.
> Brown hailed Perry in merry jest:
> 'Here's the squadron—you do the rest.'
>
> Squared with duty, without delay,
> Over the trail he rode away;
> Back to his home in New York town,
> Passed the builder whose name was Brown.

Famed is Perry in prose and rhyme;
High he poses o'er waves of time.
Take one laurel from out his crown,
Hand it gently to Noah Brown."

(Extracted from poem "Noah Brown," by W. R. Rose, in *Cleveland Plain Dealer*, September ninth, 1913.)

Noah Brown's wonderful services in his country's behalf were not altogether unappreciated, for the sailors aboard naval vessels in New York harbor used to man the shrouds when he went on board, which honor must have greatly pleased the beloved old shipbuilder.

When war came many of the ardent young men of New York, especially those who followed the sea or who had been engaged in shipping and its kindred trades, which were particularly stagnant at this time, went eagerly into the business of privateering, for it combined profit and adventure, together with service to their country. New York sent scores of privateers and letters of marque to prey upon the enemy's commerce; and formidable craft they were, being well-armed, heavily manned and ably commanded. The lucky cruiser, when many prizes were taken, brought wealth to owner, captain and crew, and the pedigrees of many New York fortunes can be traced to the letter-of-marque voyages of private-armed vessels.

Privateering flourished during the European wars of the eighteenth century, and New York newspapers of the colonial period abound in advertisements inviting "gentlemen and others" to enlist with this or that vessel fitting out under the commission of "His Majesty," while there were frequent advertisements of prize cargoes for sale. It has been at various times a useful weapon of weak naval powers or belligerents in their struggles with the great naval and commercial powers. The United States sent out privateers during the Revolutionary war, who greatly harassed and annoyed British commerce, especially in the latter years of the struggle, and the experience of sea-fighting acquired in the Revolutionary privateers prepared men for service in the young navy of the republic.

Then came the second war with Great Britain, and once

Defense During Second War of Independence 79

more American and British privateers swarmed upon the highways of commerce. Two and a half months before Congress declared war, in June, 1812, eighteen privateers were fitted out in this country to prey upon British commerce, and by October fifteenth there were twenty-six privateers hailing from New York. The first British merchant ship was captured by one of our privateers July first, 1812, and by July fourteenth there were sixty-five privateers at sea. The first privateers of this period carried less than ten guns, but towards the end of the war we licensed privateers of twenty guns. So eager were the owners to fit out private-armed vessels and to get them to sea that a contract was made at Boston to build a privateer in eighteen working days. It is estimated that during two years of the war more than 1,300 British merchant vessels were taken by our privateers, and it is believed that 250 privateers had commissions from the government of the United States. There were 106 from New York, fifty-eight from Baltimore, forty from Salem, Mass., then a great whaling port, thirty-two from Boston and fourteen from Philadelphia. The whole effective navy of the United States at the opening of the war had been seven frigates with 278 guns.

Civilized opinion is now so strong against privateering that this sort of warfare could hardly be carried on with success by any nation, since the opportunity for disposing of prizes profitably would be greatly restricted by the almost undoubted refusal of neutral nations to permit such prizes to be sold in their ports. Trade relations the world over are so much more important than they were in the days of active privateering that it may be doubted indeed whether the world would stand by and see two belligerent powers preying upon each other's commerce, to the annoyance and inconvenience of all their neighbors.

When American privateers began to reach French ports, the Emperor Napoleon issued orders for his officers to admit into all French ports all prizes captured by Americans on the same terms as if captured by the French. This was a great advantage to American privateers. They could then take their prizes into a French port for adjudication on short voyages and not run the risk of being captured by the British on their way to American ports where they must otherwise be taken. This greatly stimulated the fitting-out of privateers in America, particularly in New York. It was not long before the English channel was filled with American privateers, to the great consternation of British merchants and marine insurance companies, who refused insurance on most vessels, and on some the premium was as high as thirty-three per cent. The harrying fleets of privateers did more than the navy, imperishably glorious though its achievements were, to bring the war to its sudden end. The navy gored the British lion, but our privateers gored Britain's pocketbook, especially when they scuttled British commerce even within the gates of the English channel itself.

Before the war commenced, New York's leading merchants, who were largely engaged in foreign commerce, suffered seriously from French depredations at the time that Bonaparte, then First Consul, promulgated the Berlin and Milan decrees, which the British Government undertook to retaliate by issuing the celebrated Orders in Council. Claims were made afterward for these spoliations, and were allowed by the French Government, but never paid. These merchants, afterwards, were prominently identified not only in fitting out privateers, but also in furnishing ships to the Navy Department at their own cost, when the Treasury could not meet the expense.

Among the most noted of the privateers which the merchants of New York fitted out was a little brigantine called the *General Armstrong*. Early in March, 1813, while in command of Guy R. Champlin and when cruising off the Surinam River, she gave battle to the British sloop *Coquette*, carrying twelve more guns than she had, discovering her, when too late to retreat, a much heavier vessel. Although the *Armstrong* received considerable injury, she managed to escape, by the vigorous use of sweeps, under a heavy fire from her antagonist. For his gallant conduct on this ocasion, and his skill in saving his vessel, the stockholders, at a meeting held in Tammany Hall, New York, presented Captain Champlin an elegant sword, and voted thanks to his companions in the combat.

The privateer *Saratoga* of New York, Captain Andrew

Riker, armed with eighteen guns and 140 men, was a successful cruiser. In the autumn of 1812, she captured the ship *Quebec*, from Jamaica, with a cargo valued at 300,000 dollars. In December following, she had a desperate fight off Laguira, Venezuela, with the brig *Rachel*. They fought in sight of the town, and almost the entire population turned out to see the conflict, which resulted in victory for the *Saratoga*, after a furious combat.

We again find the *Saratoga* on a destructive errand, in February 1813, when she captured the *Lord Nelson*, one of the finest vessels in the British merchant service. At about the same time the *Saratoga* captured the British packet *Morgiana*. Previously she had been chased by a British frigate, when in order to increase her speed, she threw overboard twelve of her guns, and she only carried four guns with which to attack the *Morgiana*. Her armory was replenished with several of the fine brass pieces of the captive, and her prize was sent to Newport.

While the *Saratoga* made more captures than any New York privateersman, she was closely followed by the *Governor Tompkins*, which under Captain Joseph Skinner and subsequently Captain Shaler, captured a total of twenty vessels during her eventful career.

Success did not always attend privateering ventures. The firm of Samuel Tooker and Company went largely into that business in 1812, as did many other New York mercantile houses of that day. One vessel that they fitted out had a singular career, and we will give a detailed account of her to show how these privateering expeditions were conducted at the time. Messers. Tooker and Company fitted out a neat little brig, called the *Arrow*, with fourteen guns, selecting for commander, Captain E. Conklin, an able and very popular shipmaster, who had long been in the East India trade. They issued 65,000 dollars of stock, in shares of 1,000 dollars each. As soon as it was known that Conklin had charge, the shares were all taken, for it was known that Captain Conklin's East Indiaman had been captured by the British, and that in the *Arrow* he would do all in his power to injure British commerce and property. If she succeeded, Mr. Tooker, as agent of the enterprise, would have the selling of the prizes, thus earning large commissions, besides owning most of the shares. Everything looked bright for the *Arrow*. She was well equipped with everything necessary for a long cruise, and just as she was ready to sail, a United States vessel of war discharged her crew, so about 120 of them went on board the *Arrow* that bid fair to do well. New York harbor was then blockaded closely, but one dark night she sailed with her gallant commander and brave crew. Two other privateers left the same night, one named the *Whig* and the other the *Warrior*. They returned successful after some weeks, but the *Arrow* was never heard of from that time to this day.

Another successful privateer, owned in New York, was the *Scourge*, Captain Nicoll, which sailed for a long cruise in European waters, April 1813, and was frequently in consort with the *Rattlesnake*, of Philadelphia, a fast-sailing brig of fourteen guns. Because he found it more profitable to remain on shore and attend to the sale of prizes brought in or sent in, Captain Nicoll was often absent from the *Scourge*, while on the coast of Norway, so his first officer commanded her on cruises. The aggregate tonnage of prizes captured by the *Scourge* and *Rattlesnake*, which were nearly all sent into Drontheim and disposed of there, amounted to 4,500; the trophies being sixty guns.

New Yorkers sent out a splendid vessel of seventeen guns and 150 men, called the *Prince de Neufchatel*, in command of Captain Ordronaux, which proved a very fortunate privateer. During a single cruise, she was chased by no less than seventeen armed British vessels, and escaped them all; and she brought to the United States goods valued at 300,000 dollars, with much specie. The *Neufchatel* was finally captured and sent to England.

The most desperate and famous combat recorded in the history of privateering during the war was that between the *General Armstrong*, before referred to and now under the command of Captain Samuel C. Reid, and a large British squadron, at Fayal, in the Azores, on September twenty-sixth, 1814. This little craft, carrying only seven guns and ninety men, including her officers, lay at anchor in a neutral port,

Defense During Second War of Independence

when she was attacked by four large and well-armed launches, with about forty men in each, but they were driven off with heavy loss. Another attack was made at midnight with fourteen launches and about 500 men, and they were repulsed with a loss of 120 killed, and 130 wounded. At daybreak, a third attack was made by the brig *Carnation*, but she was very soon so cut up by the rapidly-delivered and well-directed shots of the *Armstrong* that she hastily withdrew. As it was evident that the little privateer could not maintain another severe assault, Captain Reid scuttled his vessel and then abandoned her. The British lost over 300 in killed and wounded, while the Americans lost but two killed and seven wounded. This British squadron formed part of the expedition then gathering at Jamaica for the purpose of seizing New Orleans, and the object of their attack on the *Armstrong* was to capture her, and make her a useful auxiliary in the work. She so crippled her asailants they did not reach Jamaica until ten days later than expected, and when they finally approached New Orleans, General Jackson was making competent arrangements for its defense. Had the fleet arrived ten days sooner, that city would have been an easy prey to the British.

The exports of New York City in 1791 were one-ninth of the aggregate exports of the United States; in 1794, nearly one-eighth; between 1796 and 1806, between one-quarter and one-fifth. The embargo paralyzed business. With its removal, trade revived with extraordinary rapidity and in 1811, the exports had risen again to 12,266,215 dollars. But the effects of the War of 1812, and especially of Madison's Embargo, were most disastrous. During the year 1813, the value of merchandise amounted to 1,624,574.20 dollars, against 5,223,696.45 dollars in 1810, and 10,785,354.42 dollars in 1816. In 1814, the exports amounted to only 209,670 dollars, and the Chamber of Commerce, which had kept open throughout the Revolution, was closed. Nearly all the goods imported were procured on credit. Private and public indebtedness had increased to a disastrous extent during the war, and general bankruptcy, private and municipal, State and national, was threatened.

New York City has witnessed many thrilling and exciting

scenes, but never in all its history were her sensations so rapturously played upon as on that cool Saturday evening, February eleventh, 1815, when a small boat landed from the British sloop-of-war *Favorite*, which passed through Sandy Hook and the Narrows that day, bearing the glad tidings that the Treaty of Peace had been ratified by the English government. The news was as unexpected as it was joyous. The people rushed through the streets crying "Peace!" "Peace!" "Peace!"; they hugged one another in their ecstasy. The whole town resolved itself into one grand jollification. The effect upon business was instantaneous. Prices went down with a smash; sugar dropped from 26 dollars a hundredweight to 12.50 dollars; tea and flour in proportion. All commercial and manufacturing enterprises bounded forward with an elasticity that bewildered the conservative merchant of old New York—that old New York, which, because of increased immigration and the opening of the Erie canal, was destined in a few years to pass away forever!

PART V

A PERIOD OF INVENTION, PROSPERITY
AND PROGRESS

1815—1829

V

AMERICAN COMMERCE SPRINGS INTO LIFE WITH THE ADVENT OF PEACE—AGAIN THE SHIPYARDS ARE BUSY AND SOUTH STREET BECOMES A BUSY HIVE OF INDUSTRY—MARCH THIRD, 1815, CONGRESS PASSES A LAW TO OBTAIN RECIPROCITY IN FOREIGN TRADE—VIGOROUS STRENGTH IS INFUSED IN EVERY DEPARTMENT OF OUR COMMERCE—PROGRESS AND COSMOPOLITISM OF THE NEW YORK MERCHANT—EAST INDIA MERCHANTS—SOME HISTORY ABOUT N. L. AND G. GRISWOLD—MURRAY, MUMFORD AND BOWEN, MURRAY AND MUMFORD AND GORDON S. MUMFORD—TALBOT, OLYPHANT AND COMPANY—ANENT SUPERCARGOES—INTERESTING CAREER OF THOMAS H. SMITH AND SC*.S, THE GREATEST TEA MERCHANTS IN THE UNITED STATES—HOW A SOUTH STREET MERCHANT COULD BE A "PLAY BOY"—THE "FIRE CLUB" AND WHEN THEY WERE "STUMPED"—BIOGRAPHICAL SKETCHES OF JONATHAN GOODHUE, PELATIAH PERIT, AND THE HOUSE OF GOODHUE AND COMPANY—ANOTHER "EAST INDIA FIRM," HOYT AND TOM—A SCOTTISH MERCHANT OF GLASGOW AND NEW YORK, JOHN TAYLOR—ARCHIBALD GRACIE AND HIS WONDERFUL CAREER—GRACIE'S PETITION TO CONGRESS—G. G. AND S. HOWLAND—FIRM CHANGED TO HOWLAND AND ASPINWALL—MINTURN AND CHAMPLIN, WHO CARRIED ON THE LARGEST CHINA BUSINESS IN NEW YORK—LOSS OF THEIR SHIPS AND CARGOES ABROAD CAUSES FAILURE—AFTERWARDS, JOHN T. CHAMPLIN ORGANIZES THE FARMERS LOAN AND TRUST COMPANY, NEW YORK—LIFE STORY OF ECCENTRIC PRESERVED FISH—FORMATION OF THE FIRM, FISH AND GRINNELL—POST AND RUSSELL, JOHN W. RUSSELL, MERCHANTS AND SHIPOWNERS—THE LARGEST NEW YORK MERCHANT IN IRISH TRADE, WILLIAM NEILSON—ORGANIZES NEILSON AND SON—FATHER AND SON ENTER INSURANCE BUSINESS, SERVING IN VARIOUS OFFICIAL CAPACITIES—JOHN PATRICK; SHEDDEN, PATRICK AND COMPANY; B. AYMAR AND COMPANY—INTERESTING ACCOUNTS ABOUT "BEN" AYMAR—A FEW

FACTS RELATING TO YANKEES CAPTURING BUSINESS IN NEW YORK—WHEN THE BATTERY WAS A FASHIONABLE PROMENADE; STATE STREET AND AROUND BOWLING GREEN WAS THE "SEAT OF FASHION"—WHEN NEW YORK'S WATERFRONT ELICITED ADMIRATION FOR ITS NATURAL ATTRACTIONS—STATE STREET THE IDEAL PLACE IN NEW YORK FOR A RESIDENCE—WHEN THE "PEEP O'DAY BOYS" LOOKED FOR THEIR SHIPS COMING INTO PORT FROM THE BATTERY—THE SIGNAL STAFFS AT THE BATTERY TO ANNOUNCE ARRIVAL OF SHIPS—THE OLD MERCHANT TAKES AN AFTER BREAKFAST WALK TO SEE THE SHIPPING—HOW A MERCHANT-RESIDENT OF STATE STREET BEAT HIS COMPETITORS—PROMINENT NEW YORK MERCHANTS WHO RESIDED IN STATE STREET—WHEN THE HUDSON RIVER SLOOPS ENJOYED A MONOPOLY—INTERESTING CAREER OF DAVID LYDIG, FLOUR MERCHANT AND HUDSON RIVER SLOOP OWNER—HISTORY OF THE AMERICAN SAILING PACKETS—THE FIRST VESSEL TO ENTER THE TRANSATLANTIC PASSENGER TRADE—ESTABLISHMENT OF THE BLACK BALL LINE OF LIVERPOOL PACKETS—BIOGRAPHICAL SKETCHES OF ISAAC WRIGHT, BENJAMIN MARSHALL, JEREMIAH AND FRANCIS THOMPSON—GREAT ADVANTAGES DERIVED FROM THE FORMATION OF NEW YORK'S INTERNATIONAL SHIP SERVICE—TO WHAT WE MAY ASCRIBE THE SURVIVAL OF THE AMERICAN FLAG IN OUR COASTING AND INLAND WATERS—A LITTLE HISTORY RELATIVE TO THE AMERICAN COASTWISE TRADE—*SAVANNAH*, FIRST STEAM-PROPELLED VESSEL TO CROSS THE ATLANTIC—AFTER THAT VOYAGE SHE IS DIVESTED OF HER STEAM APPARATUS AND USED AS A SAILING VESSEL—GOES ASHORE, BECOMES A TOTAL LOSS—NINETEEN YEARS ELAPSE BEFORE ANY EFFORT MADE TO CROSS THE OCEAN BY STEAM—*ROBERT FULTON*, PIONEER STEAM VESSEL BUILT FOR THE OCEAN SERVICE—LEAVES NEW YORK ON HER FIRST VOYAGE AND PROVES A SUCCESS—IS SOLD TO THE BRAZILIAN GOVERNMENT, MACHINERY REMOVED AND BECOMES A FRIGATE—WRECKED ON THE COAST OF BRAZIL—THE MERCHANTS OF NEW YORK CONVENE TO OBTAIN A FLOATING LIGHT OFF SANDY HOOK, FORM AN ASSOCIATION, THEN CONSTRUCT THE MERCHANTS EXCHANGE BUILDING—IN 1822, ON ACCOUNT OF YELLOW FEVER EPIDEMIC, MANY SOUTH STREET MERCHANTS MOVE TO "GREENWICH," UPPER BROADWAY AND OTHER POINTS NORTH—BAKER'S CITY TAVERN AND A SOCIETY CALLED "HOUSE OF LORDS"—MESSRS. THADDEUS PHELPS, PRESERVED FISH, JOSEPH GRINNELL AND OTHERS MEET THERE AND ESTABLISH THE

Invention, Prosperity and Progress 89

SWALLOW-TAIL LINE OF LIVERPOOL PACKETS—ANOTHER LINE, ORIGINATED BY BYRNES, TRIMBLE AND COMPANY, AND SAMUEL HICKS, ENTERS LIVERPOOL TRADE—THADDEUS PHELPS AND FISH AND GRINNELL, ON JULY THIRTIETH, 1822, ANNOUNCED THEIR NEW LINE OF LIVERPOOL PACKETS—CAPTAIN STODDARD CAUGHT SMUGGLING, LOSES COMMAND OF A NEW "LINER"—ROBERT KERMIT PERSUADES STEPHEN WHITNEY AND "NAT" PRIME TO ORGANIZE THE "SAINT" LINE—THEIR SHIP BRINGING NEWS OF ADVANCE IN PRICE OF COTTON AT LIVERPOOL, THEY MAKE LARGE PURCHASES IN NEW ORLEANS AND POCKET HUGE PROFITS— FIRST LINE OF HAVRE PACKETS FOUNDED BY FRANCIS DEPAU—CRASSOUS AND BOYD, AFTERWARD BOYD AND HINCKEN, WERE AGENTS OF THIS AND A SECOND LINE OF HAVRE PACKETS—WILLIAM WHITLOCK, JR., STARTS A THIRD LINE TO HAVRE—RELATIVE TO PACKET SHIPS, THEIR CONSTRUCTION, SPEED RECORDS AND PASSAGES—HOW THE PACKET SERVICE TENDED TO THE GROWTH AND PROSPERITY OF NEW YORK—THE FIRST PACKET SHIP LOST WAS THE *ALBION*, WITH NEARLY ALL ON BOARD—NEW YORK GOES IN MOURNING, ACCOUNT THIS SEA CATASTROPHE—SUCCESS OF LIVERPOOL AND HAVRE PACKETS LEADS JOHN GRISWOLD TO START A LONDON LINE—FISH AND GRINNELL'S RIVAL LINE TO SAME PORT—*EVENING POST*, JANUARY EIGHTH, 1824, DESCRIBES NEW YORK'S WONDERFUL COMMERCIAL GROWTH AND PROGRESS—IMPETUS GIVEN TO BUSINESS BY OPENING OF THE ERIE CANAL, IN NOVEMBER, 1825, EXCEEDS ALL EXPECTATIONS—INAUGURATION OF SIGNALING SYSTEM TO CONVEY NEWS OF INCOMING SHIPS—THE AMERICAN COASTWISE PACKETS EMANATING FROM NEW YORK—OLD SHIP LINE ADVERTISEMENTS IN 1827—WONDERFUL DIFFERENCE BETWEEN ADVERTISING BY THE OLD MERCHANTS AND NOW —TOPOGRAPHICAL DESCRIPTION OF NEW YORK CITY'S VARIOUS COMMERCIAL DISTRICTS IN 1828—WHAT THE *LONDON TIMES* SAID WHEN OUR MERCHANT MARINE FORGED TO THE FRONT AS A MARITIME POWER—CONGRESS ENACTS A LAW THROWING OPEN OUR INDIRECT TRADE TO THE WORLD—RESULT, GREAT REDUCTION IN OUR FOREIGN SHIPPING—THE QUESTION OF MERIT IN RECIPROCITY MAY BE JUDGED BY NORWAY AND SWEDEN SUPPLANTING AMERICAN SHIPPING, ETC.—EXTRACT FROM *JOURNAL OF COMMERCE*, NOVEMBER TWENTY-EIGHTH, 1828, IN ANTICIPATION OF A FUTURE DISPARAGEMENT OF THE OLD SAILING PACKETS—COMPARING THE COMMERCIAL PERIOD, 1820 TO 1830, SHOWS THAT THIS DECADE REPRESENTS THE MOST

FLOURISHING CONDITION OF SHIPPING IN AMERICAN HISTORY.

ONLY temporarily held in check by the War of 1812, the daring enterprise of New York merchants and of shipmasters sailing out of that port, which had been so conspicuously displayed from 1800 to 1810, sprang into life with fresh vigor as soon as peace was made. Again the shipyards along the East River became centers of active industry; whilst on South Street, there was a renewal of the characteristic din and noise made by clamorous cartmen, stevedores and others busily engaged loading and unloading the vessels tied up at the wharfs on the waterfront. And, on the one sidewalk of that "Street O' Ships," the cheerful, brisk manner of the merchants and their clerks, as they hurried to and fro, businesslike in the extreme, betokened an air of prosperity and confidence, which long had been smothered by embargoes, non-intercourse and, lastly, three years of active warfare.

March third, 1815, Congress passed a law forbidding any foreign vessel to bring goods to America, except from the country to which it belonged. This act was the legislative weapon by whose unsparing use we were enabled in the course of a few years to obtain from every foreign nation a treaty of reciprocity in trade, and to break down, one by one, the vexatious obstructions of foreign law to the free enterprise of American citizens in the carrying trade of the world. The legislative annals of Congress contain the complete record of this struggle, and our maritime career soon afterwards, proclaimed the victory.

Vigorous strength was infused into every department of commerce, on the termination of the War of 1812. The colonization of the new states of the west, the increase of new subjects of cultivation, especially that of cotton, and the augmentation of our population, together with the firm establishment of a compact and well organized government, affording free scope to national enterprise of all sorts, tended to advance with rapid strides, not only agriculture and the manufactures, but the commerce of the country; and it was soon expanded to the principal ports of Great Britain and France, Cuba and

Invention, Prosperity and Progress 91

Mexico, Spain and China, Brazil and the Hanse Towns, Russia and Denmark, Hayti, and the Argentine Republic, Sweden, Netherlands, Colombia, Peru, Malta, and Italy, adding large sums to our national wealth, and augmenting our general comforts. As we look abroad upon the ocean, we find our commerce floating from the icebergs of Greenland to the burning sands of the African desert—from the marble pillars of the Acropolis and the walls of China, to the wigwams of the remotest savage upon the north Pacific and the snow huts of the Esquimaux. Its sails are filled by the blasts of the polar sky, and the zephyr that breathes upon the sunny fields and crumbling columns of Italy. It stores its freights in the ports of Liverpool and Marseilles, or takes in its olives and macaroni by the side of the Venetian gondolier; everywhere increasing the amount of human knowledge, and acting as the agent of that liberty which is destined ultimately to brighten the world.

The East Indian trade had filled the pockets of our merchants prior to 1812 and ships from New York had found their way to the spicy and silky coasts of the Orient. It was the East Indian trafficking which proved the first to be revived after hostilities ceased.

The race of magnificent old East India merchants of the early part of the nineteenth century, and of a later period, have passed away. There was something grand in the title of an East India merchant. It conveyed the idea of large ships, long voyages occupying a year and more to the distant Oriental climes, whose commerce is still a mystery. East India merchant:—we at once think of "India's coral strand," "the golden Ind," "palmy plains," "the breezes of the Spice Islands," and a thousand other things that Columbus started to discover when he blundered upon this great continent, bearing a letter from Queen Isabella to the great Khan of Cathay. And was not Hendrik Hudson's ship fitted out to "seek westward the passage through China"? The fact is that the life of America has been continually bound up with that of the East.

Our forefathers were all accustomed to accord the highest mark of mercantile greatness to the merchant who owned his own ship, loaded her with silver, ginseng, lead, and sterling bills, and started her off on a voyage of a year, with or without a gentlemanly supercargo, to come back a wooden island of spicy perfumes, equal to any from Araby the blessed, as she lay at anchor in the East River, loaded with teas of all classes, with silks, nankeens, cassia, and a thousand other things that came from China. To us, the real East India merchant was the one who sent his ships to the Orient. We did not have much trade with British India, and the Calcutta merchant of the olden time ranked second to those firms who had, in former years, before other ports opened to the world, done a large trade with Canton.

Among those eminent East India houses in this city, well known to another generation, was N. L. and G. Griswold. It existed in 1796, at 169 Front Street, where they kept a flour store. George Griswold came to this city about two years previous to his brother Nathaniel. At that period many well known houses of merchants did not find it necessary to put the number of the street on which they were located. The city was small, and in offering merchandise for sale, the Griswolds simply made it, "apply to N. L. and G. Griswold." Everybody of any consequence knew where such a prominent concern could be found. It was so in 1803, when this house moved from their Front Street store to their new store, Number Eighty-six South Street, near Burling Slip. They did business in that spot a third of a century or more, when they moved to a new, rough, granite, double store, Numbers Seventy-one and Seventy-two South, north corner of De Peyster Street. There is "an eternal fitness in things," and that solid stone fortress was just the building for two such men as Nathaniel and George Griswold. It is there today, after they have passed away and nearly a century has elapsed since its foundation was laid.

When George Griswold arrived in this city he was only just of age, and his brother Nat, a few years old. They were very stout, fine looking young men, six feet high each, and well proportioned, and they were "six feet" men in all their business operations in after years, when they did an enormous business. They shipped flour heavily to the West Indies, and in 1804 they had become large importers of rum and sugar, receiving cargoes of these articles.

This house, like many other houses from the Eastern

Invention, Prosperity and Progress

States and ports, did an immense business by merely selling, chartering or freighting new ships. A shipbuilder "Down East" would build a large ship—about one hundred and a score years ago, a ship of 350 tons would be the very largest kind of a vessel. He would send on, for instance, such a ship, built of the best materials; her upper works being of live oak, locust and cedar, fastened with wrought copper; duck and cordage of the first quality; completely found in sails, rigging and furniture, and needing nothing whatever. They built ships strong and good in those days. There was little fancy work; all was solid and substantial, as many merchants and ship owners were their own insurers. The fact is there was not then much capital in the city of New York; ships and cargoes were generally found in Eastern ports—Salem, Boston, New Bedford, and other places. There were few houses that, like N. L. and G. Griswold, were able to own ships and make up long voyages, requiring great outlay on their own account.

In their day, or after the war, the duty on tea was enormous. Green tea paid as high as sixty-eight cents per pound; black tea as high as thirty-four cents from Canton. In all cases the duty was twice or three times the cost of the teas in Canton. The credit given by the United States Government was twelve and eighteen months. This, of itself, became an immense capital to any house engaged in the China trade. They could raise say 200,000 dollars and send it in specie or merchandise in their ships. These ships left in May. In a year they would be back loaded with teas. Merely supposing the duty double the cost in China (it was four times on low-priced black teas), the teas would be worth at least double, being 400,000 dollars. Add freight at a fair profit, would make the cargo worth 500,000 dollars at least. These teas would be sold, on arrival, to grocers at four and six months' credit. These notes would be discounted easily, while the Griswolds had to pay duty, 200,000 dollars, half in a year and half in eighteen months! Thus they really received from the Government an independent capital to do an enormous business.

The house of Griswold, however, did a safe, conservative business. That concern needed no capital but its own. Still many houses did go into this kind of business merely to get capital for other operations, as, for instance, many imported brandy that had an enormous duty then—about eighty cents a gallon. Government gave a credit of six, nine, and twelve months. Many, however, imported largely, sold to grocers, got their paper discounted, and had two-thirds of their money to use for nine or twelve months!

The Griswolds did an immense business in the China trade for years, and made a specialty of it at last. They owned the ship *Panama*, and there was not a country store, however insignificant, in the whole of the United States that had not handled large or small packages of tea, marked "Ship Panama," and "N. L. and G. G." upon it. Millions on millions of packages must have been imported from the first to last. In fact, they owned in succession three ships named the *Panama*. The first was 465 tons. When she became nearly worn out, the firm of N. L. and G. Griswold built a second ship of 670 tons burden, named her the *Panama*, and she succeeded No. One in the China trade. When the No. Two *Panama* got old, the Griswolds built a third ship of 1,139 tons burden, and named her the *Panama*. The three ships in the successive periods that they flourished must have made an uncommon number of Canton voyages. All of these were so successful that after No. Three was condemned and sold in 1867, the Messrs. Griswold had a fourth *Panama* built.

The reason for retaining the name *Panama* was that each chest of tea bore the name of the firm that had imported it and the vessel that brought it. The first lot of teas by the original *Panama* having been exceptionally fine, there was a popular demand for "Tea by the 'Panama.'" This lot was so profitable that the firm was known afterward as "No Loss and Great Gain" Griswold, but we are inclined to think it was derived from the marks "N. L. and G. G." with which all their tea, China goods, etc., was labeled.

The Griswold captains were a superior lot of men. Captain Eyre of their brig *John Gilpin* had orders to sail for China on a Christmas morning; but on that morning snow was falling, the weather was thick, seamen were scarce, and the Captain did not want to start.

"There is no wind," he said to one of the firm.

Invention, Prosperity and Progress 95

"Go and find wind," was the reply; "the wind is all ahead."

Sure enough it was: a heavy squall struck the *John Gilpin* off the west bank of Newfoundland, and not a smitch of her was left—cargo, ship, everything and everybody went under. That was a favorite expression of shipping merchants in those days—"Go and find wind." Old Commodore Vanderbilt used it whenever his captains were reluctant to start in unfavorable weather.

Many men who were afterwards prominent went out to Canton as supercargo of the *Panama*. One was a son named John N. A. Griswold, who resided out there some years. Another was John C. Green, who afterwards became a partner in the great Canton house of Russell and Co. When he retired from business and returned to this country, he married a daughter of George Griswold.

George Griswold made an excellent presiding officer at political meetings, or at popular meetings for any other purpose. He was always ready to do his part in promoting the interests of the city. He loved it. He felt the degradation of the New York merchants. He felt that here, in this great city, the merchants were what Nicholas Biddle once designated them—"wealthy white slaves." Now and then a scheming lawyer would rouse up a few of the class to take an interest in politics for some specific purpose. George Griswold mourned the degeneracy of the race of merchants in his later days. At the commencement of his career, the glorious conduct of the merchants of 1776 was fresh. Those noble old merchants were alive. He himself had met John Hancock, of Boston, and Francis Lewis, of our own city, both merchants—both signers of the immortal Declaration of Independence. When George Griswold arrived in New York in 1796, he could not turn a corner without meeting honored merchants of the city who had been the Liberty Boys of the Revolution.

In those years, none but the merchants ruled the city. There were seven wards. Of the fourteen Aldermen and Assistants, twelve were merchants. George Griswold felt that so it ought to be to the end of time. That merchants should rule—should command, and not be mere tools, as they had been. Merchants should rule the city, and represent it in the State Legislature and in Congress. He was ready with his money at any time to spend it freely to give the merchants of New York political power.

Old Nathaniel Griswold was very quiet and retiring. He cared nothing about being a bank director, or having anything to do with any one's business but his own. He differed from George in that respect, who as early as 1807 was made a director in the Columbia Insurance Company. From that time until he died he was honored with being a director in almost every society or monopoly of any importance. He was a man to be trusted, and he liked activity. The Bank of America, with its immense capital, was started in 1812, to take the place of the then defunct United States Bank, and Mr. George Griswold was, at that early period, elected a director, and he continued to be one for scores of years.

In the old times there was no name more eminent among the merchants of New York than that of Mumford. It was originally a New England family. When the New England Society was formed for friendship, charity and mutual assistance in 1805, four Mumfords joined it—John P., Benjamin M., William C., and Gurdon S. Mumford.

There was a firm of note—Murray, Mumford and Bowen, at Crane Wharf, in 1784. In 1789 they were at Twenty Peck Slip, and did an enormous business. They were in the East Indies trade, and imported largely of Hyson, Souchong and Bohea tea. In 1790 the house dissolved and the name was changed to John P. Mumford and Co., at the same place. Benjamin M. Mumford was the junior partner. Next year the firm was changed again to Murray and Mumford.

David and Gurdon formed a partnership under the name of D. and G. Mumford, and were in business together for many years. When they dissolved, Gurdon kept the commission business, and his brother David went in business with his son, B. M. Mumford, at Thirty Wall Street. In 1800 Old Gurdon died, and was succeeded by his son, Gurdon S., who for many years thereafter made his mark in New York life.

Before the War of 1812, Murray and Mumford, being largely engaged in foreign commerce, suffered seriously from

Invention, Prosperity and Progress 97

French depredations, and so forth. John P. Mumford subsequently united with other leading merchants of the city in furnishing ships to the Navy Department at their own cost, when the Treasury could not meet the expense. In addition to his mercantile activities, John P. Mumford served as President of the Columbia Insurance Co. some years; in 1810, he was elected President of the Ocean Insurance Company, and when he died, in 1821, he was President of the Merchants Insurance Company.

Gurdon S. Mumford, a much esteemed merchant, was elected to the Ninth Congress for the City of New York in 1805. He took the place of Daniel D. Tompkins, who had been appointed judge in the Supreme Court. His colleagues were the celebrated Samuel L. Mitchell and George Clinton, Jr. He was reëlected to the Tenth and Eleventh Congress, and held his seat to March third, 1811, a period of six years. During the war Gurdon S. Mumford loaned the Government 20,000 dollars. In 1816 he became a broker in Wall Street, and was one of the founders of the New York Exchange Board. He died at Fifteen Beekman Street in 1830, and his funeral was one of the largest ever held in New York.

The firm of Talbot, Olyphant and Company, in South Street, had a house in Canton which was founded by D. W. C. Olyphant, a supercargo who lived there many years. All connected with this house were pious people. Karl Gutzlaff, the German missionary, who, dressed as a Chinese, penetrated into the interior of China and afterwards translated the New Testament into Chinese, always stopped at Olyphant's in the American "Hong." They had a famed ship named the *Roman*, which, under command of Capt. Heolyn Benson, made some record voyages from Canton to New York.

There was not a port in the known world where the Stars and Stripes did not fly over some American vessel during the period of which we now write. While at first these vessels and those connected with them were mostly from New England, New York ships and merchants soon found their way to every part of the globe. Nearly all of the established American commercial houses in foreign ports were founded by the supercargoes of American vessels. At first they visited those ports, sold their cargoes, and bought return cargoes. After a while it was found necessary to remain constantly at the foreign ports. For instance, in Canton, China, when it was the only port open to foreign trade, the first supercargoes became in after years the principal merchants.

Thomas H. Smith went in the grocery business, 1800. In 1803, the firm of Thomas H. Smith and Sons began to be generally known and rose from grocers to be the greatest tea merchants in the United States. They had an enormous tea store in South Street, near Dover. It extended through to Water, and was a hundred feet wide. It was the wonder of the city when it was built; and, at night, with a myriad of gas jets brightly burning amidst ornamented cut-glass chandeliers, Smith's Tea Emporium was one of the most popular sights shown visitors from out of town. Smith's docks near it were named "India Wharf."

The firm of Thomas H. Smith and Sons went into the Canton trade on an enormous scale. Possessing originally but a few thousand dollars, they imported teas to such an extent that when the firm failed about 1827, they owed the United States 3,000,000 dollars, and, it is claimed, not a cent was ever paid. In those years there was credit given by the Government of nine, twelve and eighteen months on importations of teas.

It was a great business. A merchant who could raise 100,000 dollars in specie could soon have a large capital; and this was the working of the old system: Thomas H. Smith and Sons owned a ship, they started her from New York with a cargo of perhaps 20,000 dollars' worth of ginseng, spelter, and so forth, and 80,000 dollars in Spanish dollars. The ship went on the voyage and reached Whampoa in safety. (Canton was approached through two barriers, Macao and Whampoa.) Her supercargo in maybe two months had her loaded with tea, some chinaware, a great deal of cassia or false cinnamon, and a few other articles. The cargo, mostly tea, cost thirty-seven cents per pound on the average.

It must be borne in mind that the duty on tea was more than twice the cost, so that a tea cargo of say 100,000 dollars, when it had paid seventy-five cents per pound (which would be 200,000 dollars), amounted to 300,000 dollars. The profit

Invention, Prosperity and Progress

was at least fifty per cent on the original cost, or 50,000 dollars, and would make the cargo worth 350,000 dollars. The teas would be sold almost on arrival (say eleven or twelve months after the ship left New York) to wholesale grocers for their notes at four and six months. These notes could be turned into specie very easily, and the owner had only to pay his bonds for 200,000 dollars' duty, at nine, twelve and eighteen months, giving him time actually to send two more ships with 100,000 dollars each to Canton, and have them back again in New York before the bonds on the first cargo were due.

John Jacob Astor at one period of his life had several vessels operating in this way. They would go to the Pacific (Oregon) and carry thence furs to Canton. These would be sold at large profits. Then the cargoes of tea shipped to New York would be duly received, on which Astor did not have to pay duty to the United States for a year and a half. His tea cargoes would be sold for good four and six months paper, or perhaps cash; so that for eighteen or twenty years John Jacob Astor had what was actually a free of interest loan from the Government of millions of dollars. Astor was prudent and lucky in his operations, and such an enormous Government loan did not ruin him, when the crash came, as it did many others, among them the house of Thomas H. Smith and Sons, which had once drawn a check for 526,000 dollars to pay the duties on its imported teas.

To show how "strenuous" our old time South Street merchant could be as a "play boy," Walter Barrett, in "The Old Merchants of New York City," tells this "real hot" anecdote:

"Thomas H. Smith, besides being the greatest tea merchant of his day, was also the greatest 'Spreeite' of his day. He was the President of a club called 'The Fire Club.' It held its meetings in Franklin Square on the corner of Dover Street. Boys have a mode of amusement called 'Follow your leader.' This was adopted by the Club of which Smith was President. Many men who are now aged and respected men, or dead, belonged to the 'Fire Club,' Joseph Foulke, a trader at Curaçao, a Dutch Island in the West Indies, and the Staggs. There was old Peter Stagg, cashier of the City Bank, and John and

Benjamin Stagg. There was old Matthias Bruen, and many more whose names were on the Club list. They gave grand suppers, and their entertainments were very expensive. They would invite a guest to these suppers, explain the rules, and if he refused to join, or could not carry out the idea, the fine was one dozen of Champagne. These fines were occasioned by a refusal to follow the leader. On one occasion a great cotton merchant from New Orleans was a guest. He agreed to all the conditions. It was late in the evening, in the dead of winter. The ice in the East River was floating up and down with every flood or ebb of the tide. 'Follow leader,' shouted Smith, and out of the warm, luxurious club-rooms poured the members of the Club. Out of the Square around the corner into Dover Street. 'Follow leader,' and on rushed Smith, the President of the Club, with thirty men behind him, down Dover, past Water, past Front, into South, and thence on to the pier. One of Smith's own ships lay at the dock. A lighter lay inside of the main wharf. The ice was loose and dashed up around the vessels. 'Follow leader,' exclaimed Smith, as he plunged from the dock into the water. Some drew back, but others followed the leader, who succeeded in getting out of the ice water on to the lighter, and from thence to the dock; and shouting 'Follow leader,' he led off with frozen clothes, up Dover and into the room of the Club. Plunge, plunge, plunge, one after another, and so on until all had successfully accomplished the terrible and dangerous feat. The Southern cotton merchant was last. Some of the regular club members remained until they saw him reach the dock again safely and there they left him shivering. He did not remain long. As he walked up from the dock, he noticed a large store open in South Street. He entered. It was a wholesale and retail ship supply store. 'I have met with an accident—give me a glass of cognac, hot, with sugar and water.' It was done, and he drank it. 'Do you keep gunpowder?' he asked. Receiving an affirmative reply, he bought and paid for half a keg, and then took his way to the club room. At the door was standing Mr. Lowe and Mr. Town, two members of the Club. The latter exclaimed, 'Brave Southern stranger—you have passed the ordeal safely. You are now leader, and we are deputed to place the Club under your command, if you choose to exert your sacred privilege.'

"'Thanks, my friends, I shall do so, but I will not ask

Invention, Prosperity and Progress 101

you to go out of the room this cold night. Let us drink!' and as he entered the room, he sought a side closet where hung his cloak. There he placed the keg, and then returned and took a seat at the long solid mahogany table. President Smith called the Club to order. The stewards for the night opened a dozen of Champagne amid shouts, calls, and songs of the most stirring character. 'Order, come to order!' exclaimed President Smith. When order was partially restored, he said; 'Members of the club, our guest has passed the icy ordeal. He has now the right of becoming leader for the balance of the night, or until a failure in our sacred rites. What says he?'

"The cotton merchant took from his bosom a bundle of tow, and laid it on the table. All eyes were fixed upon him. 'I accept the command. I will lead now. Wait until I give the word and then do as you see me do.' By this time, he had spun the tow into a string, that would reach from the table to the grate. He placed a tumbler on one end of the tow, to hold it on the table, and then passed the other to the pan under the grate, and made that fast with a piece of coal from the coal scuttle. Not a word was spoken. All felt that something unusual was to occur. Cotton Merchant now deliberately went to the closet and returning with the keg took his seat. Then he went to work and removed the hoops, until he could take out the head of the little keg. Not a soul moved. Then he took a very little of what appeared to be black sand in his hand, walked to the fire, and flung it in. The considerable explosion that followed startled all. 'Powder, by Jupiter,' exclaimed Smith. Cotton Merchant took the end of the tow line from the glass, and pushed it down deep into the powder in the keg, and then reseated himself. 'Now, Mr. President and members of the club, I wish you to hear what I have to say.

"'You have tried my pluck. I come from a hot climate, and you have made me go through an icy ordeal. It is my time now, but I will not be so cruel. I will give you a fiery ordeal to go through. If you stand it, you will never need more wine; and if you do not, the fines will amount to a small fortune, and you will have wine enough to last your club a year. Look at me.' He walked to the fire, kicked off the coal lump, and placed the other end of the tow-line in the red hot coals. Then he walked back, and as he brought his fist down upon the table said in tones of thunder as he sat down, 'Keep your seats, and thus follow your leader.' The fire curled up in fitful spouts from the burning tow string—it burnt over the grate pan, and began to crawl along the carpet. It had eighteen feet to go. Sixty and odd single eyes, watched the burning train. One rose from his seat, then another, finally one exclaimed, 'We shall all be blown to old Nick,' and made for the door. The panic increased. Down stairs the club members plunged like a flock of sheep. Even Old Smith, the President, was among the first to bolt from the room. Before the tow-line had burned as far as the table all were gone but the cotton merchant. As soon as he saw that he was alone, he placed his foot upon the burning tow, and extinguished it. Then he opened the window and emptied the keg into the snow, and again resumed his seat. He waited long for the return of the club members; one by one they came back. There Cotton sat, until Smith took his seat as President. 'Now call for the fines,' he said, and a severe lecture he gave them for their follies and real cowardice."

There were three great tea houses in America at the period of which we write—Thompson, of Philadelphia; Perkins, of Boston; and Thomas H. Smith and Sons, of New York. In 1826, the market became overstocked; tea cargoes had come in so fast that the Government became scared about the duties. It must be remembered that the credit given tea importers was then nine, twelve and eighteen months—one-third at each period before they were made to pay the heavy duties. Thomas H. Smith had imported very largely, and he owed the United States probably two millions, and so Jonathan Thompson, who was then Collector of the Port of New York, refused to take his bonds.

When this upright Collector refused to take Thomas H. Smith's bonds for tea duties, Smith went at once to Perth Amboy and was told by the Collector of that port that he would take his bonds for any amount. Assured of this, Mr. Smith went to work at once and erected large warehouses, and then sent out pilot boats with orders to his captains, when they reached the Narrows, to go to Perth Amboy with his ships and their valuable cargoes. It mattered very little to Uncle Sam whether he was cheated at Perth Amboy, N. J., or at New York City. At last the firm of Thomas H. Smith and Sons failed. This failure upset the tea business for about five years, and nearly ruined every person engaged in it. Thomas H. Smith died not long after his failure.

A biographical sketch of the New York mercantile community during this period would be incomplete without including Jonathan Goodhue and the firm of Goodhue and Co. Jonathan Goodhue was the son of Honorable Benjamin Goodhue, who served two successive terms as U. S. Senator from Massachusetts. At the age of fifteen, he entered the counting room of the Honorable John Norris of Salem, a merchant of wealth and enterprise, extensively engaged in the trade of Europe and the East Indies. After a few years spent in the counting room, young Goodhue was sent as supercargo to Aden, Arabia, remaining there six months. His second voyage was to Calcutta, terminating in a year's time.

Jonathan Goodhue came to New York in 1807. In commencing his commercial career, it was his singular good fortune to enjoy the patronage of William Gray, also Joseph Peabody, the two richest and most influential merchants in New England. He was equally fortunate in being recommended to gentlemen of leading influence in New York, like Archibald Gracie, Hon. Oliver Wolcott, then engaged in commercial pursuits, and General Matthew Clarkson, and they all remained his warm friends. This was an auspicious beginning, and few men at the outset of life have been so highly favored. It was, however, an advantage which he could not have continuously enjoyed if he had not established a character which gave him a title to their confidence and esteem.

He still enjoyed the firm friendship of his early friend, Mr. Norris, who, with William Gray and Joseph Peabody, assisted him greatly in getting a great deal of Salem business, and much from Boston. His first partnership, in 1809, was with Mr. Swett, and they formed the firm of Goodhue and Swett, at Thirty-four Old Slip, afterwards moving to Forty-four South Street, one of those substantial "Modern" buildings belonging to Theophilat Bache. Goodhue and Swett did a heavy commission business for three or four years, and sold largely of foreign dry goods; acting, also, as agents for many New England shipowners, until 1811, when the firm was dissolved and Mr. Goodhue carried on the business upon his individual account till about 1816. Then it was Goodhue and Ward, and the relations of Mr. Goodhue's firm became, by degrees, more widely extended through all the commercial ports of Europe, the East Indies, Mexico, and South America.

He formed a partnership with Pelatiah Perit, in 1819, under the name of Goodhue and Company, "for the purpose of doing a general commission and freight carrying business." Mr. Perit was a Norwich boy, who had strong connections, and brought to the firm a vast amount of New England business. His graduation from Yale in 1802 made him one of the few college men in New York mercantile circles.

Large shipowners and merchants were located "Down East," in every state of New England except Vermont. Maine had her Portland and Bangor; Massachusetts had Boston, Salem, New Bedford, Newburyport and other ports; Rhode Island, her Providence and Newport; Connecticut had New London, Norwich and New Haven. Most of all the shipping emanating therefrom was owned in these New England cities, and consequently the merchant in New York who had the most extensive "Down East" connections did the largest business. Our readers must understand that to be the New York agents of these Eastern shipowners did not confine one to getting freights outward, or the consignment of the ship when she returned from a voyage to the port of New York. That was but a fraction of the business. Many of the larger New England shipowners were also merchants, so they would load a vessel for an outward voyage, and the return cargo would be on "owner's account." If it was an East Indian cargo, New York was the best port, and the Salem, Boston or New Bedford owner would order his ship and cargo to New York, consigned to his agent.

Yankee boys, clerks of the firm, went out to distant parts of the world and formed commercial houses—some in Canton, Calcutta, St. Petersburg, London, Liverpool, and so forth. Their first strike would be to open a correspondence with the "mother" firm of Goodhue and Company. The latter house ran no risk. It acted as agent for commercial firms in all parts of the world. It never deviated from its course, never speculated, and, consequently, stood as firm as the Rock of Gibraltar for many decades. The business of this world must be carried on, and there must be commercial centers, where wealth, with all its responsibilities, perils, and advantages, will be concentrated. There was never any prospect whatsoever that the pressure of care, the competition of trade, the increase of wealth, or the growth of their private fortunes, ever diminished the honest efforts of Jonathan Goodhue and his partners to straightway pursue their way in the "walks of life."

Some idea of the immensity of business transacted by large South Street merchants, like Goodhue and Company, in the days of their greatest prosperity, may be gathered from this illustration: they would sell a cargo of teas and China goods, worth perhaps 400,000 dollars, at auction or by brokers, say in an hour. They would receive their commission of two and one-half per cent and a guarantee commission of two and one-half more. If the cargo was worth half a million, their commission would be 25,000 dollars. The guarantee commission was against loss to those who sent consignments of merchandise to the South Street merchant. The latter were obliged to sell on time, say four to six months' credit to those who bought of them. If they sent notes, Goodhue and Company or other commission houses would guarantee them, and for so doing charge a guarantee commission of about one-half per cent a month. If a note was received by a house like Goodhue and Company and not paid, they lost it, and not the owner of the teas or other merchandise. It was said that their guarantee account was a losing one, for, prudent as they were, many mercantile failures occurred in New York during the half century or more that Goodhue and Company continued in business. At the same time it is safe to say that no foreign merchant would consign goods to Goodhue and Company or any other prominent New York commission house, unless they agreed to guarantee and make good the notes taken for merchandise, if not paid at maturity. This brief sketch outlines how a commercial house of the old school handled some of their financial transactions and business.

Jonathan Goodhue's commercial life extended through an interval of time fraught with momentous events, affecting deeply the position and circumstances of commercial men. The long embargo; the war with England which followed it; the various changes in the Bank of the United States, and final overthrow of that institution; the various alterations of the tariff, and the successive contractions and expansions of the currency consequent upon these events, occasioning heavy disappointments and losses to all the community, followed in quick succession. It was no small felicity to have survived these changes, and to have maintained throughout a high credit and unsullied reputation.

Another celebrated East India firm was that of Hoyt and Tom. Goold Hoyt was in early years a supercargo for LeRoy Bayard and Company, the greatest commercial house in New York for many years.

When China passages of one hundred days or so caused no little comment, their famous ship *Sabina*, on March twenty-first, 1834, commanded by Captain McEwen, backed her main yard off Sandy Hook Light, ninety days from Canton, a record unsurpassed until the clippers came into being on the China run.

From a privately printed volume, "John Taylor, A Scottish Merchant of Glasgow and New York," by Emily Johnston de Forest, we have culled this interesting account:

"In the New York directory of 1784 we find the record of John Taylor & Co. at 225 Queen Street, and from that date to 1829 all his commercial undertakings were conducted from this address. He was at first an auctioneer, and it was his custom to have 'public vendues' of his 'well known goods' on the last Friday of each month. These vendues continued long after he himself ceased to be the 'Crier.'

"He was, furthermore, a merchant and an importer, largely of woolen goods, which came principally from Manchester, England, where he had interests in several factories. There were then fortnightly packets sailing from Liverpool, and his goods were forwarded by 'every second packet.' One of his sons, either James Scott or Andrew, usually resided at Manchester or Liverpool and attended to the purchase of goods and to their shipment. In 1812 or possibly earlier James Scott had gone for this purpose to live in Manchester.

"During the War of 1812 all trans-Atlantic commerce was of course at a standstill, but our canny Scot knew that the

Invention, Prosperity and Progress

war must end sometime, and when peace was declared, he already had large stores of goods purchased and prepared for shipment. He wrote to James to divide these goods, for additional safety, and to 'ship by first two good American vessels that offer.' He also reminded him that the articles to be forwarded now were all for spring sales and that winter goods should be ordered without delay. 'But,' said he, 'I do suppose that the markets will be very much overstocked, in that case I mean to purchase here rather than import much.'

"Mr. Taylor's son Andrew was then a clerk in his father's New York office, and it was in February, 1815, immediately after the close of the war, that John Taylor took his two sons, James Scott and Andrew, into partnership, promising to give each of them one-third of his profits and to allow each one to do a commission business on his own account. The firm name was at this time changed to 'John Taylor & Sons.' Andrew went to England in 1818, when he was twenty-five years old, to make his home there and attend to the affairs of the firm, and his brother, James Scott, returned to America.

"The year 1830 found the firm established in a store which John Taylor had purchased at 72 South Street, and his business was conducted there until the time of his death in 1833. After that the affairs of John Taylor & Sons were closed up.

"It was one of his peculiarities to charge for his merchandise sixty per cent over the foreign cost. This amount, he said, represented the duty, freight, all expenses and his own profit. So invariable was this rule that he came to be known among his business associates as 'Old Saxty-per-cent.' Another peculiarity was that he never insured any shipment—and for nearly forty years he never had a single loss. Then the 'Minerva' went down with twenty-two of his cases on board. They were valued at $5,500 and there was no insurance, but the owner was undoubtedly still satisfied that his way was the best, as perhaps it was.

"For his accounts he used large ledgers of beautiful handmade paper watermarked 'J. Taylor 1795.' Many of these are still in existence and treasured by his descendants."

Among our eminent merchants (during the European wars which gave us the carrying trade of the world) none exerted a wider influence for good, or were more conspicuous for probity and honor, than Archibald Gracie of New York, William Gray of Boston, and Joseph Peabody of Salem, Massachusetts. It is said that their credit, at times, surpassed that of the Government itself, and their operations were more varied and extensive than ever conducted by individual enterprise in our country.

Archibald Gracie came out to America from Scotland as supercargo of a small vessel, directly after the Revolutionary war. He became one of the most successful merchants New York had ever seen up to his time. Endowed with rare sagacity and sound sense, to which he added great experience, his commercial enterprises were laid with judgment, and executed with zeal. His signal flag was known in most of the ports of the Mediterranean and the Baltic seas of the Peninsula, in Great Britain and China, and his name was synonymous with credit, probity, and honor. Even the Spanish government (not usually overconfiding in foreigners) intrusted to him at one time their bills of exchange, drawn on Vera Cruz, to the extent of ten millions of dollars. These bills were brought in a French frigate to New York, in 1806, and Isaac Bell, Esquire, who had charge of them, was upset in a boat, and a reward of two hundred dollars was offered to the finder of the trunk which contained them. It was picked up a fortnight after, at Deal Beach, near Long Branch. The bills were dried and collected in specie by Mr. Gracie and two other merchants—Mr. Oliver, of Baltimore, and Mr. Craig, of Philadelphia. It is needless to add, that the proceeds were remitted with scrupulous exactness and promptitude.

His firm, Archibald Gracie and Son, had ships trading to the East Indies, to Europe; in fact, they did business with all parts of the world, until the seizure of several of their ships by France, under the Berlin and Milan decrees of Bonaparte forced him to a failure. He could not get any redress during his life, but after his death, which occurred in 1829, President Andrew Jackson forced the French Government to pay this as well as other claims. Between the British and French governments, he had suffered losses estimated at over a million dollars. As many of our readers have heard about "French Claims," we will give a statement made by Mr. Gracie on the same subject. He had waited until he was heartsick for redress. None came. Finally he sent the following eloquent petition to Congress before he died:

"To the Honorable the Senate and House of Representatives of the United States of America in Congress Assembled:
The Memorial of Archibald Gracie, of New York, a citizen of the United States, Respectfully Sheweth,

"That your memorialist, in the year 1806, loaded the 'brig' 'Perseverance,' and in 1807 the ship 'Mary': that they were cleared directly for Antwerp—sailed—were captured by British cruisers, and after a forcible detention of a few days in England, arrived at Antwerp, one in March, the other in July, 1807. At the time of their arrival, the only extraordinary decree in existence which affected the navigation of neutrals was the Berlin, of the 21st of November, 1806, which, among other provisions, declared that English property, or manufactures, or her colonial produce, were good prize; that no vessel coming directly from England or going to England or her colonies, should be permitted to enter a French port; and that every vessel contravening the decree, by a false declaration, should be seized and her cargo confiscated. In consequence of an application to obtain the property in question, the French Government gave orders to admit and land the cargoes in Entrepôt. This decision evinced that the government did not consider the Relache Forcee in England as sufficient to justify the Non-admission of the vessels and cargoes; subsequently an inquiry was directed to be held, to ascertain if there were any English property on board. This inquiry was scrupulously carried into effect by the agents of the government, and a report was made that no English property was on board. The ship's papers are acknowledged to have been regular, and no ground was ever set up that there was a false declaration; nor could it have been set up; for the fact of having been forced into England was stated by the captains on arrival. Thus none of the provisions of the Berlin decree of 1806 having been contravened, all opposition to the property passing into the hands of the consignees was expected to cease; but, though the vessels were suffered to depart, upon bonds being given to abide the issue of such decision as should be made, the cargoes were still retained in Entrepôt; nor was it until their perishing condition was represented, that orders were issued to sell them under the joint inspection of the government officers and the consignees, and to place the proceeds provisionally in the *Caisse d'amortissement*. At length, by a financial decree of Bonaparte, without trial, adjudication, or any civil process whatever, the proceeds of all sequestered property were directed to be taken out of the *Caisse d'amortissement*, and placed in the public treasury. Part of the cargoes of the 'Mary' and the 'Perseverance' being ashes, had been previously, in 1809, delivered over to the Department of War, according to a decree by which the value thereof was directed to be paid into the *Caisse d'amortissement* (though such payment was the condition of the delivery, yet it never has been made,) there was a process verbal drawn up at the time by the committee appointed by the government, detailing the transaction by which the weights are given, and the value notwithstanding heavy deductions, stated to be about fr. 450,000; the remainder of the 'Mary's' Cargo produced about fr. 627,711 and that of the 'Perseverance,' about 193,212, making the claim amount to in all, fr. 1,270,923, without including interest, which, as the French nation has had the use of the money, is as fairly due as the principal; more especially as no claim is made for the depreciation of the goods by damage during the illegal detention in Entrepôt, which depreciation was great, in general, and upon the ashes amounted to twenty per cent. No possible ground exists for withholding the property.

"Enough seems to have been said of the undeniable justice of this claim; and of the duty incumbent upon the French Government (having in several instances admitted American Claims and paid them separately) no longer to withhold the same measure of justice from your memorialist. Under this statement of his case, your memorialist submits with confidence to the wisdom of Congress to such steps in relation thereto as to them shall seem fit."

G. G. and S. Howland did considerable business with both the East and West Indies. The concern stretched out and made new commercial connections in all directions. They opened a trade with the Mediterranean, and also became largely connected with England, and business went on swimmingly. The Howlands owned several Liverpool packets, among them

Invention, Prosperity and Progress

the *John Jay, William Brown,* and *Crawford;* their fleet consisting of at least seventeen or eighteen ships.

While a clerk with LeRoy, Bayard and McEvers, Gardner G. Howland was sent out to Matanzas as supercargo of a little brig. He then probably formed many connections that in after years added to his commercial grandeur.

When Gardner returned to New York, he made arrangements to commence on his own account. He did business for three years before his brother Samuel S. joined him. Meanwhile he had married a daughter of the rich William Edgar, a wealthy old merchant; and it was from Miss Edgar he received capital and credit sufficient to establish the firm of G. G. and S. Howland.

The first vessel the firm owned was a schooner, and she was named the *Edgar.* She lasted many years, and they kept her running in the Matanzas trade. This schooner was built and named the same year that William Edgar Howland (the eldest son of G. G. Howland) was born.

G. G. and S. Howland worked along by degrees, until they got into a very heavy Mexican and West India business, Vera Cruz, Campeche, and so forth, and so forth. The house suffered heavily by placing too great confidence in a person it sent out to Mexico as agent. Nothing saved them but the indomitable courage of G. G. Howland. He mastered all the difficulties. He frequently said, that on but two occasions was his house in danger. Once by the rascality of this agent in Mexico, and again in the "Greek business."

The Greek business nearly broke them. The firm contracted to build two men-of-war for the unfortunate Greeks. LeRoy, Bayard and Company shared in this contract. They employed Commodore Chauncey, under whose inspection the Greek frigates were built. But only one was sent out to Greece; the other was bought by our Government, and eventually rotted in the house at the Brooklyn Navy Yard.

The Howlands went through the cotton panic in 1826, when hundreds of houses failed. After this difficulty, Gardner G. Howland went to England. He afterwards traveled all over Europe. His pleasing address, and encouraging mode of talking, made him very popular, and he procured an enormous business both from England and from the continental cities.

William H. Aspinwall was a nephew. He was brought up in the house as a clerk. About 1832, he was taken into the firm as a partner, and in 1836 or 1837, the firm of G. G. and S. Howland was changed to Howland and Aspinwall. The two old Howlands retired as active partners, each one putting in a cash capital of one hundred thousand dollars. The general partners were William Edgar Howland, the eldest son of Gardner G., by his first wife, and William H. Aspinwall.

One of the earliest mercantile firms dealing with the East Indies, China and many other foreign countries, was Minturn and Champlin who did business at 214 Front Street as early as 1792 and up to 1816 remained a power in the Tea trade and carried on the largest business here in China goods. Beside John T. Champlin, there were three Minturns in this old firm, Nat, Jonas and Edward.

To show the widely international character of their trading, especially in China, we give below a letter which they sent out to that country by their supercargo William Law. It is addressed to the celebrated Chinese "Hong merchant" Houqua, who was the great friend of Americans in China; and, after reference to the Canton business of the Ship *Lion*, refers to the loss, some time previously, of two of their ships by Danish privateers, the brigs *Nimrod* and *Swift*, in which these New York merchants and Houqua, were both interested:

"New York, December 23, 1815.
"Mr. Houqua.
Dear Sir:

"We have already wrote you by this opportunity to which we refer—since which we have agreed with Mr. Law who will hand you this and who goes out supercargo of the ship 'Lion,' belonging to Mr. Butler that after he has done the business of that ship to remain in China another season in the hope that we shall be able to make through him some payment to you on account of the demands you may have against us, that he pay personal attention to it. We therefore request you when he applies to you to give him all the information on the subject he may require that he may communicate the same to us.

"Mr. Law was our agent in Copenhagen at the time of capture and condemnation of the ship 'Resolution,' and will hand you the papers relative thereto. We put them under his charge in the hope that you may, with him, obtain through the Danish Company's agent some compensation for your shipment in her as well as our own. We are
Very respectfully,
(Signed) MINTURN AND CHAMPLIN."

Owing to heavy losses sustained through the seizure of their ships and cargoes in foreign ports, Minturn and Champlin failed about 1816. John T. Champlin later undertook the launching of The Farmers Loan and Trust Company, which beside being a financial institution, entered the field of fire insurance, and he became its first president. This was in 1822, one of the years when yellow fever raged in the city; and as the period of 1822 to 1845 was the period of farm expansion in New York State, stimulated by the construction of the Erie Canal, the fire insurance business was discontinued, after seven years, and the Company concentrated its attention on agricultural loans and banking.

Jonas Minturn became a partner in the well known commercial house of Franklin and Minturn, and his brothers became interested in the firm of Grinnell, Minturn and Company after the dissolution of Minturn and Champlin.

Preserved Fish, senior partner in the firm of Fish and Grinnell, the members of which came here from New Bedford to attend to the oil and candle business of New Bedford whale oil merchants, but branched out in various lines until they became the proprietors of the Swallow Tail Line of Liverpool packet ships—a singular man and distinguished merchant—was born in the village of Portsmouth, Rhode Island, July third, 1766, and died in New York City, on July twenty-third, 1846, in the eightieth year of his age. His father, whose name was also Preserved Fish, descended from one of the best Huguenot families in this country, and followed the humble employment of a blacksmith.

The early history of his life was not particularly distinguished. He was a noisy, unruly youth, and though the son of an honest but poor man, he was unsteady in his habits, and it was with the utmost difficulty that he could be made to work at one employment for any length of time. He labored with his father a sufficient length of time to familiarize himself with all the secrets of the anvil, and then desired to be apprenticed to a substantial farmer. Master Fish, at the age of fourteen, was in a fair way of becoming a good husbandman, but it so happened that he sickened of his agricultural labors, and throwing away his hoe, he resolved to see what he could do upon the ocean. We then find him strolling along the wharves of New Bedford, in search of a sailors' berth. He was without money, and borrowed a few dollars of a stranger, (who took pity upon him,) with which he purchased a few necessary clothes, and in a few days he was on board of a whaling ship bound to the Pacific. He worked his way up so very rapidly that he became a captain at the age of twenty-one. He followed the sea for many years, and by industry and economy accumulated a handsome fortune.

In 1810, Captain Fish settled in New Bedford, as shipping merchant, having given up the sea. His partner in business was Cornelius Grinnell, and the firm was Fish and Grinnell. It was at this period of his life that he became engaged in politics. He was a bitter Democratic partisan, and his many quarrels and disappointments as such, were the cause of his leaving New Bedford. His manner of proceeding on this occasion was somewhat peculiar. He happened to be passing the stand of an auctioneer one day, while there was a crowd assembled, and stepping suddenly up to the gentleman with the hammer, he exclaimed in a loud voice: "I want you to sell my house!" Without any other notice the house was put up, and knocked down to a gentleman, for about one-half its value. In a fortnight from that time Preserved Fish was settled upon a farm at Flushing, New York, which he had purchased, with a view of devoting himself to agriculture.

He soon tired of this agricultural venture, and came to New York City to reside. He was appointed Harbor Master for the port, and took an interest in politics. A great number of lucrative offices were offered to him about this time, but he would not accept any of them. He was a true patriot, and desired to see his country prosper in every branch of business.

Invention, Prosperity and Progress

He was ever true to the principles of his party, but was strongly disposed to "go" for his friends, whatever their politics might be. One of these friends, whose cause he warmly advocated, was De Witt Clinton, to whom he proved faithful until the great man's death. But Captain Fish's paragon of a statesman and a man was Andrew Jackson, after whom his own strongly marked character seemed to have been molded. At this time his property amounted to about fifty thousand dollars.

In the year 1815, he formed a business connection with Joseph Grinnell. The firm was Fish and Grinnell, and they did a large shipping business. The reason why Captain Fish was always connected with the Grinnell family was because he had descended from the same stock as the Grinnells. Fish and Grinnell were the founders of that celebrated and wealthy house known as Grinnell, Minturn and Company, and they were among the first to establish a regular line of Liverpool Packets.

In 1826, Captain Fish, having acquired a fortune of one hundred thousand dollars, dissolved his connection with Joseph Grinnell, when the firm of Grinnell, Minturn and Company was organized, and he went to Liverpool. He there formed a connection with a couple of English merchants, Edward Carnes and Walter Willis, followed the shipping business for two years, lost about thirty thousand dollars, and returned to this city, completely disgusted, as he said, with the English methods of transacting business.

His last partner in business was Saul Alley, with whom he remained, however, only about six months. The immediate cause of the dissolution was as follows: Mr. Alley entered the office one morning, and seeing Captain Fish busily employed, he expressed a little surprise at his smartness, and added: "Hope you are well this morning, Captain Fish." Whereupon the Captain, who seemed to be in an unhappy mood, returned answer, "This is the place for business, sir, not for compliments." Mr. Alley answered the supposed insult in a manner peculiarly his own, and, in a few days, the firm of Fish and Alley was dissolved by mutual consent. He remained out of business for about seven years, when he was elected President of the Tradesman's Bank, to whose interest he devoted his undivided attention until the day of his death.

The causes of Captain Fish's success were his sound judgment and his unwearied attention to business, together with his daring in conceiving, and his perseverance in carrying out his various commercial plans. Whenever he said that a ship must sail, she was always sure to sail. On one occasion, when the pilot did not make his appearance at the very moment a certain ship was to sail, he went on board, and piloted her to sea himself. The integrity of Preserved Fish was never impeached, and he ever considered the fulfillment of his engagements as the most sacred of his duties to his fellowmen. He was not what we call an educated man, and not at all conversant with accounts. He was, however, a sound thinker and able reasoner. He kept his business plans to himself, and always acted upon the principle that it was better to be sure of a small profit, than risk all by an unnecessary delay. He was always devoted to business, but more on account of his passion for excitement, than on account of his love for gold.

The story that Preserved Fish had been picked up, when a child, on the ocean's shore, is a mere fiction. Its origin has been traced to the following laughable incident: While on one of his trading voyages, Captain Fish was hailed by a revenue cutter with the question, "What's the name of that brig?" "Flying Fish, sir!" "What's your cargo?" "Pickled Fish!" "Who's your captain?" "Preserved Fish." The revenue officer became quite angry, and immediately boarded the brig, to revenge himself for the insult. When he found, however, that only the truth had been spoken, he enjoyed the joke, and vowed that he would preserve the memory of Preserved Fish, as an ocean wonder.

John W. Russell was a partner of the house of Post and Russell, and prominent for many years as a merchant. They commenced as early as 1802. Their store was corner of Pine and South Streets (Sixty-nine South). Henry Post, Junior, his partner, had been in business on his own account as early as 1798.

When John W. Russell went out of Post and Russell, he took the store No. Seventy South Street, next door above that of Post and Minturn, and formed the house of John W. and Gilbert Russell. That house did an enormous business for

Preserved Fish.
From an old print
in the author's
possession

Moses H. Grinnell
From an engraving in the author's possession.

Invention, Prosperity and Progress   117

years. They had the ship *Minerva* in the Liverpool trade, 280 tons burden. The Russells owned the ship *Olive Branch*. Gilbert went out of the house in 1814, and John W. kept on in his own name doing a very heavy business for years. In 1822 there were few merchants who did more. He was then at Seventy-three South Street, and lived at Seventy White Street. He had the brig *Favorite* trading to Liverpool. He sold oil and candles of the New Bedford brands in large quantities. He owned the brigs *Hero* and *Abigail*. He had a line of packets to New Orleans. One was the armed brig *Fanny*, Captain Packard (they armed vessels in those days for fear of Gulf pirates). Another was the armed brig *Edward*, Captain Hallett; brig *Washington*, brig *Belvidere*, ship *William*, brig *Anna Maria*, brig *Wm. Thatcher*. He afterwards had a ship line of New Orleans packets; among them was the ship *Virgin*, and the ship *George*, Captain Barstow.

The Russells were receiving constantly cargoes of cotton and rice and New Orleans sugar, Kentucky tobacco, molasses, ravensduck, wines, raisins, spices, indigo, and cochineal. Mr. Russell was a clever business man. His splendid career was cut short about 1828, by his death.

His old partner, Henry Post, went with Joseph Grinnell, and after with his brother-in-law, Minturn, under the firm·of Post, Grinnell and Minturn, in 1809. Their store was at Sixty-nine South Street, corner of Pine, and they did a heavy business. They received cotton by lots of 200 and 500 bales. They had vessels for sale or charter and for freighting.

In 1812, Mr. Grinnell left the firm, and it became Post and Minturn. That year he took a store at 486 Pearl Street, and Joseph Grinnell went with him; but it was not until 1815 that the firm of Fish and Grinnell was formed—a house which grew steadily for many years, especially after it became Grinnell, Minturn and Company. How many partners in it made vast fortunes? How many clerks became eminent merchants who graduated from this house?

In 1774 just before the war, William Neilson, the elder, was doing a magnificent business. He had the ship *Needham*, Captain William Chevers, as a trader between Cork and New York. She made regular passages, lay at Lot's wharf, carried passengers, and always brought a supply of white slaves, who were advertised thus: "The times of a few servants for sale on board of said ship. Also, Irish beef, in tierces, of the best quality; with a few firkins of butter. Apply to W. Neilson."

Those "servants" were redemptionists. Some of our best families in this city came over to this country under these circumstances: For instance, the correspondent of William Neilson at Dublin, said to an Irishman who was poor, "Well, Michael, you wish to go to New York, but have no money. Now, I will advance you £100, and give you and your family passage to America."

The result would be that Michael would accept, and work out his £100, whether it was for one, two, or three years, according to the terms of the agreement. As soon as Michael landed in New York, his time was sold by Mr. Neilson. This did not apply particularly to Ireland, but also to Scotland and England.

William Neilson also had the ship *James and Mary*, Captain Workman, in the Irish trade. He was one of the largest importers of blue, white and enameled china, from England, before the war. He sold Irish clover seed. He imported and sold largely of Hibernia pig metal, also tierces of rice; lard and dry goods of all kinds; and, what was most agreeable to our citizens ninety years ago, he took "every kind of produce in pay at the highest market price." Why not?

The favorite vessel of William Neilson was the ship *Mary and Susanna*, Captain John Thompson. She traded direct to Dublin, and always lay at Robert Murray's wharf, at the foot of Wall Street. There were a great number of vessels trading from this to Irish ports a hundred and fifty years ago, and the principal cargoes they carried out were flax-seed and flour.

William Neilson was one of the first to serve as an Alderman after the war, being elected Alderman of the Dock ward in 1784, and was reëlected serving until 1787. In 1788, we find him chartering vessels and sending them to the West Indies, also carrying on a large Mediterranean business. He also owned a ship called the *Ann and Susan*, Captain Anthony Seeds. She traded regularly to Bordeaux and carried freight

Invention, Prosperity and Progress 119

and passengers. William Neilson had his counting house for several years at Forty Great Dock Street. In 1794 it became Eighty Pearl Street, when the names of streets were changed. He was an honorary member of the Marine Society in 1770, and a subscriber to the Tontine stock in 1792, naming Edward Neilson Munday, a son of Amos Munday, as holder of the shares.

He had two sons, James H. and William Neilson, Jr., and in 1797, he took the latter into the firm of William Neilson and Company. They received cargoes from Bristol, from Hull and other ports, in the ship *Joseph*, 1797, ship *Attila* 1799 to 1804—several voyages from Bristol—ship *Charlotte*, ship *Enterprise*, ship *Susannah*, ship *Adamant*, ship *Phocion*. In 1807, the firm was changed to William Neilson and Son. Up to this time, from 1800, the store had been at No. Forty-six Water Street. In 1810, they moved to No. One State Street, and William Neilson, Jr., resided in State Street. In 1810, William Neilson and Son were doing as large a business as any house in New York City. They owned the ship *Niagara*. She came in that year with an immense cargo of sugar, hides, fustic, and 4,000 bags Rio coffee.

One of the most remarkable facts is the connection of the Neilsons, father, son, and son-in-law, with Marine Insurance. When the first Insurance Company, the Mutual, was started in this city before 1789, William Neilson, Sr., was one of the Directors. He continued a Director until 1797, when the New York Insurance Company was established, with Archibald Gracie as its President. He was one of the first named Directors, and continued to be until 1802, when the Marine Insurance Company was incorporated.

In 1810, William Neilson, Jr., became President of the Marine Insurance, and his father, old William, became Director once more. In 1815, a new company called the American Insurance Company, was chartered with a capital of 500,000 dollars. Its first President, 1816, was William Neilson, Jr., and among the Directors were such prominent merchants as Nathaniel Prime, Jonathan Goodhue, Edmund Morewood, Jonathan Ogden, Goold Hoyt, James G. King and that class. In 1821, the worthy old William died, and William Neilson,

Jr., as he had been known for a third of a century, became William Neilson, President of the American Insurance Company.

John Patrick, who had taken over the immense business of Shedden, Patrick and Company, with Benjamin Aymar as partner, started the firm of Patrick, Aymar and Company, in 1815, at Thirty South Street. In 1821, when Mr. Patrick went out of the firm, Benjamin Aymar established the house of B. Aymar and Company, which later on removed to Thirty-four South Street and continued there many years. He was a son of John Aymar, also a merchant, who was the last man in New York to abandon the traditional dress of the Knickerbockers—long-tailed coat, knee breeches, silver shoe buckles, stock and ruffled shirt, and the inevitable queue.

"Ben" Aymar was a right down dollar-hunter who did not seem to care for much else than the purchase and sale of cargo, and he was known far and wide for his honesty and shrewdness. As an instance of his shrewdness, this story is told of him: B. Aymar and Company often received cargoes of mahogany and logwood. These would be generally sold at auction. On one occasion they had a cargo to be sold at Jersey City. William F. Pell was to be the auctioneer, and all hands were to start from Pell's store, in Coffee House Slip, and go over to the ferry. When they reached the foot of Cortlandt Street, Mr. Aymar noticed that one of the largest buyers slipped through without paying on the boat. He told Mr. Pell not to receive a bid from such a man. Mr. Pell expressed surprise, observing:

"Why, I thought he was good."
"So did I; but I have changed my mind, and I will not trust him a dollar."

Shortly afterwards, this merchant failed and he did not pay five cents on the dollar.

The house of B. Aymar and Company did business with all the ports of the world. They were agents for estates in the West Indies and for merchants there who shipped goods here. They had the *Emily*, the *John W. Cater*, the *Orbit*, the *Try*, the *B. Aymar*, and many more vessels in the trade between Jamaica, Santa Cruz, and other ports. They supplied all these islands with American produce. They did business with all parts of Central America. They did a heavy Russian business with William Brandt, of Saint Petersburg and Constadt.

For nearly half a century Aymar and Company was one of New York's largest commercial houses. They succeeded Shedden, Patrick and Company, who commenced when the population was about 20,000 in 1784. What a growth! Yet this great growth in population, wealth and commercial grandeur is due to such men as Benjamin Aymar and his partners and co-workers. All honor to them!

Beyond peradventure the Yankees captured shipbuilding and shipping, also the import and export business at the port of New York about this time and dominated its activity. The great rush came around 1800 and about twenty-five years later the leadership in New York commerce had definitely passed to New Englanders. New Yorkers had been strangely passive in the exploitation of their manifold advantages for commerce. They had a magnificent harbor, situated more favorably than any other in America, in its three-fold adaptability to trans-Atlantic, coastwise and interior communication. In addition to the British maritime inheritance which it shared with other ports, New York had been founded, for purely commercial reasons, by Holland at the height of its power on the seas. Yet New Yorkers had trailed behind Boston and Philadelphia through the colonial period.

When New York finally shot ahead of its rivals at the turn of the century, that easy going Knickerbocker element was crowded from commercial leadership by outsiders. Some of these came from overseas but the majority were New Englanders "more conservative in character, more grave in temperament, and at the same time, more enterprising and more insistent in action than the descendants of the Dutch and English settlers." In that respect the story of New York is quite different from that of Boston and Salem.

If the gay young people who now happen to live in Greater New York were told that the Battery was a fashionable promenade and some of the wealthiest and most socially distinguished people in the town lived in the lower part of Greenwich Street, in State Street and around Bowling Green, they would listen with incredulity. Not improbably many of them are ignorant of State Street's location, or even of its very existence. There is not a city in the world that within sixty years has so changed in its general appearance, in the aspect of particular neighborhoods, and in the character of its various quarters; and of these changes, twenty or thirty years have seen some of the most deplorable and obliterative. Cities before this have been destroyed, or wrecked by war, by decay, or by convulsions of nature; and been rebuilt, but old New York has been swept out of existence by the great tidal wave of its own material prosperity. Other cities are changed chiefly by additions. New York not only adds to itself, but incessantly rends itself in pieces. In such a city, adventurous men may push their fortunes, and they and the women and children who belong to them may lead a certain sort of prosperous life, accompanied by the enjoyment of certain sorts of pleasure. But such a city cannot be an assemblage of true homes; and it must lack certain admirable and respectable traits—outward, if not inward—which go with stability.

The Bay of New York was once one of the famous natural objects of the world's admiration. It was the pride of those who dwelt about it; and traveling strangers who had seen the Bay of Naples and the Golden Horn did not stint their praises of the beauty surrounded by which the "Metropolis of the New World" sat like a Western Venice upon the water—waters at once the source of her wealth and the occasion of her deterioration. But this is all no more. The European traveler no longer compares the Bay of New York to the Bay of Naples; and although even of old there was in this some element of surprise and some stretch of courtesy (for where is our Vesuvius and where our Capri?) it must be confessed that candor cannot condemn his silence.

Another beauty of the New York waters then was the view up the East River, where, beyond the "Wallaboght" and at the turn of the river, lay the little village of Williamsburgh, and directly east stood Brooklyn on its heights, under which great ships sailed in and out under canvas. Now the East River, from Buttermilk Channel to Blackwell's Island, is merely a tug-vexed waterway between wharves and warehouses. Williamsburg has disappeared as an individual town, and has become a part of the vast, sleepy dormitory by which it has been swallowed up; and from its loathed vicinage reek hideous smells and horrid fumes and greasy stinks. What has befallen Williamsburg has befallen many other places along New York's waterfront.

In the whole city of New York (the Borough of Manhattan, to be explicit) a better combination of conveniences, health, pleasantness and proximity to business cannot be found than State Street, and here many of the old merchants of South Street dwelt—real merchants, who traded in their own ships with Europe, the East Indies, China and the South. State Street, which is the eastern boundary of the Battery, was unsurpassed, if it was ever equaled, as a place of town residence; for comfortable living there was a park with a grand water view, where, in summer, the western breezes blew in the windows straight from the water. The sight here, on spring and summer and autumn evenings, when splendid sunsets made the firmament and the water blaze with gold and color, seemed sometimes in their gorgeousness almost to surpass imagination.

It was a matter of course that such a place should be chosen as the site of the homes of wealthy people, and, during the period of which we write, most of the City's wealth was to be found in the counting houses on South Street and its adjacent thoroughfares. From the windows and balconies of the old State Street houses across the greensward and through the elms of the Battery, the merchant-resident could look upon the ships passing up and down the North River, to and fro on the Bay, and going in and out the East River.

They were stirring times, in the days of old, when the entire business and social life of the community centered on the toe of Manhattan Island between City Hall and the Battery, so that it was easy for the "Peep O'Day Boys," as the keen old merchant shippers were called, to walk down before breakfast, and look out over the clear waters of the Harbor to see if their ships might be coming up through the Narrows from far-away ports.

There were "signal staffs" on Staten Island to notify the merchants and others in New York of the arrival of ships, and by hoisting colored balls, to convey other intelligence of interest and value to them. In those days the name of a vessel arriving off the port was known by distinguishing letters painted on her foretopsail, and a little later on, these were observed from a lookout station at the Narrows, and communicated to the observer at the Battery, in clear weather, by signal telegraph. This was the invention of Captain Samuel C. Reid, the gallant commander of the famous privateer *General Armstrong;* also distinguished as the designer of the present arrangement of the Stars and Stripes upon our National Standard.

But to return to our old merchant. After breakfast he had only to walk a few rods to his store and counting room on South Street. "Boy, give me a spy glass," he would say to his junior clerk, and raising it up, he would peer towards Governor's Island to see if his ship, telegraphed to the signal on the Battery, was coming up or not. The slip at Whitehall being only a short distance away, he could whistle or hold up his finger, and in an instant he would have one or more of the Battery boatmen rowing up to him. These boatmen were exceptionally fine oarsmen, and a few years after the period we describe, when sculling was very popular, there were some smart four- and six-oared crews among them which used to swoop down and pick up the valuable prizes offered by the Boston city fathers for competition each Fourth of July on the Charles River. Our merchant shipper could go with one of these boatmen across the Bay towards Staten Island, where his ship might be at anchor waiting a favorable breeze before entering the East River, or slowly wending her way into port. At that time one could be rowed all around the harbor without being run down by anything more furious than a slow moving horseboat, for we are now relating events that transpired long before steamboats raced up and down New York's adjacent waters.

It is related of old "Ben" Aymar, head of the well known South Street firm of B. Aymar and Company, that he would get up as early as half-past five in the morning, and go from the house where he resided so long, at No. Six State Street,

Invention, Prosperity and Progress 125

and walk up along Front and Water Streets, where the principal grocery business was done, and where his customers were located. He would see what stores were open, notice the quantity of goods, talk with the clerks, while the merchants were asleep upstairs (in a large majority of cases, merchants and shopkeepers, lawyers, too, resided over their stores or offices), and from these observations in the morning Mr. Aymar would draw pretty correct conclusions as to the goodness of this and that merchant, when they came to make purchases of him. He would go along the docks and notice what ships had come up, and notice what cargoes were discharging and going on board.

As a result of such observations, it is not surprising that he would sell two or three West India cargoes of a morning, while other merchants were selling two or three casks of rum or sugar. "Ben" Aymar was one of the best salesmen in New York City; he would see two or three large buyers, and get them to run off a cargo, dividing it up into lots, having the best names in New York,—John Johnson and Sons, Suydam and Reed, Reed and Sturgis, and others.

Then, too, our old wealthy merchant could get up at daybreak, look out of his window, and see what old cronies were walking upon the Battery. Then he could stroll over before breakfast, and, while enjoying the sea breezes, he would shake hands and talk politics with his constituents, for more than one South Street merchant, like John B. Coles, residing on State, served as alderman of the good old-fashioned First Ward,— and it was an honor to be its alderman. William Neilson, Henry Overing, Jonathan Ogden, William Bayard, Moses Rogers and his son, B. Woolsey Rogers, were among the prominent merchants who then resided on State Street.

Before the coming of the steamboat the Hudson River sloops had a practical monopoly of the transportation of the Hudson Valley. For most of these boats the passenger business was a sideline; freight was the mainstay. All the sloops advertised that they were for freight and passengers, with the freight mentioned first.

The freight handled by the sloops included a great variety of articles. From Albany came grain, flour and lumber, pork, hay, cider, potash, firewood and potatoes. Brick, stone and slate were also shipped, and live stock—sheep and cows—were carried in large numbers to supply the demands of the growing metropolis.

On the voyage up the river these vessels took a variety of manufactures, both domestic and foreign, also chests of Hyson skin tea and dry goods. The early steamboats carried little freight; "light freight" was taken at three cents a pound, or sixty dollars a ton, and as the sloops carried a ton for about three dollars, it is evident that they could hold their own.

The competition from steamboats and railroads kept on increasing, and although the sloops lingered even after the Civil War, their end was approaching.

Among the honored mercantile names of the city, none stands higher than that of David Lydig, who owned a large fleet of Hudson River sloops, and was for more than forty years the principal flour merchant in this city.

He was the son of Philip Lydig who succeeded in establishing himself in the business of supplying vessels with sea biscuit. Money was not made so rapidly in 1775 as now. It was slowly gained. This great metropolis was then but a small place of a little over 20,000 inhabitants, and those who acquired a competency reached it only after many years, by careful saving and the practice of economy.

When the Revolution was over and the business of the city revived as the new Government became gradually established, David Lydig, then a young man, found himself in possession of a very substantial property, his share, as one of two surviving children, of his father's estate. Feeling an honest pride in the pursuit by which his father had obtained his pecuniary independence, he resolved to employ his share of his parent's fortune in a pursuit directly growing out of that in which it had been gained.

Purchasing the valuable water power at Buttermilk Falls, near West Point, he erected large mills for the manufacture of flour, and commenced its manufacture upon an extensive scale, employing a large number of persons, and in connection with it purchased a building at the corner of South and Dover

Streets, as a depot for its sale, and for the transaction of the general business of a wholesale flour merchant.

Mr. Lydig owned many fine sloops plying between his mills at West Point and the city. It was his custom every summer to make up parties of friends, ladies and gentlemen, for an excursion through the Highlands, and even to Hyde Park and Albany, stopping by the way at the country places of various friends along the banks of the Hudson. It was like yachting at the present day, but more impromptu and infinitely more sociable.

Under his excellent management his business steadily increased, and the mills at Buttermilk Falls not affording a sufficient supply of flour, he purchased another water power nearer to the city, with a mill attached. This was the beautiful country residence of the De Lanceys, in Westchester County, adjoining the village of West Farms, situated on both sides of the Bronx River, embracing a large number of acres, in which was included the family mansion on the banks of the river. In this purchase was included a mill power near to the city, and accessible by water, together with a beautiful country seat.

When the great project of DeWitt Clinton, the Erie Canal, was approaching its consummation, Mr. Lydig foresaw with the foreshadowing sagacity of the penetrating merchant, that flour would be ultimately manufactured in the great grain-growing valleys of the West, at a cost in production that would annihilate all competition on the part of manufacturers in the southern portion of the State, and to the astonishment of all those engaged in the business, he sold out his extensive mills at Buttermilk Falls at what appeared to be a foolish sacrifice, commenced to curtail, and finally wound up his business.

The history of the American sailing ships known more than a century ago as "Packets," and of those enterprising individuals who started them, is very interesting. They contributed an important part to every-day life in the principal ports along our Atlantic coast, New York, Boston and Philadelphia. Up to 1815 there were nothing but transient ships, old trading vessels, whose sailing date being dependent upon the time necessary to receive sufficient cargo, kept persons who had engaged passage to Europe waiting days and days before actually sailing. European travel, however, was almost wholly confined to purposes of business, and even this was of rare occurrence. The arrival of a vessel at this time was heralded as bringing news "forty days later from Europe."

It is said that when Benjamin Marshall was returning to New York in 1815, from a tour of European cities, and had put up with all these inconveniences and uncertainties, he met as fellow-passengers, Francis Thompson and his brother, Jeremiah, and Isaac Wright, and the outcome of this accidental meeting was the formation of the famous Black Ball Line.

The first vessel of which we have any record, to cater to the trans-Atlantic passenger, was the *Pacific*, owned by Isaac Wright and Son and Francis Thompson. Their advertisement appeared in the New York *Gazette and General Advertiser*, February eighteenth, 1815, and reads as follows:

"FOR LIVERPOOL—The well known fast-sailing coppered ship 'PACIFIC,' will be prepared for sea without delay; and is intended to be the first vessel from this port. She will take in cargo only sufficient to put her in ballast. The object being to obtain passengers, to whom every attention will be given for their convenience. Her accommodations are extensive and complete."

Some months afterwards, the enterprise of the Wrights, Thompsons and Benjamin Marshall, all wealthy merchants in New York, led to the establishment of the lines of packets between that port and Liverpool, which, under the names of the "Black Ball Line," and the "Old Line" of Liverpool packets, was, until the era of ocean steam navigation, one of the chief means of communication between the Old World and the New, and which maintained its place as an important vehicle of commerce many years.

In the conveyance of cabin passengers the packet ship was superseded by the ocean steamer, just as in the transmission of news, the ocean steamer was, in its turn, superseded by the Atlantic cable. But, in 1817, when the Black Ball Line of packets was formed, it was a movement of no little vigor and enterprise and was a marked step in the advance of our commerce. Up to that year, the passenger from New York to Liverpool, or Liverpool to New York, was compelled to find a place on a merchant vessel, having at best but a very small cabin, poorly furnished, and inadequately supplied. There were no passenger vessels, and the idea of encouraging or providing for travel on an ocean route was unknown; the stray passengers who crossed in the merchantmen accepting the discomforts of the voyage as the inevitable condition of going to sea, and the master and crew regarding the passengers as a species of live freight, entitled to but little more consideration than the rest of the cargo.

The circular which announced the formation of a line of passenger packets, to sail interchangeably from New York and Liverpool on a certain day in every month, throughout the year, was a novelty and an experiment. The shipmasters were divided in opinion as to its practicability, many of them doubting whether it was possible to dispatch the vessels with any regularity.

The Black Ball Line was originated by Isaac Wright and Son, Francis Thompson, Jeremiah Thompson, and Benjamin Marshall, a member of a different family from that of Captain Charles H. Marshall, who in later years became the principal owner of this line of packets. The prospectus, signed by the proprietors, was dated "New York, November 27th, 1817," and stated that in order to furnish frequent and regular conveyances for goods and passengers between New York and Liverpool, they had undertaken to establish a line consisting of four vessels, the *Amity*, the *Courier*, the *Pacific*, and the *James Monroe*, each of about four hundred tons burden, fast sailers, with uncommonly extensive and commodious accomodations for passengers, and declared their intention to dispatch these vessels monthly, one to sail from New York on the fifth and one from Liverpool on the first of every month. Contemporaneous with this circular were announcements by other enterprising New York carriers of a new line of post chaises to Philadelphia, and a tri-weekly steamboat line to Albany!

It was not, however, until January 1818, that the first unit of four vessels consisting of the four packet ships previously referred to, went into commission. The Black Ball Liners were the only packets from New York to Liverpool until the establishment of the Red Star Line in 1821.

The Black Ball adopted as its private signal, a large painted black ball below the close-reef band in their foretopsails, and throughout the various changes of management they carried a crimson flag with a black ball in the center. Their little vessels were well built of oak and put together in the strongest possible manner, with spars and rigging to stand up under hard driving in all kinds of weather.

It may be remarked here, that in the pioneer packet ship period, whenever the days of departure fell upon a Friday, it was customary for the captains, out of deference to the superstitious feeling then existing among sailors, to drop down to the outer soundings, cast anchor for the night, so as to discharge their pilots, and make sail early next morning. The superstitious feeling gradually wore away, and then, rain or shine, blow high or low, they proceeded to sea, as per schedule; and, for many years, when the Black Ball liners sailed on the first and sixteenth of each month, these were the European mail days throughout the United States.

Isaac Wright, of Isaac Wright and Son, one of the founders of the Black Ball Line, was an English Quaker from Sheffield, England, who had originally engaged in the dry goods business. He lived at Third Avenue and Thirty-eighth Street, and walked down to his business and back to his home every day. There were no stages or horse cars in those days. He certainly was a conspicuous figure, his tall form topped off with a broad-brimmed Quaker hat, walking stick in hand, nodding pleasantly to passers-by on the old Bowery road or the more recent Third Avenue, as he daily wended his way, back and forth.

Benjamin Marshall, one of the original owners of the line, was a wealthy Englishman. He soon retired from the shipping business, and became interested, with his brother, Joseph Marshall, in the establishment of those great cotton works, the New York Mills, at Troy.

Jeremiah Thompson was a successful cotton merchant. His firm succeeded that of Isaac Wright and Son as agents

Black Ball Packetship "Montezuma"
From a painting by Charles R. Patterson—Courtesy of W. R. Grace & Co.

Invention, Prosperity and Progress 131

of the Black Ball Line, after they had failed by speculating in cotton. They in turn failed, and were succeeded by Thompson and Oddie. The next agents of the Line were Goodhue and Company, Jonathan Goodhue and Pelatiah Perit.

Jeremiah Thompson was a bachelor, but kept house and entertained in the most hospitable manner. Doing a vastly extensive business, for, in addition to being one-fourth owner of the original Black Ball Line, he owned several ships and traded all over the globe. He was by far the largest shipper of cotton from this country to Europe, and had his agents in every Southern port to attend to his ships, purchase his cotton, and draw on him for payment. He was also the heaviest importer of British cloths, having special agents in New York and Philadelphia to effect sales for him; and the shipwrights of New York no sooner fitted out one ship for him than he laid the keel of another. Yet so systematic was he in his accounts, that with all his large business, he had but one clerk. Next to Brown Brothers and Company and Prime, Ward and Sands, he was the largest bill drawer in America. But like many others, he pushed the thing too hard, and the crash in the autumn of 1827 suddenly extinguished his career as a merchant. He lived but a short time afterwards.

Francis Thompson was his elder brother, and after trading several years in his own name, with success, associated with him his nephews, Messrs. Francis Thompson, Jr., and Samuel Thompson, under the firm of Francis Thompson and Nephews. They failed, too, about the year 1829, but Samuel Thompson afterwards retained a large Liverpool trade until his own death.

We are now getting right into the midst of bright days for the American merchant marine. Every wind that blew brought fresh fortune to its unfurled sails. It has been claimed that the War of 1812 settled nothing, that the whole question of impressments and neutral right, the ostensible cause of the war, was not disposed of by its issue or by the treaty of Ghent, which settled the terms of peace; but in fact the war settled the whole question of the rights of the American marine and of the freedom of the seas as definitely as if every advancing step in the progress of our commerce had been provided for by treaty stipulations. The war, as fought and finished, was as decisive on every point involved, although the decision was not formally embodied in public records, as the 1861-65 struggle with rebellion, although no traitor had been tried, convicted, or hanged. It did the work which was needed. It swept away every hindrance from the path of our shipping in all the seas, and the new impulse which it gave to our commerce was felt in every fiber of the national life. The long, dull years between the breaking out of hostilities and their close, during which American seamen were pent up in foreign ports, or exiled to the wilderness in search of a livelihood, were not lost; they were years of preparation and training, in which strength and courage were gained for the great work which was to be done, and we have seen with what alacrity the well-trained seaman sprang to his post the moment it could be regained. The rapid advance in the size and capacity of vessels, the growth of our registered tonnage, and the reputation gained and kept by our ships, were due to the character of the men who commanded and manned them. The packet service, which, with its system and order, replaced and superseded the irregular voyages of the merchantmen, was brought to its perfection by the labor and fidelity of those who vied with one another in winning for the commerce of their native country the supremacy of the ocean. The packet master was not a mere carrier of passengers and freight, nor a mere instrument of the traffic in which he was engaged. He was the representative and exponent of the enterprise and patriotism which sought expression in every effort to raise the commerce of the United States to its predestined height. And his ship, staunch and thoroughly appointed, well officered and manned, a model in build and rigging for sea service and for speed, furnished with comforts and luxuries before that time unknown in ocean travel, was more than a mere vehicle of merchandise or passengers; it was the medium of communication between the two worlds, the Old and the New; it brought the news after an interval of fifteen, sometimes twenty, or even thirty days from all Europe to America; while the limited number of passengers which it conveyed embraced a large proportion of cultivated and intelligent persons, foreigners visiting our country, Americans indulging in what was then the comparatively rare luxury of European travel, business men engaged in operations important enough to require the long passage across the ocean, or the representatives of our own and foreign governments, passing and repassing to and from their posts of duty. The master of such a ship, if he were capable of discharging his duties and equal to their high responsibilities, deserved the success which usually followed faithful service in so difficult and perilous a career, and it was a natural transition for him to step from his ship's deck into the most important commercial relations on shore.

The sailing of the old packet-ships at regular intervals first built up the New York Shipping trade. From New Orleans, Charleston, Baltimore, Philadelphia and Boston came goods to be shipped to Europe, providing a living for the handlers of the freight, and a handsome return for the capital invested in the ships. And, curious to relate, the initiative in establishing New York's pioneer packet service, which did so much to promote, not only the shipping of that port but proved of great benefit to the whole country, came from a group of English importers.

To this is what we may ascribe the survival of the American flag in our coasting and inland waters. In 1817, under President James Monroe, the United States of America closed its coastwise trade to all foreign flags and all foreign-built vessels. And, marvelous to relate, that law has been permitted to remain upon the statute books! It enables us, after the lapse of one hundred and twenty-four years, to point with pride to the achievements of American clippers that so speedily sailed from New York, via Cape Horn, to San Francisco's Golden Gate; it enables us to enjoy possession of the large, handsome fleets of coastwise steamships and various other craft, now traveling up and down along our Eastern and Western seaboards; allows us possession of those beautiful steamers and an interminable number of other boats plying our inland waters; such as, the Great Lakes, Mississippi, Missouri, Ohio and the Hudson, and many other rivers and lakes throughout the country. Again, the American shipyard on our lakes, rivers and coast has remained an institution, and a source of fortune and of pride to our people because this Navigation Act of March first, 1817, has been preserved to us.

The American coastwise trade, having been exempted from foreign competition and other ills, has a history quite different from that of our foreign trade. When the tonnage duties were adopted in 1789, in the third act of the First Congress, it was provided that American coasting vessels should pay the duty declared once a year, and that foreign vessels, which it was not thought expedient to exclude wholly at this time from our coasting trade, should pay the advanced duty at each entry. Subsequent acts adopted from time to time, with reference to registration and enrollment, placed additional obstacles in the way of the employment of foreign vessels in coastwise traffic, and the Act of April 1808, which was one of the supplements to the Embargo Act, excluded them altogether. In the following year, however, the coasting trade was in a measure set free. It was finally closed altogether to foreign vessels by what is called the "American Navigation Act," to which we have previously referred.

The growth of our coasting trade shows an increase of tonnage almost without a break from 1789, when it amounted to 68,607 tons, over the turn of a century, up to 1932, when it amounted to 10,727,564 tons, which was its most prosperous year since the foundation of the United States. Coastwise trade tonnage advanced until 1860 with remarkable steadiness, and during those seventy years, 1789 to 1860, although it showed occasional fluctuations, suffered no important setbacks except in the period of overproduction following the year 1828. The next year our total Merchant Marine decreased twenty-seven and six-tenths per cent., but from this it rapidly recovered. While the registered tonnage in our foreign trade decreased from 2,496,894 tons in 1861 to 726,213 tons in 1898, its leanest year, American coastwise trade has gone on steadily increasing, until it reached the peak of 10,727,564 tons during 1932, which amount, by the way, shows a ship tonnage increase of 8,082,697 since the Civil War.

To a New York-built vessel, the *Savannah,* is universally conceded the honor of being the first steam-propelled vessel that ever crossed the Atlantic. By some writers it is claimed that

Invention, Prosperity and Progress 135

"only out of courtesy can she be called a steamship," as her engines and movable paddle-wheels were only used in calm weather, and *can therefore only be regarded as auxiliary to her canvas.* The *Savannah* was not built to be steam-propelled, and entries in her log many times record the wheels being "shipped."

In 1818 a sailing vessel, 100 feet long by twenty-eight feet broad and fourteen feet deep, lay on the stocks in Crockett and Fickett's shipyard at Corlear's Hook, when Captain Moses Rogers, who became her master on a historic voyage, conceived the idea of fitting her with a steam engine, driving a pair of paddle wheels. Rogers had been associated with Colonel John Stevens and his son Robert L., commanding the *Phoenix,* after the latter had relinquished command, and those pioneer efforts to navigate the high seas by steam, seems to have whetted Rogers's appetite for something even bolder and more venturesome.

The *Savannah* was of about three hundred tons burden, packet built and full ship-rigged. She was propelled by one inclined engine, not unlike those now in use, with a cylinder forty inches in diameter and a piston stroke of six feet. The boiler carried a steam pressure of only twenty pounds. Her paddles were of wrought iron with only one flange and were entirely uncovered, though it is probable that a canvas wheelhouse was made to cover them soon after the voyage began. These wheels were so attached to the shaft that their removal and shipment on deck could be accomplished in fifteen or twenty minutes. There were two fine cabins for passengers, both handsomely furnished, and the thirty-two berths were in staterooms that were provided with all the comforts and conveniences then demanded.

The *Savannah* sailed from New York on March twenty-ninth, 1819, to Savannah, Georgia, where she was owned. Thence, she went to Charleston to take President Monroe to Savannah; and from Savannah, on May twenty-fifth, 1819, sailed for Liverpool, where she arrived in twenty-two days having had steam up fourteen days of the voyage. By steam alone she could make eight knots an hour.

After returning home the *Savannah* was divested of her

steam apparatus, and used as a sailing vessel between Savannah and New York. In November 1821, while under the command of Captain Nathaniel Holdredge, who also owned her, she was driven ashore on Long Island and became a total loss. Her machinery, which had been removed, was bought by James Allaire who exhibited the cylinder at the fair in the Crystal Palace, New York, in 1856.

Singular as it may seem, nineteen years elapsed before any further efforts were made to cross the ocean by steam, and the fact of this successful voyage appears to have been entirely overlooked. It was really the all-important factor of speed on the Atlantic that gave steam its chance, for the trans-Atlantic packet service was the first on which fast voyages were attempted. The owners of the early packet ships having found that speed would pay, it was only one short step to insuring speed and regularity by introducing steam. There were many obstacles to overcome, not the least being prejudice and the firm belief in the minds of many people that it was quite impossible to cross the Atlantic with steam as a commercial proposition. It was not only the ignorant layman who considered it impossible; the celebrated English scientist, Dr. Dionysius Lardner, who had studied the question thoroughly, was convinced that steam vessels could never cross the Atlantic; that a ship could not carry sufficient coal to propel her across the ocean.

The first steam vessel especially designed for the ocean service was the *Robert Fulton*, constructed by Henry Eckford between 1819 and 1820 at his shipyard in Brooklyn near the United States Navy Yard. This ship was built for David Dunham and Company for their "triangular trade" between New York and Cuba, touching at Charleston, South Carolina, and New Orleans, Louisiana. It is thought that Cadwallader Colden and Henry Eckford were interested in the building and operation of this vessel.

The *Fulton* left New York on her first voyage April twenty, 1820. Her schedule time between the various ports she touched was about as follows: New York to Charleston, four days; Charleston to Havana, four days; Havana to New Orleans, three days. She was a success as a sea-going steamer, having encountered at times very severe weather without any serious damage. After running for about five years, the business was found to be insufficient to make the enterprise a success financially, so the line was abandoned. Mr. Dunham dying in 1825, the vessel was sold to the Brazilian government, her machinery removed, and then she was fitted and equipped as a second-class frigate. She was finally wrecked on the coast of Brazil.

In February 1822 the merchants of the city convened for the purpose of asking for a floating-light off Sandy Hook, also for the formation of an association to construct a Merchants Exchange. Action on these and other projects of benefit to shipping and commerce had to be postponed owing to an epidemic of yellow fever breaking out early in the summer, which by July was spreading with fearful rapidity. Business was entirely suspended in August and a part of September, and while the pestilence was at its height we notice that many of our South Street merchants and shipping houses moved uptown, to what is now called "Greenwich Village," to what was then "Upper Broadway," also to "Bowery Hill" and other points "north," distantly removed from the lower, downtown section of the City, where the epidemic prevailed.

John Griswold advertises from 459 Broadway, with Samuel W. Coates, whose address is now "Greenwich," that they have the coppered packet ship *Corsair*, which has been unexpectedly detained on account of health conditions prevailing in the City.

Noah Talcott is doing business at Bowery Hill, in connection with Goodhue and Company, the latter being located on Broadway, near Vauxhall Garden, and advertise their brig *Emma* for New Orleans, sailing from the foot of Clarkson Street, below the State Prison, North River. William Whitlock, Jr., has removed from South Street to the corner of Washington and Clarkson Streets; Spofford, Tileston and Company are at 504 Broadway temporarily; while John W. Russell, from his residence at Seventy White Street, is conducting the business of his New Orleans line of packets.

However we note that one prominent shipowner, L. M. H. Butler, remained at 107 South Street, and continued business during the epidemic. The Black Ball Line of Liverpool packets and other well known shipping interests do not appear to have joined the exodus uptown. With the coming of cold weather, we soon see business continued at its old haunts, and a prominent array of New York's leading merchants greeted the famous English actor, Charles Matthews, at the Old Park Theatre when he opened there with *Monsieur Tonson* in November 1822.

There was a society to which some of the most influential merchants in New York belonged at this time, called the "House of Lords," and also "Under the Rose." They held their meetings at Baker's City Tavern, No. Four Wall Street.

Joseph Baker was originally a brass founder, at this address, and in 1804 he got it into his head that he could do better by adding a "porter-house" to his business. Soon it became so profitable that he dropped the brass business, and became a publican. His place became famous as the City Tavern, and it was frequented by the best men in the city as late as 1822.

In the days of the great glory of Baker's City Tavern, the "House of Lords" met there every week day night, at half-past seven, and adjourned at ten o'clock. Each member was allowed a limited quantity of liquor and no more. The merchants discussed business, and important commercial negotiations were made. In those days nearly all the prominent men lived downtown, and here one would generally find a lively crowd of well known citizens. Among the members most prominent in the House of Lords were Robert Maitland, Thomas H. Smith, Preserved Fish, Captain Thomas Carberry, old Gulian Verplanck, Peter Harmony, Robert Lenox, William Bayard, Thaddeus Phelps, Samuel Gouverneur, Solomon Saltus, and Jarvis, the painter.

It was at one of these meetings that Thaddeus Phelps, with Preserved Fish and Joseph Grinnell, first proposed the establishment of a line of Liverpool packets. It was not in any sense bitter competition with the Black Ball Line, for American trade with England had assumed proportions beyond the capacity of one line of sailing ships. To that can be attributed the formation of the Swallow Tail Line of Liverpool and London packets, which for many years achieved unapproach-

Invention, Prosperity and Progress

able success in both passenger and freight carrying on the North Atlantic, under the control and able management of Messrs. Grinnell, Minturn and Company.

The Red Star Line was originated by Byrnes, Trimble and Company, flour and grain exporters, and Samuel Hicks, a large shipowner of New York, in 1821. Their ships were the *Manhattan,* 390 tons; *China,* 533 tons; (both built at New York in 1818 for Samuel Hicks,) also the *Panther, John Wells, Meteor,* and *Hercules,* one of these ships sailing on the twenty-fourth of the month. It was not until the close of 1821 that the Red Star Line was able to live up to their schedule in sailing dates for their packets. Previously the firm of Hicks and Jenkins, who were contemporaries of Byrnes and Trimble, owned a line of Liverpool ships, not packets, but traders. Like Byrnes and Trimble, they were Quakers, a class of citizens who, in those days, had a fancy for the shipping business, and, as a rule, were extremely successful. Byrnes and Trimble conducted the Red Star Line of Liverpool packets, in their day almost next in importance to the Black Ball Line, until about 1835, when they sold out to Robert Kermit.

On July thirtieth, 1822, Fish and Grinnell and Thaddeus Phelps and Company announced the formation of a Line of Liverpool Packets to sail regularly on the eighth of each month. To initiate this service Captain Henry Holdredge, long an outstanding figure in packet ship circles, was to leave New York on the eighth of August in the *Robert Fulton,* a ship of less than 400 tons. The *Cortes,* Captain Nash DeCost, was second, while for the October sailing it was announced that "a good ship would be provided." The fourth vessel, *George Canning,* was in process of construction and would have been commanded by Henry Stoddard, but for the fact that he was caught smuggling from one of Fish and Grinnell's ships a short time previous to that packet's launch.

The occurrence which was hushed up, to a certain extent of course, because the ship belonged to Fish and Grinnell and the guilty captain stood at the head of his profession, happened in this wise:

Captain Stoddard was coming down the wharf towards his ship, when he saw a bale of hay going on a cart.

"What are you going to do with that hay?" he asked of the customs house officer, superintending the loading.

"Send it to the public store," was the reply.

Captain Stoddard was surprised, and addressed the mate, who was ignorant of all that was going on, asking what had happened. The mate told him. It seems the cow had been kept aboard and not "struck ashore," as she ought to have been. The mate had ordered the cabin boy to go and cut some hay for the old cow from one of the bales. The boy returned and told the mate, in the presence of the customs house officer, that he had cut through hay into fine broadcloth. The customs house officer immediately smelt a very large mouse and ordered all the bales of hay sent to the public store, where a large quantity of first-quality broadcloth was confiscated. This disgrace preyed upon Captain Stoddard's mind so much that he soon retired from the sea.

Captain Robert Kermit, an owner in the ship *Saint George* (an earlier ship than the Red Star ship *Saint George*), persuaded merchant Stephen Whitney and banker "Nat" Prime to become owners of a new ship, *Saint Andrew,* and thus was started the Saint Line. Ships later added were the *United States, Virginia, Sheffield, Birmingham, Waterloo, West Point,* and *Constellation.* This line is said to have never been much of a success, although a very short westward passage made by the *Saint Andrew,* arriving at New York the day before Christmas 1834 was the means of making a large amount of money for her owners. Walter Barrett, in his "Old Merchants of New York," describes how the ship brought intelligence of an advance in the price of cotton in Liverpool, which news could not become public property until after Christmas. Details are given as to how Whitney and Prime dispatched a special messenger to New Orleans with letters of credit in the amount of one million dollars to be used in buying up all the cotton found in first hands. The messenger bribed stage drivers and Mississippi steamboat captains not to make stops except when absolutely necessary, and so reached New Orleans in eleven days from New York, three days ahead of the Great Southern mail, which had left two days before him. Before night fifty thousand bales of cotton had been purchased at about sixty dollars per bale.

Invention, Prosperity and Progress

This was sold at an advance of twenty-five to thirty dollars per bale. The messenger, who was Walter Barrett himself, was awarded the profits of 200 bales, but Captain Kermit was only nominally benefited and the Saint Line finally went down. Its flag was a red star in the center of a blue swallow-tail.

Contrary to the general supposition, the packet ship was not of sharp model, although in the early fifties a few clippers were built for that business. These were the *David Crockett, Invincible, Racer,* and *Staffordshire,* the latter running out of Boston, but none of them was more than a few years in the service and the two last mentioned were wrecked after a short career. It was claimed that ships with bluff bows, wall sides, and heavy, square sterns were the best adapted to trans-Atlantic trade, although later day packet models were not so blunt forward as were their predecessors. The celebrated *Dreadnought* was of a class between clipper and early day packet. The best speed of the latter type was about eleven knots; that of the average of their successors, twelve to thirteen, under favorable circumstances.

Much has been written about speed records made by the packets, but only a few of these statements can be fully substantiated. One such passage, frequently quoted, is that of the *Ashburton,* twelve days to Liverpool. Her log of this run shows that on the twelfth day out she was in longitude twenty-eight, latitude forty-eight, and that her whole time on the voyage was fifteen days, eighteen hours. Another instance is that of *Avelaior,* eighteen days instead of the twelve days, eight hours often claimed. As a matter of fact, more depended on the "driving" qualities of the officers of these ships than on their models and, operating as they were, over the same short course for a number of years, it would appear unlikely if at some time or another, each did not meet with sufficiently favorable weather conditions to allow the making of some short passages. A run of fifteen to seventeen days to the eastward was made by most of these ships at some period, while to the westward with anything under twenty-one days being rare, nearly all had one or more runs of twenty-five days to their credit.

These several lines of Atlantic packets rendered illustrious service to the growth of New York City as the commercial metropolis of the Union. In their presence the English and French trading vessels were absolutely insignificant. Their agents, builders, and captains speedily became rich, for all were owners—the agent owning, say, an eighth of a vessel; the builder another eighth, in order that he might secure the job of repairing her, which cost about five hundred dollars a round trip; the captain another eighth, that he might have the strongest of all motives to vigilance and prowess; the block-maker and sailmaker each a sixteenth, perhaps; and other persons the remainder, a packet of 500 tons being worth 40,000 dollars.

The first packet ship that was lost, the intelligence of which sent a thrill of horror over both hemispheres, was the packet ship *Albion* of 447 tons, commanded by Captain John Williams. She weighed anchor in the port of New York upon the first of April, 1822, and set sail for Liverpool, carrying twenty-nine passengers and a crew of twenty-five. Nothing unusual transpired until the eighteenth day out of port, when the ship encountered a terrific gale and storm off the coast of Ireland, near Old Kinsale. The ship being heavily laden, labored hard. The seas were running high, and, as night came on, the storm increased in fury, causing the vessel to ship a heavy sea that laid her on her beam ends, and completely swept the decks, filling the cabins and staterooms with water, carrying overboard one or more passengers and some of the crew. It soon became apparent that the vessel must be lost, driven to pieces during the night by the fury of the sea, lashing against the rocks, and the boats having all been swept away, there was nothing but death in prospect. In a short time, the ship was driven against the rocky coast and went to pieces. The captain and all the passengers were lost except one, William Everhart, an invalid who had to be carried out on deck, and a portion of the crew. Mr. Everhart was saved by clinging to a projecting rock, from which he was drawn up by persons on shore, so exhausted that he was confined for several weeks.

New York went into mourning for the loss of the *Albion*. The loss of life it occasioned led many persons to design life preservers, the first that was submitted to the public being an adaptation of an ordinary mattress, patented by a vender of beds and bedding, a Mr. Jackson in Pearl Street, who was long and well known as "Moccasin" Jackson, an eccentric character.

The great success of the Liverpool Lines led John Griswold to start a London line of packets in 1823, afterward E. E. Morgan and Sons, with the ships *Sovereign, Cambria, President*, and *Hudson*, the last named being commanded by Captain E. E. Morgan. At first they sailed on the first of each month from London and from New York, touching at Cowes. Fish and Grinnell became interested, and they started a rival line, the first representatives of which were the *Corinthian*, Captain D. Chadwick; *Cortes*, Captain Benjamin Sprague; *Brighton*, Captain William S. Sebor, and the *Columbia*, Captain Joseph C. Delano, which left for the British capital the first of the month; and these pioneers were followed by at least twenty other vessels in the service.

Referring to New York's wonderful commercial growth and progress towards the end of 1823, this appeared as an editorial in the *Evening Post* of January eighth, 1824:

"We do not think that we can be charged with exaggeration when we state that there is not a city in the world which, in all respects, has advanced with greater rapidity, than the city of New York, within the last ten years. Whichever way we turn, new buildings present themselves to our notice. In the upper wards particularly, entire streets of elegant brick buildings have been formed on sites which only a few years ago were either covered with marshes, or occupied by a few straggling frame huts of little or no value. Nor can it be doubted that the trade consequent on the navigation of the Grand Canal and the branches connected with it, will in a few years cause the whole of the shores of the North River to be covered with stores and yards for receiving, packing, and shipping our western countries' products to foreign ports. Already our coasting trade is unrivalled; and the amount of duties on imports and tonnage is greater than the whole of Boston, Philadelphia, Baltimore, Norfolk and Savannah put together. Last year, from a report of foreign arrivals compiled by the Custom-house, these duties extended to within a trifle of ten millions of dollars, while the amount collected at the places named, fell about eighty thousand dollars short of that sum. The number of vessels arriving at this port during the same period aggregated 1217; of which

1087 were American, 91 British, and the remainder Dutch, French, Swedish, Spanish, Portuguese and other nationalities, having on board 4,999 passengers, and laden with the products of our sister states, of the European nations, the West Indies, and the new republic of South America. On the 1st of January 1824 there were 326 vessels in our harbor.

"We have, in New York, likewise a greater number of packet ships than all the ports of the Union collectively. There are sixteen which sail regularly betwixt this port and Liverpool. In the Havre line there are four; in the Savannah, seven; in the New Orleans, four; in the Charleston, ten; besides the brigs, sloops and schooners, which sail on regular days to Boston, Providence, New London, New Haven, and various ports in the South."

At this epoch the history of modern New York properly begins. The impetus given to business of every description by the opening of the Erie Canal, early in November 1825—the increase of commerce and of wealth—exceeded all expectations. The rapid building up of towns and villages in the great grain growing valleys of the West was only equaled by the extension of New York City northward and its development in altitude, for business edifices of only three or four stories soon sprung to seven and eight.

When the Erie Canal was finished and opened for the use of commerce in 1825, those small but useful boats that plied between New York and Buffalo were located at the foot of Broad and South Streets. They brought the grain and produce of the West to New York, and carried back large cargoes of merchandise in exchange. Some of these canal boats had plain but convenient cabins, fitted up with all the accommodations of a river steamboat, and carried passengers from Albany to Buffalo, or any town or village on the canal, at the rate of two and a half cents a mile with board, or one and a half cents a mile without. This easy and comfortable way of traveling was preferred by many to the long and tiresome ride in the stage coach or wagon, and was the great emigrant route to the West until the railroads were completed.

The merchants of this city, under the direction of Captain Samuel C. Reid, who commanded the privateer *General Arm-*

strong, which held the British fleet in check at the Azores and prevented them from joining General Packenham in time for him to successfully carry out his plans at the battle of New Orleans, erected a telegraph station at Staten Island to convey news of incoming vessels. This signaling system was the invention of Captain Reid, and at a test given June twenty-third, 1821, a boy at the Battery flag-staff translated the messages with scarcely a single mistake.

On March sixth, 1824, Isaac Wright and Son and other merchants petitioned the Common Council for a lease of the flag-staff at the Battery, where the signals were received, for the ensuing year, as they found the telegraphic establishment of great utility to merchants and shipowners.

Following the completion of the Merchants Exchange in Wall Street, May first, 1827, the marine telegraph, previously communicating from Staten Island to the Battery, was extended from Wall Street to Sandy Hook via Staten Island.

Late in the thirties, Holt's Hotel, on the corner of Fulton and Water Streets, was used as a telegraph station for the mercantile interests of the city. On the roof was built the signal house, where the signals to and from Sandy Hook, announcing the arrival of ships, were operated. Then telegraphing was done by signals from station to station, at various distances, until Morse invented the electric telegraph, which did away with Stephen Holt's plan.

Section IV. of the Act of 1817, was intended to exclude foreign vessels from participation in our domestic trade—coasting, lake and river—because the London Convention of July, 1815, and its disappointing results, had admonished our statesmen that owing to the great extent of our coasts and lakes, American transportation thereon must be secured. Within the next decade, we see emanating from New York, according to some of the earliest daily issues of the *Journal of Commerce*, a Southern States Service consisting of the following:

New Orleans Packets, Old Line: Ships *Azelia S. Thacher, Frances, Russell* and *John Linton,* John W. Russell, agent, Number Seventy-three South Street.

New Orleans Packets, New Line: Ships *Kentucky, Illinois,*

Talma, Tennessee and *Louisiana.* Agents, Silas Holmes and Company, Number Sixty-two South Street.

Line of Packets for Mobile: Ships *Extio, Indiana, Elisha Denison, Amelia* and *Henry Hill.* Agents, E. D. Hurlbut and Company, Eighty-four South Street.

Line of Packets for Savannah: Ships *Emperor, Savannah, Statira* and *Louisa Matilda.* Agents, J. and C. Seguine, Eighty-six C. H. Slip, and William Whitlock, Jr., Seventy South Street.

Charleston Packets, Ship Line: Sailings every four days, with the ships *President, Salunda, Calhoun, Othello* and *Empress.* Agent, George Sutton, 181 Fulton Street, corner Burling Slip.

Charleston Packets, Union Line: Sailings weekly, with the schooners *Eliza, Coral, Ohio, Spy* and *Orbit.* Agents, H. Dudley and W. Cowing, Ninety South Street.

Regular Line for Norfolk: Weekly sailings, with the schooners *Transport, Tell Tale, Dusty Miller,* and the sloops *Independence* and *Norfolk Packet.* Agents, E. P. Cady and W. Lockwood, Eighty-five Coffee House Slip.

Petersburgh Packets: Sailings weekly, with the schooners *Planet, Eclipse, Ann, Petersburgh* and *Independence.*

Alexandria, Georgetown and Washington City: Regular line, with the schooners *Columbia* and *Increase* and the sloops *Chauncey* and *Vernon.* Agents E. P. Cady and W. Lockwood, Eighty-five Coffee House Slip.

Philadelphia and New York Packets: Regular Line, Sailings Wednesdays and Saturdays with the schooners *Triton, New York, Socrates, Leaper, Reaper* and *Boston Packet.* Agents, Baldwin and Forbes, Ninety-six Coffee House Slip.

Baltimore Packets, Todd's Line: Sailings weekly with the schooners *Control, Little William, Martha, Mary Ann, Post Boy* and *Vineyard.* Agent, W. W. Todd, corner Old Slip and Front Street.

Baltimore Packets, Despatch Line: Sailings every Saturday with the schooners *China, Rolla* and *Atlantic* and the sloop *Commodore Perry.* Agent, David Anderson, Eighty-eight Coffee House Slip.

Philadelphia Packets, Union Line: Sailings Wednesdays

Invention, Prosperity and Progress

and Saturdays with the schooners *Diana, Georgetown, Waterloo, Mary Ann* and *Valiant* and the sloop *Virginia.* Agents, N. L'Hommedieu and John W. Brown, New York.

Services to the New England States were maintained as follows:

Boston Packets, Despatch Line: Sailings Wednesdays and Saturdays with the schooners *Sun Turk, Greek, Mirror, Eclipse, Warrior* and *Advance.* Agents, S. H. Herrick and Company, Twenty-three South Street, and Van Nortwick and Miller, Twenty-four Coenties Slip and James Skelding and Son, Thirty-three Front Street.

New York and Boston Steamboat Line, via Hartford: Sailings Monday, Tuesday, Thursday and Friday of each week with the steamboats *Oliver Elsworth* and *Macdonough.* Both passengers and freight were carried and passengers traveled by stage from Hartford to points beyond.

For Sawpits and Norwalk: Sailings daily except Sunday with the steamboat *John Marshall* from the foot of Catherine Street, New York. Passage to Sawpits, fifty cents and to Old Well, Norwalk, one dollar.

Shortly afterwards we find various steamboat lines contributing to the activity and growth of American commerce, which were listed as follows:

Citizens Line, for Philadelphia, Baltimore and Norfolk: Sailings daily, Sunday excepted, from pier two, foot of Beaver Lane, North River, with the low pressure steamboats *New York* and *Pennsylvania,* carrying passengers through to Philadelphia in one day via Washington and Bordentown, with twenty-four miles of land carriage. Connection was made at Philadelphia with the boat for Norfolk. Union Line for Philadelphia and Baltimore: through to Philadelphia in one day, with twenty-five miles land carriage, via New Brunswick, Princeton and Trenton. Sailings daily except Sunday, at six A.M. and noon, with the steamboats Thistle and Swan in New York Bay, connecting by stage with other steamboats on the Delaware. On the morning boat four dollars, and on the evening boat three dollars, because the latter involved a stopover of a night in Trenton. Offices were maintained at York House, Five

Cortlandt Street; at One Washington, corner of Marketfield Street, and at the Northern Hotel, foot of Cortlandt Street. The line was operated by Letson and Bayles.

Swiftsure and Towboats, operated by the Steam Navigation Company for the transportation of passengers and freight between New York and Albany, with the 200-ton freight barges *Atlantic, New York, Albany, Ontario, Niagara, Detroit, Superior* and *Inspector,* leaving New York every Wednesday and Saturday evening at five P.M., two barges being towed by one steamboat. Passage in the barge cabins, one dollar, and in the steamboats, two dollars. Agents, A. Van Santvoord, Number Seventeen Coenties Slip, New York.

Safety Barges, between New York and Albany: Sailings four days a week with the safety barge *Lady Clinton* and the steamboats *Commerce* and *Swiftsure.* Fare in the steamboats, two dollars, and in the barge, four dollars. Offices of the Steam Navigation Company, Number Eighty-two Cortlandt Street.

There was a wonderful difference in the manner of advertising by the old merchants years ago and now. Then all the merchants advertised by the year. The regular price was forty dollars—and that price included the paper, which was left by the carrier. Without the paper it was thirty dollars. Strange as it may appear, there was no limit fixed to the amount of advertising in those days. A mercantile firm, like Goodhue and Company, advertised all they desired. No respectable house would overdo the thing. There was a sort of self-respect about the articles advertised. Goodhue and Company and no other respectable house would have advertised cotton. The reason was that cotton was an article sold altogether through cotton brokers; and to have advertised 1000 bales of cotton, even if a house had that quantity for sale, would have appeared like a "bombast" or an attempt to show off. A cotton purchaser did not look at the newspapers. He went directly to the offices of the different cotton brokers. The cotton brokers were even then an institution. The principal ones were Noah Talcott, G. Merle and D. Crassous.

In the fall of 1827 one finds this Old Ship Line advertising in the columns of New York's *Journal of Commerce:*

Invention, Prosperity and Progress 149

"London Packets.—Old Line.—Fish, Grinnell & Company, 136 Front street. Sail on 1st of month:—October, ship 'Columbia'; November, ship 'Corinthian'; December, 'Cortes'; January, 1827, ship 'Brighton.' Sailings from London on 25th of each month. Touch at Cowes each way.

"London Line of Packets.—John Griswold or C. C. Griswold, No. 69 South Street—September 15, ship 'Cambria'; October 15, 'Acasta'; November 15, 'Hudson'; December 15, 'Robert Edwards.' Touch at Cowes each way.

"Old Line of Liverpool Packets.—Leave New York and Liverpool on 1st and 16th of each month: Ships 'New York,' 'James Cropper,' 'Manchester,' 'William Thompson,' 'Pacific,' 'Florida,' 'Canada,' 'Britannia.' These ships were all built in New York of the best materials; are coppered and copper-fastened and fast sailers. Their accommodations for passengers are uncommonly extensive and they are commanded by men of great experience. The price of passage to England in the cabin is fixed at 30 guineas for which sum passengers will be furnished with beds and bedding, wine and stores of the best quality. For further particulars apply to Isaac Wright & Son, Francis Thompson, Benjamin Marshal and Jeremiah Thompson, New York; Cropper, Benson & Co., Liverpool.

"Liverpool Packets.—Ship 'Napoleon' sails 8th October; new ship, 8th November; 'Silas Richards,' 8th December; 'York,' 8th January—Fish, Grinnell & Company, 136 Front Street.

"Packets for Hull, England.—Brigs 'Freak,' 'Dapper,' 'Diana'; Brig 'Dapper' now here, will sail September 15.

"Havre Packets.—Old Line.—The ships of this line will sail hereafter from this port on the first of each month and from Havre on the 15th of each month, consequently the ship 'Montana' will sail 1st October; ship 'Henri Quatre' will sail 1st November; new ship 'Sully' will sail 1st December; ship 'Stephanie' will sail 1st January. These ships are all built in this city, copper fastened and coppered and too well known to need any further description respecting their solidity, swiftness, elegant accommodations and the characters of their commanders. The price of passage is fixed at $140, for which sum the passengers will be furnished with beds and bedding, wines and stores of all kinds. For freight or passage apply to the captain, on board, next to Rector street wharf, North River, or to Frs. Depau, 66 Washington street.

"Havre Packets.—First and Second Lines.—Leave hence or from Havre on the 1st and 15th of each month. Ship 'Edward Bonnaffe' sails September 15; 'Bayard,' October 1; 'Queen Mab,' October 15; 'Don Quixote,' November 1; 'Cadmus,' November 15; 'Edward Quesnel,' December 1; 'France,' December 15. Crassous & Boyd, New York, or Bonnaffe, Boisgerard & Company and Edward Quesnel, owners, Havre."

This topographical description of New York's commercial district, in 1828, is found in "Goodrich's Guide":

"South Street, in its whole extent, is exclusively occupied by the merchants owning the shipping, and by those connected with that line of business, and it forms a range of warehouses, four and five stories in height, extending from the Battery to Roosevelt-street, facing the East River. Front and Water Streets, together with the various Slips intersecting them from South-Street, are occupied by wholesale grocers and commission merchants, iron dealers, or as warehouses for the storage of merchandise and produce of every description. Pearl Street, is the peculiar and favorite resort of wholesale dry good merchants, earthenware dealers, etc. from Coenties Slip to Peck Slip; and in it also, are the auction stores. Sales at auction are also made in Wall-street, between Pearl and Water Streets. Wall Street commences at Broadway, and leads to South Street, and comprises the Custom House and its appendages, the principal banks, insurance offices, brokers, and bankers; also the Merchant's Exchange, with the Post Office, and offices of several important daily papers; in short, *it is the money depot of the city*, and from ten to three o'clock, it displays a busy scene, and gives a favorable impression of the extensive trade, wealth, and importance of New York."

In the memorable decade, from 1821 to 1830, American vessels were carrying over ninety per cent. of all American exports and imports, a record excelled only in the year 1810, and then but slightly. The American tariff of 1824, and the American merchant with his superior ship directly prevented England's commercial and maritime success.

It was not surprising, therefore, that the *London Times* sounded this note of alarm in May, 1827:

"It is not our habit to sound the tocsin on light occasions, but we conceive it to be impossible to view the existing state of

South Street, New York City — View in 1828 with Packet Ship "Leeds" at Her Pier.

Invention, Prosperity and Progress

things in this country without more than apprehension. Twelve years of peace, and what is the situation of Great Britain? The shipping interest, the cradle of our navy, is half ruined, our commercial monopoly exists no longer. We have closed the West India Islands against America from feelings of commercial rivalry. Its active seamen have already engrossed an important branch of our trade to the East Indies. Her starred flag is now conspicuous on every sea, and will soon defy our thunder."

Evidently, it then looked to the British like a tough job to run American merchants and mariners out of business. As acknowledged by the *Times*, England closed her West Indian ports against us "from feelings of commercial rivalry"; and, because we were shut out there, our merchants had been forced to seek other and more distant markets for their goods as well as for return cargoes.

Our statesmen must have had pity for England when they passed a bill for her relief, May 24th, 1828,—termed "A Reciprocity Act," which would allow her to carry to and from the United States, and from and to all the world. And for this she wished to give nothing.

It is said that the main principle of the bill was "Free Trade"; but it was free-trade reasoning for the benefit of other countries than ours, upon which was founded the stripping of protection from our merchant marine. Our competitor shipping nations in Europe embraced this opportunity to seize American carrying trade and commerce, under the guise of "indirect trade"; and, at the same time, the President was authorized to open our direct West Indian trade to Great Britain on equal terms, if she would let us carry our own goods to her possessions.

The question of merit in Reciprocity may be judged by Norway which proposed "Full Reciprocity" during President Monroe's administration; who, in one of his messages, stated that:—

"The Government of Norway has by an ordinance opened the ports of that part of the dominions of the King of Sweden to the vessels of the United States, upon the payment of no other or higher duties than are paid by Norwegian vessels, from whatever place arriving, and with whatever articles laden. They have requested the reciprocal allowances for the vessels of Norway in the ports of the United States. As this privilege is not within the scope of the Act of the 3d day of March, 1815, and can only be granted by Congress, and as it may involve the commercial relations of the United States with other nations, the subject is submitted to the wisdom of Congress."

In its wisdom, Congress did not touch the subject. Norway was prompted by self-interest to propose this innovation. She had already found advantage in partial reciprocity. She was a country living chiefly by navigation, to which long experience had adapted her. She could only hope to become of consequence upon the sea. She never needed protection for the encouragement of shipbuilding or navigation. The full reciprocity which she sought in 1821 would have been great encouragement, as our trade with the world was a prize such as no nation, hitherto, had ever granted another. In a few years, however, Norway received the boon desired. In 1827 the arrivals of Swedish and Norwegian tonnage in our ports were 2,458; in 1837 they had increased to 25,660 tons, and monopolized the traffic. Reciprocity with these countries has been no use whatever to the United States, in commerce direct or indirect. Hundreds of vessels under their flags carry on our foreign trade with all parts of the world, and ply in no other. They never enter the Baltic Sea after leaving it behind. These two royal flags have been enabled to supplant our own on the ocean—as a consequence of our "liberality," and the heed which we have given to "the spirit of our enlightened age."

It should be stated here that the Reciprocity entered into after the Act of 1828 was more than twice as deadly in its effects as that under the acts of 1815, and of 1824, which revived it. This applies to all flags able to compete in our foreign trade against our own ships coming from or going to all parts of the globe. Several of our reciprocity nations never had any trade of their own worth reciprocation to us.

An interesting anticipation of possible disparagement of the records of the sailing ships which served as pioneers in the development of the trans-Atlantic passenger service is shown in an extract from *The Journal of Commerce* of November eighteenth, 1828. The opening paragraph presumably was written by the editor as an introduction to the statement of the packet line. The extract follows verbatim:

"We believe the following statement was published in some of the papers several months ago, yet it will be interesting and valuable to some of our readers. Besides, it is possible that some one of our papers may be in existence a century hence. If so, we warn the men who then shall be, not to make themselves too merry at the tardy pace of their great grandsires.

"OLD LINE OF LIVERPOOL PACKETS
"(Black Ball Line)

"The following is a statement of the passages made by the different ships and masters employed in the OLD LINE, from 1818 to 1827 inclusive, embracing a period of ten years, and comprising 183 complete voyages. The passages from New York to Liverpool, during the said period, have averaged 24 days each.

"Those from Liverpool to New York, during the said time, have averaged 38 days each.

"The shortest passage from New York to Liverpool was made by the ship 'New York,' Capt. George Maxwell, in December 1823, being 16 days.

"The longest passage from New York to Liverpool was made in the ship 'Nestor,' Capt. R. J. Macy, in December 1820, and January 1821, being 37 days.

"The shortest passages from Liverpool to New York were made by the ship 'Amity,' Capt. George Maxwell, in April 1818, and by the ship 'Columbia,' Capt. Rogers, in February 1824, being 22 days.

"The longest passage from Liverpool to New York was made by the ship 'Pacific,' Capt. Crocker, in December 1827, and January and February 1828, being 71 days.

"The passages are not reckoned from land to land, as is sometimes the case, but from one city to the other."

The period, from 1820 to 1830, may be said to present the second culmination of our carrying trade. During this decade the disturbing causes that had existed almost from the beginning of the government, including European wars and the accompanying restrictions upon neutral trade, national war and its manifold consequences, and domestic embargoes and other destructive measures, ceased to be operative, and the result was a healthy, normal, and steady maintenance of the same high plane of commercial activity, which had distinguished the period from 1794 to 1810. The proportion of commerce carried in American vessels was the same as in the earlier period, namely, about ninety per cent. The diminished volume of foreign commerce, chiefly in the matter of imports, was to be expected from the inflation of the preceding period. Comparing the period from 1816-20 with that from 1821-25, the reduction in the annual average of exports amounted to eleven millions and of imports to thirty-three millions. Tonnage increased from its previous low figures until it reached seven hundred and fifty-seven thousand tons in 1828, after which a fall took place which we shall have further occasion to notice. In every respect we may say that this period represents the most flourishing condition of shipping in American history. Although in the years preceding the Civil War our registered tonnage was three times as large, yet we have never since 1830 reached the position in respect to the carrying trade to and from American ports that was maintained during this decade, but, on the contrary, have receded from it.

PART VI

THE THREE MOST WONDERFUL PERIODS OF NEW YORK'S COMMERCIAL PROGRESS, IN THE DAYS OF SAIL,—WHEN HER FAMOUS SAILING PACKETS AND THE NEW YORK AS WELL AS "YANKEE" CLIPPERS GLORIOUSLY CARRIED THE STARS AND STRIPES INTO EVERY PORT OF THE WORLD: 1830—1840; 1840—1850; 1851—1860.

VI

THE FIRST PERIOD

1830—1840

COMMERCIAL TIES BETWEEN GREAT BRITAIN AND THE UNITED STATES BOUND BY "THE ATLANTIC FERRY"—NEW YORK CITY'S GREAT TRANSITION PERIOD—INEQUALITIES AMERICANS HAD TO CONTEND WITH IN 1830—TRADE EXPANSION CAUSES INCREASE IN NUMBER AND TONNAGE OF VESSELS—NEW YORK SHIPYARDS ASSUME ACTIVITY—SHIP OWNERSHIP CHANGES FROM MERCHANTS TO TRANSPORTATION COMPANIES—ROBERT L. STEVENS PRODUCES MODEL OF FIRST T-RAIL WHILE CROSSING ATLANTIC—WHY MORSE'S INVENTION OF THE TELEGRAPH HAS A "NAUTICAL TOUCH" —ACCOUNT OF PACKET *PHILADELPHIA* LAUNCHED BY CHRISTIAN BERGH—"SHE HAS A PIANO AND CARRIES A PHYSICIAN"—GOODHUE AND COMPANY PURCHASE BLACK BALL LINE—WHEN NEW YORK'S EUROPEAN NEWS WAS OVER SEVENTY DAYS OLD—FRANCIS DEPAU AND HIS PIONEER LINE OF HAVRE PACKETS—FOX AND LIVINGSTON—NEW YORK AND HAVRE STEAM NAVIGATION COMPANY—BOYD AND HINCKEN, AGENTS SECOND HAVRE PACKET LINE—JOHN J. BOYD— WILLIAM WHITLOCK, JR., STARTS THIRD LINE OF "FRENCH PACKETS"—WILLIAM WHITLOCK, JR.—HIS SHIP *CADMUS* BRINGS LAFAYETTE TO AMERICA—MANY EXPERIMENTS IN SHIPBUILDING MADE 1830-40—NEW YORK SHIPYARDS LAUNCH FINEST SHIPS AFLOAT—BIOGRAPHICAL SKETCHES OF CHRISTIAN BERGH, ISAAC WEBB, SMITH AND DIMON, BROWN AND BELL, JACOB A. WESTERVELT, AND OTHER SHIPBUILDERS—SHIPYARDS ALONG THE EAST RIVER—NEW YORK SHIPOWNERS, MERCHANTS AND SHIPBUILDERS FURNISHED MEANS FOR AMERICA'S SUPREMACY AS A MARITIME AND COMMERCIAL POWER—LAUNCHES IN SAILING SHIP DAYS—RELATIVE TO DRYDOCKS, MARINE RAILWAYS, ETC.— FIRST TOWBOAT IN NEW YORK HARBOR SERVICE, *RUFUS W.*

KING—OLD STEAMBOAT *SUN*—PECK BROTHERS RUNNING STEAMBOATS AND DOING TOWING—APROPOS A PRIZE FIGHT AND CAMP MEETING—WHEN THE CAPTAIN RAN HIS TOWBOAT AGROUND—PIONEER SCREW-PROPELLING TUG *RESOLUTE* BLOWS UP—DESCRIPTION OF GREAT FIRE, DECEMBER SEVENTEENTH, 1835—DISTRESS IT CAUSED—HOW THE OLD SCHOOL MERCHANT TRAINED HIS CLERKS—JOHN I. MUMFORD, MERCHANT AND EDITOR—SCHUYLER LIVINGSTON—BOORMAN, JOHNSTON AND COMPANY—FOSTER AND GIRAUD—ANDREW FOSTER AND SONS, AND THEIR SHIP *COURIER*—CHARLES H. MARSHALL, SHIPMASTER, MANAGER AND OWNER OF BLACK BALL LINE—INTERESTING CAREER OF E. K. COLLINS—RETURNING TO EAST INDIA MERCHANTS—HOW F. AND N. G. CARNES FLOODED THE NEW YORK MARKET WITH VARIOUS IMITATION ARTICLES AND MERCHANDISE MADE IN CHINA—SALES BY AUCTION A LEADING COMMERCIAL FEATURE—SOME PROMINENT NEW YORK AUCTIONEERS—JACOB HAYES, NEW YORK'S HIGH CONSTABLE, STOPS A STEVEDORE STRIKE—PACKET SHIP RACING ON THE ATLANTIC—HEAVY BETS LAID ON THESE OCEAN RACES—THE *ANN McKIM*—HOW A FEW RESOLUTE SAILORS ESTABLISHED THEIR RIGHT TO DECENT TREATMENT—CONVEYING FOREIGN NEWS TO NEW YORKERS OF A FORMER GENERATION—ADVENT OF THE STEAMSHIP ON THE ATLANTIC—OWNERS OF S.S. *BRITISH QUEEN*, CHARTER *SIRIUS*, THE FIRST STEAMER TO CROSS FROM THE OLD WORLD TO THE NEW—ARRIVES AT NEW YORK SAME DAY AS *GREAT WESTERN*, AND THE CITY CELEBRATES—COMMENTS ON S.S. *BRITISH QUEEN*, BY THE DIARIST HONE—YEAR 1839 AS DISASTROUS TO NEW YORK PACKETS AS TWENTY YEARS PRECEDING—TRIALS AND TRIBULATIONS OF A MARINE REPORTER IN 1840—COMMERCE AFTER MAKING EXTRAORDINARY ADVANCES, 1830 TO 1839, LOSES TOWARDS THE END OF THAT PERIOD—A NEW FACTOR ENTERS OCEAN GOING TRANSPORTATION, STEAM VESSELS—SAMUEL CUNARD AND ESTABLISHMENT OF THE CUNARD COMPANY—PACKET *GARRICK'S* FAST PASSAGE TO ENGLAND—NEW YORKERS HAD TO WAIT WEEKS TO READ CONTINUATION STORIES BY EUROPEAN WRITERS—RÉSUMÉ OF BUSINESS CONDITIONS AT NEW YORK BETWEEN 1836 AND 1840—FINANCIAL CRASH OF 1837—IN 1840 NEW YORK BANKS COULD RESUME SPECIE PAYMENTS; THEY SERVED A SHIPPING PEOPLE.

The First Period

THE most glorious and the most triumphant illustration the world has ever seen of the omnipotence of commercial intercourse in binding two nations over to eternal peace, between whom the most angry hostilities have existed was in great part brought about by the establishment in New York of what has been termed "The Atlantic Ferry," which made possible proper water communication between Great Britain and the United States. Thenceforward is to be seen in practical operation, between the two great branches of the Anglo-Saxon race, a friendship that has become a commercial necessity. And, as it is the spirit of commerce that is the first to penetrate new seas, and to explore unknown regions, and to communicate from man to man the mutual knowledge of himself and his character, of his country and its productions, the American Merchant Marine, then past its infancy, conferred upon this country those great benefits which foreign commerce alone confers.

It may be said that the half decade of years immediately preceding the year 1830 embraced the great transition period in the life of New York City; in fact, this was the period of awakening to a new and prosperous life of the whole country. Business of every kind had been readjusted after the great disruption caused by our second war for independence, and the growth of the city and its trade was abnormal, despite a commercial revulsion in 1818-19, in which New York merchants suffered severely. Commerce rapidly revived, in this transition period; and the opening of the Erie Canal in 1825 gave a great impetus to commerce, causing New York to become the great eastern gateway of the United States.

By 1828-30 our shipping and commercial strength was considerable, but our merchants commanded scanty capital; interest here was double the rate in Europe; our government had from the first to give credit on the payment of duties; we had no capitalists with surplus wealth; about all the real advantage we had was ten per cent. in customs tariff, enterprising merchants, resolute seamen, and the improved vessels due to skillful shipbuilding, but the chances for their employment in carrying for foreign nations, the British in particular, were not equal to the chances which foreign flags were given to carry in our commerce.

Great Britain was then, as now, the best naturally protected maritime nation known on earth. She had long made claim to "sovereignty of the seas." She then had the largest navy and merchant marine. She had the oldest and the strongest shipping houses, and the richest bankers, merchants, and corporations in the world. London long had been the center of international exchange. The marine insurance written at Lloyds exceeded what was done in all other marts of trade. The great merchants, shipowners, and underwriters of England had long known each other, and were used to active coöperation. Their habit of commercial duty towards one another had acquired the force of centuries. Such were some of the inequalities of the situation when West India free freighting competition began in 1830.

The universal expansion in trade during this time caused an increase in the number and tonnage of vessels, of fifty to one hundred per cent. each year, for four years previous to 1829, when a general stagnation came on, which grew out of the revulsion in 1825, and continued into the next year. That revulsion, caused by too great an expansion in credit, did not affect shipbuilding, it appears, till some years after it had affected other branches of trade and until nearly every other branch had passed the ordeal. Agriculture was affected at the same time. In every revulsion when the credit system is carried too far and trade expanded to an unhealthy limit, it is invariably the case that agriculture and shipbuilding are the last to feel its effects. When they recover, everything is again in a healthy state—they are the barometer of commerce.

The money paid for labor, in the period of which we write, was about one-fifth of the total cost of a vessel. As a consequence of the low state of shipbuilding in 1829, great distress existed among the laboring classes, who were dependent thereon for support. There was scarcely any work to be obtained and when vessels were built, wages ruled remarkably low—only one dollar and fifty cents per day, and out of proportion to the cost of rents, clothing and food. At the close of 1830, however, shipbuilding recovered its wonted activity and

South Street about the Year 1831, with Warehouses, etc., at Dover Street. From a drawing by A. J. Davis.

wages rose to one dollar and seventy-five cents when the overjoyed mechanics resolved to strike for a day of ten hours instead of the prevailing fifteen hours. The bosses offered them two dollars a day at the old hours, but the offer was rejected and a day of ten hours ushered in. In order that the advantages so won should not by any possibility be impaired, the workmen passed around the hat and raised enough money to buy a bell —the old Mechanics' Bell—which they erected on a small tower in Lewis Street, between Fourth and Fifth Streets. They hired a saw filer in the neighborhood to ring the bell four times daily—at seven o'clock, twelve o'clock, one o'clock, and six o'clock—and were insatiable in their demand that he should be prompt, paying him for his services fifty dollars a year. It is said that the silver tones of this bell, which lingered long in the memories of thousands of New York shipwrights, could be heard across the river by the shipyard workers in Williamsburg.

The shipyards of this city assumed a look of activity, in the spring of 1831, which had not been seen in them for five years previously. One first rate vessel was launched on May fourth, and contracts were entered into for building ten others, of which six were on the stocks at this time. Besides these large vessels, great numbers of small craft and steamboats were under construction along the East River shore, and vessels of every burden were undergoing repairs. The reality and strength of this new impulse given to commerce may be judged from the remarkable fact that within two months the value of shipping had risen in this port from twenty-five to thirty per cent.

The business of shipping, especially in the transatlantic and American coasting trades, had now gradually passed from the speculative voyages of merchant owners of vessels, to transportation companies as common carriers. Regularity of service was itself an incentive in the development of trade and the transportation of passengers, and the volume of both freight and passenger traffic increased, quite out of proportion to the increase of population. In this year there were fully nine lines of foreign sailing packets: Belfast, Carthagena, Greenock, Havana, Havre, Hull, Liverpool, London, and

Vera Cruz; and of domestic there were four: Charleston, Mobile, New Orleans, and Savannah.

The packet ship *Charlemagne*, in May 1831, brought to Philadelphia a shipment of 550 rails,—the first T rails ever made. It was Robert L. Stevens, of Hoboken, who invented the "T" rail, which insures safety to travel to this day, and he had these rails made by Sir John Guest, at Dowlais, Wales. While crossing the Atlantic aboard the *Hibernia* to buy "any iron rails he chose, with any other desirable material" for the newly organized Camden and Amboy Railroad and Transportation Company, of which he was President and Chief Engineer, Mr. Stevens picked up a billet of wood left on deck by some careless foremast hand. He began whittling it to pass away the long hours of the voyage. Naturally enough, his fingers turned to the design that just then most interested him —rails. When he had cut a section of the popular British rail— the Birkinshaw—he realized that this would require a special "chair," a costly thing in an America where iron was dear and metal workers scarce. Looking for something better, he produced, in his final section from that billet, the world's first T-rail—standard for the United States ever since.

It is not generally known that there is a "nautical touch" to the invention of the telegraph. While on board the Havre packet *Sully*, returning to America, in October 1832, to enter upon his duties as professor of painting and sculpture in the University of the City of New York (now New York University), Samuel F. B. Morse conceived the great invention which won him more honors, here and abroad, than were ever before bestowed upon an American.

A fellow passenger, Charles Thomas Jackson, led the dinner conversation one day to electricity and exhibited apparatus that he had acquired in Europe. Morse remarked, "If the presence of electricity can be made visible in any part of the circuit, I see no reason why intelligence may not be transmitted instantaneously by electricity." There is evidence that his mind had already toyed with the idea, but the conception of an electro-magnetic recording telegraph came to him now with the power of a revelation, and during the rest of the crossing he lived in a state of intense intellectual excitement, sketching in his note book a rude but sufficient plan of his invention. We can almost see the figure of the illustrious inventor as he paced the deck full of this thought, or gazed dreamily into the sea, devising mechanical contrivances to give it expression. Before the packet reached New York the essential features of the electro-magnetic transmitting and recording apparatus were sketched upon paper.

The story of the long baffled efforts and final success of Professor Morse is as remarkable as any in the annals of discovery. The lesson it teaches is as old as human genius and human ambition.

On June nineteenth, 1832, the well known shipbuilding firm of Christian Bergh and Company launched the packet ship *Philadelphia*, sister ship to the *Montreal*, which was built right afterward, for John Griswold's London Line. Here's a glowing account, taken from the New York *Commercial Advertiser:*

"The competition in shipbuilding is so great and the rivalship between the owners of the different lines of packets sailing from this port is prosecuted with so much enterprise, that there is no anticipating the extent to which the art of shipbuilding will be carried, or the perfection of taste and beauty with which they will be finished. Indeed, for ten or twelve years past, we have been invited to visit ship after ship, each successive vessel presenting new claims to admiration for beauty of model, or for some new and improved internal arrangements, together with such additional points of elegance in the finish as an improving taste can devise, and profitable returns afford to bestow.

"In one word, we may say that the 'Philadelphia' is in all respects the most convenient and beautiful vessel that we have ever seen. On her bow stands the figure of Commerce, holding the key of wealth in her right hand; and on her stern are the arms of the fair city whose name she bears."

The good ship *Philadelphia*, which became exceedingly popular when commanded by that prince of sea captains, E. E. Morgan, "was sumptuously fitted up with a piano," and we learn that "a physician will be on board." Times had changed since passengers between this port and Europe were so scarce that the packet ships were fitted only for a few, and a lady desiring to meet her husband in England, applying for passage in one of the "Old" or Black Ball Line, was refused, as "she being the only woman, her presence would be inconvenient to the male passengers." "With a physician on board," "Mister First Officer" (if he had a liking for medicine or thought he knew something about surgery), and his "mysterious medicine chest," generally containing a half dozen or so "cure-alls," was now being superseded by a real "medico."

On Wednesday, January twenty-ninth, 1834: The Old Line (or Black Ball Line) of Liverpool packets, originally established by Isaac Wright and Francis Thompson, was sold out, and Goodhue and Company became the agents. Six fine ships were purchased for 216,000 dollars or 36,000 dollars each. The establishment of this line of packets and the punctuality with which it had been conducted served as a patttern to all other lines which were subsequently established between this port and London, Liverpool, Havre and Vera Cruz, and contributed more than any other cause to the commercial prosperity of New York. The original proprietors, Wright and Thompson, were well calculated for such an undertaking; bold and enterprising, they were distinguished for habits of industry and methodical correctness in business, peculiar to the religious sect (the Quakers) of which they were members.

In the days of sailing ships and early ocean-going steam vessels, no part of the world afforded a more difficult or dangerous navigation than the approaches of the northern coasts of the United States in winter. Before the warmth of the Gulf Stream was known, a voyage at this season of the year from Europe to New York, Boston and even to Baltimore was many times more trying, difficult and dangerous than it now is. In making this part of the coast, vessels were frequently met by snowstorms and gales which mocked the seaman's strength and set at naught his skill. In a little while the ship became a mass of ice; with her crew frosted and helpless, she remained obedient only to her helm.

It was due to such ice-bound coastal conditions that a curious state of affairs existed at New York in the early part of February 1834. Out of forty-six packet ships plying between New York and London, Liverpool, and Havre, but two were

The First Period

in port, both of which, in the ordinary course of things, ought to have sailed February eighth. New York's latest advices from Liverpool were seventy-one days old, London seventy-two, and Paris seventy-five. This had never before happened since the establishment of regular lines of American packets forty years previously, it is said, when there were only British packets running between here and Liverpool, one leaving each port monthly.

Old Francis Depau must have been in business as an importing and commission merchant long before 1806, and he was the merchant who first organized a line of packets from this city to a port in France. He lived on the west side of Broadway, between Leonard and Franklin Streets, until he built Depau Row, at the southeast corner of Bleecker Street and Depau Place.

The first line of Havre packets, founded by Francis Depau about 1822, commenced with the *Stephania*, Captain John B. Pell; the *Montano*, Captain Smith; the *Henry IV*, Captain William W. Skiddy; and the *Helen Mar*, Captain Harrison. Other early Havre packets were the *Cadmus*, Captain Allyn; *Edward Quesnel*, Captain E. Hawkins; *Bayard*, Captain Henry Robinson; *Howard*, Captain Holdredge; *Edward Bonnaffe*, Captain James Clark. For most of these vessels, Crassous and Boyd, then Boyd and Hincken were the agents.

During the most prosperous times of the "Havre Liners" or "French Packets" as they were often called, 1830 to 1836, Francis Depau built and named one of his crack ships, the *De Rham*, after his friend Henry C. De Rham. Coming here from Switzerland in his early twenties, Henry C. De Rham became prominently identified with New York's commercial interests before becoming senior partner in De Rham and Iselin, afterwards De Rham, Iselin and Moore, the largest importers in the city of what was termed "French Goods." The *De Rham* was placed under command of Captain Augustus DePeyster, probably the oldest active ship master going in and out of the port of New York, and one of the most popular, too. Commencing as a boy on one of John Jacob Astor's ships, he had been sailor, mate, and finally master in the same employ; then we find him fighting French privateers; joining in our Naval

War of 1812, in command of various privateers, New York owned and manned. He commanded the brig *Seneca*, belonging to Mr. Astor that carried the Proclamation of Peace, in 1815, in fifty-five days, to the Cape of Good Hope, and then to Java and China. He had been engaged in the China trade many years previous to entering the North Atlantic trade, in which he commanded the *Sheridan* of Collins' Dramatic Line and other European packets. In 1845, Captain DePeyster became Governor of Sailors' Snug Harbor at Staten Island, in which office he succeeded Captain John Whetten, under whom he sailed several voyages on John Jacob Astor's ships.

The business of Francis Depau was continued by Bolton, Fox and Livingston, the firm consisting of Curtis Bolton, Samuel M. Fox and Mortimer Livingston; and after the death of Mr. Bolton, becoming Fox and Livingston. These two gentlemen had served as clerks for Mr. Depau and both were married to his daughters. They added to the old line the *Sylvie de Grasse, Louis Philippe* and other ships. Francis Depau had married a daughter of the Compte de Grasse, celebrated in our Revolutionary War Naval history, and the *Sylvie de Grasse* was named after her. One of the best known of their later packets was the *Isaac Bell*, of 1400 tons, which made three passages from Havre to New York in eighteen days.

Fox and Livingston became the agents and were the principal proprietors of the New York and Havre Steam Navigation Company, running the United States Mail side-wheel steamers *Humboldt, Franklin, Arago* and *Fulton*.

They continued in business long after the death of Mr. Depau. Financial difficulties overtook them, in 1857, but when they failed it is said they secured all their captains from loss, by giving them security on the ships, and so forth. That is the way some of them came to own heavy amounts of stock in the Havre Line when it was finally liquidated upon very favorable terms.

Boyd and Hincken were the agents of the second line of Havre packets, started about 1825, with the ships *Charles Carroll, Erie, France, Utica, Oneida, William Tell, Baltimore, Mercury,* and *Rhone*. This line was advertised in a Havre paper as follows: "Our ships are fast sailing, copper bottomed, copper fastened, and offer intending passengers all sorts of advantages, which include staterooms having locks and keys, a captain who speaks French, and French cooking."

When fourteen years of age, John J. Boyd entered the counting house of the celebrated firm of Le Roy, Bayard and McEvers, then in its greatest glory, and doing business with all parts of the world. Their office was in Washington Street near Carlisle. Old William Bayard used to say that he never had a more efficient clerk than John. It was a great school to learn business. Mr. Boyd remained there for many years.

When he left the house of Le Roy, Bayard and McEvers, he formed a partnership with Dominick Crassous, under the firm name of Crassous and Boyd. After the retirement of Mr. Crassous, he continued the business in his own name, and when the first regular line of Havre packets was organized in February 1823, he became their agent. He then took into partnership Mr. Edward Hincken, and the firm was active in ship brokerage business until his death.

John J. Boyd was a man universally respected and very popular. All the French people in the city called him "Metternich," because he closely resembled that celebrated Austrian diplomat and statesman, Prince Clemens Metternich. Mr. Boyd was a Whig in politics, and in 1834 was elected Assistant Alderman of the First Ward, where he was born and raised. He was superstitious about Friday, never on that day beginning any business on his own account, nor taking an order from a customer.

Having furnished supplies for Wilkes' exploring expedition, he sent to Lieutenant Wilkes for vouchers for the same, and was told that the goods had not yet been examined with sufficient care, that the barometers especially must be tested before any receipts could be given. Tired of the delay, he went to Naval Agent James K. Paulding, who, upon one pretext or another, put him off from day to day. Mr. Boyd finally met Mr. Paulding in the street, and gave him a piece of his mind. "It is impossible," he said, "for an honest man to do business with the government. I will never do it again." And he never did. So strictly did he keep his resolution that the steamer

Washington, of which he was agent, having been awarded a contract for carrying the United States mails to Havre and Bremen—the price to the latter city being double that to the former—he immediately withdrew from his agency. The vessel became a financial failure, and so did the *Hermann,* built by the same company that owned the *Washington.*

Mr. Boyd, like Mr. Collins, had considerable knowledge of commercial law, and was often chosen arbitrator by his contemporaries. His favorite haunt in the evening, and on Sunday morning before church, was the office of the *Courier and Enquirer,* where Mr. Smith, afterward superintendent of the Maritime Association, then an editor of that journal, used to entertain him and other shipping merchants who lived downtown with early marine news from Australia by way of Brazil. The announcement of arrivals of vessels in the Lower Bay was received in New York by signal from Staten Island only a minute or two more slowly than at present by telegraph.

About the year 1832, William Whitlock, Jr., founded a third line to Havre, with the *Albany, Duchesse d'Orleans, Formosa, Gallia, Carolus Magnus,* and other vessels. He had previously operated his ships in conjunction with Francis Depau's fleet of "Havre Liners" and now went along upon an independent basis as a third line.

William Whitlock, Jr., was one of the independent ship owners, who when freights were dull, had capital to invest in cargoes, so as to load his ships quickly. He was always fortunate in such purchases, not only getting plenty of freight for his ships, but deriving a handsome return on his investments. His name was rarely used for any purpose except in banks and insurance companies, when he could facilitate his own business by being a director, and getting aid if he needed it. He never let a note lay over and regarded his commercial credit as beyond anything, and probably no earthly calamity—not even death itself in any way or shape—would have filled him with such horror as a failure to pay his mercantile obligations.

A son of William Whitlock, who was a sailing master out of New York as early as 1790, retiring from the sea with a competence, William Whitlock, Jr., started in the grocery business, at Seventy-one South Street, having organized the firm of

"Mr. Boyd Finally Met Mr. Paulding."

Whitlock and Jenkins, which was soon dissolved. He then went to Augusta, Georgia, where he remained a couple of years, buying cotton on commission. In 1824, young Whitlock started a line of Savannah packets, in connection with J. and C. Seguine as agents, operating the ships *Emperor, Savannah, Statira* and *Louisa Matilda*. Scott and Morrell, afterwards Scott, Shapter and Morrell, continued this line for many years after Mr. Whitlock gave it up to embark in other ventures.

For some years he conducted a large South American business, especially with Brazil. Then he organized the First Line of Havre packets, having as competitors, Francis Depau with his Old Line, and, also, the Second Line. In April 1825, he owned only four ships, the *Bayard, Cadmus, Edward Quesnel* and *Desdemona*, sailing from New York on the fifteenth and from Havre on the first of each month. While there were three lines of Havre packets for years, they all made money. Old Mr. Depau retired very rich, Mr. Whitlock made a mint of money, and so did every one connected with them.

It was the *Cadmus*, Captain Francis Allyn, that brought General Marquis de Lafayette out to America, on that memorable visit he made during the summer of 1824. She was to sail from Havre to New York with a full freight and a long list of passengers, but all were patriotically sacrificed to make room for General Lafayette, the nation's guest, his suite, and their baggage. As the *Cadmus* neared the Narrows, two gentlemen came on board from a rowboat, and after holding a private conference with Captain Allyn departed. No one except the commander of the *Cadmus* knew the object of their mission, and, to the surprise of all on board, the vessel anchored alongside Staten Island. Presently a long line of vessels appeared in sight, coming down the bay with flags flying. They approached and encircled the *Cadmus*. The Mayor of New York, General Jacob Morton, and other eminent personages, presently reached the deck of the *Cadmus* and paid their respects to America's illustrious visitor—whose tears fell like rain as he received unexpected congratulations, and learned of the plans for his public reception in the city next morning. Although Lafayette visited the United States by invitation of the Government, Mr. Whitlock received no compensation whatever for all the trouble and expense he had incurred, and he never carried another great man free after that trip in any ship that he owned.

In 1830 when William Osborne, the well known South Street merchant, failed, which failure created quite a panic, Mr. Whitlock bought Osborne's one-third share of the ship, *Salem;* the other third share being held by Captain Richardson, who originally commanded this vessel. She proved a fast sailer, made quick passages, and coined money.

It is a singular fact that a merchant rarely buys real estate, because they want to keep their capital in active business and will not lock it up in a store or warehouse and lot. About the first real estate purchase Mr. Whitlock made was the store and lot Forty-six South Street, which he bought from old John Aymar, about 1830, and continued to occupy for many years, proving an excellent investment.

William Whitlock, Jr., and his brother, Sidney B., bought a corvette built for the Colombian Government, which they fitted up and sold to Commodore Fornier of the Buenos Ayrean navy. She was to be paid for, part in cash and the other part by a draft of Commodore Fornier upon the Buenos Ayres Government. The Commodore had a letter of credit, authorizing him to draw for such a purchase. The cash and the drafts had just got into the possession of the Whitlocks, when Jonathan Thompson, who was then collector of the port, seized this corvette, on the ground that she was going to sea to act in hostility towards a power friendly to the United States.

Here was a stumper for any man but William Whitlock, Jr. He at once purchased the schooner *Rehoboth,* and loaded her with flour. Orne was a smart young fellow who had been recommended to him, and he at once placed him in command of this schooner, and gave him orders to proceed to Buenos Ayres, anticipate the news of the seizure of the corvette by the United States, get the money for the drafts, and come home as speedily as possible. The schooner made a splendid run out, ran the blockade of the "Banda Orientale," and managed to get into Ensenada. From that port Captain Orne went up by land to Buenos Ayres. It was with the greatest difficulty he could do anything; but finally he paid a liberal discount to the nephew of the Governor of Buenos Ayres, cashed his drafts, and hurried away to Ensenada, dreading every moment that the news of the corvette's seizure in New York would arrive. He sold the outward cargo at a tremendous profit, loaded the schooner with hides and specie, and returned to New York, making a famous trip, for which he deserved and received great credit.

The corvette was eventually released, and proceeded to sea through Long Island Sound. The news came down to the collector that boats were constantly passing from her to the shore. He supposed she was shipping a war crew, and he gave orders to a revenue cutter to go up the Sound and bring the corvette back to the city. The cutter went, but found no corvette. She had proceeded to sea the night previous, and from that day to this has never been heard of.

The Whitlocks made a large sum of money out of this venture, but it led to a quarrel between the two brothers, and from that time they never spoke to each other.

Probably more experiments and alterations were made, from 1830 to 1840, on both sailing and steam vessels in New York, than during any other decade in the history of our merchant marine. It was then that so many experiments were made in the form of vessels as well as in the motive power. Shipbuilders found that more was required of them and, in order to hold their own and maintain the reputation of their yards, they were forced to study the scientific principles involved in the form and sparring of ships. They did not sufficiently know what made one ship bad and another one good. The old spoon-shaped bow was giving way to vessels with an easier entrance line, and a finer run aft; in fact, by the early thirties, not only was the very shape of ships changing, but they had doubled in size.

From New York's shipyards on the East River, at this time, were launched the finest specimens of marine architecture afloat—the New York Sailing Packets, which so successfully maintained international communication between that port, Great Britain and the continent of Europe. In the construction of these vessels the best talent of the day was employed, and they were constructed only by builders who had attained some celebrity. The rivalry of the various North Atlantic packet lines was keen, and it was this eager competition principally which led to the continual improvement in models, rig, workmanship and the general excellence of New York built ships, each vessel being expected to excel some rival or all the predecessors of its own fleet in some desirable quality. In consequence, there grew up a race of acute and daring shipbuilders, whose achievements were the wonder of the world, and whose productions were imitated, both on this and the other side of the ocean, by everybody who built ships.

Unlike the productions of those whose genius is recorded in buildings, railroads, or bridges—structures resting on solid earth, which often perpetuate their fame for centuries—the handiwork of the shipbuilder is quickly perishable, exposed as it is, from the moment it touches the water, to the action of the most destructive elements. For this reason he who would know of the achievements of shipbuilders and naval architects must look to the musty records of history, and to form a correct estimate of their importance as contributors to a nation's progress and prosperity, he must learn what they had to contend with in the production of their works, and be conversant also with the development of the mechanical arts. We indulge in no empty rhetorical phrase when we say that this country could not be what it is to-day if former generations had not been incurably maritime. These men were not blind to the blessings of that sea power which enabled them to build up a foreign trade, the profits from which contributed to the wealth and prosperity of the entire nation.

Shipbuilders have always been men of mark, as well as men of "brains and brawn," among their contemporaries. In the case of the first shipbuilder, Noah, can be seen an illustration of this fact, for he was undoubtedly superior to all human beings at that time, or else his name would never have been so prominent in the oldest traditions. Again, it should be borne in mind that New York's earliest settlers were shipbuilders, and the first mechanic art practiced on her shores was shipbuilding.

Among the eminent shipbuilders in New York during the thirties, Christian Bergh stood out prominently. Most of the Havre and some of the London Line packets were built at his yard, on Water Street corner Scammell, extending to the East

River over what is now South Street. The register of vessels built at that yard shows that Christian Bergh, Robert Carnely or Connolly and Jacob A. Westervelt were the master builders, which would imply the two latter having an interest in "C. Bergh & Co." Mr. Bergh retired from business in 1837, and was succeeded by his sons, Henry and Edwin Bergh, who continued the business until just after their father's death in 1843, when the yard was closed.

Isaac Webb, the father of William H. Webb who became New York's most prominent designer and builder of ships in the following generation, began business at the foot of Montgomery Street about 1818. He was born in Stamford, Conn., in 1794 (where Noah and Adam Brown also came from), the son of Wilsey Webb, himself afterward a ship carpenter in Henry Eckford's yard. Isaac Webb learned his trade with Mr. Eckford, and when his term of apprenticeship expired, was in possession of 1,000 dollars, which he had received during his term of service, in addition to his stipendiary dues. It was Henry Eckford's chief object to have New York shipbuilders excel all others, and he would not withhold any means when he could find a suitable opportunity for encouraging his men, especially the apprentices, with extra pay and rewards. Isaac Webb, in his turn, was very considerate of his apprentices (the writer's grandfather, Donald McKay, afterwards Boston's leading ship designer and builder, also his grand-uncle, Lauchlan McKay, who commanded the famed clipper ship *Sovereign of the Seas*, both "served their time" with Mr. Webb); and when he had occasion to find fault with a mechanic who had done a piece of work to the best of his ability, but not exactly in the best style, he would say, "John, if I had had this to do, I should have done thus and so," indicating the way; but if the man offered to do it over again, he would invariably say, "No matter," thus sparing his pride while teaching him a lesson.

Improvements and increase of business forced the shipyards uptown, Mr. Webb's along with the rest, and he moved to the foot of Stanton Street, where he associated himself with John Allen, a half-brother of Henry Eckford, and a Mr. Rathbone, under the firm name of Isaac Webb and Company. While there, they built the ships *Superior*, in 1822, of 575 tons, and

Splendid, in 1823, of 642 tons; *Silas Richards,* of 454 tons; *Oliver Ellsworth,* a New York and Hartford steamboat, in 1824; and some of the Liverpool packets. This last named vessel was built just after the embargo on steam navigation, in the State of New York, had been raised by the decision of the United States Supreme Court, and she was the first steamboat to run between Hartford and New York.

The *Superior* and the *Splendid,* were built for the China trade, but they were unfortunately too large. There being no demand for such cargoes of teas and silks as the *Splendid* brought in from China, she became a Havre packet. Her Captain, "Bully" Hall was a character; he once fastened his mate in a chicken coop and tantalizingly called to him as to a chicken to be fed with corn.

The introduction of steam as a motive power, although introduced in 1807, did not sensibly enlarge the demand for vessels adapted to that mode of propulsion. Until about 1820, Charles Brownne built all the steamboats; but it was resolved that others could do quite as well, and Isaac Webb and other builders were employed to try.

In 1837, Isaac Webb and Company built the *Sheridan,* of 895 tons for Collins' Dramatic Line to Liverpool; and, here is a curious contradiction—that ship was regarded as too large for a Liverpool packet, and after a few voyages was placed in the China trade. Conditions had changed since the *Superior* and *Splendid* were launched.

On the spot where Fourth Street tumbles overboard stood Smith and Dimon's yard where among other vessels built at this period, were the packet ships *Roscoe* and *Independence,* the ship *Mary Howland,* the North River steamboats *Rochester, James Kent,* and *Oregon,* and the Greek frigate *Liberator.* When they built the packet *Corinthian,* and other vessels in the 'twenties, the firm was Blossom, Smith and Dimon; then it became Smith, Dimon and Comstock in the 'thirties, which partnership did not last long enough for them to achieve fame; afterwards the firm became Smith and Dimon, which is the name by which it was best known in shipping circles.

Stephen Smith, of Smith and Dimon was, like Isaac Webb, a native of Stamford, Connecticut, and an apprentice of Henry

Eckford's. His partner, John Dimon, attended principally to the business of repairing vessels—usually the most profitable department of a shipbuilding firm's enterprises—and is supposed to have said on one occasion, "Smith builds the ships, and I make the money." The ship *Mary Howland* had great celebrity in her day because of her size; crowds thronged the wharves to see her—she was about 500 tons. The *Independence* was one of the most celebrated of the Liverpool packets. Commanded by Captain Ezra Nye, she for several years sailed regularly on the sixth of March, and carried the President's Message.

It was in Smith and Dimon's yard where John Willis Griffiths, father and founder of the modern science of naval and marine architecture, dreamed his *Rainbow*, the first out-an-out clipper, and in launching her, on a freezing January morning in 1845, launched a new idea into the world's destiny. Not so much as a tablet marks this historic spot. In all the city there is not a memorial to Griffiths' genius nor yet a remembrance of the fact that it was New York which contributed what is popularly known as the "Yankee Clipper" to the needs of mankind. We will, later on, tell more about Smith and Dimon and other East Side shipbuilders who long made New York famous as a shipbuilding center.

A little to the south of the *Rainbow's* cradle were the yards of Brown and Bell. David Brown and Jacob Bell were both originally from Darien, Connecticut, "a circumstance almost sufficient in itself to insure them their well earned and richly merited success."

And now to continue quoting from a biographical sketch of David Brown.

"What State in the Union has given wings to commerce, genius to the mechanical arts, enterprise to every pursuit, and intelligence to the world in a greater degree than Connecticut? Every intelligent son of this world-known State feels an almost intuitive inspiration stimulating his energy, and inviting him to enterprise and triumph."

David Brown and Jacob Bell came to New York and served a regular apprenticeship at shipbuilding with Adam and

Noah Brown, young Brown being their nephew and the adopted son of Noah Brown.

In 1817, after having learned their trade, they went to Saint Stephens and there built the first steamboat (the first vessel of any kind) ever built in Alabama. They remained in this place about a year, and removed to Blakeley, Georgia, where they stayed about a year and a half, and returned to New York in 1819.

They took the yard of their former employers in 1819, and commenced business. They had no capital, but their credit being good they were able to go on until March twenty-fourth, 1824, when they were burned out, with a loss of 20,000 dollars. By their own exertions and the assistance of their friends they again started business.

In 1821, they launched their first ships, the *William Tell* and *Orbit*. The firm was known as Brown and Bell until the former's death about 1848, when Bell conducted it in his own name until his death (1852). Their yard held its own with the principal local rivals, William H. Brown, Smith and Dimon, also Isaac and William H. Webb. They seem to have been equally successful in turning out fast sailing vessels and in keeping up with the latest developments in steamships.

The firm was in close relation with Edward K. Collins. In 1834, they joined with him in starting the New York Marine Dry Dock Company, and shortly afterward built the *Garrick*, *Roscius*, *Sheridan*, and *Siddons* for his trans-Atlantic Dramatic Line of sailing packets. They are credited with building in 1840, the first ocean steamships launched in New York, the *Lion* and the *Eagle*, which became Spanish warships. A year later, they built the fast little schooner *Angola* for the opium trade.

David Brown's favorite ship was the *Roscius*, of E. K. Collins' Dramatic Line. "Nothing," he used to say, "can beat the Roscius." They built many ships for Liverpool packet lines —the *Liverpool*, of 1,174 tons, in 1843; the *Queen of the West*, of 1,168 tons; *Henry Clay*, of 1,228 tons; also the *Constitution*, of 1,334 tons.

Brown and Bell's clippers were surpassed only by the

David Brown

Jacob Bell

Jacob A. Westervelt

Three Famous Shipbuilders of New York

The First Period

products of Jacob Bell's pupil, Donald McKay.* The partners built the *Houqua* (1844), *Samuel Russell* (1847). Afterwards, Jacob Bell built the *White Squall* (1850), *Trade Wind* (1851).

Mr. Brown received from the Emperor of Russia a diamond ring in acknowledgment of some drawings lent to that monarch. One midnight he was awakened by loud rapping at the door of his house. The Seventh Ward Bank was in trouble, and some of the directors had called to beg him to take the presidency as the only hope of carrying them through the crisis. Very reluctantly he consented, and from that hour the bank's distress ceased.

About 1848 Mr. Brown determined to retire from business, in spite of the remonstrances of his friends. He had long desired to spend his days in the country, and his ample fortune made him independent. Four years afterwards on Christmas day, 1852, he died at Princeton, New Jersey, and when his body was brought to New York for burial, his friends noticed that many flags in the shipping were at half-mast.

Jacob A. Westervelt was a native of Hackensack, Bergen County, New Jersey, and the son of a shipbuilder. He learned the "art, trade, and mystery" of his profession by serving as a common sailor, and as an apprentice of Christian Bergh. Having finished his time with Mr. Bergh, he established himself in business in Savannah, and built several vessels there; but on the invitation of his old "boss" he returned to New York, and became a member of the firm of C. Bergh and Company, Mr. Robert Connolly being a third member, and so continued until 1837, when each partner retired with a fortune. Indeed, all the old shipbuilders that have been mentioned became rich, with perhaps the single exception of Isaac Webb. After a trip to Europe, Mr. Westervelt became associated with Nathan Roberts, and built two ships in Williamsburg. He went back to New York, entered into business with George Mackay, and built many ships. While a member of the firm of C. Bergh and Company he constructed most of the Havre packets and London packets that were launched previous to 1837. In 1852

* When released from his "indenture" by Isaac Webb, Donald McKay entered the employ of Brown and Bell. Jacob Bell quickly realized his ability and sent him to construct a ship at Wiscasset, Maine; from there he went to Boston, where he built many of the finest ships that ever sailed the seas.

he was elected Mayor of New York City, and on leaving office was awarded the contract for building the United States steam frigate *Brooklyn*. He finally took his sons into partnership, under the style of Westervelt and Company. Mr. Connolly and Mr. Westervelt built houses for themselves side by side, in East Broadway, facing Grand Street, and over the front door was a large stone cap on which was carved a representation of a ship's taffrail.

We are still among the shipyards, on the banks of the East River. Lawrence and Sneden, whose yard was near the foot of Corlaers Street, made a specialty of steamboat construction and had a high reputation as builders. At the foot of Montgomery Street was the shipyard of Thorn and Williams—Stephen Thorn and "honest old Jabez Williams"; below that the shipyards of Carpenter and Bishop, Ficket and Thomas, James Morgan and Company, and one or two other yards.

There were two yards opened in 1834 that were subsequently widely known for the steam vessels built there: Bishop and Simonson, foot of Walnut Street (now Jackson), builders of the *Lexington* in 1835 and many steamships; and William H. Brown, who built many Hudson River steamboats and Coastwise steamships. A few years later Bishop and Simonson's yard was located between Seventh and Eighth Streets, which afterwards became Westervelt and Mackay's. There were many other builders or repairers of ships who occupied the same interesting shore of the East River at about the same time or later.

Between 1830 and 1836 we were in a state of marine advancement. The American Merchant Marine increased twelve and three-quarter per cent a year, while the British increased only one and one-half per cent. Nations are like men; they concede no rights that are not asserted. To assert our rights at sea, we must sail it with our ships, and New York shipowners, merchants and shipbuilders furnished the means of winning and holding our deservedly foremost rank as maritime, also a commercial power, among the nations of the world.

Americans in those days were known to possess a skill and economy in building vessels, second to no nation in the world; a cheapness in fitting them out; an activity in sailing them,—

all of which gave us an advantage in coping with any commercial power in existence. Furthermore, such was the accurate calculations of our merchants, the ability of our seamen, and the intelligence of our shipmasters, that American vessels could, on an average, make three trips to Europe while a foreign vessel was making two.

The launching of a large vessel in the old sailing ship days brought people from all parts of the city and even from the surrounding country, for an event of that kind was most always an item of news, especially during the "clipper epoch." The builders invited their friends, and the owners invited theirs. Christian Bergh did not like the *saturnalia* which the occasion often invoked—almost everybody in the neighborhood was more or less under the influence of liquor—but the proprietors of the packet and clipper lines always insisted upon giving the workmen a "blow-out," and usually paid the bills for the biscuits, cheese, and rum punch, and also for the champagne drank by the guests, in the mold loft.

It was a day of anxiety to the builder until the ship was successfully launched. He had so much at stake: the ways might be insufficiently greased; the chains beneath the vessel might break; she might tumble over on her side, as the *Switzerland* did in Westervelt and Mackay's yard; she might acquire momentum enough to drive her into the opposite bank of the river.

There was no finer sight in New York four or five score years ago than that of a noble ship sliding easily into the water, while a young woman broke the christening bottle of wine over the bow, and the sailors heaved anchor, and the saluting cannon boomed, and the wild throng of spectators on river and shore rent the air with cheers. A friend of the late Reverend Dr. James W. Alexander relates that one day at a launch in Brown and Bell's yard the doctor was trembling with emotion when the ship began to start. "There! there she goes!" he exclaimed, adding, as the gun was fired, "That serves as an outlet to my feelings."

For the launching of the *General Admiral*, in William H. Webb's yard, the mechanics had erected, the previous evening, a stage for "their really fine-looking families," wrote an eye witness of the scene, who was on board the vessel. "A slight jar, a rush to the sides, roar of cannon, loud huzzas from outsiders, Dodworth's Band playing 'Departed Days,' and through the port-holes it was seen that the vessel was in motion. So gentle and steady was the movement, so slight was the dip, and so gradually was she brought up by her anchors before passing twice her length from the shore, that a person standing on board, with closed eyes, could not have realized that any change whatever had been made in her position."

The crowd began to separate immediately after the flag-bedecked ship was off the ways, and the rush for the various entrance gates of the yard was tremendous.

In the *Chronicle Express* of January sixth, 1803, we find this interesting account relative to the first drydock patented in the United States:

"John Gardiner of this City has obtained a patent for erecting Dry Docks (where there is little or no ebb and flow of tide) to repair ships in. On his construction a steam engine that costs $4,000. will dry eight docks in twenty-four hours and may be applied to any number of docks. The fuel consumed by the engine is ninety pounds weight of coals per hour whilst at work."

For many years the need of a drydock or marine railway was felt badly in New York. Meanwhile ships in service had increased so largely, for the foreign as well as the coastwise trade, that some better means of preparing a vessel for inspection or repairs to the hull below the waterline had to be made here than the usual "heaving down" process then in use. When coppering of the bottom or serious repairs had to be made to our naval vessels and large merchantmen, we were obliged to send them to European drydocks.

Two shipbuilders, Henry Steers and John Thomas, after furnishing plans for the construction of an immense shiphouse and an inclined plane, by means of which they were successful in hauling up the frigate *Congress* for repairs at the Washington Navy Yard, came to New York, in 1824, and a little later built, at the foot of Tenth Street, on the East River, the first ship-railway ever seen in the United States. It consisted of rails laid on an inclined plane, upon which a cradle was run for the purpose of drawing vessels up out of the water in order to repair them; and in consideration of their enterprise the Legislature granted to the New York Dry Dock Company a charter for a bank, to last "as long as grass grows and water runs." Thus was founded the Dry Dock Bank, afterwards the Eleventh Ward Bank. The only other institution that ever received such a charter was the Manhattan Company.

Henry Steers was the father of James R. and George Steers, both of whom achieved fame and fortune as shipbuilders, and it was said that they were stockholders in that bank for nearly fifty years. This marine railway was 300 feet in total length, and was operated at first by horse power, but a few years later steam power was substituted. The first trial with this slipway was not made until March, 1826, in taking out a brig-rigged vessel, which was so successfully done, that shortly after several other vessels were taken out for repairs. The first use of the diving bell in this country is believed to have been made for cutting off the wooden piles for the outer end of the ways for this railway.

As the number and size of vessels continued to increase, the inventive faculty of the American mechanic had been brought into play to devise more adequate methods to take a vessel out of the water and properly repair her. The "Marine Railways," above referred to, had been found inadequate for efficiently handling the continually larger sailing vessels and steam-propelled craft which were being constructed, within a year after they were projected. The invention of a hydraulic or "screw dock" was therefore hailed with joy. The New York Screw Dock Company began the operation of a screw dock at a slip on South Street, between Market and Pike Streets, in September, 1827, the company being incorporated April twenty-first, 1828. This dock, which was the first of its design, is thus spoken of by an engineer of that period:

"The vessel to be raised by this apparatus was floated over a platform of wood sunk to the depth of about ten feet below the surface of the water, and suspended from a strongly built wooden frame work by 16 iron screws 4½ inches in diameter. This platform has several shores on its surface, which were brought to bear equally on the vessel's bottom, to prevent her from canting over on being raised out of the water. About thirty men were employed in working this apparatus, who, by the combined power of the lever, wheel, pinion and screw, succeeded in the course of half an hour in raising the platform loaded with a vessel of 200 tons' burden to the surface of the water, where she remained high and dry, suspended between the wooden frames.

"The first vessel raised was the steamship *Great Britain* in June, 1835. After being secured in the dock she was raised out of the water in forty-five minutes. The mode of raising a vessel on this dock was to bring the vessel in between the two wharfs exactly over the cradle; the chains were then tightened so as to make the blocks come in contact with the keel; water was then forced into the cylinder through a small tube by means of a pump, which caused the ram to be forced out, drawing with it the sliding beams, raising the cradle with the vessel in a slow but steady manner, to the required height."

The New York Sectional Dock Company built a sectional dock from plans of Phineas Burgess and Daniel Dodge in 1839. This concern was incorporated as the New York Floating Dry Dock Company on April eighteenth, 1843, having a capital of 100,000 dollars. Their dock was located at the foot of east Eleventh Street, on the East River, and it was the largest drydock in the city; and, as there were other floating docks in the vicinity, the whole section from Stanton Street to east Eleventh Street was known as the "Dry Dock." While this name has no significance now, when linked with early associations it is very appropriate.

Towing with steamboats began on the North River with the opening of the Erie Canal (1825) and the steamboat *Henry Eckford*, built in 1825, was the first steam craft to make a special business of towing barges on the North River. But the first regular towboat engaged in harbor service was the *Rufus W. King*, which craft was built in 1828 by the New York Dry Dock Company. She was legislated into existence, as the company could get no charter for their scheme, to repair vessels on railways, unless they provided a steamboat to tow all ships that might need repairing to their place. This building and repairing yard was thought then to be so far up town as to be useless for the needs of shipping without the adjunct of a steam tug, and the solicitude manifested by legislators in those times for American shipping is in marked contrast to the contemptuous disregard shown nowadays. John R. Skiddy was the president of the company, and John Dimon, Russell Stebbins, Jesse Woods, and others were interested.

The old boat would look queer enough now, but she was as stanch as she was ugly, with her square stern—like a North River sloop—and a bow as round as the full moon. Her timbers were live oak, and you could wash your hands overboard from her guards, she floated so deep. She was about ninety-eight feet long, twenty-two feet wide and seven feet six inches depth of hold. Her paddle wheels were very far forward and the boiler was abaft the engine which was, of course, of the "steeple" pattern, a type now nearly extinct. She had no upper deck, but was steered from a pilot house about as wide as the gallows frame, over the companion way leading down below deck to the forward cabin. There was also a small cabin below deck aft, just forward of which and projecting some three feet above deck was the boiler, made of pure copper. The engine was six by thirty-six, and there was trouble sometimes when it got caught on the "dead center," for it took all hands with capstan bars to pry it over. In those days they burned pine wood, which, piled up along the deck fore and aft, made the old craft look like a floating wood yard. The system of signals between the pilot and engineer at that time was crude indeed. She had only one bell, a "jingle," to start her ahead, and to back they would ring the "church" bell—a big brass affair perched on top of the gallows frame. To go fast either way they had to stamp once or twice on the floor of the pilot house to notify the engineer who was stationed just below. Her engine would look absurd to a present day engineer. Crankshafts, and so forth, all were of cast iron, and its greatest working pressure was about eighteen pounds.

There was some towing done in those days of United States naval vessels, and many foreign men-of-war which visited the port often required repairs. The Dock Company had also to heave down vessels that were too heavy for their ways, and the tug *Rufus W. King* would assist in the operation. Passengers on the "Old" or Black Ball Line had good reason to remember the *King*, for she long remained the connecting link between America's shore and their departure for Europe, as is indicated by the following notice in the New York *Commercial Advertiser* of September fifteenth, 1832:

"Ship 'CANADA' for Liverpool—
The passengers of the 'Canada' are requested to be at the Battery Place, formerly Marketfield Street, tomorrow morning at 10 o'clock, when the steam-boat 'Rufus King' will be in readiness to convey them on board."

The *King* would sometimes tow the trans-Atlantic packets out to the Sandy Hook Light Ship, but that tugboat never hunted outside of the Hook for work. When they left the ship below, after towing her down the harbor, though the tugboat men were paid by the hour, there was no time lost in getting back to their dock, for the Captain of the *King* was a "rounder" and always in a hurry to get back among the "b'hoys" or up in the third tier of the Old Bowery Theater in the evenings.

The old steamboat *Sun*, built to run on the North River, was the first towing boat to hunt after incoming vessels outside of Sandy Hook. Our Congress had enacted a law, which, on and after a certain date, affected very seriously the value of all importations from Europe, and the merchants interested in these goods chartered the *Sun* to cruise "along the beach," with pilots on board and tow all the incoming ships up the Bay immediately on their appearance.

About 1837, the Peck Brothers were running steamboats on the East River to places on the Sound. They also did some towing by contract in the summer, and in the autumn and winter had the tow-boat signal flying always on their boats that were docked at Fulton Market. Captain Curtiss Peck began with the *Fanny* and then he built the steamboat *Linnæus* (called after his large gardens where he raised flowers for the market), afterward he had the *Fox*, next the *Comet*, *Statesman* and *Fairfield*. Captain Peck commenced harbor towing with the *Comet* and the *Statesman*, which craft ran to Flushing in the summer. All this time, however, the *Rufus W. King* was the only regular tow-boat in New York harbor.

The *Jacob Bell* was built by Brown and Bell for Captain Yates, especially for towing, and was owned by Dackerty and

Sons, who, although they had made their money in the African slave trade, were strait-laced in some things, as is attested by the following story, which was told to an old *Herald* reporter many years ago, apropos a prize fight and camp meeting:

"We worked around the harbor, docked vessels, etc., with the 'Bell' for a time and were then engaged by the Allen Street Methodist Church to attend their camp meeting at Sing Sing, but a day or two before the time that we were to convey the brethren and sisters to Sing Sing, Captain Yates took a party of prize fighters (the Yankee Sullivan-Bell fight) up the Sound to Hart's Island. They paid us $150 for the trip and well I remember it. We anchored off the island and all hands went ashore, when the ring was pitched and the 'mill' began. Yankee Sullivan had the worst of that fight, when his friends broke into the ring, and it was some time before order was restored. He thus got his second wind, and Bell, losing heart, apparently, was whipped very handily. The church people, as you can easily imagine, made some severe comments on our prize fighting charter, which our captain cared very little about, but our owners were much chagrined and called Captain Yates to order for disgracing their new boat. However, we took the church people on board and started up the North River for the camp grounds. The captain had been out all the night before with the boys, and the owner and his sons, who were on board, picked a quarrel with him, in which some pistol shots were fired, when I ran down from the pilot house to see what was up. The captain immediately ordered me back to the wheel, saying that he could take care of himself, etc. We were then just off the Palisades, above Fort Lee, and approaching a shoal spot, that was situated well in under the bank of the river. I had given her wheel enough while steering to offset the sheer which flat bottom steamboats always take when they 'smell the bottom,' but the captain, in his excitement and rage, and from his position on the lower deck, thought differently and so up he came into the pilot house and took the wheel from me, saying as he did so, 'Why don't you keep in there?' giving her a few more spokes himself. Hardly had the boat felt the increased pressure than with her heavy load of passengers she took a rank heel and submerged. Of course one of her paddlewheels was elevated considerably, when, with a noise like young thunder, smash went the engine. I thought the bottom of the boat had been crushed out and there was consternation among the passengers, I can assure you. A glance aft from the pilot house showed me that the engine was a wreck, for the shaft had broke close to the crank, in the journal, the cylinder head was smashed, the connecting rods were all twisted around the cranks, and the main crosshead unshipped—a terrible mess. There we were, helpless as a log, and the owners would have it that the captain did it purposely, which opinion they held till they died."

There were many powerful side-wheel towboats in the harbor when the screw propellers were introduced here for towing, but they were expensive crafts to run, they burned so much coal. In 1849 and 1850 the screw-propelling tugboats came here from Philadelphia. They were not like the tugboat of today and their boilers were very slight affairs built to run with fresh water. One of the first, the *Resolute*, blew up one day at the foot of Wall Street and killed all hands. When she was running, the jar of her engine shook the safety valve so much that they were compelled always to tie it down. But this time they forgot to remove the fastening when at the wharf so the steam made up and blew the bridge wall of the boiler out while all hands were at breakfast in the cabin abaft of the boiler. This accident hindered the use of that type of tugboat very much, but improvements in engines and boilers and high pressure steam have made them superior to the old side-wheel tow-boats.

New York suffered from an unparalleled calamity by fire on the night of December seventeenth, 1835. Perhaps one of the best descriptions of it is that contained in the "Diary of Philip Hone" from which this is extracted:

"The greatest loss by fire that has ever been known, with the exception perhaps of the conflagration of Moscow, and that was an incidental concomitant of War. I am fatigued in body, disturbed in mind, and my fancy filled with images of horror which my pen is inadequate to describe. Nearly one half of the first ward is in ashes; 500 to 700 stores, which with their contents are valued at $20,000,000 to $40,000,000, are now lying in an indistinguishable mass of ruins. There is not perhaps in the world the same space of ground covered by so great an

View of the Great Conflagration of Dec. 16th and 17th, 1835 from Coenties Slip. From a sketch drawn by J. H. Bufford.

amount of real and personal property as the scene of this dreadful conflagration. The fire broke out at nine o'clock last evening. I was writing in the library when the alarm was given and went immediately down. The night was intensely cold, which was one cause of the unprecedented progress of the flames, for the water froze in the hydrants, and the engines and their hose could not be worked without great difficulty. The firemen, too, had been on duty all last night, and were almost incapable of performing their usual services.

"The fire originated in the store of Comstock & Adams in Merchant Street, a narrow crooked street, filled with high stores lately erected and occupied by dry goods and hardware merchants, which led from Hanover to Pearl Street. When I arrived at the spot the scene exceeded all description; the progress of the flames, like flashes of lightning, communicated in every direction, and a few minutes sufficed to level the lofty edifices on every side.

"The fire has been burning all day in the direction of Coenties Slip, and was not fairly gotten under control until towards evening.

"A calculation is made in the 'Commercial' this afternoon that the number of buildings burnt is 570, and that the whole loss is something over 15,000,000 dollars. The insurance offices are all of course bankrupt. Their collective capitals amount to 11,750,000, but those down town have a large proportion of the risks, and will not be able to pay 50 per cent of the losses; the unfortunate stockholders lose all."

Two days afterwards, December nineteenth, this eminent diarist writes:

"I went yesterday and to-day to see the ruins; it is an awful sight. The whole area from Wall Street to Coenties Slip, bounded by Broad Street to the river, with the exception of Broad Street, the Wall Street front between William and Broad, and the blocks bounded by Broad Street, Pearl Street, the south side of Coenties Slip, and South Street, are now a mass of smoking ruins. Nineteen blocks are destroyed." (Later Hone estimates the number of buildings burnt at 674.)

"It is gratifying to witness the spirit and firmness with which the merchants meet this calamity. There is no despondency; every man is determined to go to work to redeem his loss, and all are ready to assist their more unfortunate neighbors. A meeting of citizens was held this day, at noon, at the Sessions Court Room, on the call of the mayor. A committee of 125 was appointed, which met in the evening at the mayor's office and appointed sub-committees on each branch of duty submitted to them. I am of the committee to make application for relief to the State Government. That committee is to meet to-morrow evening at my house. The utmost spirit and harmony prevailed at the meeting, which embraced all the best and most influential men in the City."

Then, on the 22nd, he continues:

"Goods and property of every description are found under the rubbish in enormous quantities, but generally so much damaged as to be hardly worth saving. Cloths, silks, laces, prints of the most valuable kinds, are dug out partly burned, and nearly all ruined. A mountain of coffee lies at the corner of Old Slip and South Street. The entire cargo of teas arrived a few days since in the ship 'Paris' lies in a state not worth picking up, and costly indigo and rich drugs add to the mass of mud which obstructs the streets."

One of the amusing stories told about the "Great Fire," relates to Black Joke Engine 33, the members of which were nearly all employed in the shipyards along the East River:

It seems that Engine 33 was run on the deck of a brig at the foot of Wall Street, and supplied water to the engine playing on the fire further up the street. The weather was bitterly cold, and the boys were frequently obliged to leave the brakes, and get into the brig's cabin to "thaw out." When their comrades on deck judged that their turn at the stove had come the expedient of placing a fire hat over the stove pipe speedily smoked out those below. After working all night the engine became so encased in ice that further work was impossible.

The buildings in the burnt district were occupied chiefly by New York's largest shipping and wholesale dry goods merchants and grocers. Among the well known business houses which were burned out, were Halsted, Haines and Company, Howland and Aspinwall, James Bleecker and Son, and many others, but the firm names afterwards were so much changed that they cannot be recognized readily. The greatest consterna-

The First Period

tion was presently awakened in view of the probable financial consequences of the disaster. One firm after another failed. Howland and Aspinwall, B. Aymar and Company, and S. V. S. Wilder, three of the largest mercantile houses, gave notice promptly after the fire that they would cash all their paper which was out in the hands of the sufferers, and their example was followed by many others.

It was a winter of distress—three thousand clerks, porters, and car men, were thrown out of employment, many of them having families to support. And, to add to the distress, every insurance company in the city was made bankrupt. There was little English insurance capital here, owing to restrictive laws against foreign companies, and the loss fell almost entirely upon American companies.

As it was universally conceded that the fire in its magnitude had been the direct result of a water famine, this calamity gave the Croton Aqueduct project an impetus which carried it to a successful conclusion earlier than would have been the case otherwise.

Very few merchants of the old school brought up their own sons to business in their own stores. A business education was a severe one in old times. Every duty, from sweeping out the office to bookkeeping, was minutely exacted. It was a regular apprenticeship to commerce, and it created thorough merchants. The progress was as regular as clock work. Sweeping out office, doing errands, taking letters to post office, copying letters, copying accounts, entering goods at the Custom House, delivering goods sold, taking an account of goods received from the ships, keeping the store-book, making sales, assisting the bookkeeper, going out as supercargo to East or West Indies. The habit of neatness and correctness in copying letters, when once acquired follows a man through his life. The old school merchant took ten times more pains with his clerks than is taken in Columbia College. When they were set to copying letters, their work was read to the first blot or error and then destroyed, and the unhappy clerk was set at his task again, and made to copy correctly. This achieved, he was promoted to making duplicates, and even triplicates of letters, and he had the honor of knowing that his "fist" went to ports in the uttermost parts of the earth—for in the days of sailing ships, while one ship took the "original" letter, succeeding vessels carried "duplicates" and "triplicates," and not unfrequently the last reached their destination first.

John I. Mumford went into business at Fifty-one South Street, in 1816, under the firm name of Mumford and Muir. At that time his father, John P. Mumford, was a member of the firm of Murray and Mumford, and one of the best known merchants in New York. John I. dissolved with Muir in about two years, and continued on his own account until 1823, when he formed a partnership with Henry Underhill, at Number One Tontine Coffee House. The firm was Mumford and Underhill, and continued until 1828, when he became editor of the *Mercantile Telegraph*, and soon was well known as a writer on commercial affairs.

After some editorial experience in other journals, he became editor of the *Daily Standard*. He sustained General Jackson in his veto of the Charter of the United States Bank, and the proclamation against the nullifiers of South Carolina. The services he had to render and duties he was called upon to perform at this period of his life were of the most laborious character. He was often called to act as Deputy Collector of the port of New York, by reason of his accurate commercial knowledge. He also took a lively interest in local and national politics, although never seeking political office. He filled the office of secretary to the commission which was charged with the adjustment of our difficulties with Spain. He was, at the same time, engaged in arduous editorial duty, superintending the daily issues of the *Standard*, one of New York's leading Democratic organs. Old Jackson loved him. It was his only organ here in this great city after James Watson Webb of the *Courier and Enquirer* betrayed him, and went over to the United States Bank.

General Jackson wanted to do something for John, and one year sent for him to come to Washington. It was just before the annual message was to be delivered to Congress.

"Colonel John, would it be of any use to you if you had a copy of my message to take on to New York with you?" said the President, kindly.

"It would be, indeed, if I could print it in advance of any other paper, General."

"No, not exactly that; but I will tell you what I will do. You shall have a copy. Promise me the utmost secrecy, so as not to compromise me, and I will give the copy to you. Start at once for New York. When you reach there, have it set up and strike off as many copies as you think you can sell. The moment the regular copy reaches New York, you can throw yours upon the market—not a minute before."

This was agreed to. It was an act of pure kindness and John I. did not intend to deviate from it. Alas! there is no use of disguising the fact, John I. Mumford loved liquor, and it had the same effect upon him as it does upon many other clever persons. If he drank one glass, fifty followed. A tremendous reckless spree was sure to follow. It was a disease. John got safe to Philadelphia, stopped over night at the old United States Hotel, kept by Billy Dorance. He was drinking, and the next morning started early to drink again. He was pretty tight, and went into a barber shop to get shaved. The talk among the intelligent customers gathered there was about the President's expected Message. One said it would contain such recommendations about the bank; another said it would not. John I. took a hand. He said it would contain such sentences. He was laughed at. He got angry, took out the real article and read from it. This was not convincing, for his audience believed he was lying. However, he got sober—got to New York—was ahead of all the papers. They got wrathy. This set the barber audience in Philadelphia to thinking. The result was several affidavits as to Mumford's reading a genuine Message. An explanation followed, and General Jackson was outraged. He never tolerated Mumford from that day to his death.

While in business John I. Mumford was very active in starting new ideas. He originated the "Prices Current," and the obtaining of news by express, news-boats, public reading-room, and so forth, which proved of immense advantage to a former generation. Of course the telegraph and cable superseded those methods of news gathering, but the public reading room is a beneficial institution in our large city libraries to-day, although it may be said to have "lost caste" in newspaper offices, and commercial men do not gather there nowadays "to get the news."

Schuyler Livingston was a true New York merchant. He was educated to it, serving a regular clerkship of five years, as nearly all of our great shipping merchants have done. In 1819, when sixteen years old, he entered the counting-house of Henry and George Barclay. Their office was at Number Three, in the famous Phoenix stores, that stood at the corner of Water and Wall Streets, as late as 1830.

In 1824, when Schuyler Livingston became of age, he was taken in as a partner, but his name did not appear on the letter head, nor was the style of the firm changed from H. and G. Barclay until 1834, when it became Barclay and Livingston. This change was due to the law passed that the name of no person should be kept in a firm when he was not in it. They were the agents of Lloyds, London. For nearly half a century this house continued in business, and for forty years Schuyler Livingston was its main pillar. His whole life, from boyhood, was devoted to the mercantile profession. He had no ambition outside of it; since he swept out the "office" as under clerk, he had probably never been out of New York over a week at a time.

To rise early in the morning, to get breakfast, to go down town to the counting-house of the firm, to open and read letters —to go out and do some business, either at the Customs House, bank or elsewhere, until twelve, then to take a lunch and a glass of wine at Delmonico's; or a few raw oysters at Downing's;* to sign checks and attend to the finances until half past one, to go on 'change; to return to the counting-house, and remain until time to go to dinner; and, in the old time such things as "packet nights" existed, to stay down town until ten or eleven at night, and then go home and go to bed;—this for forty-three years had been the twenty-four-hour circle for Mr. Livingston.

The credit of the house—its standing at home and abroad

---

* Theodore Downing, long known as a caterer, had his place at Five Broad Street, where he continued until the building was removed to accommodate the Drexel building, to enjoy a widespread reputation for the excellence of his oysters, and the superior manner in which he cooked plain dishes.

The First Period

—was dearer to his heart than all the national difficulties of Europe. He thoroughly understood his business and never neglected it. He was careful, prudent and just; but the moment a merchant failed, then good-by to any further feeling of equality on the part of the managing partner of the old and respected firm of Barclay and Livingston. He might give charity to such a man, but never his countenance. To fail, and not pay one hundred cents on the dollar, exhibited in the eye of Mr. Livingston something wrong—a lack of moral qualities that he could not comprehend. He never failed—why should other people fail? Schuyler Livingston would not have accepted the Presidency of the United States at any period of his long mercantile career, unless its duties could be performed as secondary to those of the house of Barclay and Livingston. If by taking the Presidency he could have extended the business connections of the "firm," he would have accepted the office—just as he became a director in a bank or insurance company, if it helped him in the successful pursuit of his business.

One of the oldest, wealthiest and largest commercial houses, conducting a most varied business in New York for a long time, was Boorman, Johnston and Company, which commenced shortly before the war of 1812. Originally the firm was Boorman and Johnston.

Both of the partners were Scotchmen, and their business at first was selling Scotch goods, bagging from Dundee, and so forth. The firm did a very large business with Virginia, and at one time sold nearly all the tobacco that came to this market from Richmond. They also did a large iron business, receiving cargoes from England and Sweden. They always had Swedish vessels coming in loaded with cargoes of iron to their consignment.

The store of Boorman and Johnston was at Fifty-seven South Street for a long time. About 1829 they removed to One Hundred and Nineteen Greenwich Street, directly opposite Albany Street. It was an immense store, with a very large yard. Here were erected sheds and iron bins. In 1835 Boorman, Johnston and Company received a consignment of immense iron pillars, which they did their best to sell, but nobody wanted them. Finally they set a mason at work, took out the under front wall of their great store and placed the pillars underneath. These were the first iron pillars ever used in New York for building.

The business of this mammoth concern became so large that they had to give up portions of it. They were the largest Madeira merchants, and received immense quantities of that wine every year. From Italian ports they received large consignments of wines and other goods.

From a biography of John Johnston by Emily Johnston de Forest, we cull this interesting item:

"John Johnston continued to be a member of this firm for thirty-one years and only severed the connection in 1844 because of ill-health. Many years later, after Mrs. Johnston's death, when the contents of her house were divided among her heirs, huge demijohns and magnums of Madeira and other wines were found in the attic, labeled, 'Sent on voyage to India and back in 1819,' some labels showing that the journey had been made twice. These undoubtedly had been so sent by Boorman, Johnston and Company, as a sea voyage was supposed greatly to improve the flavor of these wines."

Both James Boorman and John Johnston were prominently identified with building up the north side of Washington Square, where they both resided, and took an active interest in that neighborhood's welfare, both as to the character of the houses erected there and as to their owners or inmates, not forgetting their politics.

Andrew Foster, one of New York's foremost merchants, was in business on Greenwich Street, about 1800, and later moved to Sixty-five South Street, where he remained during the War of 1812, and for many years after. His firm was, afterwards, Foster and Giraud, consisting of Andrew Foster and Jacob Post Giraud. For years they were important factors in the "Rio" or coffee trade. Jacob P. Giraud, who had commenced life as a cooper, maintained a close friendship with Mayor Philip Hone, and that most interesting diarist refers to Mr. Giraud being in his company upon more than one occasion.

Foster and Giraud, with J. and N. Heard and Company, operated the ship *Caroline Ann*, Captain Betts, between New

York and Liverpool in the Spring of 1815, and she proved a pretty successful "trader" before the North Atlantic trade came under control of the Black Ball and other lines of packets. After Jacob Post Giraud died, the firm became Andrew Foster and Sons, the partners being Andrew Foster and Andrew Foster, Jr., Frederic Giraud Foster and George T. Elliott.

Numerous importations were offered for sale in the columns of old New York newspapers, but this advertisement in the *New York Gazette and General Advertiser*, January fourth, 1834, attracted especial attention:

"Elephant's Teeth—5000 pounds prime, averaging 51 pounds for sale by Andrew Foster and Sons, Sixty-five South Street."

It was the firm of Andrew Foster and Sons, who gave that eminent ship-builder, Donald McKay, his first commission to design and build a ship in 1842, when he was at Newburyport, before going to East Boston. This was the little ship *Courier*, of 380 tons, which, it has been claimed by such authorities as Captain Arthur H. Clark, had the first "clipper hull" ever designed. She was built to sail in the coffee trade between this city and Rio de Janeiro, and the idea that such craft as were demanded by the competition in that trade could be built outside of New York and Baltimore was scouted by commercial men in those days. Her success, when sailing side by side with the finest vessels in the trade, was a little wonder, and as quick passages meant money then, her builder was at once brought prominently before the maritime public.

The *Courier* was still running to "Rio" in May, 1850, when she reached New York with 2300 bags of coffee, for Foster, Elliott and Company, and 600 bags, for Grinnell, Minturn and Company. The firm of Andrew Foster and Son had then become Foster, Elliott and Company. Later, in the same year, under command of Captain Norton, this gallant little craft joined the fast growing California fleet and embarked for San Francisco, via the Horn, sailing from Pier Ten, East River, under the house flag of David Ogden, shipping agent, who continued to fill her with freight in the California trade, until she piled up on the bleak shore of the Falklands; but she was still owned by Foster, Elliott and Company, representing the same interests for whom she was built.

The interesting career of Charles H. Marshall, seaman, shipmaster, manager, afterwards principal owner of the famous Black Ball Line of Packets, is so closely welded to South Street's continued growth and welfare that no history of New York City's shipping would be complete without some account of him. We have drawn the following from a "Memorial of Charles H. Marshall" written by his talented son-in-law, William Allen Butler, one of this country's leading admiralty lawyers, but more generally known as the author of that poetic masterpiece of trenchant wit—"Nothing to Wear!"

Captain Charles H. Marshall, one of the corps of shipmasters, who, by their skill and fidelity, gave to the vessels of the Black Ball Line their high reputation on both sides of the Atlantic, left the sea in 1834. Besides a whaling voyage, an East India voyage, and his coasting voyages, he had crossed the Atlantic Ocean ninety-four times. After this long apprenticeship he took his place among the shipping merchants of New York. The control of the ships of the "Old Line" in 1836 had passed into the hands of Messrs. Goodhue and Company, and other owners, when Captain Marshall assumed their entire management. Subsequently he purchased the interest of Messrs. Goodhue and Company, and became the principal proprietor and active manager of the line. The undertaking was, to a great degree, an experiment with him, as up to this time he had acquired but little experience in mercantile affairs, and the business required large resources and constant vigilance. Captain Marshall retained the management of the line for thirty years, identifying himself during all this period with the leading movements of commerce in this city, and bringing into practical exercise the experience he had gained in his long training as a seaman, and in his varied intercourse with men. He superintended the building of new vessels to replace the earlier and smaller packets of the line, and many of the finest carrying ships in our port were constructed and equipped under his practiced eye. The vessels thus added by him were the *Oxford, Cambridge, New York, Montezuma, Yorkshire, Fidelia, Isaac Wright, Isaac Webb, Columbia, Manhattan, Harvest Queen,*

Great Western, and *Alexander Marshall*, ranging from six hundred tons to fifteen hundred tons burden. Under his administration the ships of the "Old Line" made eight hundred voyages to Liverpool. He carried the packet service to its highest point of utility and profit, and, as he had seen its first beginnings, and brought it to its fullest development, so he saw it gradually superseded, first as to cabin passengers and the transmission of intelligence, and then, to a large extent, as to freight and steerage passengers, by the ocean steamers and Atlantic cable.

When Charles H. Marshall bought Goodhue and Company's interest in the Black Ball Line, the Swallow Tail Line added new vessels of increased tonnage, and received notable accessions, and the Dramatic Line of E. K. Collins was organized and entered the Liverpool trade. There were twenty ships now to take the place of three or four little English packets of 179 tons, some of them registering 900 tons—more than the aggregate tonnage of all little old New York's fleet of packets.

Edward Knight Collins was a great naval architect as well as shipping merchant, whose career was, on the whole, more noteworthy than that of any man engaged anywhere in similar pursuits. This public spirited citizen, son of Captain Israel G. Collins, the owner and commander of a ship that traded between the United States and England, was born on the fifth of August, 1802. In his fifteenth year, he entered as a clerk, at Number Forty-one South Street, the store of Messrs. McCrea and Slidell, the latter gentleman a brother of the Confederate minister John Slidell, who was captured on board the *Trent* by naval officers of the country he had disowned.

Five years afterward Mr. Collins was making trips to the West Indies as supercargo for John F. Delaplaine, sharing in the profits of the ventures of his new employer, and experiencing several hair-breadth escapes from pirates and two disastrous shipwrecks on the coasts of Cuba and Florida, so that when, in 1825, he became the partner of his father in the firm of Israel G. Collins and Son, on the north corner of South Street and Burling Slip, he was fully equipped for a notable commercial performance which may be called the foundation of his subsequent prosperity. The ship *Canada*, a regular Liverpool trader, had arrived in New York, after a short passage, with the news of a great rise in the price of cotton in England, and a number of speculators forthwith combined to buy all the cotton they could find. Several merchants, also seized with a similar purpose, determined to send an agent to Charleston, South Carolina, and at one o'clock on the day of the Canada's arrival proceeded to the office of I. G. Collins and Son, and asked the junior member of the firm to act in that capacity. A few minutes' reflection was enough to enable him to accept the appointment, and in reply to their question, "How soon can you start?" he said, quietly: "As soon as I can charter a pilot-boat and ship provisions and crew—about three hours. I will be ready to sail at four o'clock this afternoon."

"But the regular Charleston packet leaves at that hour, and the speculators will go out by her, and get there before you."

"Gentlemen," was the reply, "I will go in the way I have named, or not go at all."

Enough said. At precisely four o'clock from the pier at Burling Slip, the packet hauled in her hawsers, and the pilot-boat, under command of E. K. Collins, cast loose her moorings, the vessels proceeding down the East River together, much to the amusement of the speculators on board the packet, who mercilessly chaffed the "boy," as they called him, for his temerity in undertaking to beat them. But Collins, being an accomplished navigator, and sailing in a boat of so light draught that it could keep close to shore and take full advantage of tides, currents, and land breezes, was soon out of sight of the Merry Andrews, and reached Charleston long enough in advance of them to buy all the cotton in that city and on the Cooper and Ashley rivers, to arrange his exchanges, make out his invoices, and set sail for New York in his saucy little craft. She was crossing the bar homeward bound, with her whip at the main, when the packet and the speculators hove in sight, and as the two vessels passed each other within speaking distance, an eyewitness relates that the would-be cotton-buyers on board the bigger one laughed this time the other side of their mouths. That was certainly a splendid start for a young business man of twenty-three years.

In 1830, under the firm name of E. K. Collins, he established a line of full-rigged packets between New York and Vera Cruz. This venture was so profitable that he soon built additions to the line, and organized a regular line of fast sailing schooners between New York and Tampico, and, in October 1832, the first regular line of packets between New York and New Orleans. Never had the city of New Orleans seen such vessels as those that Collins sent. They revolutionized the packet service of the American coast.

Here began the cordial and long continued relations of this ship-controller with the great shipbuilders Brown and Bell, in whose yard had been laid the keels of the *Congress, Vicksburg,* and *Mississippi.* The plans for these vessels, and for all his later vessels, were devised by Mr. Collins himself, in consultation with the builders who were to execute them, and no persons had a higher respect for his ability as a naval architect than those eminent naval architects David Brown and Jacob Bell themselves.

At the time of her launching from Brown and Bell's yard (1833), the *Mississippi* was the largest ship under the United States flag in the commercial marine, being of 750 tons and 2,600 bales of cotton capacity; but larger still was the *Shakespeare,* which followed her in 1834, and began her first voyage to New Orleans on the twenty-seventh of January 1835, commanded by Captain John Collins, an uncle of her owner. She was constructed to resemble a man-of-war, and having made several round trips to the Louisiana port, was despatched with a cargo to Liverpool. Entirely different in model from the ships then engaged in the trans-Atlantic packet service, and much larger than any of them, she awakened much curiosity on sailing up the Mersey. The pier heads of that river were crowded with spectators, and after she had been docked, the crowd of visitors from all parts of the neighborhood made it necessary for the captain to ask for the interference of the police, he promising, however, in a public notice, to show the ship as soon as her cargo had been discharged and her decks cleaned. He kept his word, and for one week held a continuous reception on board.

What could have been more natural for a man like Mr.

Collins than to make the glowing success of the *Shakespeare* the occasion for establishing between New York and Liverpool a packet line of his own? He had sent one ship to that port, and she had returned to him overflowing with profitable passengers and cargo, after rejecting for lack of room three times the number of people and the quantity of freight. Prosperous as were the ocean packet lines already in operation, not one of them sailed a ship that could approach within hailing distance of the *Shakespeare*. Already he had in frame in Brown and Bell's yard the *Garrick* and the *Sheridan*, which had been intended for the New Orleans service. He proceeded to add to them the *Siddons*, and his famous Dramatic Line—nicknamed the "Theatrical Line"—was an accomplished fact. They were successful until Collins, in 1850, started running his line of large wooden side-wheel steamers under a subsidy from the government, after which his sailing fleet was neglected and allowed to go to destruction in hull and rigging.

One of the most remarkable of all newspaper wars broke out in May 1840. It was declared by the Wall Street press, aided by a few disappointed small papers of New York, and several of the Whig papers in Albany, Boston, Philadelphia and Baltimore, against the New York *Herald*. Nearly every paper in the country, Whig, Democratic or neutral, became engaged on one side or the other before there was a truce. Between Mr. Collins and James Gordon Bennett a warm friendship existed, for Mr. Bennett always lent his influence and aid to the furtherance of New York's shipping.

Mr. Collins was sitting at his desk in South Street one bright beautiful day early in June 1840, when three well known politicians and merchants entered his office.

"We have called, Mr. Collins," said this self-constituted committee, "in regard to your advertisements in the *Herald*. You are aware, Mr. Collins—"

"Yes, yes," replied Mr. Collins, in his quick, decided tone, "yes, yes, I understand. Charles," calling to a clerk in another room, "how many advertisements have we in the *Herald* this morning?"

"Three, sir," answered the polite Charles.

"Three—yes, yes— Well, Charles, put in three more to-

Edward Knight Collins.

The Signal Gun of Distress on the "Arctic."
From a lithograph in possession of the author.

morrow morning." Then turning to the committee, he said, "That is my answer, gentlemen. Good morning."

When the English steamers *Sirius, Great Western, British Queen, Royal William, Liverpool* and *President* had successfully crossed the Atlantic, Mr. Collins said, "There is no longer chance for enterprise with sails; it is steam that must win the day." To his friend William Aymar, Mr. Collins said, in the autumn of 1840, "I will build steamers that shall make the passage from New York to Europe in ten days and less." It took him ten years to get his line in operation, but he kept his word.

In 1850-1 the summit of his ambition was reached, and the splendid steamships of the Collins Line were launched—the *Arctic, Baltic, Atlantic* and *Pacific*. A fierce competition ensued between them and the steamships of the Cunard Line. In twenty-six passages to Liverpool in 1852, the average time of the Cunarders was one hour and forty-three minutes faster than that of their American rivals; but in the same number of passages from Liverpool to New York, the average time of the Collins steamships was not less than twenty-one hours and thirty minutes faster than that of their English rivals, and the American line had the cream of the trans-Atlantic trade.

The misfortunes that soon befell the line—the sinking of the *Arctic* in September 1854, with the loss of more than three hundred persons, among them Mr. Collins's wife and two of his children; the foundering of the *Pacific* not long afterward; and the withdrawal of the government subsidy—were too disastrous to be survived. This, combined with the panic of 1857 and with sectional opposition to New York subsidies in Congress, led to the ultimate failure of what had been the most ambitious effort to establish a steam American merchant marine. The country felt grateful to Mr. Collins, and sympathized with him in his misfortunes. He died in 1878.

But to return to the "East India" merchants. The large capital required in this business kept the mass of merchants from operating in that quarter of the world. During the year 1835, our China trade underwent a complete change. A new class of men entered into it and enlarged it very much. Up to 1834, the cargo of an East Indiaman, from China, was principally tea. A small quantity of China ware, some preserved ginger, boxes of firecrackers, some two or three thousand mats of cassia or Chinese cinnamon, each weighing a pound or more, used principally in stowing cargoes. This trash cinnamon was the only kind used in the United States, the real cinnamon from Ceylon, such as then used in London, coming too high for American use. The nasty stuff from China called "cinnamon," impregnated with bilge water, was ground up and sold by all the grocers in the United States. It cost about one cent per pound in Canton. The cargo was commonly completed with silks.

A house called F. and N. G. Carnes was located in Paris, also in this city. Frank Carnes resided in Paris and N. G. Carnes in New York. They had made a fortune by importing drugs, fancy goods, and so forth, from Paris. These gentlemen took it into their heads that as the Chinese were a very imitative people, they could send out samples of every fancy article made in Paris and have it imitated in China at one-tenth part the cost. An experienced clerk in their employ was sent out in a ship which they purchased called the *Howard*. The speculation succeeded, and such a cargo was never brought to the United States before. The profit was immense. Only small quantities of Chinese matting had been brought into this country up to that time. But the *Howard* had over 6,000 rolls and her owners doubled their money.

The next trip of the *Howard* was to be a great one. N. G. Carnes had a tongue, great energy, and plans sufficient in his head to load and employ ten Chinese ships; but he lacked the needful money; so he inveigled two other houses, both blessed with plenty of money, into the Chinese trade. One of these firms, Gracie, Prime and Company was composed of A. Gracie, Rufus Prime, and John C. Jay; the other firm was Henry and William Delafield, twin brothers, red-headed and perfect images of each other. The arrangement for a fair share of profits was duly made and N. G. Carnes was told he might "sail in." He did.

The ships *Washington, Romulus,* and *Thomas Dickinson,* were respectively chartered, and added to the China Fleet, of which the *Howard* was number one. B. T. Obear, who commanded the *Howard*, was changed to the *Washington*, and a Captain Wainwright to the *Howard*, Mr. Butler being sent out as supercargo of the *Romulus*. That ship made an awful business of it. She was gone eighteen months.

The captain, one Haring, was "one of the boys," that is, mad as a March Hare. Once when he thought the ship was sinking, he locked up Supercargo Butler in his cabin while he and the crew fled to the boats. Seeing however that the ship did not sink, they shortly after returned and brought her home. But Butler got the best of the old fellow in a trial which occurred in New York, after the arrival of the ship. He made the old captain pay swinging damages. The *Romulus* however brought home a very valuable cargo, and did well.

The *Thomas Dickinson* carried out a supercargo, younger than the rest; but what he lacked in experience he made up in luck. The ship made the passage out in ninety-seven days, and returned home in ninety. But such cargoes were never heard of before, and in most cases the quantity of articles ordered was so extensive that the market was overstocked, and prices actually soon ranged lower in New York than in Canton!

In these cargoes every fan ever made in France was recopied by the Chinese and hundreds of cases of feather, palm, silk, ivory, mother-of-pearl and peacock fans were included. Palm leaf fans were abundant, and one of these ships brought 20,000 dollars' worth of them alone. Some of the finer fans cost five dollars each. In addition to this, every drug known in Europe Carnes had imitated in China. There is a wood in China, which when cut up into proper sizes resembles the real Turkey rhubarb. It is yellowish and has a taste like our American sumach. Carnes ordered a hundred tin cans (just as the genuine Turkey rhubarb is packed) to be packed with this yellow wood, and sold it for the original article, thus clearing several hundred times its cost. After that this mock China-wood called rhubarb became a regular article of trade and superseded the genine Turkey rhubarb.

Carnes also sent out a sample of pure attar of roses worth twenty-five dollars an ounce. The Chinese Samski made a capital imitation, costing about sixpence an ounce. About 10,000 ounces came out in one ship, and New York druggists and perfumers bought it up rapidly at from ten to fifteen dollars an ounce. Cassia buds, Chinese camomile flowers, and in fact every known drug were imported.

From Paris and London the most famous sauces, condiments, preserves, sweetmeats, syrups, and so forth, were procured. The Chinese imitated them all, even to the facsimiles of the printed London or Paris labels, and 20,000 dollars' worth at least of these imitations were imported at prices underselling the London and Paris manufacturers. An immense profit was realized.

But the fireworks that Carnes ordered were tremendous. Every pattern, shade and name appeared: firecrackers, rockets, revolving wheels, and all the rest, but these did not take so well.

Every species of lacquer ware, ever made in London or Paris, was imitated closely by the Chinese, and New York was flooded. Chessmen, backgammon boards, fifty in a case; they came in cargoes almost. Every article of horn was imitated—one invoice containing 100,000 horn scoops, to be used in the drawers of grocers and druggists to ladle out sugar, salt, or any powdered stuff, so there was hardly a druggist in the city who did not possess some of these Chinese horn scoops.

There had been, up to 1833, but a few varieties of China silks imported. Carnes sent samples of Italian, English and French silks, and the Chinese imitated them not only to perfection but actually improved on the patterns sent. But the tendency of these importations from China was to reduce the price of all silks. The shawls imported by the Carnes concern were never equaled, and the South American markets were supplied from New York for ten years after with the most costly crimson, scarlet, white, cream-colored and pink shawls, at prices varying from fifty to two hundred and fifty dollars each. The result of the combination was not such as was expected; the business was overdone. Some few articles paid enormous profits, others did not bring here the first cost in Canton. Duty was high, and of course, the freight on such cases of goods as fans, woodenware, and baskets, was enormous. It was decided by these firms to close up, and to abandon the China trade. Their losses were heavy; and so the old ship

Howard was sold, and bought in by Gracie, Prime and Company, to place in the Liverpool line of packets.

The appointment of auctioneers had an early date in the history of the country, and laws were from time to time passed regulating the manner in which they should conduct their business, and fixing the amount of duties they should pay to the Government. The law passed by the State Legislature in 1817 created a new era in the history of auctions at New York City. For many years after that, a fierce warfare was carried on between the importing and jobbing merchants and the auctioneers. Strong influence was brought to bear to repeal or alter auction laws, but the State was reaping too great a harvest from that source, which afforded the solons of Albany good grounds for not interfering. Even though many New York merchants and storekeepers organized to prevent sales by auction, pledging themselves not to purchase anything at them for a certain time, the auctioneers continued to flourish.

After the passage of the 1817 auction law, as business begets business, and the pioneer commercial connecting link between New York and England—the Black Ball Line of Packets—was well under way, the auction sale of much of these ships' cargoes added greatly to the auctioneers' commission accounts. To this merchant shipping factor, the success of New York was ascribed, and packet lines were established from Boston and from Philadelphia, but in neither instance were they successful. When auction sales were prominently identified with New York's commercial welfare, a Boston ship from the East Indies was sent to this port (all previous cargoes having been sold in Boston); and afterwards all the India vessels were sent here; few attempts were made to sell a cargo of India goods east of New York. The truth was that both in Boston and Philadelphia the free and absolute sale of goods by auction was not encouraged. It did not appear to be understood.

Evidently the auction law previously referred to gave the first impulse to the extensive auction trade of this city, and followed, as it was afterwards, by the establishment of lines of packets, and the construction of the Erie Canal in 1825, together with all the natural advantages of New York, auctioneering was eminently successful and advantageous.

Prominent among those who were identified with auction sales in New York were Joseph Samson, who founded the great auction firm of Boggs, Thompson and Company—he formed the "company." There seems to be little attention nowadays paid to the auction commission business, but during the thirties, forties, and fifties it was an extensive and lucrative branch of mercantile business. In 1830 the directory showed thirty-nine prominent houses in the business. Among these, Hicks, Lawrence and Company were at the top; the second member in the firm, Cornelius W. Lawrence, became Mayor, Congressman, and Collector of the Port.

Haggerty, Austen and Company were auction kings, with whom L. M. Hoffman competed largely. The first named firm began as dry goods traders at Eighty-two William Street and next took consignments to be auctioned to jobbers. John and Philip Hone grew rich in the auction business and it gave New York another Mayor; nor must Austen and Spier, Wilmerding Priest and Mount, and Adee, Simpson and Company be forgotten in the same line; nor the witty Simeon Draper, who afterwards became one of Lincoln's Collectors of the Port. His cleverness descended in the same manner to his son, John H. As general auctioneers, James M. Miller and Thomas Bell became popular favorites and ranked in the "going, going" parlance with the London auctioneer of the same period, George Robbins. Bell was commemorated thus in a burlesque at Mitchell's Olympic Theater:

> "Her voice as any bell was sweet and clear
> E'en tho' that bell was Bell the Auctioneer."

Attendance at the first auction sales was more or less confined to New York merchants and a speculative element which followed them up closely and displayed much shrewdness in buying; but, in later years, country buyers by the scores came to auctions, and the high standard set by the auctioneers of the early '20s and the buyers of that period, too, was not maintained.

One of the earliest merchants just after the republic was

formed was an Irish exile named Daniel McCormick, who was of the house of Moore, Lynsen and Company, auctioneers, afterwards carrying on the "Vendue" business alone, at Fifty-seven Wall Street, and he made a large fortune in the sale of prizes captured during the War of 1812. He lived above his store, and was noted for his hospitality; of a fine afternoon, he would sit with his friends upon the stoop of his house for hours. In 1834 every other resident had sold his house or had altered and rented it for offices, but McCormick remained, and in that year he died. He was the founder and first president of the St. Patrick's Society, and had he lived another year, he would have seen the house which for thirty-four years he had occupied, vanish in the great fire of 1835. This last resident of Wall Street wore to the last short breeches and shoes with buckles and hair powder and peruke.

While the Griswolds, Goodhue and Company, Grinnell-Minturn, Howland and Aspinwall, and other large and powerful mercantile houses held commanding positions in many branches of New York commerce, they had little to do with the handling of New York's heaviest import item, textiles from England. These were usually consigned to manufacturers' agents, the "Yorkshiremen," and were sold at auction. The little group of licensed auctioneers who gathered their two and one-half per cent on the tremendous volume of business passing through their hands was headed by John Hone and his debonair brother, Philip.

During June 1836 the men employed in the loading and unloading of vessels in New York harbor—stevedores and laborers—decided to demand an increase of pay. Being denied, they proceeded to prevent from working those who were willing to continue for the existing wages. So formidable was the number of "strikers," as they were termed, that some captains of vessels in progress of being discharged or loaded armed their crews to defend their work. Whereupon "Old Hays," the High Constable of New York, proceeded to where the strikers had assembled and addressed them literally as follows:

"Gentlemen and Blackguards—Go home or go along

with me. 'Tain't no way this to raise wages. If your employers won't give you your price, don't work; keep home and lay quiet—make no riots here, I don't allow them things. Come, march home with you; your wives and children want you—no way this to raise wages."

Jacob Hays lived, reigned rather, in the time when the guardians of the City were watchmen, who, with their old camlet cloaks and huge lanterns, prowled about the city at night, and were known as "Leather-heads," from the leather cap they wore. Hays was a regular autocrat, and held the monopoly of catching thieves. So successful was he as a detective, that his fame spread over the whole world. He was as well known in London as in New York. He was a terror to evil-doers, and "Old Hays is after you!" would send scamps off at any time.

The stand taken by the stevedores was followed by that of the laborers at work upon the ruins of the late fire in the removal of bricks, and so forth, and so formidable was their attack upon those who were willing to work that it became necessary to resort to military power to control them.

The latter part of 1836 saw this strike fever dying out, a presidential election was then on the way, and in a few months the business panic of 1837 had brought on a stagnation in the industries that threw very many of the laboring classes on their own resources, and the trade unions were left without support by the members, and as the leaders did not see a very promising field of labor for the near future, dropped the whole thing, and the organization fell from the want of support. When business revived again during the following year, most of the trade unions had ceased to exist, and wages of mechanics and laborers were at a lower level than they had been for a long time. Thus ended the first trade union fever in this country, and it was many years before it broke out again.

About 1836, ships of a faster type were beginning to make their appearance in the North Atlantic passenger trade, and here too a certain amount of ship racing was going on.

The first packet ship race of any note was that between the *Columbus*, 597 tons, Captain Palmer; the *George Washington*,

734 tons, Captain Henry Holdredge, of the Swallow Tail Line; and the *Sheffield,* Captain Allen. These three ships left New York on the eighth of July, 1836, in the midst of a crowd of other vessels, all bound for Liverpool. We are told that heavy betting on the result of the race took place in New York. The racing packets were in company on the Banks of Newfoundland but did not meet again. The *George Washington* was the first to signal Holyhead, followed two or three hours later by the *Sheffield.* Both ships arrived in the Mersey on the afternoon of the twenty-fifth, seventeen days out. The *Columbus* arrived on the following morning.

In 1837, the *Columbus,* of the Black Ball Line, under Captain De Peyster, and the *Sheridan,* of the Dramatic Line, commanded by Captain Russell, then on her first voyage, raced to Liverpool for stakes of 10,000 dollars. Though the *Sheridan* was only 895 tons, she carried a crew of forty before the mast with regular pay of twenty-five dollars a month and the promise of a bonus of fifty dollars each if the ship won. The ships sailed together, and the *Columbus* won in sixteen days, the *Sheridan* arriving two days later.

Large wagers were placed upon these Ocean Races, and many longshoremen and others employed along the waterfront, also old habitués of South Street—those knowing ones, so prone to croak "I told you so"—went badly "broke" after some of these contests.

To be first in anything—whether the race be run by human being, a fast horse, a fast ship or yacht—always carries a distinction that is lasting; and this distinction goes on down through the ages to be talked and written about, making whatever is thus declared first, a matter of world history. So much controversy has arisen concerning which of the *Ann McKim, Rainbow, Houqua* or *Sea Witch* was the first clipper ever designed or built, that we do not want to enter the lists as contenders for any one of these vessels.

It is claimed that no one had ever attempted to reproduce the lines of a small, swift vessel in a large one, until in 1832 Isaac McKim, a wealthy merchant of Baltimore, commissioned Kennard and Williamson of Fell's Point, Baltimore, to build a ship embodying as far as possible the lines of the famous Baltimore clipper brigs and schooners. This ship, named in honor of the owner's wife, was the *Ann McKim*, of 493 tons register, a large vessel for those days. She measured: length, 143 feet; beam, thirty-one feet; depth, fourteen feet; and drew seventeen feet aft and eleven feet forward. She possessed many of the striking features of the Baltimore clippers of that period; namely, great dead-rise at her midship section, long easy convex water-lines, low free-board, and raking stem, stern-post and masts, and was really an enlarged clipper schooner rigged as a ship.

The *McKim* was a remarkably handsome vessel, built as the pet ship of her owner without much regard to cost. Her frames were of live oak; she was copper-fastened throughout, and her bottom was sheathed with red copper imported for this purpose. The flush deck was fitted with Spanish mahogany hatch combings, rail, companions, and skylights. She mounted twelve brass guns, and was equipped with brass capstan heads, bells, and so forth, and carried three sky-sail yards and royal studding sails. She proved to be very fast, though of small carrying capacity, and the latter quality together with her elaborate and expensive fittings caused the older merchants to regard her unfavorably so that for some years they still adhered to their full-bodied ships. The *Ann McKim* sailed in the China trade for a number of years, and upon the death of Mr. McKim in 1837, she was purchased by Howland and Aspinwall, of New York.

That this little vessel proved a success in making quick voyages soon attracted the notice of this far-sighted firm. As she sailed to and from this port, she was, no doubt, an object of considerable interest to New York shipbuilders of the time who were on the *qui vive* for improving their ships; and, beyond a doubt, her graceful lines influenced them to try and get out something after her model. It is certain that during the years following her appearance, more determined efforts were made in the United States to improve the model and sailing qualities of ships.

After having put many dollars into the treasury of the New York firm during the ten years they owned her, the *Ann McKim* was sold at Valparaiso in 1847, and she ended her days under the Chilean flag.

To tell the truth, the crew of the good ship *Columbus*, Captain Frederick A. DePeyster, of the Black Ball or "Old" Line of Liverpool packets, in the Fall of '37 were for the most part, in no great need of sea chests. Thanks to the attentions of the pawnbroker, the rum-seller, and the boarding-master, they were comparatively unimpeded with baggage, for not a few veteran "packeteers," time after time, faced the winds and waves of the Atlantic in a suit of dungaree. The swaggering roystering packet sailor was an enigma, an object of apprehension and disgust, and they were looked down upon by their brother tars of the American merchant service, who styled themselves "deep sea sailors."

Now, reckless as that class of seamen were, they did not fancy insults, curses, blows, and kicks as a steady diet, and on this voyage Captain DePeyster had as mates two most brutal men—of the "raw-head and bloody-bones" type. An account written some years ago, by one of the *Columbus* crew, George Davis, shows how a few resolute sailors established their right to decent treatment:

"About two in the afternoon (the wind having hauled round to our starboard quarter, we were shifting our stun' sails over to starboard), one of the new hands, Cornelius Emery, a Boston boy, was aloft on the starboard foretop-sail yard-arm, rigging out the fo'to'-gallant-stun' sail boom, when the second mate, Huntington, wishing, no doubt, to assert his authority, sung out: 'Bear a hand, you son of a b——h!' The newcomers, scattered all over the deck, cast a glance aloft to see who was thus addressed, and an ominous tightening of belts ensued. Cornelius Emery instantly laid in from the yard-arm, and, shaking himself well together, came rapidly down the fore-rigging, and, jumping on deck, made a rush for the astounded Huntington, knocking him down and kicking him. Huntington shouted for assistance, and Cornish, hearing the uproar, first shouted for Captain DePeyster, and then, armed with his favorite weapon, an iron belaying-pin, came rushing forward, frothing with rage. 'I'll teach you, you mutinous scoundrel. I'll let you know that—'

"His didactics were cut short. Starting from his work in the fore-rigging, a sailor named Joe Winrow thrust his athletic form between Emery and the chief mate, wrenched the belaying-pin out of his grasp, and then with one terrific blow split his cheek from his eye to his mouth, and tumbled him in a heap upon the deck, the blood spouting in torrents from the wound.

"You wanted first blood, did you? Now you've got it! I've writ 'Joe Winrow, his mark,' on your figure-head, anyhow. Let the beggars up, Corneil; here comes the after-guard.'

"Sure enough, Captain DePeyster, hurrying on deck upon Cornish's call, was just in time to see Huntington lying helpless, Cornish felled like a log by Joe Winrow, and the whole crew rushing to take part in the fray. Fearing the worst, he hurried into the cabin, and opening the arm-chest, distributed pistols to the more resolute of the cabin passengers, and, hastily explaining to them the dangerous turn things had taken, bade them follow him and returned on deck.

"Joe Winrow, who was now tacitly acknowledged as leader, saw the captain come on deck and return to the cabin. Divining his purpose he determined to prepare for defense.

" 'See here, lads, them two fellows aren't so badly hurt, but what they can point a pistol. The old man will muster the cabin gang. Any of you got pistols better get them lively. Jump for them capstan bars and handspikes; get them heavers, some of you.'

"We were pretty well armed, and had thrown up a sort of breastwork across decks, when the captain appeared with the officers and about ten of the cabin passengers.

"Cornish and Huntington had had their wounds dressed, and now advanced flourishing their pistols, Cornish breathing death and destruction. The captain, when he saw the barricade and the whole ship's company ranged, armed, silent and resolute behind it, grew pale, and, turning aft, began a hurried consultation with the passengers.

"This hesitation did not satisfy the officers, and they vehemently insisted upon crushing out the mutiny and making an example of the ringleaders. They were exasperated beyond endurance by the indifference with which DePeyster treated their alleged injuries and wrongs, and continued to demand that measures should be adopted which would strike terror into the hearts of the crew.

"The captain now came forward to within a few feet of our barricade, motioning to the others to remain at the main hatch.

" 'Now, men,' began he, 'put the scoundrels in irons,'

shouted Huntington. 'No parleying with mutineers, Captain DePeyster. Come on; let's shoot them like dogs,' roared Cornish.

" 'Mr. Huntington, you may retire to the quarter-deck. Mr. Cornish, go to your state-room; you are relieved from duty until further orders.'

"At these words Cornish and Huntington slunk away like whipped curs, and the men raised a hearty shout, 'Hurrah for Captain DePeyster,' and, throwing down their weapons, removed the barricade and came to meet him.

" 'Now, men; now, men; what's all this? What's the use of all this? Come, now, turn to and let's hear no more of it."

" 'Captain DePeyster, sir, we all know you, a gentleman and a seaman; and we know Cornish and Huntington, and they're a pair of d——d tyrants. Now, if this thing is to be called square we're satisfied, always providing that you let them gents understand that they're not going to kill any one on this passage if we can help it.'

" 'Well, so be it, my men, and now turn to and do your duty like men.'

" 'Aye, aye, captain,' and so the 'mutiny' ended."

Newspapers of the day, for instance, *The Spirit of the Times*, (a New York Chronicle of the Turf, Field, Sports, Literature and the Stage,) would have a column headed *"News by the 'Siddons' "* and therein state that by the arrival of that Liverpool packet they received Liverpood and London papers, of such and such a date. Then would be given the foreign political and commercial news, also what happened in the sporting world abroad, etc.; and New York merchants, men of Wall Street, too, placed so much dependence upon these somewhat belated reports, as to be guided by them largely in their business transactions.

At this time the "great event" was the "slashing passage of arms" between Burke, known as the "Deaf-un," and Bendiga, which ended in a victory for the latter. It is stated editorially that hundreds of citizens called at the *Spirit* office to learn the particulars and result of the fight, and this was over a month after the battle had been fought in England—but no news could be imparted until issued from the press.

Perhaps there would be a last minute paragraph in this

interesting news organ of a former generation, reading: "This morning the packetship *Shakespeare* brought dates two days later." From this one can readily conceive how important was the coming and going of these little trans-Atlantic packets, that tied up along South Street in the year 1837.

At London, the British and American Steam Navigation Company set the hammers of Thames shipworkers clanging on a steamer named *British Queen*. At Liverpool, the construction of a steamer named after the city was begun by the Atlantic Steamship Company. The Great Western Railway Company was the third to enter the shipbuilding contest. Their engineer, Isambard P. Brunel, designed a paddle-wheel ship called the *Great Western*, which was the first steamship to be completed for the transatlantic trade. She was 236 feet long, of 1,430 gross tons, and fitted with an engine of 750 horsepower. In April, 1838, she was ready to make the westward voyage.

The *British Queen* was still several months short of completion. At the head of the latter enterprise was Junius Smith of Plymouth, Connecticut, who had gone to England seeking capital to help exploit his ideas. In dread of being outdone by his rival, he hurriedly chartered the *Sirius*, a vessel built for the coastwise trade and which attained the distinction of being the first steamer to cross from the Old World to the New. She was of 703 tons gross, 178 feet long, twenty-five feet beam and had a speed of seven and one half knots. She left Cork on April fifth, 1838, and was followed three days later by the *Great Western*. Arriving in New York's upper harbor, with bunkers empty, the *Sirius* stoked her small engine with spare spars and rosin, and to the gratification of those aboard reached her wharf under her own steam after seventeen days at sea. The hour was midnight, yet reports of the "wonderful thing tied to Jones' Wharf" had spread. Curiosity awoke the waterfront. Sailors and citizens lighted bonfires, beat pans, and held celebrations until morning. The shouts had hardly died when cannon booming in the harbor heralded the arrival of the *Great Western*.

Prior to the entry of the *Sirius* into this port, a steamer schooner, fifteen days from Kingston, Jamaica, had made its appearance. The latter is entered on the books at the Barge Office as coming in on the ninth of April, 1838. Whether any of the New York ship-builders or owners of that period then and there saw with prophetic vision what the future had in store for them is not of record. Yet, by theorizing we may say that this was the first deadly blow dealt American shipping, although the harm then given did not exhibit any alarming symptoms until nearly twenty years afterward. The *Great Western* returned again on the seventeenth of June with fifty-eight passengers, and the *Sirius* a day later from London with forty passengers, but she never returned again.

The *Sirius* ran afterwards on the line of steam packets between Dublin and Cork, and went on the rocks of Bally Cotton, January sixteenth, 1847, and was wrecked with twenty lives lost. Incidentally it may be remarked that she was one of the first ships to be fitted with a condenser instead of using salt water in her boilers.

The *Great Western* made seventy-four trans-Atlantic voyages before passing into the hands of the West India Company, then New York saw her no more. She averaged fifteen and one-half days on the westward voyages and thirteen and a half days on the eastern run. Her fastest voyage was in 1842, when the ocean was spanned in twelve days and seven hours. This vessel of the Great Western Steamship Company inaugurated an era of ocean transportation that ever has been changing for the better. She dissipated the uneasiness in the minds of a great number of the doubters; and created, both directly and indirectly, a competitive scale between later steamship companies that resulted, step by step, in improved service, greater safety and much more comfort.

On July twenty-ninth, 1839, the diarist Hone records that

"The long-expected steam packet, the 'British Queen,' arrived in New York, on her first voyage from Portsmouth, yesterday morning."..."The 'British Queen' sailed on the 12th. She is commanded by Captain Roberts, formerly of the 'Sirius,' the Columbus of steam, who first of British steam-men reached our shores. She is the largest steamer ever built, being of the following dimensions: length from figurehead to taffrail, 275 feet; length of upper deck, 245 feet; breadth within the paddle-boxes, 40 feet 7 inches; breadth including the boxes, 64 feet; her engine is of 500-horse power; burthen, 2,016 tons. The 'British Queen' arrived in New York on the 28th."... "Her greatest distance in one day was two hundred and forty miles; the least, one hundred and thirty miles."

On February thirteenth, 1839, the New York *Gazette and Commercial Advertiser* announced, in an editorial article:

"Twenty years have now elapsed since the first establishment of packet ships between Liverpool and New York. During that long period, though the ships comprising the various lines have sailed in all weathers, both foul and fair, only three of them, up to the close of last week, had met with any serious disaster.

"The 'Albion' from New York for Liverpool was, some eighteen years ago, totally wrecked on the Old Head of Kinsale, when the Captain, most of the crew, and all except one of the passengers, were drowned. The 'Liverpool,' also from New York to Liverpool was subsequently lost, in the ice, on the Banks of Newfoundland, but every soul on board was saved; and later still, the 'Panthea' was lost in Holyhead Bay.

"Three of New York's Packet Fleet have been wrecked recently on Britain's shores. One of them, the 'Pennsylvania' was a total loss, while the 'Oxford' and 'St. Andrew' suffered serious damage.

"The year 1839 has been as disastrous to the New York Packet ships as the whole twenty years preceding have been. Poor Captain Smith of the 'Pennsylvania' has gone, never to return, but Captain Rathbone of the 'Oxford' on shore in Bootle Bay, and Captain Thompson of the 'St. Andrew,' on shore at Leasowe, have sympathies, etc.

"We may state as a proof of the strength and admirable construction of our New York Packet Ships that though the 'Pennsylvania' had been lying in the surf on the banks for six days, exposed to the beating of the sea, she was as straight (yesterday) as when she floated gracefully in smooth water; while the 'Oxford,' which had been exposed a day longer to the 'pelting of the pitiless storm,' is as stanch as she was on the day she arrived at Liverpool, from her maiden trans-Atlantic voyage—her copper scarcely showing a wrinkle. The 'St. Andrew's' hull is in the same state. The condition of these vessels, after their disasters, must give great confidence to

The First Period

passengers in the safety and strength of the liners sailing out of New York."

To show the trials and tribulations of a marine reporter, at the port of New York, in March 1840, when "Old Jim" Gordon Bennett was strenuously pushing ahead with his *Morning Herald*, we have extracted the following:

"On Monday evening our efficient news collector, Commodore Martin, boarded the Canton Ship 'Morea,' Captain Western, a long time in advance of any of the Wall Street loafers. [The "Herald" was then strongly contending against the "Courier and Enquirer" and the other newspapers then located on Wall Street.] As soon as he announced himself as the boarding officer from the office of the 'Herald,' Captain Western furnished him with all the latest intelligence from Canton, embracing list of vessels, etc.

"When the 'Morea' reached her dock, up the East River, Captain Bancker, the boarding officer from the Wall Street prints, all puffing and blowing, like a porpoise out of water, boarded the vessel and demanded the news, lists, etc., for his employers. 'I have been boarded,' replied the Captain, 'and gave my lists to the news collector.' 'That was only for a penny paper.' 'I am the only one authorized by the respectable Wall Street papers.' 'I know nothing about your relative degrees and respectability,' replied Captain Western, 'I give my news to the first that comes—thinking, very probably, that the rule of first come first served, is fair play.'

"And on this point [contends the "Herald"] Captain Western was right—perfectly right. In our competition with the Wall Street Press, we want nothing but fair play. We expend more money for news of all kinds than any paper in Wall Street—we employ better collectors, reporters, and writers and pay them better and far more honestly. Why then should we not have the rightful benefit of our activity? As to the ridiculous charges of the Wall Street press against our industry, our enterprise, our respectability and character, we are perfectly willing to let the community be the judges of our relative merits.

"We return our thanks to Captain Western for his justice and impartiality, and shall pray that he may always have prosperous breezes and plenty of sea room—whether he sails along the dark blue ocean of Time, or the deeper and darker blue ocean of Eternity."

By the *Morea*, the first report was received at New York that the Canton authorities had interdicted all the foreign trade, including the American, in the war then prevailing between the English and Chinese.

Commerce, after making extraordinary advances between 1830 and 1839, lost a part of its gains toward the end of that period, while the registered tonnage showed a steady and marked increase, reaching in 1846 nearly the maximum figure of 1810. This rise in tonnage is noticeable as being the beginning of that extremely rapid production in shipbuilding which was destined a few years later to lead to a second and more fatal reaction. The shipping industries, on the whole, were prosperous. The world was at peace, reciprocal agreements had thrown open an extensive trade to all competitors on an equal basis, and, notwithstanding the slight fall in our carrying trade from our own ports, the era was one of prosperity.

But a new factor was now entering into the calculation. Steam vessels, whose advantages in river navigation had been demonstrated by Fulton in the early part of the century, and whose use had advanced rapidly since the days of the *Clermont*, not only in river but in coastwise traffic, had up to this period taken no hold upon long voyage ocean commerce.

In 1839 the future of steam navigation was assured when Samuel Cunard founded the English line that bears his name. This line actually started business in 1840 with four wooden steamers capable of carrying 115 cabin passengers and 225 tons of cargo, with a speed of eight and one-half to nine and one-half knots—the *Acadia, Britannia, Columbia,* and *Caledonia,* which probably cost between four and five hundred thousand dollars each. The mail contract with the British Government, under which the line began business, provided for a compensation of 425,000 dollars per annum. It is beyond question that the sum paid to the Cunard Company in its early days, amounting to about twenty-five per cent. per annum on the cost of the running plant, subsequently increased to 550,000 dollars, then to 750,000 dollars and later to 850,000 dollars was clearly a subsidy. It was given with the plain intention of establishing firmly in English hands the trans-Atlantic traffic; and it accomplished the desired result. Without it the

Cunard Company may possibly have survived, but it would certainly not have built up a career so monumental in its success.

From the "Packet News" in the *Spirit of the Times*, under date of December nineteenth, 1840, we learn that "they have received English papers up to the 15th of November"; also that "the Dramatic Line sailing packet 'Garrick' went out on her last passage to England in fifteen days." The steamers must look to their laurels. "We look to the steamer of the Cunard Line by Monday next. It will doubtless bring us 'O'Malley' and 'Ten Thousand A Year,'" continues this article. Thus New Yorkers had to wait weeks at a time to read any stories by European authors which were running serially at this time in the *Spirit of the Times* or other papers.

Between 1836 and 1840, New York suffered a loss in import freighting, but gained somewhat in export carriage, the packet-ship lines having increased their numbers in 1836. In the following year occurred a severe panic, with bank suspensions, and our carriage fell off. The financial crash of 1837 was the most formidable in New York's history up to that time; and, coming so soon after the fire of 1835, it seemed at first an irretrievable blow; but our merchants did not lose heart. New York's bankers were thoroughly trained, and moreover had the advantage of the advice of the most experienced financier of the day, Albert Gallatin, who, after long service at home and abroad, had made his home in this city. During the period of these events foreign merchants and their ships kept on at work, while ours had to slacken sail. In 1838 the banks partially resumed, only to fail again in 1839. In 1840 the New England and New York banks resumed specie payments—they served a shipping people—whereas those in States having no active commerce in shipping took years to recover.

PART VII
THE SECOND PERIOD
1840—1850

VII

THE SECOND PERIOD

1840—1850

A PACKET-SHIP SAILS UP THE EAST RIVER—SAILORS CHANT "LEAVE HER, JOHNNY, LEAVE HER," AS SHE DOCKS—TRANSATLANTIC PACKETS—THEIR COMMANDERS A HIGH TYPE OF MEN—CAPTAIN E. E. MORGAN—"ODE TO THE *DEVONSHIRE*" —ENTERTAINS QUEEN VICTORIA—HIS FRIENDSHIP WITH JOSEPH BONAPARTE—ON INTIMATE TERMS WITH DICKENS, THACKERAY, SYDNEY SMITH, ALSO MANY CELEBRATED ENGLISH ARTISTS—ONE OF DICKENS' FAVORITE STORIES—PACKET *SOUTHAMPTON* MAKES A RECORD TRANSATLANTIC PASSAGE —MORGAN BECOMES MANAGER, LONDON "X" PACKET LINE —BRITISH WAR WITH CHINA, 1840-43—THEN AMERICAN MERCHANTS DO ALL THE TRADING—WILLIAM S. WETMORE —THE HOUSE OF GRINNELL, MINTURN AND COMPANY, MOSES H. GRINNELL—HENRY GRINNELL—ROBERT B. MINTURN—HOWLAND AND ASPINWALL—WILLIAM H. ASPINWALL —COASTWISE TRADE, NEW YORK TO CHARLESTON, SAVANNAH AND OTHER SOUTHERN PORTS—SPOFFORD AND TILESTON—THOMAS TILESTON AND PAUL N. SPOFFORD— STEAMSHIPS INTRODUCED BETWEEN NEW YORK AND CHARLESTON—PIONEER COASTWISE STEAMSHIPS *SOUTHERNER* AND *NORTHERNER*—THE LINE GETS CONTRACT FOR CARRYING MAIL TO CHARLESTON, SAVANNAH, KEY WEST, AND HAVANA—S.S. *ISABEL*, AFTERWARD BLOCKADE RUNNER *ELLA WARLEY, MARION* AND *JAMES ADGER*—AS LATE AS 1860, COAST FLEET SAIL TONNAGE OUTNUMBERED STEAM—SPOFFORD AND TILESTON START LIVERPOOL LINE, 1852—THEIR SHIP *ORIENT* RUNS AGROUND AT HAVRE—WHAT MR. SPOFFORD OWNED SO DID MR. TILESTON—MARINE INSURANCE— FOUNDING OF ATLANTIC MUTUAL INSURANCE COMPANY —JOSIAH L. HALE AND WALTER R. JONES—DESCRIPTIVE OF SOUTH STREET AND ITS ENVIRONMENT—EXPERIENCE AND SKILL OF NEW YORK SHIPBUILDERS ENABLE THEM TO PRO-

DUCE CLIPPERS SUCH AS NEVER BEFORE SAILED THE SEAS—TRUE STORY OF THE *RAINBOW*—CHEESE, ONE OF THE GREAT EXPORTS TO ENGLAND—S.S. *PRINCE ALBERT* TAKES COAL TO LIVERPOOL—DESCRIPTION OF HER CARGO—AN EAGLE CREATES SENSATION ON SOUTH STREET, PERCHES ON FOREMAST TRUCK OF THE *PRINCE ALBERT*—WONDERFUL PERFORMANCES OF THE *NATCHEZ*—HOW CAPTAIN "BULLY" WATERMAN ESCAPED TO SEA—SQUARE-RIGGERS WERE STILL THE WORLD'S REAL SEA CARRIER IN 1845—AMERICA'S COMMERCIAL VENTURES IN CHINA—HONG MERCHANTS AND CHINESE BUSINESS METHODS—ADVANTAGES OF AMERICAN TRADERS OVER EUROPEANS—WRECK OF THE *HENRY CLAY*—CAUSED BY NEGLECT OF USE OF LEAD SOUNDINGS—THE AMERICAN SHIPMASTER—PRESIDENT POLK'S MESSAGE RELATING TO DISCOVERY OF GOLD IN CALIFORNIA—RUSH FOR THE NEW "EL DORADO"—TRANSIT ACROSS THE ISTHMUS—PANAMA RAILROAD AND ITS SUCCESSFUL OPERATION—ONE OF THE MOST IMPORTANT RAILROADS EVER CONSTRUCTED—"THE PATHFINDER OF THE SEAS," MATTHEW F. MAURY—SECRETARY OF NAVY, GEORGE BANCROFT, FOUNDS UNITED STATES HYDROGRAPHIC DEPARTMENT—MAURY'S OCEAN LANES AND THEIR BENEFITS—START OF THE OCEAN STEAM NAVIGATION COMPANY—S.S. *WASHINGTON*, FIRST VESSEL TO CONTRACT FOR UNITED STATES MAIL—CHARLES H. MARSHALL AND COMPANY HAS S.S. *UNITED STATES* BUILT—REVIEW OF NEW YORK SHIPBUILDING IN 1847—FOUNDING OF THE CUNARD STEAMSHIP LINE—SAMUEL CUNARD SECURES MAIL-CARRYING CONTRACTS, ETC., FROM BRITISH GOVERNMENT—ESTABLISHES LINE OF STEAMSHIPS AT NEW YORK—PACIFIC MAIL STEAMSHIP COMPANY IS ORGANIZED—THEIR EARLY CAPTAINS—NEW YORK AND HAVRE STEAM NAVIGATION COMPANY—A NINETEENTH CENTURY ROMANCE, IS THE STORY OF STEAMBOAT *SENATOR*—SHE PROBABLY EARNED MORE MONEY THAN ANY VESSEL EVER KNOWN—UNITED STATES GOVERNMENT CONTRACTS FOR MAIL FROM NEW YORK TO ASPINWALL AND FROM PANAMA TO SAN FRANCISCO—GEORGE LAW—DANIEL WEBSTER WINS FAMOUS STEAMBOAT CASE, AND BREAKS MONOPOLY—COMMODORE CORNELIUS VANDERBILT—CHARLES MORGAN—CLIPPER SHIP *ORIENTAL*—GOLD RUSH OF '49—LEAVING NEW YORK'S BATTERY, FOR "FRISCO'S GOLDEN GATE"—"BOB" WATERMAN AND THE *SEA WITCH* MAKE A RECORD—THREE STEAM VESSELS, COSTING MORE THAN A MILLION DOLLARS, LAUNCHED IN SUCCESSION AT WILLIAM H. BROWN'S SHIPYARD—HOW

The Second Period

CAPTAIN "NED" WAKEMAN GAVE THE SHERIFF A "SEA RIDE"—THESE WERE BOOM TIMES FOR NEW YORK SHIPYARDS—WILLIAM H. WEBB'S TRIPLE LAUNCH—ANENT UNITED STATES TONNAGE LAWS—JOHN WILLIS GRIFFITHS SHOWS HOW DELETERIOUS THEIR EFFECTS—GREAT EVENT OF THE PERIOD, START OF THE COLLINS LINE—ITS CAREER AND END.

A FINE sight it was to see a returning packet come up the East River and brought right alongside her pier with all sails set. The news of her arrival had been conveyed by signal telegraph from Sandy Hook to Staten Island, and thence by another signal telegraph to New York, though perhaps she had been two days in sailing her last twenty miles from the Hook to the River. Tugboats were seldom used in leaving or making harbor until after 1835, and long afterwards captains took pride in dispensing with their services and in sailing their ships right up to their berths. There is a powerful current in the East River and the packet-master would have to go up that stream, on the port tack, under "working canvas," standing well over to the Brooklyn side until the ship's pier, say at Pine Street where the Swallow Tail packets docked, had been passed to the exact distance needed. Then he turned his vessel to the starboard tack, reached across to the pier, and while the crew hauled up the clewlines and buntlines, and yanked at the downhauls hand over hand, to the tune of that favorite farewell chanty of a deep sea voyage:

LEAVE HER, JOHNNY, LEAVE HER

Moderately

1. Oh, the times are hard and the wa-ges low,
Leave her, John-ny, leave her; I'll pack my bag and go be-low; It's time for us to leave her.

2

Solo   It's growl you may but go you must,
Chorus   Leave, her Johnny, leave her;
Solo   It matters not whether you're last or first,
Chorus   It's time for us to leave her.

3

Solo   I'm getting thin and growing sad,
Chorus   Leave her, Johnny, leave her;
Solo   Since first I joined this wooden-clad,
Chorus   It's time for us to leave her.

4

Solo   I thought I heard her second-mate say
Chorus   "Leave her, Johnny, leave her;
Solo   Just one more drag and then belay,
Chorus   It's time for us to leave her."

Now the gallant little packet, with perhaps the skipper himself at the helm, the first mate being as busy as the devil in a gale of wind, would slip into her berth gracefully as a swan. Then the crowds thronging along South Street, admiringly watching this feat being performed, would render cheer after cheer, as the tie lines were skillfully made fast, snugly berthing the vessel in her accustomed place.

The packets were conspicuous for sailing regularly at their advertised time, wind or no wind, gale or calm. Eighty cabin passengers were considered a good list, and the freight consisted of breadstuffs, tobacco, lard, cheese, oil-cake, woods, and staves, with barrels of turpentine and pitch for ballast. Such a cargo was paid for by weight and measurement—barrels by the piece, wheat by the bushel, cheese by the ton, tobacco by the hogshead—and from 5,000 dollars' to 10,000 dollars' freight money, and from 2,000 dollars' to 5,000 dollars' passage money, were the usual returns of an outward voyage, although occasionally the sum was much larger. All freight was insured for its full value, and usually the vessel was insured also. The Atlantic Mutual Insurance Company would carry from 20,000 dollars to 30,000 dollars on the hull of each packet, the yearly rate for the hull being from eight to twelve per cent., paid by giving a premium note due in twelve months; and for the cargo, according to the season of the year, from two and one-half to four per cent.

The packet captain, no matter what his age might be, was usually spoken of as "the old man," a title frequently embellished by the crew with vigorous epithets, which seemed to them appropriate, but which must now, I fear, be left to the imagination of the reader. Few if any Americans sailed regularly before the mast on board of these vessels, the crews being largely composed of the most abandoned scoundrels out of British and continental jails.

Among the famous New York packet captains, and there were many of them, were Charles H. Marshall, of the *South America*, *James Cropper*, and *Britannia*; N. B. Palmer, of the *Siddons*, *Garrick*, *Huntsville* and *Hibernia*, and his brother, Alexander, later of the *Garrick*; F. A. DePeyster, of the *Columbus* and *Ontario*; John Collins, an uncle of E. K. Collins of the *Shakespeare*; John Eldridge, of the *Liverpool*, and his brother Asa, of the *Roscius*, and Oliver, another brother, who was mate with Captain John; Ezra Nye, of the *Independence* and *Henry Clay*; William Skiddy, an older brother of Francis Skiddy, of the *New World*; Benjamin I. H. Trask, of the *Virginia*, *Jamestown*, and *Saratoga*; Joseph Delano, of the *Columbia* and *Patrick Henry*; John Britton, of the *Constitution*, later United States consul at Southampton; Ira Bursley, of the *Hottinguer*; Philip Woodhouse, of the *Queen of the West*; James A. Wooton, of the *Havre*; William H. Allen, of the *Virginia*, *Waterloo*, *West Point*, and *Constellation*; E. E. Morgan, of the *Hudson* and *Victoria*; John Johnston, of the *Rhone* and *Isaac Bell*; and a host of others.

It required an unusual combination of qualities to command these Western Ocean packet ships successfully. Above all things it was necessary that the captains should be thorough seamen and navigators; also that they should be men of robust health and great physical endurance, as their duties often kept them on deck for days and nights together in storm, cold, and fog, and there were frequently desperate characters among the crew and steerage passengers, who had to be handled with moral courage and physical force.

Then the captains were men in whom every confidence was reposed, at a time when the passage to Europe was not the holiday jaunt it is today in this age of floating steam palaces. They were the chosen guardians to whose care were committed the invalid wife, the timid daughter, the infirm parent, compelled to risk the perils of a long uncertain voyage in search of health, or from other cause of dire necessity; and so momentous a step was the sea voyage then considered that relations to the third and fourth remove flocked to the dock to bid a tearful adieu to the adventurers.

Many of the captains made the City Hotel their headquarters when in port, and their company was eagerly sought by a band of *bon vivants* who frequented that popular hostelry and were well known characters in the city. They were all on the *qui vive* when a fresh arrival was announced from Sandy Hook, and they would proceed in a body to the Battery to obtain the first glimpse of some boon companion who had been charged with a momentous commission to procure some gastronomical luxury which was anxiously awaited.

The quality of the men who officered and sailed the New York packets was no mean factor of the environment that enabled the old shipping merchants to acquire fame and fortune. Most of them came from New England, and had been trained on board the whalers, which, before the passage by Congress of an act to establish United States Naval Schools, in tardy response to a memorial drawn up by Adam P. Pentz in the year 1837, were almost the only source of the supply of American born seamen for the merchant marine.

Take, for instance, a commander like Captain Benjamin I. H. Trask, master successively of the *Virginia, Yazoo, Garrick, Jamestown, Switzerland, Saratoga, William F. Stover* and *Hamilton Fish*, for whom, when he died, on the twenty-third of December, 1871, the flags on the shipping in the harbor were at half-mast. "No braver or better man," said one of the newspapers, "ever commanded an American ship. He was about the last of the old sea kings of the past."

This was the kind of man he was: His good ship the

Saratoga was about to leave Havre for New York at the time when, in honor of the birth of the Prince Imperial (son of Eugénie and Louis Napoleon), many convicts had been liberated from prison. Some of these rascals—the ugliest set of mortals he had ever associated with—shipped as sailors on board his vessel, their character and antecedents, of course, quite unknown to the captain. The first day out the new crew were very troublesome, owing in part, doubtless, to the absence of the mate, who was ill in bed, and who died after a few hours. Suddenly the second mate, afterward Captain G. D. S. Trask, son of the commander, heard his father call out, "Take hold of the wheel," and going forward, saw him holding a sailor at arm's length. The mutineer was soon lodged in the cockpit; but all hands, the watch below and the watch on deck, came aft, as if obeying a signal, with threatening faces and clenched fists. The captain, methodical and cool, ordered his son to run a line across the deck, between him and the rebellious crew, and to arm the steward and the third mate. "Now go forward and get to work," he said to the gang, who immediately made a demonstration to break the line. "The first man who passes that rope," added the captain, drawing his pistol, "I will shoot. I am going to call you one by one; if two come at a time, I will shoot both." The first to come forward was a big fellow in a red shirt. He had hesitated to advance when called; but the "I will give you one more invitation, sir," of the captain furnished him with the requisite resolution. So large were his wrists that ordinary shackles were too small to go around them, and ankle shackles took their place. Escorted by the second and third mates to the cabin, he was made to lie flat on his stomach while staples were driven through the chains of his handcuffs into the floor to pin him down. After eighteen of the mutineers had been similarly treated, the captain himself withdrew to the cabin and lay on a sofa, telling the second mate to wake him in an hour. The next minute he was fast asleep, with the stapled ruffians around him.

Given, a clever, ambitious boy, a district school, a kindly clergyman, a first "chance" offered by friend or stranger, and you have in one form or another the solution—success. One scarcely needs to fill up the outline, it is so familiar; and the boy of whom I write found, like many another of his day, that the road to fortune, albeit long and hard, was straight enough to feet that had been trained in ways of industry and thrift. In Captain E. E. Morgan's case the road lay over the sea, and his first voyage was made in a little packet ship of 420 tons, belonging to the well-known Black "X" line, with which he afterward became identified. For years in the early part of the nineteenth century this line carried the mails and monopolized the cream of the passenger trade, between New York and London, and when, after an apprenticeship of six years, the young sailor found himself captain of the *Hudson*, he must have felt that his fortune was, so far as any man's can be, in his own hands. Those were the palmy days of ships and sailors, when the regular packets left New York once a month, and their departure made an event for the whole city, and when the captain of a favorite vessel (especially if he chanced as well to be a favorite captain) might be sure of sitting for weeks at a time at the head of a table whose guests represented the best society of England or America. In those days it was not every one who traveled, and a certain dignity still remained to an Atlantic voyage, while with the knowledge that it might not improbably be prolonged to forty or fifty days it became even a "deed of derring-do." Then, too, the enforced companionship induced intimacies which often refused to wither away at sight of land, and the long confinement developed the general resources in the line of amusement to an extent undreamed of on solid earth.

Captain E. E. Morgan commanded in quick succession four of the finest packets sailing from the port of New York and afterward became the principal owner of the London Line of packets named after him. He was a calm, self-possessed officer, whose reproval for a delinquent mate rarely took a form more severe than, "Never mind, I'll attend to it myself this voyage." While on deck during a storm he seemed to preserve his equilibrium by chewing the end of an unlighted cigar. Thackeray and the artist Leslie once sailed with him from London to Portsmouth, just for an excursion; and in the fury of a gale, while the captain, with hands to his mouth, stood shouting to the sailors up on the yards, Leslie, who had taken refuge under the gunwale, exclaimed, "Great heavens, what a picture!" and proceeded to make a sketch of the commanding officer, which he afterward filled in with his portrait —a work of art long in the possession of Captain Morgan's family.

The London "X" Line packet *Devonshire*, built by Westervelt and Mackay at New York, was placed under the command of this popular shipmaster, and a passenger who sailed with him in that vessel, thus recommends her, in the *Spirit of the Times:* "so great are the improvements and facilities in all departments of maritime conveyance that a voyage across the Atlantic has become almost as easy as a trip to Saratoga"; and afterward he, or she, inscribes the following:—

"Ode to the 'Devonshire'

"Here she goes, and there she goes,
    Wind ahead, and billows foaming;
Once more ashore where 'Hudson' flows,
    Catch me the broad Atlantic roaming.

"How she pitches, how she rolls,
    Dipping her bowsprit in the water;
A lady walking with 'cork soles,'
    Made a mis-step, but Captain caught her.

"Mothers sick, and children crying—
    Dinner tumbling on the floor,
Boys upon the couches lying,
    Others blocking up the door.

"Water washing upon deck—
    Creaking beams, and groaning masts;
See my stateroom, what a wreck
    Of desolation, while it lasts.

"But for romance, the true sublime,
    We have it in perfection here—
Take passage, friends, if you have time
    On board the good ship 'Devonshire.'"

Far different from the foregoing, was this recital:—

"Two Jesuits on their passage to America were desired by Captain Morgan to go down into the hold, as a storm was coming on. He told them they need not apprehend any danger as long as they heard the seamen curse and swear; but if once they were silent and quiet, he would advise them to betake themselves to prayers. Soon after the lay-brother went to the hatches to hear what was going forward, when he quickly returned, saying, all was over, for the sailors were swearing like troopers and their blasphemy alone was enough to sink the vessel. 'The Lord be praised for it,' replied the other, 'then we are safe.'"

"Come with me," he said one morning to a friend in New York, "and see my new ship launched. I am going to have a yachting voyage next time." It was of the *Hendrick Hudson*, then on the stocks in Westervelt and Mackay's yard, that he spoke.

In 1843, he had the pleasure of entertaining Queen Victoria at luncheon on board the *Victoria*, which had been named in her honor. The Duke of Newcastle, one of the party, expressed his surprise that the captain had not called a ship after her Majesty before. "We never before built a ship that was worthy of her," quickly replied the American officer. She was a wonder at that time, by reason of her long poop and her cabin on the main-deck, the cabin previously having invariably been between-decks.

At three different times the ship under Captain Morgan's command was chartered by Joseph Bonaparte, ex-king of Spain, for himself and suite, and these voyages were full of interest and pleasure to the captain, who was a faithful admirer of the genius of the first Napoleon, to whom he bore in person a curious resemblance, and Louis Philippe, who knew Captain Morgan well, styled him *"mon ami le Napoléon de Connecticut."* Joseph was himself a man of little apparent force of character, and his time seems to have been largely spent at chess or draughts—a game at which he had a truly royal objection to being beaten. He had his share too of the family peculiarities, and, while usually kindly and generous, was quick-tempered and willful to obstinacy. His exhibitions of temper

The "Victoria", New York-London Packet, Entering New York Harbour. (Lithograph in color by T. G. Dutton).

were sometimes amusingly childish, as on one occasion, when, Captain Morgan having been so unwise as to beat him three times in succession at backgammon, he shut the board in a pet and told his successful opponent to take it out of his sight, for he would never play on it again—a promise which he persistently kept, leaving the board in Captain Morgan's possession.

The friendship which was begun during these voyages lasted until Joseph's death, and Captain Morgan not only visited him more than once at his domain at Bordentown, but also received from him certain proofs of especial regard, which were of scarcely less than priceless value to one who had so keen a sympathy with the fallen fortunes of the great emperor.

Captain E. E. Morgan was sort of a "social lion" in London, the only honorary member of the exclusive London Sketching Club chosen in forty years of its existence, and on intimate terms with Dickens and Thackeray, Sydney Smith; the celebrated English artists—Turner, Leslie, Stanfield, the two Chalons, Alfred and John, Sir Edwin Landseer, and Richard Doyle, whose name was a household word to all friends of *Punch*, as well as some of the most celebrated men and women in Great Britain, and on the Continent.

What is said to be one of Charles Dickens' favorite stories, "The Wet Lovers and the Dry One," is worth retelling because a story over which the creator of "Sam Weller" had a hearty laugh ought to be perennially good. It is taken from an old article in *Scribner's Magazine*, entitled "A Yankee Tar and His Friends":

"On one of Captain Morgan's voyages from America to England, he had under his care a very attractive young lady, who speedily distinguished herself by reducing five young gentlemen to the verge of distraction. She was quite ready to marry one; but what could she do with five? In the embarrassment of her riches she sought the captain, who, after a few moments' thought, said: 'It's a fine calm day; suppose, by accident, you should fall overboard; I'll have a boat lowered ready to pick you up, and you can take the man who loves you well enough to jump after you.' This novel proposition met the young lady's views, and the programme was accordingly carried out, with the trifling exception that four of the young men took the plunge, and, being picked up by the boat, presented themselves, a dripping quartette, upon the ship's deck. The object of their undampened ardor, no less wet than themselves, fled to her state-room and sent for her adviser, the captain. 'Now, Captain,' cried she in despair, 'what am I to do?' 'Ah, my dear,' replied the captain, 'if you want a sensible husband, take the dry one'—which she did."

While in command of the *Southampton*, Captain Morgan left New York, June eighth, 1850, and landed his passengers at Falmouth in thirteen days, twelve hours, the best passage that had ever been made over that course; one that is comparable with the fast run of the clipper *Red Jacket* in January 1854.

While at heart a sailor, Captain Morgan's voyages from the time that he established himself as managing head of the London "X" or Morgan Line of packets, were only occasional, and, therefore, his intercourse with his English friends became more and more dependent upon correspondence; and, although he identified himself closely with the commercial and philanthropic interests of New York, he felt strongly the separation from the pleasant life with which he had been so long familiar.

As the sky darkened with the oncoming of our civil war, Captain Morgan had the pain of seeing many of his English friends range themselves upon the side of rebellion and slavery, or at best hold themselves aloof from the struggle, which to Americans meant national life or death. It was undoubtedly hard for him to bear this disappointment, coming as it did in the last years of his life; but his hopefulness never failed, and in the darkest days he did not doubt as to the end. Dickens writes:

"And you think the South will come back within the winter and spring? May I whisper at this distance from Fort Lafayette that I don't. I wish to God, in the interests of the whole human race, that the war were ended. But I don't see that end to it, no, nor anything like that end—with my best spectacles."

Before the war ended the genial heart which had drawn to itself so many friends was stilled; the life which had seemed to bear promise of so many rich years yet to come was quenched. The intense energy of the typical New England temperament seems scarcely compatible with length of days, and Captain Morgan died, as such men must always die, in the midst of his work.

From 1840 to 1843, the first British war with China took place. This increased insurance rates on British vessels in Asiatic trade, and ultimately led to the building of American clippers for the Chinese and Indian trades. During the continuation of hostilities, the Chinese refused to do business with English commercial houses, so American houses did all the trade and the New York firm of Wetmore and Company received the lion's share.

The founder of that house was William S. Wetmore, who, at the age of twenty-three, was shipwrecked near Valparaiso, to which port he had gone as supercargo of one of the ships of Edward Carrington and Company, of Providence. Samuel Wetmore, an uncle of young William, was the partner of Mr. Carrington. The latter was one of the largest ship owners and East Indian merchants in the United States. The sending of Mr. Wetmore to South America, as supercargo of one of his ships, by Mr. Carrington, was the stepping stone to his entrance in the house of Alsop and Company, and this eventually led to the formation in 1824 of the great house of Alsop, Wetmore and Cryder in that city.

Alsop, Wetmore and Cryder, of Valparaiso, did all the English and American business of the old Chilian city. William S. Wetmore left the house of Alsop and Company in 1831, retiring from it with a large fortune. He came back to the United States. Not long after he went to Canton, China, and in connection with Joseph Archer of Philadelphia, established the house of Wetmore and Company and succeeded to the large and profitable business of Nathan Dunn and Company and he remained in Canton, personally superintending his large business, until 1839, when he returned to New York and again established himself in this city.

Throughout New York's history, there are few men more prominently identified with her commercial growth and prosperity, also in the advancement of her shipping, than Moses Howland Grinnell. Until he was sixteen years old young Grinnell was kept regularly at school, at which time he had completed the course at the academy of his native town, New Bedford, Massachusetts. He was not burdened with special predilections for scholastic pursuits, and determined to become a shipping merchant. Leaving school he entered as a clerk the store of William H. Rotch and Company, then large importers of Russian goods, and also largely engaged in the whaling trade. The munificent salary of 100 dollars a year was paid him for three years, from which he was expected to board himself. His employers, as a special mark of their appreciation of his services, allowed him to make business ventures on his own account, many of these yielding him good financial results. Not yet twenty years old, young Grinnell determined to get beyond the narrow horizon of the then small, quaint seaport town of New Bedford. He shipped as a supercargo in a vessel bound for Brazil, disposed of his goods on exceptionally good terms, owing to the Dom Pedro revolution then in progress, and, loading with coffee, sailed for Trieste. Arriving safely he sailed for Liverpool in another vessel and spent some time in England and on the continent. From Liverpool he took passage on a packet ship for this city.

A story which long ago went the rounds of New York business circles relates that after young Moses H. Grinnell settled in New York he was soon on intimate terms with Mr. Preserved Fish, then head of the firm of Fish and Grinnell.

One day Mr. Grinnell met Mr. Fish on the wharf.

"I want to have a few moments' talk with you. Will you step on board the packet ship 'Leeds'?" said Mr. Fish to him.

"Certainly," answered Grinnell, going on board and following Mr. Fish into the cabin.

"You are out of employment," said Mr. Fish, in that thoroughly practical manner in which he generally spoke.

"Yes, sir," replied Grinnell.

"And you like the shipping business?"

"Yes, sir."

"I know that you understand the business thoroughly," said Mr. Fish. "Now to the point. On the first of January your brother will retire from the firm; I sail in this very ship for Europe on Saturday next. I want you to take my place during my absence and your brother's place in the firm on his retirement."

"But I have no capital and . . ." interrupted young Grinnell.

"None is required," retorted Mr. Preserved Fish in his blunt way. "You have youth, health, ability and honesty, and that is all the capital I require from you; I will furnish the rest. Will you accept my terms?"

"I hardly know what to say; you are very kind; but . . ." stammered young Grinnell.

"No buts; yes or no?"

"Yes," answered Grinnell, promptly.

"When can you take my place?"

"Immediately."

And within half an hour young Grinnell had entered upon his duties in the place of Mr. Fish. The latter sailed for Europe, established a branch house there and remained abroad, while Joseph Grinnell retired, returning to New Bedford, where he later became a railroad president and congressman, and attained great success in promoting the cotton industry. Robert Bowne Minturn succeeded him, and thus was the house of Grinnell, Minturn and Company formed in the year 1828, the senior partner being twenty-two years of age.

Thus also was established a co-partnership, which through the financial shocks of nearly fifty years stood firm and unblemished. To trace the history of the house of Grinnell, Minturn and Company would be a long chapter. In 1841 the business was located at Seventy-eight South Street, and their ships grew in number until they were seen in every sea. It had not been ruined by the bad legislation of Western Congressmen who never had seen a ship. They established two lines of ocean packets between New York and Liverpool and London. "The Blue and White Swallow Tail" cleared for the former, "the Red and White Swallow Tail" for the latter. At one time the house owned, wholly or in part, nearly fifty vessels which, laden with valuable freight, were traversing every sea. In 1860 Mr. Grinnell retired from active work, leaving to the house the prestige and unexampled success and an unblemished name. With this is closed the chapter of his business life.

There were few men better known to the citizens of New York than Moses H. Grinnell, and no one has been held in higher estimation for plain and persistent rectitude in business, for honesty in political life, for zealous fidelity to public and private trusts committed to his control, and for those high and generous attributes of the heart, probity of life, warmth of friendship and charming geniality which give completeness to character and stability to reputation. He was a clean-cut type of the ideal New York merchant. He belonged to that class whose progress to wealth was by slow and honest means, that class to whom mercantile credit was as dear as honor and life itself. These dominant motives are seen whatever part of his career is encountered; whether he is seen as bank president, as director of other monetary institutions, as member of Congress, or as president of the Chamber of Commerce.

Henry Grinnell became a clerk in the commission house of H. D. and E. B. Sewell, remaining there seven years and acquiring an intimate knowledge of the shipping business. In 1825 the firm of Fish and Grinnell, in which his brother, Joseph, was a partner, was dissolved by the retirement of Preserved Fish, whereupon Henry joined Joseph and their younger brother Moses H., in forming the new firm of Fish, Grinnell and Company. Compelled by ill-health to retire, Joseph Grinnell left the firm January first, 1829. Robert B. Minturn took his place and some years later the firm became Grinnell, Minturn and Company. Under the new name the scope of their operations was greatly expanded by the firm's entry into the general shipping business, and it became one of the strongest mercantile houses in New York. For twenty-one years Henry Grinnell continued an active member of the firm, his high standard of commercial morality and aversion to speculative ventures being important factors in the increasing prosperity of the business, and when he retired in 1850 he was a wealthy man.

Mr. Grinnell's early connection with the whaling industry had caused him to take great interest in all matters connected with the sea and more particularly the Arctic regions and their exploration. When no tidings had been received of the Franklin Polar Expedition, he bore the entire expense of fitting out two vessels, the *Advance* and *Rescue,* which under the command of Lieutenant De Haven, sailed from New York in

The Second Period

May 1850 in search of the lost explorer. Though the main object of the expedition was not achieved, land was discovered beyond Davis Strait and Baffin Bay which was named Grinnell Land.

Undaunted by this failure, in 1853, Henry Grinnell placed the *Advance* at the disposition of Doctor Elisha Kent Kane, for a second search, and again contributed financial assistance. Though this second expedition was equally unsuccessful and the *Advance* was lost, it attained the highest latitude ever reached by a sailing vessel. On later occasions, Henry Grinnell manifested his unabated interest in polar explorations.

Robert Bowne Minturn, of Grinnell, Minturn and Company, was born to the purple in New York's social and commercial circles and went even further in both fields, winning general respect for his philanthropic as well as his business success. His grandfather, William Minturn, had moved a profitable business from Newport to New York. His father, William Minturn, Jr., was a partner in the firm of Minturn, Champlin and Company. In 1829, Robert B. Minturn entered the counting-house of Fish, Grinnell and Company as a clerk, but in 1832, the two original partners retired, then the firm was reorganized as Grinnell, Minturn and Company and he became a partner.

Under its new name the firm attained a secure position as one of the greatest commercial houses in New York, ranking with the Griswolds, Howlands and Lows. In Latin America, they were behind the Howlands, though their Cuban business was so extensive that Mr. Minturn sent his son to Spain to learn the language. In China they competed successfully with the houses of Griswold and Low which virtually specialized in that trade. They did a great deal of business with England and extended their influence into almost all parts of the world. They seem to have shared with the Welds of Boston the honor of being the greatest American shipowners of the day. They owned the *North Wind* and *Sea Serpent* and above all the greatest of American clippers, Donald McKay's *Flying Cloud*.

Robert B. Minturn's fortune was estimated at 200,000 dollars as early as 1846. He and his partners were more public spirited than many of the other New York merchants of the day. He himself served as Commissioner of Emigration to improve the condition of the incoming foreigners. His wife was Anna Mary Wendell, who has been credited with the idea of establishing Central Park, and he supported her in the project.

The firm of Howland and Aspinwall replaced LeRoy, Bayard and Company in the primacy of New York commercial circles. While trading with all parts of the world, they specialized in commerce with Latin America. In almost every port from Vera Cruz and Havana around to Valparaiso and Mazatlan, there were agents in their service and ships bearing their flag. They ran two lines of packets to Venezuela, where they had a special hold on the trade through an understanding with President José Antonio Paez, and their mixed cargoes to the Pacific ports were sometimes worth a quarter of a million dollars. In 1834 the two elder Howlands retired from active direction of the firm, retaining only a special interest. The control descended to Gardiner's son, William Edgar Howland, and to their nephew, William H. Aspinwall. The senior Howland became interested in railroads, at first in the New York and Harlem, and more particularly in the Hudson River railroad. He was one of the principal promoters of the latter road and was one of the thirteen original directors in 1847. His fortune, estimated at a half million in 1845, was reckoned at twice that amount at the time of his death, while Samuel was also rated as a millionaire. After retiring, Gardiner G. Howland spent much of his time at his "noble farm" at Flushing. He died suddenly of heart disease at his home on Washington Square upon hearing of the death of a friend.

William H. Aspinwall was admitted as a partner in the firm of Howland and Aspinwall in 1832 with a fourth interest which meant an annual profit of about 15,000 dollars. In 1837, his uncles, Gardiner G. and Samuel S., turned the business over to him and William Edgar Howland, a son of the former, with a capital of 200,000 dollars. Howland and Aspinwall withstood the panic of that year, continuing to handle the largest general trading, exporting, and importing business of any house in New York. The years following were treacherous ones for a newly established mercantile house. The credit for successfully carrying on was probably due to the well-established reputation of the Howlands as much as to the executive ability and farsightedness of their young successors. At any rate, the firm retained its heavy trade with England and the Mediterranean countries and remained without a rival in the Pacific trade and scarcely an equal in the West and East Indies shipping. Favored by the president of Venezuela, they had almost a monopoly of the American trade with that republic. With this and the Mexican business as an entering wedge, the concern made great strides in the Latin American countries. Its fleet of ships was well known in the chief ports; and its profits rapidly made Aspinwall a leading merchant and capitalist in New York.

Affected by the gold fever of 1849-51 he resigned active leadership in the firm to enter the Pacific Railroad and Panama Steamship Company. In 1850, largely through his efforts, the New York legislature granted a charter for the Panama Railroad incorporated at 1,000,000 dollars. He and his associates, Lloyd Aspinwall, a brother; Samuel W. Comstock, Henry Chauncey, and John L. Stevens, obtained from New Granada the privilege of building a railway across the Isthmus, and within five years the forty-nine miles of road were completed under the ingenuous George M. Totten and John C. Frankwine. The town of the Eastern terminal was named Aspinwall in honor of the man who more than any one else was responsible for the success of the hazardous undertaking.

In 1847, William H. Aspinwall, Henry Chauncey, Richard Alsop, the Howlands, and Edwin Bartlett founded the Pacific Mail Steamship Company, incorporated under a New York statute for twenty years. This was considered highly speculative for such a conservative investor as Aspinwall, and its failure was generally predicted. California gold soon decided otherwise. Two years later, its capital was increased from 400,000 dollars to 2,000,000 dollars, so large were the returns from carrying, by way of Panama, men and supplies, to California and gold back to the East. With the completion of the railroad, the Aspinwall interests had control of a through water rail route from New York to San Francisco and a monopoly of the carrying trade until the completion of the Union Pacific Railroad in 1869. By 1859, the railroad alone had netted about 6,000,000 dollars. When Aspinwall resigned the presidency of this corporation (1856), he was one of the richest men of New York.

During the Civil War, William H. Aspinwall was an active supporter of the Lincoln policies, a founder and vice-president of the Union League Club, and along with John M. Forbes a secret emissary of the President to urge the British Government to stop the building and outfitting of iron-clad rams under construction at the Laird shipyards for the Confederacy. After this time, Aspinwall was not actively engaged in business, though he or a representative of his house held a place on innumerable boards of directors of railroads, shipping concerns, banks and insurance companies. Indeed, Howland and Aspinwall had become more of a banking than trading firm. Aspinwall never sought or held political office, though his interest in politics was keen. He was long a leader in the Chamber of Commerce, active in social life, a trustee of the Lenox Library, a charter member of the Society for the Prevention of Cruelty to Animals, a patron of the drama and of fine arts, and owner of one of New York's finest art galleries, which he opened to the public. His later years were spent in his town house, which his hospitality made a social center; in his show place near Tarrytown on the Hudson, and in extended travel. On his death, the wealthy old merchant could be described as a good man, generous, if not open-handed, lenient to debtors, and willing to meet bankrupt merchants more than half way.

There was a time when our most important coastwise trade between New York and Charleston, and Savannah and other South Atlantic ports, was carried on largely by brigs which handled all the freight and passengers between the ports named. The coast at that time was imperfectly lighted, and not thoroughly surveyed as at present, but these little brigs were commanded by old sea dogs who knew every point, every headland and every current, and made their passages with wonderful regularity. It was not infrequently that during the winter months these vessels would be enveloped in fog during their entire passage; but so thoroughly familiar were these men with the soundings, and the nature of the bottom along the coast, that they carried sail with about as much confidence in foggy weather as they did when the sun was shining. It was little use those men made of chronometer or sextant, if indeed they ever owned one; their "lead" (sailors then called it "the blue pigeon") was their dependence, and it rarely, if ever, failed them, for they knew every foot of water and the composition of every mile of bottom, and the conformation of every headland was indelibly photographed upon their memory. Of course if the sun shone bright at noon, and they were out of sight of land, they brought up their time-worn quadrant at noon; or if they wanted to regulate a clock they took a sight in the morning or in the afternoon; but after all it was only perfunctory, and to entertain their passengers and impress them with their vast scientific knowledge; but their lead line was their main dependence. These little brigs, also the sailing packets which came later, were superseded late in the forties by steam vessels, most of them being owned by Spofford and Tileston, shipping merchants, who brought wealth and honor to New York.

Thomas Tileston, born in Boston in 1793, was setting type in a printing office in his thirteenth year.

"By going into a printing office, mother," he had said, "I hope to educate myself and others, and to become able to support you and the whole family."

At twenty-five he was in New York, a member of the firm of Spofford and Tileston, commission agents of New England manufacturers.

He was in the newspaper publishing business in Haverhill, Massachusetts, when he and Paul N. Spofford agreed to go to New York and go into business together, selling shoes on commission. They started a place at 125 Pearl Street, in 1819, and did a commission business for many years. There was a line of sloops of 120 tons running between New York and Boston, and by becoming the agents of this line, Spofford, Tileston and Company entered the shipping business. The shoes and brogans consigned to them, when the New York market was overstocked, they sent to parts of the Southern

States, and also to ports in the West Indies and South America, getting back produce in payment, cotton and rice, coffee and sugar. They sent such quantities of brogans to Cuba for the slaves, that eventually the return produce became so important that they chartered vessels and sent for these cargoes of coffee, sugar, and so forth. They then built vessels expressly for the Cuban trade. Spofford, Tileston and Company received a large amount of cotton and rice from Charleston, and they became acquainted with Captain Berry, who had been for years in the Charleston trade.

From about 1840 the question of a more rapid and certain intercourse between the coast cities began to be agitated, as the slow and uncertain sailing packets were often detained on their voyages by calms and fogs, thus delaying the passengers en route, and often putting merchants in despair by the non-arrival of merchandise that was much wanted for consumption. Probably what gave a stimulus to the matter was the contract made by the Post Office Department of the government for the transportation of the mails to foreign countries, March third, 1845, as it was under this act and that of March third, 1847, that the mail was carried to foreign countries and the Southern States by steam vessels.

About 1844 the subject of a steamship to run between New York and Charleston was discussed between the firm of Spofford and Tileston and a few Charleston capitalists, with the result that in 1845 it was determined to build a vessel of about 800 tons. A contract was entered into with William H. Brown, of New York, to build the hull, and the Novelty Iron Works, of the same city, to construct the machinery. The hull was 191 feet long, thirty feet eight inches beam by fourteen feet deep, with a "side-lever" engine, sixty-seven-inch cylinder by eight feet stroke, operated under a steam pressure of fifteen pounds to the square inch. This was the same type of engine as used in the Collins steamships a few years later. This vessel had a wide square stern and a very full bow, with other features that, taken as a whole, would not pronounce her a nautical beauty. One authority said her stern was like the side of a house. There were many changes in the next few years in the form of our ocean steam vessels. The opening of the various

The Second Period

lines on the Atlantic and the Pacific Ocean called for the construction of many vessels, and almost every vessel built was a great improvement upon those preceding it.

This pioneer steam vessel of our coastwise trade was named the *Southerner*, and sailed from New York on her first trip to Charleston, South Carolina, on September thirteenth, 1846, arriving there after a period of fifty-nine hours. Her date of sailing was about every fourteen days from New York until the *Northerner* was finished as a consort, her initial trip being made September twenty-ninth, 1847. The latter vessel was somewhat larger and had more power than the *Southerner*. Such were our two first coastwise steamships.

The line had the benefit of a mail-carrying contract, through M. C. Mordecai, a merchant of Charleston, South Carolina, who received for carrying the mail to Charleston, Savannah, Key West, and Havana, 50,000 dollars per year for seven years, and 60,000 per year for three years, the contract ending in 1860. The same parties also ran the *Isabel*, of about the same size as the *Southerner*, between Charleston, Key West, and Havana, for several years. This vessel was a blockade runner during the Civil War, and known as the *Ella Warley*. The *Northerner*, sold for service on the Pacific coast in 1851, was wrecked when on a voyage to San Francisco, on January fifth, 1860. The Company subsequently built the *Marion*, of about the same dimensions as their second steam vessel, and the *James Adger*, in 1852, which was of increased dimensions and more power. The speed of these coastwise steamers was not much more than ten knots an hour, and they could not keep up with a smart sailing vessel in a fresh, fair breeze. As late as 1860 the sail tonnage of the coast fleet outnumbered the steam tonnage.

Spofford and Tileston's Liverpool line was started about 1852 with the *Orient*, the *Henry Clay* (the rebuilt *Henry Clay* of Grinnell-Minturn's Swallow Tail Line), the *Webster*, and the *Calhoun*, Captain Truman. The *Orient* and the *Webster* were built in Portsmouth, New Hampshire, by George Raynes.

In 1856, the *Orient* was chartered by the French government to take freight from New York to Havre. She carried 80,000 bushels of wheat, or 2,100 tons, at the rate of twenty-five cents a bushel, and 1,000 barrels of flour, but on arriving at Havre, she ran aground through the stupidity of a French pilot, and swung directly across the entrance to the harbor, and while some steamboats were trying to tow her off, she brought up on the old wall of a fortification and broke herself in two. Her master had her towed to Liverpool for repairs. On one of her trips to that city and back, Captain Hill collected 50,000 dollars in freight money; and Captain Joseph J. Lawrence, of the *Webster*, of the same line, once grossed 60,000 dollars.

It is a remarkable fact, that Thomas Tileston and Paul N. Spofford were within a few years partners in everything. When they first came to New York, they boarded together; Mr. Tileston married first, and then Mr. Spofford boarded with him. They kept no separate accounts. Becoming prosperous, in the early thirties, they built two dwelling houses, side by side, Thirty-seven and Thirty-nine Barclay Street; both belonged to the concern, and not to them individually. Ten years later, when they built two houses up Broadway, 733 and 735, they belonged to the firm, and each partner occupied one house. Again, when they built in Fourteenth Street, corner Fifth Avenue, it was joint property. The corner house was the most valuable, and they drew straws to decide which should occupy the best one. Their houses adjoined and there was a passage inside from one to the other, without going into the street. All their real estate was owned jointly, so, too, were ships and steamers, and every other species of property. What Mr. Spofford owned so did Mr. Tileston.

In conducting the great and growing commerce of the port of New York, marine insurance was deemed indispensable and received the ready support of our merchants. Before iron and steel ships supplanted wooden vessels, the influence and power of the Atlantic Mutual Insurance Company tended greatly to the growth and benefit of New York ships and shipping. It must be borne in mind that previous to 1854 only foreign vessels trading to Great Britain could get inspection for Lloyds' book, sometimes styled the "Book of Life."

New York was a city of less than 300,000 inhabitants in 1829 when Josiah L. Hale, a New Englander, discussed with his friend, Walter Restored Jones of New York, the prospects of forming a new organization to transact marine insurance. As a result of their conversations, the Atlantic Insurance Company, a stock company, with a capital of 350,000 dollars, was formed in November 1829, with Mr. Hale as President, Mr. Jones as Vice-President, and Mr. John Hale as Secretary.

The organization under Josiah L. Hale and Walter R. Jones prospered from the very beginning. In 1842, it was decided to liquidate and organize a new company on the mutual system. At that time, the business of marine underwriting was conducted principally in the interest of merchants who were engaged in the trading business, owning their vessels and sending them with cargoes to the East and West Indies and South America. The insurance, therefore, was for their own account, and any system giving promise of minimizing the cost would, of course, commend itself to them.

New York is the meeting point of two worlds—the commerce of the continent and the trade of the ocean; yet it may be said, as an onlooker views the city from the Battery, that one's dreams are quickened, not broken, by the distant whistle of steamboats or loud-puffing tugboats, the noiseful elevated railroad or the many other "roars," characteristic of it.

There was a time when "the rush of commercial life greeted you" as you stepped off a boat at South Ferry and meandered up South Street. Concerning South Ferry, it may be of interest to state here, that the Common Council of the City of New York, on September twenty-first, 1818, granted to Governor Daniel D. Tompkins and Noah Brown, New York's well known shipbuilder, the privilege of erecting a ferry house at Whitehall Street, "not more than eleven feet square and fifteen feet high." This was a preliminary towards the erection of a terminal there, which has so well served the transportation requirements of generation after generation of New Yorkers, Brooklynites, Staten Islanders and others.

The "Flour District" began along lower South Street, then up the side streets and around Coenties Slip. In those days the canal boats, which were the principal carriers of grain, were moored at Whitehall and Coenties Slips. They were tied so close together that the East River at this point looked like a floating village, every boat being inhabited by the "Captain" and his generally numerous progeny, together with a dog or two and a sleek-looking, well-fed cat. There were also canal boats stowed away, for the winter, here and there in other slips and places along the East River, while the "canawlers" enjoyed a season of Metropolitan life.

In the palmy days of South Street, every pier was a scene of busy life and money making. There were many busy places when square-riggers from every port pointed their jib-booms far over the pavements, and the forest of tall masts extended from below Wall Street away up beyond Market and Pike Streets. The only break in the line was just at the balance-docks, where half a hundred sloops "snuggled" themselves into place, and made things generally lively with their trade in merchandise and market stuff from the big and little places on the Sound. Palmy days those were for the harbor masters, the shipping agents, the stevedores, 'longshoremen, and the shipowners. The monthly fees from registered vessels and the perquisites from coasters made the harbor masterships the plum worth struggling for in the distribution of patronage. Politicians sought them for their friends and secured them for themselves. When there were seven harbor masters the wire-pulling was energetic. Then there were nine, and the wires were still taut. Then there were eleven hungry officials to bite at the cherry, and yet the wire-pulling continued, and the skilled talent in requisition at the old Capitol chambers, the Delavan House and Stanwix Hall in Albany, successfully engineered non-confirmation by the Senate, and the stubborn harbor masters held over for more than one term. And this, too, while stubborn old Commodore Vanderbilt was fighting against paying the fees. The fight amused the Commodore, who was as much of an autocrat, in his way, as the harbor masters. But the old Commodore failed to win, and finally paid for his amusement.

There was much to be seen along the docks, and the rural visitor had reason to wonder where all the big ships came from. The Southern coasting trade was an important factor in the revenues to the merchants of New York. From Beekman Street to James Slip the "two dollar fellows" (for the schooners, as a rule, paid this amount for the berths provided by the harbor masters, and the schooner district was the pet one on the East River) had their regular places. Such firms as Dollner, Potter and Company, Jonas Smith and Company, R. M. Demill and others, had the cream of the naval store trade. The North Carolina and Virginia ports did their heaviest business with these houses. The "Down Easters" had a trade of their own. The lumbermen from Maine and the traders from New England east of Boston made their headquarters among the Wall Street offices near the river. Among them J. W. Elwell and Company and the circle of merchants who originated and supported the Marine Bank were the leading spirits.

As one walked up or down South Street he would be jostled by a continuous stream of men, of wonderful diversity, of every shade of cleanliness, honesty, industry, and intelligence. In fact, every species seemed to be represented; some labeled by their ragged coats, and others mislabeled in the same way. At last he would come to a crowd of peculiar aspect at the foot of Pine Street and Maiden Lane, where Grinnell, Minturn and Company's Liverpool and London packets docked, also the Savannah sailing packets. Here was a hundred or more 'longshoremen, standing in two parallel lines, between which two of them were competing for drinks at "hop-skip-and-jump." They were ragged and dirty; they were heavy, lifeless, and even monotonous in various shades of ignorance, but those men capably handled the most valuable cargoes that were brought in or taken out of the port of New York.

Presently a dark man with an important air walked up the Pine Street pier, and stepped in front of the crowd who were waiting for the jumping. His movements were closely watched by the 'longshoremen; and when he came to a halt in the street, they all hurried over and bent all their attention upon him. He was a boss stevedore seeking a few more hands to help unload one of the Swallow Tail Line packets. He looked gravely and slowly up and down the line, and finally nodded to one of the men, who then left the ranks and walked toward the ship. The rest stood motionless, and kept their eyes fixed on those of the stevedore, while they silently chewed their quids with the vigor of expectation. They seemed subject to the severest discipline. When a dozen men had been selected, the stevedore turned to follow them to the ship. The rest of the crowd broke up into groups of loungers leaning against the wall, and relapsed into their habitual stolidity and inertia.

A livelier scene was in action on the pier at the foot of Wall Street, where both the Norfolk and the New Orleans packets landed their cargoes of cotton, sugar and tobacco. Hundreds of bales of cotton, hogsheads of sugar, and so forth, covered the quay, and men were busily loading them upon trucks that drove up every few minutes.

We are now writing of a time when modern methods of refrigeration were unknown. The docks for river craft and coasting vessels, also those whereon were landed tropical fruits from the West Indies at Burling Slip, were a busy place, even at night in the early summer; for at that time large quantities of fruit, and other perishable articles arrived every day. They had to be delivered to the market men (the commission merchant was not the factor he is today) before daylight, to be ready for sale in the early morning. Wagons began to arrive about midnight; the piers were soon crowded with vehicles, with men working at top speed in unloading boats and loading wagons. It was a bedlam of boxes, baskets, and barrels, lighted with lanterns, some of which being continuously carried to and fro, gave an odd illuminative effect to the scene.

All was not honesty and simon pure commercialism along the docks of South Street in the days of long ago. The waterfront was a dangerous region for the unwary stranger. Here the most expert of all thieves—the confidence-man—met him as he landed, and commenced one of those games so plausible while they are being played, so absurd when they are over. Besides this cunning class, the docks had many ordinary thieves —always will have—who depend on their "heels and hands." The wharves were then the general market of the city, where every kind of produce was landed and kept until bought and stored in shops or warehouses. The irregular nook-and-corner structures along the North and East River-fronts offered abundant shelter for prowlers, preying on every kind of prod-

Stevedores Unloading a Ship on South Street.
From an old print in the author's possession.

uce landed at the wharves. Some of them were organized into gangs and accomplished quite important results. The cotton thieves, for example, operated with much daring and success. A squad of boys, with sheath knives in their sleeves, would steal up to the side of a truck-load of cotton, cut open the bales, pull out armfuls of cotton and escape to their nooks and corners. If they were noticed and molested, a squad of men joined, ostensibly, in the charge or pursuit, but really to defeat the capture of the rascals.

The great rush of life along the East River was the late afternoon crowd at the ferries. Naturally the ferries were the forerunners of all development, for Fulton, Catherine and South Ferries all ministered to the Village, afterwards the City of Brooklyn. The establishment of Wall Street Ferry in the fifties enabled the "Heights" to boast of a ferry all its own. Its influence made itself felt in bringing across the river a class of inhabitants which were to make Brooklyn Heights forever famous. Running as it did from the heart of the financial and shipping district, it made access easy and pleasant for bankers, brokers, merchants and lawyers, the very best of New York's business community. Shipping men especially felt drawn to the Heights, as from it they could view their own gallant ships arriving and departing. The cargoes from "India and Cathay" were unloaded almost at their very doors. Such families as the Lows, Mallorys, Clydes, Flints, Spicers, and the Hewitts, Captains N. B. Palmer, "Sam" Samuels, and many others, are indelibly associated with Brooklyn Heights as well as New York ships and shipping.

Then there was Peck Slip, Grand and Houston Street ferries, running to Williamsburg, also Jackson Street Ferry which crossed over to Hudson Avenue, Brooklyn. South Street was thus crossed by sparkling streams of wealth and fashion, flowing down from the upper and lower reaches of the metropolis.

In January, 1821, a fire destroyed a great number of wooden buildings, occupying the premises on Fulton, Front and South streets, and Fulton Market was erected thereon to replace the Fly Market at Maiden Lane, which was insufficient in area and inconvenient in its location. About November of the same year Beekman Street was extended from Pearl Street to the River, and Fulton Market was opened for business. It was especially welcome to the people of Brooklyn and Long Island, but many of the New York citizens who lived further downtown refused to patronize the new market, and Franklin Market, at Old Slip, between Water and Front streets, was built for them.

Fulton Market has been properly called "The American Billingsgate," and it is the only commercial institution which has consistently maintained its prominence on South Street for more than a century. The fish bins are the same, and the ancient sea smell has survived. Some years ago, one could see a fishing smack unloading, with a scoop net, live codfish from the well in her hold to a crate or car alongside. This car was a large covered box floating in the water like a raft; it was about twelve feet square and five deep; its sides and bottom had cracks for the flow of water in and out, and it would keep alive 4,000 pounds of live fish. New Yorkers of a former generation were thus enabled to get plenty of fresh fish, but nowadays, owing to the contaminated condition of all our nearby waters, such a use of these cars is prohibited.

Fulton Market does not supply New York City alone; indeed, much of the fish is shipped by rail and steamship to points hundreds of miles away, and they were doing that "before the war." Fish is also brought to this market from the fresh and salt water grounds in all parts of the United States and from Canada, too, and a supply of nearly all kinds of fish is kept in the market all the year round.

Here one can still see twenty or thirty vessels (fishing smacks) of varying tonnage, driven by motor power now, instead of Nature's own force, variable winds, discharging their cargoes at once.

It was a pretty sight to see one of those old coasters enter the wharf and unload in the moonlight, her crew, a rough-visaged, brawny set of men with bare legs and arms, being gathered on the deck over the glittering cargo, and working silently in the pale light. The sails clung loosely about the masts, dripping with spray, and not furled, as they were so soon to taste the breeze once more. Soon the fishermen hauled out into the stream again; there was a creaking of ropes, the brown and well-worn sails were hoisted, and with helm hard up to the wind, the boat speeded down the broad bay and into the ocean. Soon as the old craft was out at sea again, her nets were trailing in the gray depths for prey.

North of Market Street, the surroundings were entirely maritime. The houses were full of ship chandlery—great cables, blocks, anchors and wheels; the signs of sail-lofts flapped from the upper stories; boats ran their bows out-of-doors; spar-yards were full of men hewing great timbers; and shipsmith shops glowed with forges and echoed with blows on the anvil; whilst the echo-like repetition of sound, emanating from where the ship-caulkers were at work, carried a cadence, all its own. Here and there a window was full of quadrants, compasses, chronometers and other navigating instruments. On the waterside were the drydocks where some large sailing vessel or a steamer was being repaired by gangs of men.

The scene depicted in our illustration "Landing From An Emigrant Ship" is one which occurred on the arrival of the packet *Kossuth,* at the foot of Rutgers Slip, and is of characteristic interest. This ship landed 590 passengers and one wonders how so many human beings could be accommodated in such a small vessel, during a long trans-Atlantic voyage. On this passage, when the *Kossuth* was some six hundred miles off our coast, in the European track, she was run into by the packet-ship *Henry Clay,* and thus had her bows stove in, and was otherwise seriously injured. The *Henry Clay* put into Saint Johns for repairs.

The artist has given us here an actual scene. On the right, is an immigrant hearing of the death of a relative; near by, is represented the meeting of a man and wife after long separation; then there is a son shown supporting an aged father, while in the background two lovers are greeting each other; while a man is superintending the loading of a dray, a dock loafer is picking his pocket. The scene, altogether, is one of the most suggestive character, and furnishes an epitome of scenes often witnessed upon the arrival of emigrant vessels, during the Sailing Packet Era.

A well known social economist then estimated the capital value of the male laborer at one thousand five hundred dollars, and the capital value of the female at seven hundred and fifty dollars, making the average value of persons of both sexes eleven hundred and twenty-five dollars.

James Gordon Bennett thus writes on the value of immigrants to this country:

Let us look at the following table of the number of souls that have arrived in this city (New York) alone for the last ten years, with a low estimate of the actual amount of wealth they have brought with them.

PASSENGERS ARRIVED IN THE PORT OF NEW YORK

1832	38,815	$1,500,000
1833	39,440	1,600,000
1834	39,461	1,600,000
1835	43,959	2,000,000
1836	49,922	2,000,000
1837	51,676	2,200,000
1838	24,213	1,000,000
1839	47,688	2,000,000
1840	60,722	3,000,000
1841	55,585	2,500,000
1842, to August 15	55,386	2,500,000
	507,137	$21,900,000

But we are digressing, so let us return to South Street and its environs.

There was a welcome sign of civilization among all the roughness of the waterfront—the Bethel ship with its cross and its church bell.* One hopes that some social pleasures awaited the sailor landing from the boisterous seas; but the miserable boarding houses and hotels for seamen in this City at that time scarcely encourage the hope. South Street had strong marine characteristics, for not only did you find a large

* The Bethel flag was first hoisted on the ship *Cadmus* (the same vessel which brought General Lafayette to this country in 1824) by Captain Christopher Prince, and appeared frequently at the mastheads of vessels wharfed around New York harbor during the thirties and forties.

Scene Showing "Landing from an Emigrant Ship". 1853.
From an old print in possession of the author.

fleet of ocean-going craft along that thoroughfare from Pier Number One, at the foot of Whitehall Street, to Pier Number Fifty, on the east side of Walnut (now Jackson) Street, but one would meet the sailors themselves, congregating within sight of their vessels. You very seldom saw the typical jolly tar in his sailor's shirt. They were generally a lot of dull-looking men, unshaven, unkempt, and their clothing, like Joseph's coat, of many colors—and many patches. They sometimes paced up and down the one sidewalk of South Street, as if still on their watch; but oftener they loafed about in small groups, or hung around in the many saloons which abounded in New York's "shiptown," as it did, and does today, along the waterfront of nearly every seaport on the face of the earth. It must be borne in mind that, at this time, say "in the roaring forties," no adequate laws had been made for the sailor's protection in America, and while a very effective code was in operation in Great Britain, here he was the undisputed prey of the most degraded and rapacious land-sharks.

Here's' something, over which the present day patriotic American, in favor of a large Merchant Marine, should ponder:

When there were nearly thirty thousand vessels of all kinds under the American flag, with an aggregate capacity· of over four million tons, and about three hundred thousand seamen were required for the demands of American commerce, sailors were shown by mortality tables to be the most short-lived of all men, averaging only twelve years of sea-service to each man.

That the rapid growth of our maritime commerce had very far outstripped the capacity of old American laws and safeguards is certain; and most of the abuses of the sea, the sailing of unseaworthy ships, the incompetency of seamen and the cruelty of masters, the loss of life and property, and the suffering of individuals, arose out of the fact that the shipping business had grown beyond the control of those who used to guard it against abuses.

From the middle of the nineteenth century, when the American showed to the world that he could not only build the better vessel, but also that he could get more out of it when built, the American Mercantile Marine was moribund. Foreign sailors were preferred, because there was less assertion of equality, less social assumption among them; foreign captains were also found convenient. They were bred where social ranks had legal status, and also dishonest owners found them more pliable than full-blooded Americans. It was of this period, and of the largest and finest class of sailing ships the world ever saw, the "Old Packets," of which Hawthorne wrote, that the system of government and intercourse, of the ships, captains and crews, was as bad as it could possibly be. Hawthorne's opportunities for observing whereof he wrote, were, while United States Consul at Liverpool, exceptionally good. But his daily intercourse with the captains, who were bound to defend their use of the belaying-pin and handspike, as best they could, left him with the mistaken idea that the result of the system was a self-reliant and useful officer, when in truth it was a slave-driver, scourging the American seaman out of existence.

In conclusion: During all this time the sailor kept on improving his vessel and learning its way, and it is curious to note the simultaneous growth and mechanical improvement of the vessel, and the deterioration and social degradation of the mariner. The two facts had no real connection, no bearing upon each other; the sailor was degraded as labor sank in the social scale; the vessel was improved as the natural result of the growth of the mechanical arts. And such improvement of the vessel continued to go on, and the business, although no longer a prime necessity of existence, continued, until the downward course of the sailor crossed the upward path of the vessel. A short struggle ensued and the degradation, almost extinction of the American sailor was complete, *but he carried down with him the ship he sailed in!*

The experience gained by New York builders in constructing packet ships prepared them for the highest achievements in producing great white-winged clippers, such as had never previously sailed the seas, and which for years were the wonder of the world, carrying the name and fame of American ship designers and builders to the remotest corners of the globe. The size, as well as the performances, of these vessels may well be

Preaching in the Open Air — Along the New York Docks.
From an old print in the author's possession.

considered phenomenal and mark a proud era in the history of American sea commerce.

There were few ships built in 1841 and 1842, in consequence of the low rate of freights. About that time some improvements were proposed, which, in connection with certain casual circumstances, brought out a course of lectures (the first in this country) on the science of shipbuilding, at the rooms of the American Institute, by John Willis Griffiths, who was then a draughtsman with the shipbuilding firm of Smith and Dimon. In the *Herald's* Résumé of New York Shipbuilding, December thirty-first, 1852, Griffiths' innovation in ship construction, which had been inaugurated some years before, is thus described:

"The suggested improvements consisted in relieving the bows of their abrupt termination, by carrying the head of the stem forward. This, while it materially eased the shock of the sea, caused the bows to appear lighter in their continuation of flare to the knightheads. Another improvement consisted in rounding upward the ends of the main transom, for the purpose of relieving the quarter of its cumbrous buttocks, and more nearly equalizing the weather and lee lines of flotation, thus allowing the vessel to carry less of a weather helm. These suggested improvements were for a time suffered to slumber, waiting for an opportunity to develop their utility, when they were silently adopted, and the author was employed to accelerate the onward momentum which they then received. Subsequently they were universally adopted."

It must be borne in mind that the shipbuilding period of which we write was one of study, experiment and discussion. Ship-builders did not sufficiently know what made one ship bad and another ship good, and therefore began to study and they sought every source of information. Merchants and ship-owners, whose expectations had to be met, were demanding faster and better ships, and it needed only one or two successful ships to prove that the way was clear for all who chose to embark their capital in larger vessels of an improved model. Among the leaders in New York maritime progress was the well known shipping firm of Howland and Aspinwall, and they determined to test the effect of these improvements on a ship for the Canton trade, so they contracted with Mr. Griffiths' employers, Smith and Dimon, for a ship of his designing, and named her the *Rainbow*.

This vessel, of seven hundred and fifty tons' measurement, may properly be said to be the first extreme clipper ever built. The radical departure in her design, especially in connection with the bow, was such a marked change from anything previously attempted, that there was considerable doubt expressed by shipping men as to the practicability of a vessel embodying such drastic alterations in the generally accepted plans for ship construction. Such great interest was manifested in the *Rainbow* during the period of her construction and such a variety of opinions were expressed as to her seaworthy qualities, that her owners delayed her completion for more than a year. The masting of the vessel was a matter which received the most careful consideration; and as it appears that one of the owners, William H. Aspinwall, had come to the conclusion that his new ship should have the benefit of foreign aid, he had called upon the best recognized European experts for assistance in placing the masts. Accordingly, a spar draft and elaborate calculations were prepared and forwarded to New York,—but the builders paid little attention to them. Finally, on January twenty-second, 1845, the *Rainbow* was launched.

It was generally admitted by the recognized shipping authorities on South Street, that she was a handsome vessel, but whether she could be made to sail fast was a question, some of these old waterfront wizards claiming that her bow "was at the wrong end" and she would not go outside of Sandy Hook. She sailed from New York for China on February first, 1845, and soon proved herself to be a fast ship. Upon her return home, her commander, John Land, declared that no ship could be built to outsail her and was enthusiastic about her sailing qualities.

On her second voyage, she left New York, October first, 1845, and reached Hong Kong in ninety-two days, having sailed against the northeast monsoon, and she romped home in eighty-eight, bringing the news of her own arrival at Canton.

The gallant little *Rainbow's* career was short. On her fifth voyage, in 1848, she was lost while bound from New York to

"Rainbow" — Pioneer New York-Built Clipper. 1845-1848.
Courtesy of the artist, Warren Sheppard.

Valparaiso, in command of Captain William H. Hayes, and it is supposed that she foundered off Cape Horn.

Now as to the *Houqua*. While she was of a sharper and finer model than many vessels which had been constructed up to that time (1844), she was not an out-and-out clipper. She made a number of very fast passages, but it was not until 1850 that she made a record breaker—Shanghai to New York in eighty-eight days. Neither Brown and Bell, builders of the *Houqua*, nor their ship can take from John Willis Griffiths and the *Rainbow* the glory that is theirs!

William H. Aspinwall, not to be outdone, defied tradition and built a ship of 907 tons, which he called the *Sea Witch*. That was the signal for A. A. Low and Brother to go Aspinwall one better, and they placed an order for a ship of 940 tons, which was called the *Samuel Russell*. All these ships became famous and it was said that there was not a port in the world of active commerce that had not harbored them.

On November 17, 1843, Hone makes an almost unbelievable statement in his celebrated diary, which is to this period of New York's history what Pepys is to London during the reign of Charles II:

"One of the great articles of exportation to Great Britain at the present time is cheese. Every packet takes out immense quantities of this article. Who would ever have thought of John Bull eating Yankee cheese? It sells in England at *forty to fifty cents a hundred pounds* [we think that "cents" means "shillings" here] which pays freight and charges, and leaves Brother Jonathan a pretty good profit."

Continuing he states that in 1843 we were sending "Coals to Newcastle":

"The 'Prince Albert,' Grinnell, Minturn & Co.'s splendid new ship, which sails on her first voyage on the first day of December, takes out as freight a quantity of anthracite coal! America shipping coal to England! Who knows how soon we may fit out Chinamen with outward cargoes of tea consigned to the successors of our old acquaintances, Houqua, Chinqua, & Co.?"

From what the diarist writes on November twenty-seventh, the present day reader may gather some idea of the cargoes carried by our packets in the North Atlantic trade:

"I went with Moses H. Grinnell on board his splendid new packet ship 'Prince Albert,' which is loading to sail on her first voyage to London on Friday next. She is equal to the noblest; the best and more beautiful of her unrivaled class. This vessel is taking one of those anomalous cargoes which we send nowadays to John Bull, consisting of provisions, oil, lard, oil-cakes, cheese, coals, and Yankee clocks. This last is one of the triumphs of Yankee skill and ingenuity. Five hundred thousand clocks are made annually in Connecticut. I saw one of these clocks the other day in a merchant's counting house. It was enclosed in a handsome mahogany case, with a looking-glass plate in front, as fair a face as many of its betters can boast, keeps good time and goes well, of which it gives striking proofs; and all this costs $1.75. John Bull thought when he first traded in this article at $7 or $8 that Brother Jonathan had stolen them. They seized some at the custom house in Liverpool as undercharged. But Jonathan told them he would supply them with as many as they wanted at half the price."

Then he goes on to say:

"An eagle towering in his pride of place. A circumstance occurred on Saturday which among the ancient Romans would have been considered an omen of high importance. Augurs and soothsayers would have drawn from it presages of victory and triumph, and legions would have marched with confidence under its auspices. A large eagle, after sailing in the air of this busy city, so unlike his usual haunts, until his gyrations had attracted the notice of a large number of spectators, perched upon the truck of the foremast of the 'Prince Albert,' now preparing for her first voyage at the wharf in South Street near Fulton Market. He sat there for some time, looking down in solemn dignity upon the busy scenes beneath him, and wondering, I suppose, how the 'unfeathered bipeds' could make such fools of themselves. After resting himself sufficiently he spread his wings and took to flight again; not, however, without receiving a shot from some fellow below (privileged to kill game, I presume) which made the feathers fly a little, but did not impede the progress of the 'bird of Jove.'"

There was one ship that earned a reputation as a fast sailer, in the China trade, at the time of the pioneer clippers that should be mentioned. Howland and Aspinwall extended their trade with South America to China with the *Natchez* in 1842. This vessel sailed from New York, June fourth, 1842, for Valparaiso, where she arrived in seventy-five days. Left there, stopping at Callao, for Macao, China, where she arrived January fifteenth, 1843. Left Macao for New York, where she arrived June fifth. Then sailed from New York for Valparaiso, June twenty-fifth, where she arrived in eighty-two days; stopped at Callao for a cargo, and sailed for Canton, where she arrived December seventeenth, 1843; and left Canton January fourteenth, and arrived at New York, April twentieth, 1844. Again sailed from New York for Canton via Valparaiso on May twentieth, and arrived at Canton, November twentieth. Left Canton, January fourteenth, 1845, and arrived at New York, April third, same year. Her first voyage around the world from New York in June, 1842, to June, 1843, was made in one year, with two stops, while the second voyage was covered in nine months and twenty-six days, including stops at three ports in discharging and receiving cargoes; and the third voyage in ten months, fourteen days, including stops at two ports discharging and receiving cargoes.

The *Natchez*, a New York built vessel, constructed long before the clipper ships, was a flat-bottomed craft, which had formerly been used in the New Orleans trade, and for her type of vessel shows she was a fast sailer and commanded by a "driver," Captain Robert H. ("Bully") Waterman. Altogether he made six successive trips from China, the longest of which was only ninety-eight days, reaching this city eight or ten days before his rivals, who had started at the same time. It was believed by many people that he had actually found out the secret of the tradewinds, and knew just how to sail to take advantage of them.

A story long-current on South Street relates to one of Howland and Aspinwall's captains, we daresay "Bully" Waterman or George W. Fraser, both ardent disciples of "belaying-pin gospel" and other forms of ill-treating their crews. It was in the days when the warehouses along that busy thoroughfare stored teas and spices and aromatic goods from matted packages, bamboo wrappings, marked with the "chops" of famous Oriental merchants in the Far East—and the ships that freighted these fascinating cargoes poked their long jib-booms across South Street and almost into the iron shuttered windows.

"Sailing time was nigh," when one of those "maritime bugbears," a sea lawyer, accompanied by a metropolitan police officer, appeared at Howland and Aspinwall's warehouse, Fifty-five South Street, with documents to be served upon their shipmaster. At the moment he was taking leave of good old Gardner G. Howland and receiving his parting instructions from William H. Aspinwall, the very active member of the firm, before making the long voyage to China. The minions of the law stationed themselves near the door leading into South Street, at the bottom of the stairway leading to the private offices and counting-room upstairs, sure of their prey, for there was no other means of exit.

An observing shipping clerk promptly told Mr. Lane, the chief accountant, and he quietly informed the Captain regarding the unwelcome visitors. A brief consultation was held, then one of the mates, who accompanied the Captain, was told to return immediately to the trim-looking vessel, lying in the East River directly across the street. A boatswain's chair, some rope and a tackle-block were soon obtained (your old South Street shipping merchant's cellar always contained a plentiful supply of "gear" as well as ships' stores and what not). These things were carried to the top of Howland and Aspinwall's building, Fifty-five South Street, where the rope was securely tied to the flagstaff on the roof, and properly rigging the boatswain's chair took only a few minutes. Then the rope was thrown down to the sidewalk to a foremast hand who was waiting for it, and he ran swiftly across to where the well known Howland and Aspinwall clipper ship *Sea Witch* lay, tugging at the full length of her hawsers as if yearning to get away. Here the ship's officer, previously referred to, taking the rope from the now panting sailor, wound it around the lower foremast in a jiffy, signaled to the waiting captain on the roof, who, without hesitation, pushed off in the boatswain's chair and soon reached his own ship's deck. Immediately orders were given to cast off, when a squat-looking, sidewheel tugboat, snorting and puffing loudly, quickly pulled the ship out into the East River, down the harbor and through the Narrows, and she was well out on her way to sea before the "limbs of the law" discovered they had been outwitted.

The steamships afloat upon all oceans, in 1840, and even in 1845, were still only a petty squadron as compared with the vast fleets of sailing vessels. It was the square-rigger, the ship, bark or brig, that was still the world's real sea carrier. To this period belongs the swift growth of our commerce with the Far East. Americans in their peace and new prosperity, developed a large demand for the strange wares of the Orient. Discriminating duties protected American ships in the traffic between our ports and the East until 1834. By that time our merchants had secured a hold upon this romantic and profitable trade that could not easily be shaken. The great houses of New York and Boston that brought teas, silks and spices from China and India owned their own ships and supplied them with both outward and homeward cargoes. These American firms had established branches in Hong Kong or Canton, or Calcutta. In 1840, twenty-one cargoes were brought to the United States, amounting to 17,000 tons, valued at 1,250,000 dollars. Our oriental trade had doubled since the first years of the century, and it was destined to a further and much greater increase.

Let us look for a moment at the history of America's early commercial ventures in China. Canton, the only port where foreigners were allowed to do business before the middle of the last century, was approached through Whampoa, about fourteen miles away. Those who went to Whampoa or through to Canton were confined to their ships or to the "factories" or warehouses where the goods were stored.

There was a prominent body of men in China called "Hong merchants." This class of merchants—there were about twelve Hongs at Canton—were licensed by the Chinese Government to carry on its foreign trade, and they were held responsible for the good conduct, as well as for the collection of the imperial duties on imports and exports. Their places of business were in the suburbs of Canton, near the points called "factories," which were the foreign places of abode, and were termed "Hongs," the meaning of which is a block of houses fronting on the river.

Upon the arrival of an American ship at Whampoa, the anchorage place of foreign vessels trading with Canton, the supercargo or consignee, applied to the Hong merchant, to "secure" the ship, which was nothing less than receiving the cargo into his warehouse, and undertaking to pay the duties to the Chinese Government. It was customary for the Hong to purchase himself a considerable portion of the cargo which he received, also to sell teas largely on his own account.

Besides the port charges which were comprised under the general term of "cumsha and measurement," there were also charges for inward and outward pilotage, and the "linguist" and "compradors'" fees, amounting to between 600 dollars and 1,000 dollars on a ship of five or six hundred tons.

As the "linguist" was one of the prominent actors in the foreign trade of China, it may not be uninteresting here to consider his character. He was a sort of public servant, being the "runner," as he has been called, between the office of the Hoppo (or collector of customs); the foreign merchant, and the Hong merchant, bearing the burdens and encountering the complaints of all three, in case anything went wrong. He was always ready to act as the agent for these three parties, providing a consideration was granted to him, and he was the slave of each. Lacking a sense of honor, he was expected to utter falsehoods for his masters, and was admitted on all sides to be a thorough and unscrupulous rogue. While the entire trading population of China established a character for knavery in our early dealings with them, the Hong merchants were uniformly honorable, intelligent, accurate accountants, punctual to their contracts, and as respectable in their character as the merchants of any country, seeming to prize highly a good reputation.

When all the pros and cons are summed up, it is an undeniable fact that the Americans were absolutely at the mercy of the Hong merchants. That the trade was mutually profitable cannot be denied. But there is nothing in the records to show that the Americans, who were regarded by the Chinese as barbarians bringing tribute to the Celestial Empire, gave the Chinese the short end of the deal.

And yet Europeans were obliged to purchase all they wanted of the Chinese for the most part with ready money or silver bars; the Americans, on the contrary, were not obliged to carry on the Chinese trade with the precious metals. They carried to the Chinese market either various articles of their own production, like ginseng,* which were highly esteemed there, or others which they had obtained in exchange for them.

Another long distance commerce, in which the Stars and Stripes were conspicuous, was that with the west coast of North America. This region was still a no man's land, and ventures thither were full of hazard. The furs of wild animals and the hides of cattle were the chief objects of export, and they were secured by barter with the Indians and Mexicans. Nobody dreamed as late as 1845 of the golden possibilities of California.

On May fifth, 1845, the *Henry Clay*, belonging to the Liverpool line of Grinnell, Minturn and Company, the finest and largest merchantman in the United States, sailed on her maiden trip from New York, and within ten months, on March twenty-fourth, 1846, she "piled up," at Squan Beach on the Jersey coast. The sea made a complete breach over her, and her commander, Captain Ezra Nye, ordered the masts cut away, in order to ease her. Six persons were drowned in attempting to go ashore in a boat; two sailors, two steerage and two second cabin passengers, out of the three hundred people on board, mostly immigrants. The ship was valued at 90,000 dollars; and her cargo, which was light, was mostly insured. For twenty days she lay "broadside to" on the beach, but she was finally hauled off, brought up to the city, repaired and refitted for efficient service at a cost of 30,000 dollars, a large sum at that time.

In connection with this marine catastrophe an old story is told:

"Neglect of the lead or 'blue pigeon' as sailors call it, has occasioned the loss of many a noble ship through overconfidence. At the 'Waterloo Inn,' a noted hostelry in Liverpool, largely patronized by American packet captains, news had

---

* Ginseng—The Chinese in those days called this plant a precious gift of nature, sweeter than honey, more valuable than fine gold, and jewels, and pearls, a glorious gift of heaven, bestowed by the Gods upon mortals for their happiness and their enjoyment on earth.

just been received of the loss of one of our fine liners by going ashore on the New Jersey Coast. Of course the shell-backs there assembled had much to say on the subject, when Captain Nye of the 'Henry Clay,' rather astonished his audience with the remark that, 'No shipmaster who understands his business need ever lose his ship by putting her ashore when making New York Harbor.' This remark struck all those present as rather arbitrary, and did not meet with ready assent; but, as if to punish him for his over-confidence, in less than one month from that time he piled his ship high and dry at Squan Beach, on a moonlight night, with studding sails set alow and aloft—and all because he neglected the use of his lead."

At this time in our history, when the American flag was frequently seen in foreign ports, those shrewd New York merchants, who, sensing the possibilities in world trade, dispatched their ships, little traders, packets and clippers, on long voyages that brought substantial profits,—fully recognized that the firm basis of a merchant marine was not only ships but men. The American shipmaster then had lifted his profession to new heights. He was recognized as an able coadjutor of the merchant. He was as intelligent in trade as in navigation and combined all the requisites of seaman and commercial agent. He served his rough apprenticeship in the forecastle and entered the cabin door through many a hard gale and weary night watch. His anxieties commenced with his promotion. Responsibility was thrust upon him. Life and character and fortune depended on his skill and vigilance. He mingled with men of all nations, gathered information in all climes, maintained the maritime reputation of a country, and showed his model of naval architecture wherever there was sunshine and salt sea. He heard strange languages and he learned them. His hours of leisure were given to cultivation and to prepare him for well earned ease and respectability in those halcyon days to come so earnestly looked for, when he should hear the roaring wind and pelting rain about his rural retreat and would not feel called upon to watch the storm.

"A national debt has become almost an institution of European monarchies. It is viewed in some of them as an essential prop to existing governments. By a judicious application of the revenues not required for other necessary purposes, it is not doubted that the debt which has grown out of the circumstances of the last few years may be speedily paid off."

President James Knox Polk delivered the above in his Inaugural Address, March fourth, 1845. Three years later, when many were unemployed and this country was in the throes of a financial and commercial crisis, critical in the extreme, "Gold was discovered in California!" What probably had more to do with developing the California gold craze to such proportions as it assumed, was that part of the President's Annual Message of 1848 on the discovery of gold in California coming as it did at this time. Of course, it must be borne in mind that full accounts of the mineral wealth of the new country had been laid before the people in the daily journals.

The part of President Polk's message relating to the discovery of California's precious metal was as follows:—

"It was known that mines of the precious metals existed to a considerable extent in California at the time of its acquisition. Recent discoveries render it probable that these mines are more extensive and valuable than was anticipated. The accounts of the abundance of gold in that territory are of such an extraordinary character as would scarcely command belief were they not corroborated by the authentic reports of officers in the public service, who have visited the mineral districts and derived the facts which they detail from personal observation. Reluctant to credit the reports in general circulation as to the quantity of gold, the officer commanding our forces in California visited the mineral district in July last for the purpose of obtaining accurate information on the subject. When he visited the country there were about 4,000 persons engaged in collecting gold. The explorations already made warrant the belief that the supply is very large, and that gold is found at various places in an extensive district of country. Labor commands a most exorbitant price, and all other pursuits but that of searching for the precious metals are abandoned. Ships arriving at the coast are deserted by their crews and their voyages suspended for want of sailors. Our commanding officer there entertains apprehensions that soldiers cannot be kept in the public service without a large increase of pay. Desertions in his command have become frequent. This abundance of gold and the all engrossing pursuit of it have already caused in California an unprecedented rise in the prices of the necessaries of life."

Right after this glowing account of the wealth of gold in our new possessions, and coming from such a high authority as the President's Message, preparations were made by American merchants on an extensive scale for the forwarding of merchandise, and so forth, to the newly found El Dorado. Vessels sailed almost daily from the principal ports on the Atlantic coast for San Francisco. These sailing vessels went by way of Cape Horn.

There were other means of transit—across the Isthmus of Panama. Before the railroad was in operation, canoes were used, which were propelled by natives some thirty miles up the Chagres River, the remaining distance to the Pacific Ocean being traversed on land by mules. A small side-wheel steamboat named *Orus* and an iron-hull side-wheeler named *Gorgona*, were run on the Chagres in connection with the railroad before its completion. Passenger fare through was first class, 600 dollars; deck, 300 dollars; sailing vessel, 300 dollars. By the summer of 1849 the first mad rush had expended itself.

> "Beyond the Chagres River,
> 'Tis said (the story's old)
> Are paths that lead to mountains
> Of purest virgin gold;
> But 'tis my firm conviction,
> Whate'er the tales they tell,
> That beyond the Chagres River,
> All paths lead to Hell!"
> (*Gilbert the Poet of Colon*)

No other enterprise undertaken by the American people did so much to change the established currents of the world's commerce as the completion of the railroad across the Isthmus of Panama. The near approach of the Atlantic and Pacific at this Isthmus, led the early explorers of Central America to conceive the project of a ship canal which should practically unite the two oceans, and thus save the weary and dangerous voyage around Cape Horn. Each one of the principal European nations, at one time or other, attempted this work, and at least three of them had believed themselves upon the point of carrying it to a successful issue. Not a few preliminary surveys of the Isthmus have been full of promise, but in every instance a further acquaintance with the difficulties of the route has led to the abandonment of the attempt. The Panama Railroad was strictly an American enterprise. After all hopes of a canal at this point were given up, the project of a railroad was originated, and amid difficulties, and in the face of obstacles which would have daunted ordinary courage, carried to a successful issue. It was a new channel for commerce, and not a mere improvement of an old thoroughfare. It broke through the barrier of unsubdued wilderness, and for the first time since the continent was discovered, opened a broad pathway from the Atlantic to the Pacific. The old channel of trade swept for 10,000 miles around Cape Horn, and could not be diverted in a day. Thousands of eager passengers poured over the Isthmus, in their transit to and from California, as soon as an avenue was opened, but commerce could not buy a ticket and set out at once upon its travels. It needed ships of established lines, including regularity and certainty of conveyance; it hesitated for precedents of safe voyages and speedy deliveries; it waited to disencumber itself of the trappings and dead weight of the old thoroughfares. Merchants were ready to ship their goods by the new route, but where were the vessels to take them? Shipowners were anxious to send their vessels, but the freight was not stored upon the wharf, and they could not count upon a cargo without collecting it. Through steamship lines, already established in communication with New York and San Francisco, it had a growing trade, yielding a profit of from ten to fifteen per cent upon its capital stock. But it was not satisfied with this; with far-reaching sagacity it had been the pioneer in the enterprise of demonstrating the advantages of this route to the world. It had loaded its coffee at Costa Rica, brought it across the road, and taken it to New York, where it had been sold, retailed, roasted, and drank, before the tattered vessel that carried a rival cargo around stormy Cape Horn in the old track appeared off Sandy Hook. It had delivered Yankee calicoes to the western coast, where they faded into dinginess before the cargo that preceded them had doubled the Horn and gained its destination. It had been almost ubiquitous in combating the fears of the timid; encouraging the spirit of the pioneer adventurers, whose fugitive ships came like white-winged heralds into the strange harbors; and making known to the Atlantic nations, that the Pacific, whose waves once rolled on the other side of the world, was now harnessed by an iron band at their very doors.

The road being finished, the greatest difficulty was, perhaps, in the want of freighting vessels in the Pacific. Nearly all the craft sent to our Pacific Coast went there for a specific purpose, not like numbers of ships in our ports, commissioned to look for business, but this evil was slowly cured, by dispatching freighting vessels and steamers around the Horn. Large amounts of the produce of the West Coast of South America consisting of Peruvian bark, cocoa, pearl shells, India rubber, and hides was brought to New York, together with large quantities of coffee. A contract was made to transport, by this new route, a considerable portion of the new coffee crop from Costa Rica to New York, and this caused a considerable stir in the coffee trade, because the traders in "Rio" had controlled the market for a considerable time. Less than fifty miles in length, the Panama Railroad was one of the most important lines of railroad ever constructed.

The spirit which had been awakened in this country by the discovery of the gold mines in California, and by the authentic facts published concerning them, under the authority of the Government at Washington, exceeded everything in the history of commercial advantage that had occurred in many ages.

When the relative performances of the American sailing ship were a matter of international discussion, the study of the winds and currents of the sea had a vital interest, and the name and fame of Matthew Fontaine Maury, deservedly called "The Pathfinder of the Seas," was established. He prepared a series of wind and current charts that attracted the attention of all the mercantile nations in the world and revolutionized the methods of sea-borne commerce. And it was his observations and knowledge that made possible the laying of the first Atlantic cable. Cyrus W. Field said at the time: "Maury furnished the brains, England gave the money and I did the work."

For his magnificent services in charting pathways across the oceans and in introducing rule, system and security into navigation, we are, more or less, indebted to George Bancroft, Secretary of the U. S. Navy in Maury's time, but more renowned as an historian. He wrote this communication to Lieut. Maury:

"Navy Dept.—March 6, 1846.
"Sir—
"Desirous that the numerous and able corps employed at the National Observatory at Washington may produce results important to maritime science and to the navy, I approve your course in making a series of astronomical observations more immediately necessary for the preparation of a nautical almanac.

"The country expects, also, that the observatory will make adequate contributions to astronomical science. The two most celebrated European catalogues of the stars, 'Bessel's Zone Observations' and Sturve's 'Dorpat Catalogue of Double Stars' having extended only to fifteen degrees south of the equator, and the Washington observatory, by its geographical position, commanding a zone of fifteen degrees further south, and being provided with all instruments requisite for extending these catalogues, you are hereby authorized and directed to enter upon the observation of the heavens, commencing at the lowest parallel of south declination which you may find practicable. You will embrace in your catalogue all stars,— even of the smallest magnitude—which your instruments can accurately observe. You will, when convenient, make duplicate observations of stars for each catalogue; and when time permits, you will determine with precision, by the meridian instruments, the position of the principal stars in each pair of multiple stars.

"Simultaneously with these observations you will, as far as practicable, determine the positions of such stars as have different declinations or right ascensions assigned to them in the most accredited ephemerides.

"You will, from time to time, report directly to this Dept. the progress of the work.
"Respectfully yours,
"George Bancroft.
"Lt. M. F. Maury
"Supt. of Observatory,
"Washington."

Matthew Fontaine Maury, born in Virginia, 1806, was of Dutch sea captain ancestry naturalized at Jamestown, 1671. When twenty-five years of age he theorized that the sea had its laws. The waves, winds, storms, currents, depths and temperatures of the sea constituted a cause and effect—constant in its regularity, perfect in its orderliness and mathematically inter-related, that by patient investigation he would be able to understand its phenomena, to forecast its processes and to reduce them to writing so that they could be readily interpreted.

Delineating a Lane to Rio, Maury saved ten days in time over previous routes. His Lane* to the Coast was tested by four clipper ships competing in a New York-San Francisco race of 16,000 miles. The two ships following Maury's indications arrived within three hours of each other; two, following their own route, arrived eight and twenty-four days later. McKay's swift *Flying Cloud*, sailing along Maury's Lane, negotiated a New York-Coast trip in eighty-nine days. Racing from England to Australia, along the Lanes laid out by this master of oceanography, the gold ships cut their transit time from 124 days to ninety-seven days. Maury continued to determine the duration of winds and ocean currents, assembling a mass of pertinent material from the Log Abstracts of our war ships for further foundational recommendations. Meanwhile, the California gold discoveries initiated a period of sailing competitions between fleets of famous clippers plying the economical Maury tracks between the Coasts.

There came from his office in 1853 charts of the Atlantic on which two Lanes, each twenty-five miles wide, were mapped

---

* Forty-six thousand "Abstracts" from as many ships' logs went into the charting of Maury's "Lanes" across the oceans. In this connection, it must be borne in mind that there are well-defined "Lanes" across the sea and ships follow them.

for the use of steamers between America and Europe. These tracks outlined a method by which collisions, similar to the one occurring a short time previously, off our Atlantic coast, which had arrested his attention, could be avoided. He pointed out that, at that time, the British roadway and the United States of America roadway overlapped and wrote of the possibilities of accident. His exact words are:

"Suppose we take this same breadth of ocean and lay off a Lane 20-25 miles broad near its northern border, and another 15-20 miles broad near its southern border, and recommend steamers, when coming westwardly to use the former, and when going eastwardly, to take the latter, would not the adoption contribute to the safety of vessels, passengers and crews? I think so. If steamers would agree to follow two such routes, or Lanes, I think I could lay them off so as to have them quite separate, except at the two ends, without materially lengthening the passage either way."

On February one, 1873, Matthew Fontaine Maury laid aside his beloved charts and confidently sailed out across the Unknown Sea to drop his anchor in the Ultimate Haven from which no voyager returns. But on the seas his personality lives for all time, and his works shall pass only when the tides cease to run.

"The stars had no secrets from him; seas
Revealed the depths their waves were screening;
The winds gave up their mysteries;
The tidal flows confessed their meaning.
Of ocean paths the tangled clue
He taught the nations to unravel."
(*From:* "Through the Pass";
Verses by Margaret J. Preston.)

In the twenties and thirties of the last century the American packet ships plying in the trans-Atlantic trade were superior to any other vessels then in operation and had a practical monopoly of the passenger traffic as well as of the transportation of the choicest description of cargo traffic. In spite of the good showing made by the *Savannah* in crossing from Savannah to Liverpool in twenty-seven days, and the extensive operation of steamboats in local waters, no steamships were operated in the trans-Atlantic service by an American company until the organization of the Ocean Steam Navigation Company of New York in 1847. This company started with two sidewheel steamers, the *Washington* and the *Herman*, built by Westervelt and Mackay of New York.

These vessels are described as long, square sterned three deckers of the regular sailing ship type, built of wood, with a white streak along the sides broken by black painted ports. They were bark rigged and the engines were of the side lever type with six-foot by ten-foot stroke. The dimensions of the *Washington* were 230 feet long, thirty-nine feet beam and thirty-one feet draft and those of the *Herman* were 235 feet long, forty feet beam and thirty-one feet draft. They were run twice a month to Bremen, touching at Cowes in both directions and were operated under a contract to carry the United States mails for the sum of 200,000 dollars a year, this subvention being granted as an offset to the subsidies given to the foreign lines. The *Washington* started on her first voyage on June first, 1847, and the *Herman* on March twenty-first, 1848.

The *Washington* was the first United States government mail vessel intended for England and the continent, that went to sea. She took out an agent of the Post Office Department, who established an international system of postage with the European governments. At that time the postage from New York to Europe on letters was twenty-four cents per half ounce or less, forty-eight cents for weights of a half ounce to one ounce and fifteen cents for every additional half ounce. Newspapers and pamphlets were rated at three cents each. When Congress refused to renew the mail contracts in 1858, the vessels were withdrawn from service and subsequently were transferred to the Pacific.

When the *Washington* began her trips, in 1847, Charles H. Marshall and Company, owners of the famous "Black Ball" line of packets, gave a contract to William H. Webb to build the steamship *United States*. This vessel made one round trip from New York to Liverpool, and not proving a success from a commercial point of view, she was withdrawn and shortly afterwards sold to the Prussian government and turned into a steam frigate. Later she found her way into the merchant service where she plied for years.

Observations of a stroller along the shipyards in the banner year of 1847, taken from the New York *Herald* of March thirteenth, 1847, concerning shipbuilding in New York and activity in our shipyards:

"The unprecedented demand for vessels of all descriptions, but especially for large ones, the immense profit resulting to owners from their employment, and the prospective business of our mercantile marine, are causes which result in the greatest activity at the shipyards in this city. All of our shipbuilders have their hands full, and are continually turning away orders, which they cannot procure hands to enable them to fulfill. The government has taken all the vessels their agents could procure, and those engaged in the merchant service are sought at almost any price, either purchased or chartered, for the corn trade, which is carried on to such an extent between this country and Europe. Foreign governments, seized with admiration at sight of our floating palaces, are anxious to avail themselves of the benefits of our skill in naval architecture, and send in proposals of the most liberal kind to New York ship-builders.

"All these things combined, have brought about a perfect mania for shipbuilding. There is a constant rush to the offices of the Dry Dock. The yards are filled with materials, upon which the carpenters are at work. The berths in the yards along a line of the river are all taken up by the rising fabrics, and the din of a thousand axes, hammers, saws and mallets, is heard in admirable confusion, by the visitor whose ear is not dead to the tremendous clatter. In consequence of the activity to which we allude, demands, in some cases exorbitant, have been made upon the builders by dealers, in the material which is requisite for the performance of their contracts. Lumbermen demand the highest prices for ship timber, and every farmer who has a tree for sale refuses to part with it except at an enormous price. Workmen being in demand, not only here but elsewhere, ask and receive the highest rates of wages; consequently ships built at the present time cost much more than formerly."

When the first Cunarder arrived at Boston, in June 1840, it was supposed that making Boston the terminus would seriously interfere with the passenger business of New York, and Boston went wild with joy over the prospect of such rivalry; but, as it turned out, some natural law, like that which makes great rivers run by great cities, brought the ships here, after all.

As the steamers of the Cunard Line were the first to bear a regular and Government mail between England and this country, a detail of its early operation is of interest, and worthy of record for future reference.

An able and enterprising merchant in Halifax, Mr. Samuel Cunard, was among the first to give serious thought to the problem of ocean navigation. He had managed for many years a line of brigs which carried the mails between Halifax and Falmouth, England, and he foresaw at an early day that the time would come when such a service, in the interest of dispatch as well as security, must be performed by steamers.

When the *Great Western* and the *Sirius* arrived in England with the news of their great achievements, they were received with the greatest enthusiasm. The Lords of the Admiralty, who had charge of the ocean mails saw that the time was come for instituting radical changes in the packet service of the empire, and their first step was to advertise for tenders for the conveyance of the royal mails by steam from Liverpool to Halifax, Quebec, and Boston.

Whether Mr. Cunard went to England on hearing the announcement of the plans of the British government, or whether he happened to be there at the time, we do not know; but he saw that the time for action on his part, for which he had long been waiting, had arrived. He made the acquaintance of Robert Napier, already a celebrated engineer on the Clyde, and by him was introduced to George Burns and David MacIver, of the firm of Burns and MacIver, proprietors of a line of steamers plying successfully between Glasgow and Liverpool. All the details of the new undertaking, the size of the ships, the power, the cost of construction, the probable running expenses, and so forth, were thoroughly discussed by these able and practical men; the aid of a few capitalists was secured, with subscriptions by them to the amount of 270,000 pounds; and the British and North American Royal Mail Steam Packet Company was brought into existence. In behalf of this company, Mr. Cunard made a tender for the conveyance of the mails across the Atlantic, in accordance with the proposals of the government, and his tender was accepted. The only other bid came from the Great Western Steamship Company.

The contract was for ten years, 55,000 pounds a year, payable quarterly. The steamers were to run between Liverpool and Halifax, with branch lines to Boston and to Quebec, by way of Pictou. The business men of Boston were not disposed to be satisfied with a branch line from Halifax; they insisted that the trans-Atlantic passages should be made to and from Boston, and at a meeting held in that city, a series of vigorously worded resolutions to this effect, drawn and proposed by Mr. E. Hasket Derby, were adopted.

These resolutions, confirmed by many private letters, reached Mr. Cunard as he was getting ready to sail for America in the *Great Western*. He went with them at once to the Lords of the Admiralty, and offered to increase the size and power of his ships, and to extend the main route to Boston, promising also, half jocosely, to settle the northeastern boundary question, then pending, if they would add 10,000 pounds per annum to the subsidy. His proposition was accepted, and a new contract was signed in May.

Mr. Cunard then went to Glasgow, where the keels of four steamers had already been laid. These were broken up, and four ships of about 1,200 tons each were started in four different shipyards, Mr. Napier's firm agreeing to build the engines. These ships were, of course, of wood, with paddle wheels, and afterward made a reputation for themselves as the *Britannia*, the *Arcadia*, the *Caledonia*, and the *Columbia*, the first leaving Liverpool on the fourth of July, 1840, and arriving in Boston after a fine passage, in fourteen days, eight hours, to the great delight of Bostonians and their anticipation of commercial advancement in consequence. For seven and a half years thereafter Boston enjoyed the monopoly of the Cunard steamship service, and whenever any question arose as to the present or future prospects of the cities of Boston and New York, we were uniformly met with, "We have a line of Liverpool steamers," which was held to settle the question of commercial superiority.

On September eighth, 1846, the Cunard Line announced its intention of establishing a line of steamships "between Liverpool and New York direct." The Line's first agent was D. Bingham, Jr., with an office at Harnden and Company's, Six Wall Street.

Late in the following January, the Cunard Company arranged to make Jersey City the terminus of their steam packets. Later on, Vernon H. Brown and Company became the Steamship Company's agents here, being located in "Steamship Row," Bowling Green, for several years.

Another and most successful enterprise belongs to this period. In 1847 was founded the famous Pacific Mail Company, which with many and varied fortunes continued for many years as a connecting link between the Atlantic and Pacific oceans; in fact, the line was called into being by the sudden development of the Pacific Coast. Its early operations were conducted under extraordinary difficulties, which were only overcome by great skill and judgment in the management. Its first steamer, the *California*, left New York, October sixth, 1848, for San Francisco. After the building of the Panama Railroad, the company's steamers ran from New York to Aspinwall on the Atlantic Coast, and from San Francisco to Panama on the Pacific. Other lines of the same company were subsequently established to Honolulu, to Japan and China, and to Australia.

Their second steamship, the *Oregon*, sailed on December ninth, 1848, and arrived at Panama on February twenty-sixth, 1849. The third vessel, the *Panama*, left on February fifteenth, 1849, but became disabled when several days out from New York, and had to return for repairs to her engine, and subsequently sailed for the Pacific Ocean. These vessels were built, the *California* and the *Panama*, by Wm. H. Webb, and the *Oregon* by Smith and Dimon. They were loaded when leaving New York with material for buildings, tools for the shops, duplicate pieces of machinery and supplies of all kinds that were necessary to install a plant for the repairs of the vessels and the machinery, all of which had to be sent from the Atlantic coast.

The running of a line of steam vessels on the Pacific coast at this period was very expensive in the matter of coal alone, as the supply had to be brought from the United States or England, and cost not less than twenty dollars a ton, and in one case fifty dollars a ton was paid. The company had as many as nine vessels in operation, consuming as much as 35,000 tons of coal a year.

A good story is told of two of the early Pacific Mail Steamship commanders. At that time there were only four American steamships running out of New York, the *Washington* and *Herman* to Bremen, and the *Northerner* and *Southerner* to Charleston, all of which subsequently went to the "Coast." Richard L. Whiting and W. L. Dall were first and second officers on the *Oregon*, in 1851, when the New York local agent, of the Pacific Mail tendered them positions as commanders of the steamships *California* and *Columbia*.

Both Whiting and Dall had been masters of sailing vessels, and when Captain Pearson, the senior commander of the Pacific Mail Steamship Company, asked Whiting what his experience had been in steam navigation, he replied, "The same that you have yourself, sir—going on the ferry to Hoboken." Pearson did not know whether to laugh or get angry, when in stepped Dall, to whom a similar question was propounded, and he replied: "None at all; but I'm engaged to be married to a lady in Hoboken, and I hope to learn something in traveling back and forth on the ferry."

Dall made a good record for himself on the *Columbia*, 700 tons register. On the round trip to Oregon he had to cross eight bars. On reaching one of these, he would call up his pilot, lash him to the bridge, and then send his little steamer through the surf whether it were fair or foul weather.

In 1851, the company built the *Golden Gate*, and in 1853 the *John L. Stephens*, both of them much larger and of more power than their first three vessels. They purchased six or eight steamships at different times for their service on the

Pacific Ocean, mostly vessels of under 1,000 tons. There were many vessels sent around from the Atlantic Coast when the gold fever broke out, some of them worn out in the service on the coast, and others purchased by the Pacific Mail Company. The company had built for them at New York, in 1853, by Wm. H. Webb, the *San Francisco,* and when but two or three days out from New York on her voyage to the Pacific Coast, having a number of United States troops on board for duty in California, she encountered a heavy storm and was lost through the derangement of her machinery. This occurred on December twenty-fourth, 1853. This was the first ocean steamship having feathering buckets to her water wheels.

The business of the company prospered in spite of all opposition, as there were several vessels sent to the Pacific coast by outside parties that were ill-adapted for the work.

The New York and Havre Steam Navigation Company obtained a contract from the Government in 1849 to carry the mails between New York and Havre, calling at Cowes, for the sum of 150,000 dollars a year on a fortnightly sailing basis, starting with the sidewheel steamers *Franklin* and *Humboldt,* built by Westervelt and Mackay. The *Franklin* was 263 feet long and forty-one feet beam, and the *Humboldt* was 292 feet long and ninety-two feet beam. They made the eastward passage to Havre in twelve days, ten hours and the westward passage in twelve days, sixteen hours. The Bremen steamers previously referred to made the run to Bremen in fourteen days, nine hours and the return trip in thirteen days, twenty hours.

The *Humboldt* was lost at the entrance of Halifax harbor, December fifth, 1853, and the *Franklin* went down off Montauk Point on July seventeenth, 1854, but the line continued operations with chartered ships until the *Arago* and *Fulton,* slightly larger vessels, were built in 1855. These vessels had oscillating engines and were considered a great improvement on their predecessors. They continued in the Havre trade until 1861, when they were withdrawn from the service and chartered by the United States Government for war service.

Steamer "Franklin" Leaving New York for Havre and Southampton. From a picture in possession of the author.

NEW YORK ARGONAUTS' SONG OF THE DAYS OF 'FORTY-NINE

"Then Goodbye to old Manhattan, our boat is on the tide;
Farewell to father, mother, to sister, wife and bride;
And when her shores are fading, we'll bless her through our tears,
She filled the cup of happiness through many pleasant years.
And the friends who dearly love us, within our hearts are set,
Whose tenderness and kindness, we never can forget;
Yet we go with dauntless spirits, and go with hearts elate;
To build another Empire—to found another State."

A nineteenth century romance is this tale that should now come to life, of a group of young Americans, who, in the racy, adventurous past, when the quickest way to California was the shortest road to fortune, established a record for making money with a little wooden paddle-wheel steamboat, which has never been equaled in the history of the world.

It was before the Yankee Clipper came into being, and heavy, bluff-bowed, wallowing old craft consumed three hundred days making the trip from New York to San Francisco, and the crossing of the Isthmus was attended with many risks and hardships and at much expense. Attracted like so many others by the glowing accounts of the auriferous treasure buried beneath the soil of the long-considered barren desert of California, which set men to dreaming of wealth as never before, was Lafayette Maynard, who had been a lieutenant in the United States Navy. He conceived the idea of sending a steamboat out to California, by way of the Straits of Magellan, to monopolize the trade just springing up between San Francisco and the mines, via the Sacramento River. This trade was then carried on by means of small sailing craft, ships' launches and scows, and although the distance was a little more than one hundred miles, the average passage was two weeks in ascending the river, and in coming down about seven days; the passage money from forty dollars to sixty dollars, and freight charges in proportion.

Lieutenant Maynard, appreciating the vast and growing volume of emigration, and foreseeing that a steamboat could command any rates she chose to ask, in casting around for the proper vessel at last hit upon a small side-wheeler named *Senator*, built to ply between New York and New England ports, via Long Island. She registered only 750 tons, was 220 feet long by thirty feet beam, with a 450 horse power single beam engine of fifty inches by eleven feet stroke. Her original owners were old "Deacon" Daniel Drew, whose great efforts to promote American steamboats is overshadowed by his gigantic failure in Wall Street trying to "corner Erie," and James Cunningham, a retired marine-engine builder of New York.

About that time Charles Minturn had failed as a Liverpool packet agent, and his brother, Edward, a millionaire, belonging to the prominent New York shipping firm of Grinnell, Minturn and Company, agreed to take an interest provided Charles should be the agent on the steamboat's arrival at San Francisco.

So hazardous seemed the enterprise of sending an ordinary river steamboat on the long, long, dreary voyage of seventeen thousand miles between Sandy Hook and the Golden Gate, where wreckage marked the journey, and death and disease claimed men at every intervening port, that the insurance companies refused the risk on any terms. When friends congregated at Burling Slip, East River, on the morning of March tenth, 1849, to see Lieutenant Maynard and his adventurous comrades sally forth into the (then) Great Unknown, it was more like a funeral than an ordinary leavetaking.

Observing that steam was an important element in his profession, and in the Naval service there were so few chances offered of becoming fully acquainted with it, Lieutenant Richard Bache, one of the most popular officers in our Navy, had requested to be detached from the Coast Survey and granted leave for six months in order to take command of this steam vessel. His officers were Cortlandt Benham and Harry Porter, brother of Admiral D. D. Porter. Lieutenant Maynard and Charles Minturn went along as owners' representatives, although the former had been given a share in the enterprise as a *quid pro quo*.

New York presented extraordinary traits of enthusiastic emigration, when "Ho! for California! and the Gold Mines!" was the most popular slogan, yet the *Senator's* sole passenger was "Jack" Addison, who had been a law partner of Beverly Tucker in Washington and afterwards became a well known man in California. Many prospective passengers had turned away when they saw how small a craft she was, and her departure created an unwonted stir amongst the shipping along South Street, where many predictions from the habitués of that waterfront thoroughfare were made, pro and con, as to the little boat reaching her port of destination.

The little side-wheeler pulled through many a hard gale, while her "gentlemen adventurers" suffered through many a weary night watch along both coasts of South America, and when "feeling their way" through the tortuous Straits of Magellan, before they reached Valparaiso. Those aboard the *Senator* had the unusual pleasure, on arrival at Panama, of reading flattering obituaries published in the New York dailies, their craft having been given up as lost!

Many were awaiting passage to San Francisco when the *Senator* arrived there. From that time this lucky little steamboat's wonderful money-making career commenced, for every nook and corner of her capacity was filled with passengers at any rate that her agent, Charles Minturn, chose to demand. She reached San Francisco, October twenty-seventh, 1849, with about 200 passengers, at 500 dollars per head, having made the passage from Panama in twenty-one days, despite heavy seas and contrary winds, while loaded almost to her gunwales.

There was no more hospitable place on the face of the earth than San Francisco during the Gold Rush. Everybody knew the signal on top of Telegraph Hill for a side-wheel steamer,—two black boards, one on each side of the long black signal pole like two uplifted arms. So delighted were the citizens to see this sign, which meant "some tidings of home," that they suspended all business, took a drink, and then wended their way to the steamship wharf. Here assembled a large portion of the City's population, among whom the safe arrival of this pioneer steamboat, after her wonderful voyage from New York, created a great sensation; and a hearty welcome was accorded to the passenger and crew of the *Senator*, for her arrival had been eagerly anticipated, and all of them were soon lined up alongside the El Dorado, Eagle, or one of the other many bars, with hundreds of San Franciscans eager to do them homage.

Thousands of men were at San Francisco, and hundreds daily arriving, who had no means of getting to Sacramento City and from there to the placer mines, so the *Senator* was at once put on the route to Sacramento. Being the first steamer that had ever floated on those waters, her owners were able to fix the rates of passage and freight as they pleased. For the trip, either way, which occupied from eight to ten hours, passengers paid thirty-five dollars, or its equivalent in gold dust by miners from the "diggins," with five dollars for each meal and five dollars for a berth; and merchants paid from forty dollars to eighty dollars a ton for freight, and the cargo carried was enormous for so small a vessel. Day after day and month after month, for a year or more, this bonanza boat gathered in, not unfrequently, 50,000 dollars for the trip of a few hours' time. The *Senator* probably earned more money than any sail or steam vessel ever known.

The Pacific Route which was started in 1848, was certainly a most ambitious undertaking. After the Mexican War had given us control of a vast, unknown country south of Oregon and along the Pacific Coast it was recognized in Washington that steam communication was quite as essential as forts and warships to bind California and Oregon to the Union. Contracts were accordingly made with George Law and his associates, for the conveyance of the United States mails from New York to Aspinwall (now Colon) on the Isthmus of Panama, and with William H. Aspinwall for the conveyance of the mails in the Pacific from Panama to San Francisco and Astoria.

Of a group of steamboat men, prominently identified with the progress and growth, not only of New York, but of a great part of the United States, George Law was the most picturesque, after that shrewd "bible-banging" scoundrel Daniel Drew, and pugnacious Commodore Cornelius Vanderbilt, but his name is practically unknown today. During the early steamboat days and into the forties "Liveoak George" as he was called in tribute to his rugged pugnacity, was a familiar character to Americans all over the country.

From the time George Law left his father's farm in Washington County, New York, up to the year 1839, when he contracted to build the High Bridge which spans the Harlem River, conveying the Croton water at a giddy height across that stream, he was continuously employed on the public works of different States, principally New York and Pennsylvania. He began in a subordinate capacity, but soon advanced to the position of superintending and sub-contracting, and then to be one of the most extensive contractors of his time, in which he laid the foundation of his fortune. His engagements were always in constructing railroads and canals.

In 1847, George Law embarked in the crowning enterprise of his life. In that year he commenced the preparations which ended in his becoming the owner, by building and purchase, of sixteen ocean steamers. The vast treasures of California had become partially known to the world. Colonel A. G. Sloo, of Ohio, had contracted with the United States Government to transport the mails between the Atlantic Coast and California by way of New Orleans and Chagres. Sloo had not the means to fulfill his contract, and he opened negotiations with Mr. Law in order to obtain his aid in carrying out the project. With the eye of a statesman as well as a sagacious business man, Mr. Law discerned the importance to the nation of securing this immense trade against the competition of Great Britain. The commerce of the South Pacific was monopolized by her far-seeing merchants, and nothing but the bold enterprise and almost illimitable resources of George Law prevented them from gaining possession of the entire trade of the North Pacific and California. His great movement was inspired by the highest motives of patriotism, the vast returns from the investment being a secondary consideration. The steamer *Falcon*, which he bought in 1848, took the first passengers to Chagres which reached California by steam. Soon after he built the *Ohio* and *Georgia*, which commenced running in January 1849. But we have not room for further details of his operations on the ocean.

In 1852, the great enterprise of crossing the Isthmus

from Aspinwall to Panama by rail was languishing from want of confidence in the undertaking, and the difficulty of providing the requisite means to surmount the almost invincible difficulties presented by the obstacles of high mountain ranges, deep ravines, and a climate so charged with miasma as to be dangerous to human life. The vast importance of an early completion of the road so impressed Mr. Law, that he visited Chagres and Panama in order to inform himself by personal examination in respect to the feasibility of the undertaking. After purchasing into the road to the extent of half a million of dollars, he went to Aspinwall and Panama, located a terminus, and set men at work on the road, and in constructing a dock and station for steamers, which was the first accommodation of the kind for commerce between the two oceans ever provided in that country. He came home in April 1852, having visited Havana, Jamaica, Porto Bello, San Juan, and New Orleans, and made a careful scrutiny into the resources and capacity of those important places. On his return he made a report respecting the difficulties of the undertaking, and the prospective advantages of connecting the Atlantic and Pacific oceans. The judgment of Mr. Law was accepted as undoubted authority, and the money to complete the work was forthcoming.

It was a great day, in February 1824, when Daniel Webster and Attorney General William Wirt, acting for Gibbons, met Thomas Addis Emmet and T. J. Oakley, representing Ogden, in the United States Supreme Court, before Chief Judge John Marshall, in the long-pending Steamboat Case, Gibbons versus Ogden, which released steam navigation from the nagging control of a horde of petty bureaucracies. Already Gibbons and Ogden had fought through the lower courts; one to break, the other to save the Hudson River monopoly. Now, at last, the legal giants had it in hand, and with John Marshall on the bench it would be definitely settled. No small part of the fame of John Marshall as the soundest interpreter of the Federal Constitution rests upon this Steamboat Case. Even within our own time (1934) the precedents he then established have been invoked in connection with the George Washington Bridge cross the Hudson at 170th Street. The effect of this decision upon steamboat operation and domestic commerce was electrical. And it was Captain "Corneel" Vanderbilt who made the money, with a little steamboat that plied between New York and New Brunswick, for Gibbons to pay Webster, whose lucid arguments convinced Marshall, whose *dicta* reduced the pretensions of the monopoly.

A fine stroke for freedom, that decision. Before long Captain Vanderbilt resigned the managership and a command in Gibbons' Union Line of Steamboats, and his wife gave up the hotel at New Brunswick which she was keeping while he ran a steamboat. Embarking in the transportation business on his own account, he soon had steamboats going in various waters, on the Hudson, on the Sound, the Delaware, and so forth, everywhere seeking to have a monopoly of the business and profits.

Captain Vanderbilt's second command and the first boat he owned, the *Bellona*, was propelled by what were termed paddles, but they were strictly "palmipedes," in order to evade the Fulton claim for side-wheels, but these being condemned as useless, she was fitted with side-wheels, and from this arose the litigation between Thomas Gibbons and Gouverneur Ogden.

As the formation of paddle-wheels are such an important feature in the propulsion of a steamboat, and paddle-wheels proved a factor in the Steamboat Case, above referred to, we do not think it amiss to dwell upon that subject:

Fulton employed the ordinary paddle-wheel from the start—a large, light, double wheel, carrying boards fixed on the outer ends of the spokes, about four feet long and dipping twenty-six inches into the water. Builders were never quite satisfied with that wheel, because the buckets struck and left the water in such a way as to lose a great deal of power. An astonishing number of inventions were patented from 1807 for forty years afterward intended to introduce a better wheel, and a great deal of money was lost in experimenting with the idea. Several tried to feather the paddles, and all sorts of shapes in buckets were tried. They were patterned after fishes' tails, ducks' feet, and birds' wings, and were made of various triangular forms, with the pointed end outermost in some wheels and the base of the triangle out in others. Few of these multifarious devices were ever put to use, and none ever stood the test of more than a year or two.

Cornelius Vanderbilt entered into the hotly contested Hudson River competition with the announcement that his service would furnish better boats and lower rates. This was what the people were looking for, and he made his rivals "scratch gravel" for trade.

The rivalry for the New York steamboat speed record became so great between the *Oregon,* owned by George Law, and the *Cornelius Vanderbilt,* owned by Commodore Vanderbilt, then running on Long Island Sound, that a race for 1,000 dollars a side was arranged between them, which took place on the Hudson River, June first, 1847. The race started at the Battery and both boats got away at eleven o'clock, a great throng of people being on hand to witness the contest. For thirty miles up the river, the boats kept side by side, but the *Oregon* was bumped by her rival and her wheelhouse was considerably damaged. On the way down the river, the *Oregon's* coal gave out, but the captain and crew resorted to tactics that had been followed before, in the days of exciting steamboat racing. The woodwork of the berths, chairs, benches, furniture of staterooms and everything else that would burn was put under the boilers to keep up steam. She finished the race at the Battery about twelve hundred feet ahead of the *Vanderbilt,* having covered the seventy miles in three hours and fifteen minutes with the tide against her going north and with her on the return. The owners of the *Oregon* got the 1,000 dollars' stake and possibly expended more than that restoring the joiner work on their boat.

The interest in this race was greater than any ever manifested in this city; far in advance of that shown in the races of the Albany Line boats or the *Highlander* and *Robert L. Stevens;* it was equal to that of the later contests between the *R. E. Lee* and *Natchez,* from New Orleans to St. Louis. In order to reduce the draught of the vessels they were docked, the bottoms cleaned; furniture, ornaments, and all unnecessary

C. Vanderbilt.
From an engraved portrait in possession of the author.

articles were taken on shore; and previous to the day of the race the *Oregon's* inner bottom (that is, between her frames) was freed of water by sponges where it could not be reached by dippers. In unison with this regard of lessening of draught of water, the necessary supply of coal was carefully estimated; but in the case of the *Oregon* it fell short near the end of the course. Commodore Vanderbilt was much disappointed; the loss of the money was not considered; it was the man who had defeated him that annoyed him. But the victory did not win much for "Liveoak George," for he had to sell out to Daniel Drew, not very long afterwards. Being ground between the competition of Drew's powerful line and Vanderbilt's, both of whom had well paying lines of steamboats on the Sound and contrived to enmesh their affairs together, Law stood no chance at all.

"Commodore" Vanderbilt carried on his competition for Hudson River travel for nearly twenty years. He owned and operated nearly fifty steamboats in that period and would probably have continued in it, had not the discovery of gold in California in 1848-49 induced him to seek what promised to be a more profitable field in Atlantic and Pacific Ocean navigation, by way of the Isthmus of Panama. There was a great tide of travel and merchandise moving toward California in those days and "Commodore" Vanderbilt was among those to reap the profit.

"Clipper ships, designed to round the Horn under royals, were slipping down the ways by scores; but fast freight and passengers in a hurry preferred to pay high for steamship transportation via Central America—it was a voyage of three to four months as against three weeks," recites Arthur D. H. Smith, in his book, "Commodore Vanderbilt, An Epic of American Achievement."

Then he continues: " 'Liveoak George' (Law) already was reaping a fat harvest from this demand for haste. He and his associates had incorporated the United States Mail Steamship Company, which operated a line from New York to Aspinwall—now Colon; the Panama Railroad Company, which had begun work on a road across the Isthmus; and the Pacific Mail Steamship Company, which operated a line from Panama to San Francisco. The two steamship companies received mail subsidies from the Federal Government aggregating 480,000 dollars at this time; and they did a capacity passenger business, besides deriving a lucrative revenue from bullion and light freight. In the first ten years of their existence they transported 175,000 passengers and 200,000 dollars in gold. It was the spectacle of their early prosperity which made Corneel's (Vanderbilt's) mouth water, and directed his attention to Nicaragua. Opposition, competition, those were his watchwords."

The story of Commodore Vanderbilt's rise to fortune, anecdotes which circulated the waterfront, his pugnacious methods, especially after 1848, when he fought opposition vigorously and triumphed, secured him popularity perhaps beyond his due.

When he went to Europe, in 1853, in his luxurious yacht *North Star*, on that "memorable vacation trip," Vanderbilt had turned over to a group, headed by Charles Morgan, the operation of his Nicaragua Transit Company and its allied steamship lines, who manipulated the business in such a way as to secure for themselves large sums of money; and, on his return to New York, he found himself, for the time being, dispossessed of control. He was furious! "I won't sue you," he stormed, "for the law is too slow; I will ruin you!" Morgan survived, however, and was rated as the largest shipowner in the United States just before the Civil War.

Commodore Vanderbilt's European trip and the Crimean War determined him to enter the trans-Atlantic field, and this brought him into collision with E. K. Collins, who had organized a line of high-class American passenger steamships to compete with the English Cunarders. It had been proved, both before and after Collins' line started, that it would be impossible, without protection of some kind, to run American steamships in competition with foreign, supported by protection as the British lines were. Even on routes where opposition had not developed, it was impossible to find adequate support for lines destitute of government aid. A bill, passed by Congress, June fourteenth, 1858, gave "the sea and inland postage," in lieu of the subsidies authorized in 1845, 1847, 1852, 1854 and 1855. After the passage of the act, Vanderbilt, the best steamship manager of the time, tested trans-Atlantic steam navigation for "sea and inland postage" pay, and satisfied himself that there was no money in the business.

During his ocean steamship career Cornelius Vanderbilt owned twenty-one steamships, eleven of which he built; and, with steamboats, his entire fleet numbered sixty-six. When he abandoned the water, in 1864, his accumulations were estimated at 40,000,000 dollars. As early as 1844 he had become interested in railroads; now he turned his capital and his energies in that direction. He obtained control of one railroad after another; and at the time of his death, his various roads covered lines more than 2,000 miles in extent, and, under one management, represented an aggregate capital of 150,000,000 dollars of which he and members of his family owned fully one-half. His entire property at his death, January fourth, 1877, was estimated at nearly 100,000,000 dollars, nearly all of which he bequeathed to his son, William H. Vanderbilt, that the great railroad enterprise might go on as a unit and increase.

Of the men who have amassed fortunes in the city of New York, it can be said of Cornelius Vanderbilt that he did more for the City than the City ever did for him, and that his immense fortune was the acquirement of his own genius and not the result of lucky investment by some remote ancestor.

There is no New England name whose origin in this country has been more certainly established, whose branching lines have been followed out through all their ramifications with more absolute success than that of Morgan. In these United States, whose antiquity is but the yesterday of older nations, there are not many who can trace back their ancestry even through the brief history which the country possesses; but though it be common to speak slightingly of the desire to trace one's pedigree, few Americans, we apprehend, are anxious to hide their descent from some one or other of the Pilgrim Fathers when it is clearly established.

At the age of fourteen, Charles Morgan left his native village to seek his fortune, and arrived in the city of New York, light of heart and lighter of purse; engaged himself to a retail grocer, and patiently went through the early and late hours, and the drudgery incidental to such a life, till in a few years he had thoroughly learned the business, and saved enough to set himself up in the same line in a small way. Success followed and he began to import a little fruit from the West Indies, purchased a brig sailing to that region, then other vessels, until he became sole owner of a line of brigs and schooners trading between New York and the West Indies. His success was but suggestive of new enterprise; he turned his attention from sailing vessels to steam, beginning by purchasing an interest in the steamer *David Brown*, and sending her to Charleston, South Carolina, the first steamer that ever entered that harbor from the city of New York. She was the pioneer of others, and for a number of years he maintained a line of steamers between the two cities. Success here again prompted to new enterprise, and he now commenced the running of steamers in the Gulf of Mexico, a department of business with which his name is most prominently connected in the steamship annals of the country.

In 1835, while Texas was struggling with Mexico for her independence, before she had won it on the field of San Jacinto, Mr. Morgan, believing in the certain triumph of the Anglo-Saxon race over the mixed races of Mexico, determined to be the first in a trade which he foresaw must, in the event of the success of the Texan arms, one day rise to large proportions. He sent his steamer *Columbia* from New Orleans to Galveston, Texas. Galveston, now a beautiful and prosperous city, the "Queen of the Gulf," then consisted of but a single house; there was no wharf at which to land goods, and those carried thither by Mr. Morgan's steamers then, and for some time afterward, were taken to the shore in scows, and thence found their way into the interior upon the backs of mules and other primitive conveyances. What a change has come over that region! The whistle of the steam engine has taken the place of the howl of the wolf, and the red children of the forest and prairie have here, as everywhere else, disappeared before the aggressive and remorseless tread of the white man. Texas conquered her independence—emigrants flocked from the north into the new territory—the city of Galveston increased with unexampled rapidity—other cities sprang up on the coast—steamer followed steamer as the trade expanded, and Charles Morgan reaped the reward of his far-seeing adventure.

Discouragements, however, followed. The harbors of Texas were shallow and exposed, the bars changing and treacherous: the steamers, then, from the lack of experience, were not so suitable to the peculiar navigation as now, and their commanders less acquainted with its intricacies. Not a few were cast away on that inhospitable, because unfamiliar, coast. In rapid succession Mr. Morgan lost by shipwreck the steamers *Perseverance, Globe, Yacht, Meteor, Palmetto, Galveston, Portland, New York,* and *Jerry Smith,* on none of which was there any insurance. Adverse fortune, however, did not shake Mr. Morgan's confidence in the final result. He built other and better ships in the place of those lost, and as the business grew, improved each over its forerunner, as experience dictated, adding to their capacity, speed, and adaptation to the peculiarities of the navigation. The result was that for twenty years not an accident worth naming happened to any of his vessels, and the Morgan Line of Texas steamers, trading between New Orleans and Brashear, Galveston, Indianola, Lavacca, Rockport, Sabine, and Brazos Santiago, became as well known for regularity and safety to the inhabitants of the region bordering on the Gulf, and to all having business relations there, as the Cunard Line to Liverpool was then and is now to the citizens of New York.

Mr. Morgan also owned a line of steamers running on Lake Pontchartrain, between the cities of Mobile and New Orleans, and was the sole owner of nineteen steamships, all iron sea-going vessels of a superior class, besides several ferryboats, and other smaller craft. First and last, since he began, he built one hundred and ten vessels—sail and steam—and was for some years the largest shipowner in the United States.

He purchased the railroad connecting New Orleans (at Algiers, opposite that city) with Brashear, eighty miles in length, which he ran in connection with his steamship lines in the Texas trade. This road he owned and operated himself. Its value was not represented by shares, and he managed it without the aid of a president and a board of directors. This was one railroad in the land whose fortunes were independent of the smiles and frowns of Wall Street, and which had no stock to corner or to buy or sell in any way, short or long.

At one time in connection with others, he carried on, at the Morgan Iron Works—a large property on the East River and Ninth and Tenth streets in the city of New York—the business of engine building. Here the engines and boilers of many of the largest steamers of the navy, and of the mercantile marine have been built. At a later period, he became the sole owner of this property, which long bore his name.

Charles Morgan is said to have been worth thirteen millions at his death and his combination of steamship and railroad lines soon became a part of the Southern Pacific System.

In 1849 at New York, a clipper ship was built by Jacob Bell for A. A. Low and Brothers, which embodied the perfection of her type. She was christened *Oriental* and was built to bear the precious trade of Asia, the oldest traffic known to commerce. Her first voyages were between New York and Hongkong, but in 1849 the East India trade with Great Britain was opened to the ships of other nations; and as this trade was the most desirable, it went to the finest and fleetest ships. So in December, 1850, the *Oriental* brought to London the first cargo ever carried there from China in an American ship. Perhaps she had in her hold many gifts for the approaching Christmas season. The *Oriental* already had made New York from Hongkong in eighty-one days and returned to Hongkong in like time. Now, she made London from Hongkong in ninety-seven days, notwithstanding adverse weather. Her arrival was a sensation. Crowds thronged to the docks to see the long slender hull of this earliest of ocean greyhounds, her lofty masts that towered like spires above the dwarfed shipping of the yard, the wealth of furled white canvas that had carried her down the winds with such unheard of speed. To the editorial writers of the day she was a wonder, a menace and a challenge. "We must run a race with our gigantic and unshackled rival. A fell necessity constrains us and we must not be beat." (London *Times*.) The London *Illustrated News* published a picture of the *Oriental* and an article, part of which reads as follows:

"Although many British ships have arrived at New York and Boston from China, since the alteration in the navigation laws, the first American ship (the 'Oriental') arrived in the West India docks on the 3rd instant, and has made the fastest voyage on record from China, by a sailing vessel. We should add that the 'Oriental' brings about 1600 tons of tea at £6 per ton whilst all the ships loading at Whampoa (Canton's Seaport) at the same time only got £3 10s. Correspondents availed themselves of the opportunity even at such a high rate of freight, the 'Oriental' being known for her fast sailing qualities, which she fully verified."

Arthur H. Clark in "The Clipper Ship Era," says:

"It is not too much to say that the arrival of this vessel in London with her cargo of tea in this crisis in 1850, aroused almost as much apprehension and excitement in Great Britain as was created by the memorable Tea Party held in Boston harbor in 1773."

The Gold Rush of 'Forty-nine, that gigantic migration of human beings to California, via Cape Horn, stands out as the peak of the Clipper Ship Era. During the year 1849, a total of 91,405 passengers arrived at San Francisco, and a large proportion hailed from New York. For about three years, one or more fast clippers were always on the berth, loading day and night with supplies for California. The old piers along the East River, from Coenties Slip say to Beekman Street, New York, were busy places and scores of people visited them to see the ships.

It was customary after the clippers had finished loading, for them to drop down the East River and anchor off Battery Park, then a fashionable resort. Here they would remain a few hours to take on their crews and what passengers could be carried.* Crowds would gather to see the ships get under way; some to bid their friends good-by and others to enjoy the gayety and bustle of the event. As forty or fifty sailormen, in a capstan chanty, swear eternal devotion and recite the charms

---

* The accompanying illustration from a painting by the well known marine artist, Charles Robert Patterson, gives one a fine idea of the beautiful sight of a California clipper leaving the port of New York for the Golden Gate. It shows her just as she gathers way and some of the friends of those aboard were still able to keep abreast in their small boats.

of that much-loved lady, "Sally Brown," the yards are swung to a full and the ship's head pays off. There are tears and waving handkerchiefs as the sleek vessel, with the grace of a well-handled yacht, now picks its way down the Bay; off on a fifteen thousand mile "trek" to California!

Interestingly, under a stirring title, "Boom Days in America," Carl Cutler in "Greyhounds of the Sea," tells about a "Maritime event" in New York, outside the pale of "Ho, California!" doings, which held front-page prominence in the days of 'Forty-nine:

"It was Sunday afternoon, the 25th of March, 1849, when the watcher at the Sandy Hook telegraph station descried a large, heavily-sparred ship in the offing, coming up wing and wing before a spanking breeze from the south-southeast. As she drew near, it became plain to the operator that here was an Indiaman of the extreme clipper type. But there was no vessel of that description due. The swift sailing ships of the tea fleet were not expected to leave Canton before the 5th of January, if then, and at best would not reach port for a fortnight.

"Nearer and nearer she came, breasting the sagging tide, her studding sails crumpling one by one as the light canvas was taken in. Long before her private signal went fluttering up from the little group on the quarter deck, the watcher knew that she was indeed the 'Sea Witch,' and that Bob Waterman had set another mark for the Canton packets to shoot at. Waterman himself could not even dimly foresee that he had participated in the making of a record which would never be broken by any ship of sail, for at that time there was no imaginable limit to the possibilities of clipper ships.

"The next morning the newspapers of the city blazoned forth the fact that the 'Sea Witch' had arrived the preceding afternoon, breaking all China records by a notable margin. She had come home in seventy-four days and fourteen hours!

"By some strange twist of circumstance, this passage has been recorded by later writers as occupying seventy-nine days, and the 'Sea Witch's' passage of seventy-seven days in 1847 has been cited as the world's record to the present time.

"Nevertheless, evidence in favor of Waterman's claim in 1849 is as conclusive as any that can be adduced in substantiation of any of the early records, and the passage cannot be stretched

"The Gold Seekers, 1849". A Clipper Ship Sailing out of New York for San Francisco.

From a painting by Charles R. Patterson. Courtesy of the Columbian Rope Company.

to seventy-nine days without a grotesque distortion of every shred of evidence.

"On the negative side there appears to be no suggestion that the record was ever disputed by any contemporary report, although there were many rivals in the China trade whose ships were arriving almost daily, who would undoubtedly have been glad to set 'Bob Waterman' down a bit. Two fast ships are definitely known to have sailed from Macao for New York on the 5th of January, the last day for Waterman's departure, if his passage was to occupy seventy-nine days. These were the 'Oneida,' commanded by Cressey, and the 'Carrington,' under Abbott. Although fine ships, neither were in the class of the 'Sea Witch.' The 'Oneida' passed Anjier nine days later on the 14th, one day ahead of Waterman.

"Aside from the possibility of accident—of which there is not the slightest hint in the marine records of the times—it is unthinkable that the comparatively slow sailing 'Oneida' could have beaten the 'Sea Witch' on the run to Anjier. It is far more likely that the 'Sea Witch' beat the time of the 'Oneida' on this leg by at least two days, since she arrived at New York twenty-six days before the 'Oneida.'

"The 'Carrington' also arrived at New York nineteen days after the 'Sea Witch.' Both the 'Oneida' and 'Carrington' were reported as sailing in company on the 5th, but nothing was said of the 'Sea Witch.' If there had been any doubt about the time of the 'Sea Witch,' it would surely have been raised by the arrival of the two later ships, if not before. Nothing would have been simpler than for Cressey, for example, to have reported that he had sailed in company with the 'Sea Witch,' if such had been the case. It appears to be the fact that the question was never raised by any of the numerous shipmasters who lay at anchor at Whampoa with Waterman, or, for that matter, by any contemporary writer, in this country or elsewhere.

"The log of the 'Sea Witch' was evidently open to inspection, as witness the following particulars published in the New York *Commercial Advertiser* three days after the arrival of the ship:

" 'The splendid ship "Sea Witch," Capt. Waterman, arrived here on Sunday in seventy-five days from China, having performed a voyage around the world in 194 sailing days.

" 'During the voyage she has made the shortest direct passages on record, viz.: 69 days from New York to Valparaiso;

50 days from Callao to China; 75 days from China to New York. Distance run by observation from New York to Valparaiso, 10,568 miles; average 6–2/5 miles per hour. Distance from Callao to China, 10,417 miles; average 8–5/8 knots per hour. Distance from China to New York, 14,255 miles; average 7–7/8 knots per hour. Best ten (consecutive) days' run, 2,634 miles; average 11–1/10 knots per hour."

"This passage of the 'Sea Witch,' in some respects the most remarkable voyage of the entire clipper ship age, received, relatively, as much publicity as the famous eighty-nine day run of the 'Flying Cloud' in 1851. Thereafter it vanished, unaccountably, from the lists of record passages, a curious and not uninstructive example of historical vagaries. 'Fables agreed upon.' "

Three steam vessels of the aggregate cost of more than 1,000,000 dollars were launched in succession from the shipyard of William H. Brown, at the foot of Twelfth Street, East River, on the morning of January twenty-eighth, 1850. The *New World*, intended for the navigation of the rivers of California; the *Arctic*, belonging to the Collins Line of New York and Liverpool steam packets; and the *Boston*, intended to run on Sanford's Line between Boston and Bangor. They were all put afloat within an hour and a half, which was a skillful piece of work considering the very cold weather prevailing and the liability of the tallow freezing on the ways. It was estimated that there were fully 20,000 people to see the launching of these vessels, as it had been widely advertised, and was the first time more than one vessel has been launched from one yard in a day.

The *New World* was launched with her machinery all in place and ready for service, as was shown by a few revolutions of her water wheels while on the ways prior to launching. She started on her trial trip in less than half an hour after being put overboard. This was a most novel feature of the occasion; for as soon as she touched the water, the ship was set in motion; her paddle-wheels revolving, the smoke ascending and steam whizzing with its usual vivacity.

A rush now took place of the multitude to the nearby plant of the Novelty Iron Works, where anxious faces were seen from every dock, vessel, storehouse and roof, looking toward the great object of attraction, the S.S. *Arctic*,—the largest vessel that had then been built in the United States, costing nearly 600,000 dollars, and which was approximately the cost of each of the other Collins liners, *Atlantic, Pacific, Antarctic* and *Adriatic.*

Whilst the crowd was waiting for the crowning glory of the occasion, the steamer *Boston,* of 800 tons, took her departure from the land alongside the leviathan of the ocean.

However, soon after the *Boston* left the ways, the *Arctic* began to move slowly and gracefully, heralded by the shouts of the immense multitude, who had been anxiously looking for the event.

The novel features attending the *New World* launching, with steam up and then immediately going to sea, is thus explained. There were some financial differences regarding the vessel between her owners, one of whom was the builder, and the vessel having been placed in the sheriff's hands, the builder desired to send her to the Pacific Coast. The officers wined and dined the law officers in charge of the vessel who permitted the captain to make a "trial trip" down the bay, and when he was well into the lower bay gave them the choice of California with him or he would send them ashore in a small boat. They accepted the latter. It was a well planned scheme to get away from New York, for the vessel had been regularly cleared at the Custom House the day before. Captain "Ned" Wakeman who thus ran the *New World* out of New York, when she was supposed to be in charge of the sheriff, was a "diamond in the rough." He made a great reputation in California, and some years after this event, when he was in command of the steamship *John L. Stephens,* he allowed her to be captured by Frank Dana and others at San Blas.

William H. Brown, later in the same year, launched two more vessels, named *Pacific* and *Independence,* with steam up. Shortly afterward he sent them to sea, engaging in the Panama-California trade on our West Coast.

On March second, 1850, the next Collins Line steamer, the *Baltic,* was launched, with the ship *St. Louis,* for the New

York and New Orleans trade, from Jacob Bell's shipyard, at Stanton and Houston streets.

These were boom times for the East River shipyards. Another notable event was the double launching by William H. Webb, on June ninth, 1850, when he sent overboard within a few minutes of one another, the ship *Celestial* for the China trade and a steamship named *Alabama* for the New York and Savannah Line; both vessels going off without mishap.

The next year William H. Webb added one more to the list by the triple launching, on January twenty-first, 1851, of the steamship *Golden Gate*, for the Pacific Mail S.S. Company's service on the Pacific Ocean; the trans-Atlantic sailing packet *Isaac Bell* of 1485 tons, for Livingston and Fox's Havre Line; and the clipper *Gazelle* of 1500 tons, for Taylor and Merrill in the China trade.

It was of no little surprise to scientific men in the old world, that a country like ours, during all the years that we were successful as a maritime power, continued in force laws so detrimental to her commercial interests as the tonnage laws proved to be; our ship-builders had long witnessed its baneful effects, and nothing but an indomitable energy saved us from defeat in our race with England for the ascendancy in building ships. The hoary and venerated prejudices of their fathers influenced American ship-owners so strongly that they were reluctant to allow designers to change the character of their ships. They feared that the builders would foster their own interests in marking out a course for the measurement of ships.

Had the United States a code of tonnage laws worthy of the name, she would have had nothing to fear; but with laws actually inviting fraud, she had much to dread; the terms were unequal, the odds were against us, and the ship-owner soon found that it was not enough to have equally as good a sailing ship, and one that could carry as much per every ton of displacement as his rival, but that he must carry more, and sail faster, if he would successfully compete in this commercial race. We should remember that English ships were then built under the fostering influence of the best code of laws on the globe, while we were building under those among the most heterogeneous; and although the great bulk of English vessels had been launched prior to the alteration of her tonnage laws, yet these were not the ships that were to be our rivals. The Americans had nothing to fear when their energies could be concentrated on a single point with the world combined in the race to wealth or fame; and as they lost in this rival race, it will be found that they had foundered in the straits of avarice.

To show the deleterious effects of our Tonnage Laws upon the commerce of the United States, John Willis Griffiths, in his authoritative "Treatise on Marine and Naval Architecture," writes:

"It cannot be denied, that our tonnage laws, as they now exist, have done more to clog the wheels of improvement in marine architecture, than everything beside; whether we regard them as the parent of legalized fraud, or as the fruitful source of premature graves, their deleterious effects are alike obvious to the thinking portion of the commercial world. While the present practice prevails, of accounting the one-half or any proportion of a ship's breadth for the depth, it must be quite apparent that ships will be disproportioned, and consequently, unfit for navigating the ocean; by a diminished breadth, and an increased depth, the ship-owner registers his ship at much less than her actual tonnage, and, as a consequence, that wholesome competition which in every other enterprise is the muscle of improvement, is rendered weak and inefficient. Mechanics finding their boldest thoughts and best exertions fettered by the onerous burdens entailed upon commerce, have partially lost the laudable ambition to excel, they once possessed, and, like ship-owners, seem to have forgotten, in their haste for the dollar, that our ships perform little better, or make a voyage in no less time across the ocean than they did forty years ago. Startling as this announcement may appear, it is nevertheless true, that voyages of thirteen and fourteen days, from this city to Liverpool, by sailing ships, were as frequent forty years ago as they now are. It will not be denied that there are ships owned in this city, that under the same circumstances in which the best voyages have been made, would, without doubt, perform the voyage within eleven days; but those ships are engaged in a trade over which the tonnage laws have no warping influence; I allude to the trade with China. The profits accruing from our commercial intercourse with that remote nation, is found to consist in the quick returns, rather than the bulk of cargo; hence the reason why no notice is taken of the inducement to evade the provisions of the present law, and the results are, that Canton has already been measured as distant but seventy-five days from New York; and the day is not far distant, when the time will be reduced to sixty. There is one feature in political science that teaches us that cheerful submission to law is only rendered when based on the principles of equity; when its wholesome provisions bear alike on all its subjects. This great principle, the glorious bond of union in this republic, will be found no less advantageous to our commerce than to the country. England, sensible of this, abolished her heterogeneous code in 1836, since which time her improvements have been without a parallel in the history of the commercial world. In framing a law that will equalize the burdens, and make competition a fair and laudable enterprise, making the ship something more than a mere floating warehouse, and at the same time a source of profit to her owners, without abridging her carrying properties in the least, but rather augmenting them; and, as a consequence, making her owners greater returns than they can possibly do under the existing code, and giving them an equal chance for the rewards of energy and enterprise with their English competitors under the reciprocal navigation laws; it needs but a glance at our geographical position to satisfy the incredulous, that the United States is destined to become the great theatre for commercial improvements, and that it only remains for her legislators to enact such laws as will cherish a spirit of emulation worthy of our favoured locality, and of the age in which we live, to place her far in advance of other nations in commercial improvements. The present mode of determining the tonnage of ships by law, is a powerless aid to science and emulation, and no sophistry can make that right which common sense pronounces wrong. It only remains for our legislators to be true to the instinctive impulses that have prompted the extension of our commercial interest to the present time, and this monstrosity in commercial science shall be found only in the history of the past."

The great event of this period, however, so far as it relates to the development of the shipping industry in the United States, was the attempt at American operation of the

---

NOTE: Mr. Griffiths published his "Treatise," in 1850; a large quarto volume, which was the first work on shipbuilding of any considerable size.

famous Collins Line, between New York and Liverpool.

When Congress decided to "drive the Cunarders out of business" Collins secured the heaviest subsidies for his line to Liverpool, in which he had four of the finest steamships afloat. Under the authority of an Act of Congress, March third, 1847, a contract was made November first, 1847, with E. K. Collins and his associates, to run a line of steamers twice a month during eight months of the year and once a month during the other four, to carry the mails at an annual rate of pay of 385,000 dollars. The line began to run in 1849. The number of its trips and the rate of compensation were subsequently increased, running up finally to 850,000 dollars per annum.

Four steamers were put afloat, the *Atlantic, Pacific, Baltic,* and *Arctic*, whose internal arrangements were admirably adapted for ocean passenger traffic. They were constructed with a lavish disregard of cost, and fitted with what were at that time considered extraordinary luxuries. Many of the improvements still in use in the trans-Atlantic passenger service date from the Collins line.

On her first voyage the *Atlantic* sailed from the foot of Canal Street, North River, on April twenty-seventh, 1849, and reached England on May tenth, making the trip in less than thirteen days and thereby earning the government subsidy. The steamer *Pacific* was the first ship to cross the ocean inside of ten days. She made the voyage from Liverpool to her dock in New York in nine days and twenty-two hours. In July, 1851, the *Baltic* shortened the trip by five hours and established a record that stood for a number of years.

In the winter of 1852 the *Atlantic* broke her shaft in mid-ocean, was not heard from for forty days, and was given up as lost.* She subsequently arrived safely at Cork, having effected temporary repairs and word of her safety was brought to this country by the Cunard liner *Africa*.

A few years later, the *Adriatic*, the speediest and the last of the Collins Line steamers, was added to the fleet. She was

---

* A great crowd assembled to meet the *Atlantic* upon her return to New York after her apprehended loss. The moment Jenny Lind heard of her arrival, she hastened to the wharf to greet the vessel which had conveyed her to our shores.

built by George Steers, at his yard in East Seventh Street, New York. In connection with the *Adriatic*, Mr. Collins experienced a great disappointment in the installation of an oscillating engine, which was not a success, so that the *Adriatic*, which was of expensive construction, had to be tied up at her pier for a year before the engine was replaced. This was a serious blow to the finances of the Collins Line and it has been stated to have been the turning point in the history of the line. From that time on, one misfortune came upon another.

On September twentieth, 1854, the steamer *Arctic* left Liverpool with a large passenger list, which included the wife, daughter and younger son of Collins. Seven days later, while off Cape Race, Newfoundland, the *Arctic* ran into a fog and was rammed by the French steamer *Vesta*. An endeavor was made to reach land, but the vessel was so badly damaged that she sank with a loss of most of the crew and passengers. The news was not received at New York until two weeks later, and it has been stated that following the receipt of news of the disaster the City of New York was draped in mourning from Bowling Green to Fourteenth Street.

The *Pacific* sailed from Liverpool on September twenty-third, 1856, and was never heard of again. Her fate is one of the unsolved mysteries of the sea. The Collins steamers had records of nine days and thirteen hours to ten days for the passage from New York to Liverpool.

Feeling against the company was increased by the refusal of one of its captains to give passage to a party of two hundred American soldiers who had been carried to Liverpool on a British ship after being shipwrecked en route to the Pacific Coast, and in the following year, through a combination of Southern and Western members of the House and Senate the allowance was further reduced and finally the subsidy was discontinued, so the line decided to withdraw its steamers from the service. Thus ended the first, and with one or two exceptions the last American experiment, until 1893, in trans-Atlantic passenger steamship lines.

PART VIII

THE THIRD PERIOD

1850—1860

VIII

THE THIRD PERIOD

1850–1860

NEW YORK'S MARITIME GREATNESS IS ITS GREATEST HISTORICAL ASSET—ITS RISE AS A SHIPBUILDING CENTER IN THE DECADE, 1851–1860—BIOGRAPHY OF WILLIAM H. WEBB, MASTER SHIPBUILDER—*STAG HOUND*, PIONEER OF THE "CALIFORNIA CLIPPERS"—JAMES GORDON BENNETT DESCRIBES CONDITIONS BY THE WATERSIDE, JANUARY THIRTIETH, 1851—ILLUSTRATING INCREASE OF OUR MARITIME INTERCOURSE WITH FOREIGN COUNTRIES—ANENT COSMOPOLITANISM OF NEW YORK MERCHANT—HISTORY OF "THE CHAMBER OF COMMERCE OF THE STATE OF NEW YORK"—BIOGRAPHICAL SKETCH OF ABIEL ABBOTT LOW, FOUNDER OF THE GREAT MERCANTILE HOUSE OF A. A. LOW AND BROTHERS—CLIPPER SHIP *CHALLENGE*—"BULLY" WATERMAN QUELLS MUTINY—FOUR DIFFERENT SHIPS NAMED *PANAMA*—GEORGE AND NATHANIEL L. GRISWOLD, PROMINENT SOUTH STREET MERCHANTS, MADE MORE MONEY OUTSIDE OF THEIR BUSINESS—*FLYING CLOUD* AND HER COMMANDER, JOSIAH P. CREESY—EXTREME CLIPPER *COMET*—CONTROVERSY OVER SAILING QUALITIES OF BOSTON AND NEW YORK SHIPS—HISTORY OF *NIGHTINGALE*, THE MOST ROMANTIC AND INTERESTING "YANKEE CLIPPER"—COMMODORE JOHN C. STEVENS AND THE YACHT *AMERICA*—MORE THAN A YACHT BUILDER WAS GEORGE STEERS—FIRST AMERICAN SCREW STEAMERS TO CROSS THE ATLANTIC—BRIEF SKETCH OF JOHN ERICSSON—DONALD McKAY, MASTER SHIPBUILDER—WHEN PARTISANS OF THE NEW YORK AND BOSTON CLIPPERS LAID BETS ON THEIR FAVORITES—CLIPPER SHIP RACES 'ROUND THE HORN—BIOGRAPHY OF CAPTAIN LAUCHLAN McKAY—*SOVEREIGN OF THE SEAS*—MARINE INSURANCE UNDERWRITERS WERE ALL-POWERFUL IN THE DAYS OF SAIL—CAPTAIN FRANK SMITH AND THE *MESSENGER*—CLIPPERS LOADING FOR CALIFORNIA, OCTOBER 1852—IT

WAS A TIME NAVIGATORS WERE REAPING BENEFITS OF MAURY'S RESEARCHES—GREAT CALIFORNIA CLIPPER RACE—STRIKE OF STEVEDORES ON NEW YORK WATERFRONT IN 1852—SHIP *TORNADO* STRUCK BY WHIRLWIND—A VOYAGE TO AFRICA, "BLACKBIRDS' WOOL AND IVORY IN THE HOLD"—NEW YORK TRADE CIRCLES FEAR THE PACIFIC COAST ENDANGERING THEIR CITY'S COMMERCIAL SUPREMACY—WILLIAM H. WEBB'S FAMOUS SHIP *YOUNG AMERICA*—"FLYING CRAFT FOR SAN FRANCISCO UP APRIL TWENTY-FOURTH, 1853"—*FLYING SCUD* MAKES ONE OF THE MOST REMARKABLE VOYAGES—HOW SHIPOWNING TRANSACTIONS WERE CONDUCTED IN THE FIFTIES—"SAM" SAMUELS AND THE *DREADNOUGHT*—MAMMOTH CLIPPER *GREAT REPUBLIC*—DESTROYED BY FIRE WITH SHIPS *JOSEPH WALKER* AND *WHITE SQUALL*—REBUILT AND BECOMES PROPERTY OF A. A. LOW AND BROTHERS—HER EVENTFUL CAREER—PACKET SHIPS INCREASE IN TONNAGE—FOURTEEN-DAY PASSAGES TO LIVERPOOL—NAMING SHIPS IN DAYS OF SAIL—*RED JACKET* AND HER COMMANDER—*COMET* MAKES RECORD PASSAGE, SAN FRANCISCO TO NEW YORK—SAN FRANCISCO GLUTTED WITH MERCHANDISE, SO MANY SHIPS ARE DIVERTED TO TRANSATLANTIC TRADE—ANENT FIGUREHEADS—A PUZZLED CAPTAIN—NEW YORK SHIPYARDS ARE AGAIN BUSY—MEDIUM CLIPPERS COME TO THE FORE—YEAR 1855 A TURNING POINT IN AMERICAN MERCHANT MARINE HISTORY—CONGRESS REVERSES ITS POLICY AS TO MAIL SUBSIDIES—AN ENORMOUS TOTAL OF DEEP-SEA SHIPPING IS REGISTERED—FINANCIAL DEPRESSION OF 1857—CALIFORNIA AND OTHER FREIGHTS TUMBLE—NEW YORK'S SHIPYARDS ARE SILENT, AND MERCHANTS FAIL ON EVERY HAND—SOUTHERN POLITICIANS AND WESTERN AGRICULTURAL INTERESTS IN WASHINGTON CRIPPLE DEVELOPMENT OF AMERICAN COMMERCE—COLLINS STEAMSHIP LINE COLLAPSES—WHY BRITISH SHIPPING STEADILY ADVANCED WHILE AMERICAN COMMERCE AND SHIPPING WENT DOWN—NEW YORK'S COMMERCIAL PROGRESS MAKES IMPROVEMENTS OF HER DOCKS NECESSARY—WHEN MR. NEW YORK CITIZEN WITH HIS FAMILY WOULD STROLL DOWN TO THE WATERFRONT TO SEE HIS FAVORITE SHIP—HOUSE FLAGS OF PROMINENT NEW YORK MERCHANTS—ADVERSE LEGISLATION CHECKS GROWTH OF SHIPPING, AMERICAN OCEAN STEAMSHIP TRADE FALLS OFF ENORMOUSLY, 1857 AND 1858—SHIPPING BUSINESS IN THE DOLDRUMS—TWO SAILORMEN LOOKING FOR A JOB ALONG SOUTH STREET—LAYING THE ATLANTIC CABLE—SUDDENLY THE CABLE SNAPPED—SECOND ATTEMPT MADE WITH S.S. *NIAGARA*—AGAIN FAILURE, ENTERPRISE ABAN-

The Third Period

DONED, 1857—AUGUST SIXTEENTH, 1858, SUCCESSFUL LAYING OF CABLE ANNOUNCED—NEW YORK HILARIOUS WITH EXCITEMENT—ALARMING NEWS! "CABLE OUT OF ORDER!"—AMERICAN SHIP CHANTING HER "LORELEI" IN NOVEMBER, 1859—N. L. AND G. GRISWOLD OFFER THEIR SHIP *PERKINS* FOR SALE—WHEN THE SAILOR HAD HIS HOME IN NEW YORK DURING THE DAYS OF SAILING SHIPS—DESCRIPTION OF CHERRY AND WATER STREETS, SEAMEN'S BOARDING HOUSES, VILE DENS, AND SO FORTH—WITH THEIR PASSAGE WENT CRIMPS, BLOOD MONEY AND SHANGHAIING—THE STEAMSHIP *GREAT EASTERN* ARRIVES AT NEW YORK—A FEW PARTICULARS OF THE LARGEST VESSEL EVER BUILT UP TO 1860—WAS AN UNLUCKY SHIP—BRIEF SKETCH OF HER CAREER—CHIEF SOURCES OF OUR EXPORT WEALTH AGRICULTURAL—SOME FIGURES *RE* AMERICAN EXPORTS AND IMPORTS, WHEN DISCRIMINATING DUTIES WERE IN FORCE—ABANDONED IN FAVOR OF RECIPROCITY—THE SQUARE-RIGGED SHIP ADVANCED COMMERCE AND INDUSTRY—HELD ON AS "CARGO CARRIERS" AGAINST STEAM VESSELS—NEW YORK DREW ITS ADOLESCENT STRENGTH IN DAYS OF SAIL—TABLE ILLUSTRATING FOREIGN SHIPPING AT THE PORT OF NEW YORK—ONE OF NEW YORK'S GREATEST MERCHANTS, ABIEL A. LOW, MAKES A STATEMENT OF THE CAUSE THAT RUINED THE AMERICAN MERCHANT MARINE—WHEN THE PARADE OF SOUTHERN STATES OUT OF THE UNION BEGAN—NEW YORK MERCHANTS AND SHIPPING MEN SEE OUR DEEP-SEA TONNAGE DECLINE, SOME TIME PREVIOUS TO CIVIL WAR—WHEN THE WAR BECAME A CERTAINTY, NEW YORK WHARVES WERE WORTH SEEING—HER SHIPPING TAKEN UP UNDER CHARTER OR SOLD TO UNITED STATES GOVERNMENT—CIVIL WAR CAUSED A HALT IN AMERICAN OVERSEAS STEAMSHIP OPERATION—MISTAKEN MEASURES, BAD ADMINISTRATION, UNFORTUNATE SECTIONAL STRIFE, CIVIL WAR, AND PARTY SPIRIT SET AT NAUGHT THE WORK OF THE FATHERS UNDER THE CONSTITUTION!

THE Maritime Greatness of New York is its Greatest Historical Asset. Time was when our maritime development found us in the very forefront among the great powers. Sometimes, perhaps, we are carried away by our sentiment and set too great a store on accomplishments of the past. This may be a human failing, but, after all, nothing is worth while without a background. The history of New York furnishes such a background, especially during the Clipper Epoch, when both shores of the East River were lined with shipyards whose products have never been equaled in all the world, and her shipbuilders lifted the fabrication of vessels from the level of a journeyman's trade to the plane of an exact science. The ships we built, like the "runs" they made, were "quite beyond compare." Our starred banner was then the talisman of the earth's commerce and enthroned this nation as Mistress of the Seas! To have suggested in the days of our maritime effulgence that a half century later the seas would know us not, that the Stars and Stripes would be the rarest flag ever seen upon the seven seas and in the busiest ports of the world, would have provoked only ironical jeers or pitying contempt! Were we then in the chrysalis state, and now, when our American deep sea marine is ingloriously fading, are we full-fledged butterflies?

One notable event of the decade between 1851 and 1860 was the rise of New York as a shipbuilding center. Earlier in the century, Boston and the East had had the lion's share of sail-construction. But the New York merchants who owned and managed the successful packet lines preferred to have their fine ships built under their own eyes as far as possible. The long range of yards which had grown up along the East River were supplemented, when the ocean mail contracts were let to New York bidders, by several iron-working plants for the production of marine machinery. Not only the Collins and Pacific Mail liners, but the majority of the coastwise steamships were built at New York, and many high-class sailing vessels. For several years before the Civil War ten thousand workmen were called to their labors every morning by the clang of the shipyard bells. William H. Webb and one or two other masterbuilders employed each more than a thousand of the most intelligent and skillful mechanics whom the country had ever known, and the East River shipyards often had at the same time twenty or thirty great vessels on the stocks awaiting completion.

Some of the clippers were fully rigged on the stocks and launched with skysail-yards across, then hurried to their loading berths, where cargoes were shipped day and night, and when captains got to sea they never let up on their ships or crews till the Golden Gate was over the taffrail and the anchor on the ground in San Francisco Bay. It was drive, drive, drive, and

William H. Webb,
New York's Most Famous
Clipper Ship Builder.
From an old print in the author's posses

William H. Webb's Old Office.
From an old print in the author's possession.

the captain who made the fastest passage was the hero of the hour.

In the construction of many of these vessels of great speed, and capacity too, William Henry Webb took a leading part. At his yard, which extended from the foot of Fifth Street to Seventh Street, East River, he launched, during the year 1851, the *Challenge, Invincible, Comet, Gazelle,* and *Sword-Fish,* five in all, out of the total of thirty-one clippers that were launched in the whole country.

It would be impossible to name the handsomest of these ships, for while they were all of the same general design, each possessed her special type of beauty; and beauty, as we all know, is elusive, depending largely on fashion and individual taste. In order to attract the favorable attention of shippers and to secure the highest rates of freight, it was necessary that these ships should be handsome as well as swift. Ship-owners were content to spend large sums of money, not only upon refined decoration, which was but a small portion of the expense, but also in carefully selected woods, such as India teak and Spanish mahogany for deck fittings, and in the finest shipwright's and joiner's work about the decks, which were marvels of neatness and finish. Shipbuilders certainly had every incentive to exercise their best skill upon these vessels; they received very largely their own prices for building them, and each ship, as she sailed out upon the ocean, held in her keeping the reputation of her builder, to whom a quick passage meant fame and fortune.

The first vessel built by William H. Webb as masterbuilder was the brig *Malek-Adhel,* of 120 tons, in 1840, for the Pacific Ocean trade. She was a handsome vessel and fast sailer, and aided in establishing him as a marine architect.

A new era in the art of building sailing vessels at New York began in the decade 1840-1850 with a more perfect development of the famous Baltimore clipper. The New York shipbuilders had already become preëminent as constructors of fast sailing vessels for the merchant marine. The Liverpool packets built by the Webbs (father and son) and by other New York shipbuilders were the fastest sailing packet-ships of that class in the world. They had attained a speed and a regularity in their voyages in point of time almost equal to that of steamships. Fourteen and sixteen days was the average time occupied by some of them in voyages between New York and Liverpool. They carried double crews before the labor-saving invention of double topsails appeared.

The urgent requirements of the East India trade at the middle of this decade, and the rushing stream of emigration to California after the discovery of gold in its bosom, called for faster sailing vessels and transportation, so American inventive genius soon produced a greater development of the clipper principle in naval architecture. New York built vessels soon reached a higher point of excellence than had ever before been attained, and William H. Webb stood foremost among those master-mechanics who developed the clipper ship from its inception until it reached the acme of perfection, say in 1853, when he designed and built the *Young America*.

When Mr. Webb constructed the *Helena*, in 1841, for the China trade, her sharp lines drew considerable comment, as did his ship *Montauk*, which he built for A. A. Low and Brother, and the *Panama*, for account of N. L. and G. Griswold. During the year 1843 two famous packets were launched from Webb's shipyard, the *Montezuma*, of 916 tons, and *Yorkshire*, 1,165 tons; each earned renown by doing the eastward passage, New York to Liverpool, in fourteen days, and that more than once. The *Yorkshire* made the shortest western passage, sixteen days, in November 1846. In March 1845, this ship made the run in twenty-one days, the shortest up to that time.

In 1847 Mr. Webb built for Charles H. Marshall and others the steamship *United States* for the New Orleans trade, but it was sold to the German Confederation and altered into a powerful vessel of war by Mr. Webb. The next year he built the steam vessel *California* for the Pacific Mail Steamship Company. It was the first steamer to enter the Golden Gate and the harbor of San Francisco. He also built the three steamships which carried the first regular United States mail between this country, Japan and China—New York and Aspinwall, and Panama to San Francisco, and thence to Yokohama and Hongkong.

To enumerate all the important vessels that have been

constructed by William H. Webb during his career of thirty years as a master shipbuilder would be a tedious task. However, we may mention the *Guy Mannering* (Liverpool packet), the first full three-deck merchant vessel built in this country; and the ship *Ocean Monarch*, possessing the greatest freight capacity of any ever constructed up to her time, which often received on board over seven thousand bales of cotton at one loading.

From the day of the cargo ship, carrying passengers purely as an accommodation, to the time when emigrants in considerable numbers were anxious to get to this country, the packet ship had developed into the highest class of passenger vessel in the year 1850, when the last of the Black Ball liners, *Isaac Webb*, of 1,800 tons, was launched from William H. Webb's shipyard.

With marked boldness of conception and unfaltering energy, William H. Webb determined to "solve the problem of combined speed, capacity, and strength." In 1851 he put upon the stocks four clipper ships designed for this purpose. These were the *Sword Fish*, of 1,150 tons, which established the record between Shanghai and San Francisco by sailing the distance between those ports in thirty-one days, making an average of 240 miles a day; the *Comet*, 1,209 tons, "remarkable for speed, seaworthiness, strength, productiveness, and good luck"—(the round trip to San Francisco was made by her in seven months and nine days; the run home was made in seventy-six days, the shortest time on record)—the *Challenge*, of 2,000 tons; and the *Invincible*, of 2,150 tons. It is said of the *Challenge*, that "when lying at the foot of Pine Street, her bowsprit at high tide reached over the roofs of the stores on South Street and crowds went down to see her."

Of the eight extreme clipper ships launched from the Webb yard between 1850 and 1853 the *Challenge, Comet* and *Young America* were the largest and are the best known. The other five, *Celestial, Gazelle, Sword-Fish, Invincible* and *Flying Dutchman*, though smaller, were also regarded as excellent specimens of marine architecture, and the run, bow, shear, masting and general appearance of a Webb clipper were always the subject of favorable comment, no handsomer appearing vessels being seen anywhere. Of the eight, the *Celestial* (1850) was the first, as she was also the first clipper to be built expressly for the California trade, then in its infancy; and the *Young America* was the last to be put afloat. Their builder, however, subsequently constructed vessels which, although not clippers, yet established sailing records to be proud of, particularly the *Intrepid* (built in 1856, lost in 1860) and the *Black Hawk*.

In 1857, Mr. Webb built for the United States Government the *Harriet Lane* (named in honor of the niece of the bachelor President Buchanan, who was the accomplished "lady of the White House"), the first steam revenue vessel constructed for our government. The contract was awarded to him in competition with twenty-two other shipbuilders. It was the first competition of the kind ever held in this country. The vessel was a noted one. She was destroyed by the insurgents off the harbor of Galveston in 1862.

During the Civil War he built for the United States Government the steam-ram *Dunderberg*, 7,200 tons displacement, the largest iron clad vessel then built; her speed was unequaled by any vessel of war, being fifteen knots at sea, fully armed and in commission. She mounted twenty-two guns of enormous caliber in casemates. The Rebellion ended before she was completed, and the government had no immediate use for her. The combined governments of Peru and Chili were then at war with Spain, and they offered 5,000,000 dollars, United States currency, for her delivered, full armored, in the harbor of Valparaiso. He offered to refund to our government the money already paid, but it refused to release him, unwilling to have the most powerful vessel of war in the world leave the country. William H. Webb afterward obtained a law of Congress relieving him from the contract on equitable conditions, and he sold the *Dunderberg* to the Emperor Napoleon for 2,500,000 dollars, delivered in New York. The French admiral sent a French crew to man her for an Atlantic voyage, but, afraid to undertake the task, he made arrangements with Mr. Webb to deliver her in the port of Cherbourg. This was done by an American crew, under the command of Captain Joseph W. Comstock, with Mr. Webb on board. She arrived

Clipper Ship "Challenge" Just Previous to Being Launched at William H. Webb's Shipyard. — 1851.

at Cherbourg after a rough passage of fourteen days and her name was then changed to *Rochambeau.*

In 1866 Mr. Webb built the magnificent coast steam-vessels *Bristol* and *Providence,* to ply between New York and Newport. They were his first effort in this class of vessels. They were built at a cost of 1,200,000 dollars each. The *Bristol* was 375 feet in length and of 3,000 tons burden. She had four tiers of staterooms, and 1,200 berths. These steamboats were unrivaled in speed and best sea-going qualities at the time, and in appointments they were considered veritable palaces afloat.

To William H. Webb should be given the honor of launching the last square-rigged ship built in New York. This was the three-decker *Charles H. Marshall,* May twenty-sixth, 1869. She was a large carrier and proved herself a good sea boat.

Besides the building of ships Mr. Webb was largely engaged in other enterprises. He was a large stockholder of the Panama Railway at the time of its construction, but sold out long after its completion at an enormous profit. After his retirement from shipbuilding he was engaged in running steamships to California, the Sandwich Islands, New Zealand, and Australia for several years. He was the first to establish an American line of steamers to these far off countries. It was done with a view to controlling the trade which had enriched them, and to bring it to the United States. He tried to interest his own government in the enterprise, but although President Grant recommended it in two messages, Congress could not be made to see its advantages. He obtained subsidies from New Zealand and Victoria, the first ever accorded by British subjects to an American line of steamers. The enterprise proving unprofitable, the ships were withdrawn.

At the age of fifty-six Mr. Webb withdrew from active business life, and lived quietly at his beautiful and picturesquely situated country seat, *Waldheim,* at Tarrytown-on-the-Hudson. He built and endowed the Webb Academy and Home for Shipbuilders, Fordham Heights, New York. He died in New York City, October thirtieth, 1899.

The *Stag Hound* was the pioneer of the "Extreme" Clipper Fleet, vessels that were distinguished there and then by the name "California Clippers." She was launched December seventh, 1850, and according to the contract in sixty days from the signing of the documents. Her model was an "original" and she was designed and built by Donald McKay, at East Boston.

This ship arrived at New York in tow of the Boston tug *R. B. Forbes* on December thirty-first, 1850, and the following day was placed on the Sectional Dock, Pike Street, to be calked and metaled. Her loading berth was at the foot of Wall Street, there being no ferry there, and she went under the command of Captain Josiah Richardson, who had the name of being a skillful navigator, and was highly regarded in New York and Boston shipping circles.

The lines of the *Stag Hound* were so much sharper than those of any ship which had been built previously that some of the oldest and most conservative authorities were doubtful of her stability and seaworthiness. It was dubbed by the knowing ones at the times to be rash, stupid, and so forth, and in fact so much was said in criticism of the *Stag Hound* that the marine underwriters on her first voyage charged additional premiums to insure her, for she was thought to be an extra hazardous risk.

California freights were booming then and her outward cargo to San Francisco had been secured at about one dollar and forty cents per cubic foot, her freight list exceeding 70,000 dollars. Her homeward cargo of tea was sold at auction by Haggerty, Draper and Jones and a few days after, when the earnings of the voyage had been computed it was found that the ship had been absent ten months, twenty-three days and that she had paid for herself and divided among her owners over 80,000 dollars. At New York Captain Richardson left the ship to take the new clipper *Staffordshire*, belonging to his former employers, Train and Company, and was afterwards lost in that vessel.

In the spring of 1861 the *Stag Hound* was thoroughly overhauled and placed on a New York berth for a voyage to London, expecting on arriving at that port to obtain an Australian charter, and in order to facilitate matters a first-class skipper was placed in command. Now it so happened that James Gordon Bennett, hearing of the expected sailing of the *Stag Hound*, conceived the idea that there might be a possibility of the vessel reaching London before the regular mail steamer, and so he made arrangements with the captain and owners to take a copy of Lincoln's First Inaugural Address, promising that if the *Stag Hound* delivered the message in advance of the mail packet a very handsome prize would be given. The *Stag Hound* sailed from New York early Sunday morning, March third, with the precious document on board. The mail steamer *America* left Boston harbor on the afternoon tide of March sixth. The *Stag Hound* arrived off Gravesend March eighteenth. The captain hastened forward the telegraphic message to London of the inaugural address, as directed by James Gordon Bennett, and was over half-way through when word came that they were receiving a similar message via Liverpool from the steamship *America*, which had just arrived, and stopped short the message via the *Stag Hound*. The captain claimed his reward, as it was proved conclusively that the message by the *Stag Hound* was in the hands of the telegraph operator some short time ahead of the one sent by the *America* via Liverpool. The captain got the prize.

On Thursday, the thirtieth of January, 1851, James Gordon Bennett walked down by the waterside. While the entertainment afforded in the cabins of a clipper ship did not then possess the unique value that it would today, Bennett seems to have combined business with pleasure in a satisfactory manner. He records:

"We yesterday paid a visit to this beautiful craft (the clipper ship 'Gazelle'), lying at Peck slip, where she will take freight for California and China. We have seen many of this kind of vessels lately and all of the first class; but we have never met with one that came nearer to our idea of a skimmer of the wave than does the 'Gazelle.' She was constructed upon the same principle as the far-famed 'Celestial,' and by the same builder (Mr. Wm. H. Webb, of this city), but is much sharper —everything, excepting the due and proper regard for strength, being made secondary to speed.

"Shippers by the 'Celestial' were able to make their payments from returns for goods sent out, before their bills became due—such is the extraordinary speed of that vessel; and yet the 'Gazelle's' trip to San Francisco is confidently expected by many to exceed that of the 'Celestial.'

"The 'Gazelle' has a dead rise of forty inches—nearly as much as any ship ever built—with very fine lines below, which gives her the power of sailing very fast in light winds; at the same time, her great breadth at deep-load line, carried well forward and aft, combined with her deep keel, will enable her to carry a very great press of canvas in strong winds, at the same time keeping her well above water, and preventing her pitching deep in heavy weather, and enabling her to scud at all times.

"She has a very small and short cutwater, or head, totally different from the old style—which, on account of the great length, was very objectionable—and has but little ornamental carving. The cutwater is fitted or framed in the ship in so strong a manner that it will require an extraordinarily heavy sea to displace any portion of it. Her stern is very small, but carried high up out of water, and ornamented with a carved representation of a gazelle. She has but few mouldings outside, and her round, swelling sides, small and beautifully turned cutwater, and light, airy stern—the outline of which is perfection itself—gives her hull a most neat and graceful appearance."

In 1851 New York City was, and had been for some years previously, the great emporium of the western world, the very heart of commerce, whose pulsations were felt and responded to in every section of the Union. But it was not wise to rely upon its natural advantages, which made the city preeminent in the inducements it offered to commercial enterprise. It was not enough that wharves and piers should be provided for the accommodation of the fleets of sailing vessels. Accommodation should also be provided for ocean steamers, the number of which had increased with a rapidity unparalleled in the history of the world. The immense increase of our maritime intercourse with foreign countries is well illustrated by the following comparative figures of the tonnage employed in the foreign trade:

1840

Number of vessels	2,048
Tons	570,425
Men employed	23,008

1850

Number of vessels	3,233
Tons	1,178,598
Men employed	45,359

Nevertheless the tonnage of British and American steamships registered for the deep-sea trade in 1851 was practically equal—65,921 British and 62,391 American. A considerable portion of this tonnage lay in the steamships of the Pacific Mail Company. By 1855 the tonnage of American steamships had grown from the small beginning of 16,068 in 1848 to its maximum point prior to the Civil War, 115,045.

In the old Dutch days the traveler noted that ten languages were spoken on Manhattan Island, that eighteen pieces of gold coinage of the mintage of different nations circulated here. At the beginning of the nineteenth century Spanish was the language of commerce, and the knowledge of French not an exceptional acquirement in New York. Yet in the colonial days there were few who could really be called merchants who owned their vessels and their cargoes, who traded to distant ports with their merchandise, who sold in bulk and rarely condescended to retail their cargoes. The colonial warehouses in Hanover Square held a motley stock: hogsheads of sugar and molasses hobnobbed with pipes of brandy and rum and Madeira, and about every conceivable article of hardware in close companionship. Later this was changed, and commerce settled on regular lines. After 1817 the merchant became exclusive, and no man was admitted into the Chamber of Commerce unless engaged in foreign trade.

At the close of the eighteenth century and some years thereafter, the London and Liverpool merchant, the Amsterdam merchant, the Turkey merchant, the Spaniards who traded on the Spanish Main—all had their peculiar characteristics, and were typical of their races. The New York merchant, trading with them all, was more cosmopolitan than any one of them. Of that race of men who enjoyed a world-wide fame over a period of many years, it may perhaps be said that they were superior to those of any foreign nation. Not a few were college-bred at Yale or Columbia; not a few had made the continental tour, and thus joined culture to enterprise. The plain, terse, telling English contained in New York's Chamber of Commerce records is unexcelled by the documents of our statesmen, our lawyers, or our jurists.

That important institution now known as "The Chamber of Commerce of the State of New York" was founded as long ago as the year 1768, by twenty merchants who associated "for the purpose of promoting and extending all just and lawful commerce." From an interesting little booklet issued recently by the Chamber of Commerce, written by its very able librarian, L. Elsa Loeber, we further note:

"The twenty gentlemen who met in the Long Room of Fraunces Tavern and, with four not-present colleagues, formed the unique commercial body, were the recognized leaders of the business, social and political life of New York City. Many became historic personages, and their names endure to the present day in descendants, and in the nomenclature of New York City streets. They were opposed to England's high-handed measures, but had no thought of breaking with her, and, through the Acting Lieutenant Governor of the Colony, Cadwallader Colden, they petitioned for and received a charter from King George III, in 1770.

"The successful opposition to the Stamp Act gave impetus to the idea of a permanent organization for the protection and promotion of business interests. If the unorganized co-operation of the merchants of the city could produce such important results it was evident that a formal and close-knitted body could produce even greater results in the promotion of the peaceful pursuits of commerce. And the very nature of the grievances which first had united them, probably made the founders realize that a body entirely separated from, and independent of, government control would be distinctly advantageous. Hence the formation of a Chamber of Commerce which differed so greatly from the kind already functioning in other cities of the world.

"In spite of the fact that tax problems were partly responsible for its origin, the Chamber seems not to have concerned itself very much with them in the pre-Revolutionary period. Instead, it concentrated its energies and attention on matters closely affecting business and commerce. It recognized the tremendous natural endowment of the port and foresaw the possibilities of its future greatness. The work that was done in these years laid the foundations on which New York's present supremacy is built. Laxity in business methods and lack of leadership in New York had made Philadelphia and Boston the more important ports. The members of the Chamber, therefore, felt that to establish principles of fair dealing, to improve the quality of exported articles, and to eliminate fraud in the handling of goods at the port must be their first concern if they would surpass their rivals.

"The Revolutionary War presented an interlude in the activities of the Chamber, during which meetings were held irregularly and few members were added to the lists. With the close of the war and the resumption of trade the organization took up its interrupted existence. It welcomed back to its membership those who, either from necessity or choice, had left the city for the duration of the war, and it reincorporated under the laws of the newly formed State of New York as the Chamber of Commerce of the State of New York, which is the name it has used ever since. The powers conferred by the new charter were somewhat broader than they had been under the royal charter and the Chamber's sphere of influence was somewhat widened.

"Its form of government is practically the only one of its early traditions which the Chamber has retained. A student of manners and customs of the colonial and revolutionary periods will find in the records numerous illuminating details. To members of the present day these are amusing by reason of their contrast with current customs. The meetings were held monthly at six o'clock in a 'Proper room—provided at the expense of the members so that it doth not exceed one shilling per man, which each person is to pay to the Treasurer at their respective meetings.' The members talked over and debated the subjects before them as they sat around a table and smoked their pipes, ate bread and cheese, and drank beer, all of which items, including the pipes and tobacco, the Treasurer was empowered to provide.

"In any commercial community transportation is a subject of great interest. New York City has had to concern itself not alone with the handling of freight and passengers to and from distant points, but has had, as well, the tremendous problem of local transit. The New York Chamber has played an important rôle in the solution of both of these problems. It has given its best efforts and large sums of money in making and in maintaining New York's supremacy. The inauguration and development of canals and railroads have always claimed its interest. The Erie Canal and the Erie Railroad were projects which had its enthusiastic support. Later, when the first transcontinental railroad was proposed, the Chamber bent every effort to aid in the realization of the scheme. Again, through all the intricacies of an always intricate freight rate situation it has staunchly stood for New York's rights and has materially aided in the establishment and maintenance of an equitable freight rate structure. Local and selfish interests have many times been attributed to projects which the Chamber has approved in this connection, but the Chamber itself has always emphasized the broader application and pointed out that any scheme which aided New York's commercial facilities and importance must inevitably be followed by benefit to the entire country.

"No other organization has survived continuously over a period of one hundred and sixty-six years as has the Chamber of Commerce of the State of New York. It has never deviated from the fundamental purpose for which it was formed; its field of action has varied and matters have been approached from whatever angles the exigencies of the times and the particular situation demanded; it has strictly adhered to a policy which was first voiced in a report made in 1851: 'If we speak upon every topic we shall soon cease to be heard upon any. The Chamber cannot step out of its true path without lessening its dignity, impairing its usefulness and detracting from the weight of its judgment.'

"The attributes which have secured this permanence and remarkable success to the New York Chamber of Commerce may be briefly summarized. It has met a real commercial need; it has adhered strictly to the sphere of duty assigned by its founders; within its sphere it has rendered essential service

Abiel Abbott Low.

Captain Charles Henry Marshall

to the community and to public interests; it has maintained a high standard of business dealing; it has brought to bear enlightened judgment on all subjects which have been submitted to it; it has sought to gain its ends by appeal only to the best in the citizenry of the city and the Nation."

Salem was the home of the great East India merchants, whose enterprise, long broken up by the embargo and the second war with Great Britain, had again, after the treaty of Ghent, revived; and it was natural in such an atmosphere for a bright, ambitious youth to seek fortune in a career enticing to his imagination. Permitted to follow the bent of his mind, Abiel Abbott Low became a clerk in the house of Joseph Howard and Company, who traded from Salem to South America, and soon won the confidence and esteem of his employers by his conduct and business aptitude.

In 1829, he came to New York, where his father was established in the drug trade. But the Orient drew him with its promises of fortune, so in 1833, he sailed for Canton and entered the employ of Russell and Company, the largest American house in China, where his uncle, William Henry Low, was a partner. In 1837, he was admitted into the firm, and three years later, having made a fortune, he returned to this country.

Soon after his arrival at New York, he began business on his own account in Fletcher Street and laid the foundation of the great house of A. A. Low and Brothers. Familiar with every branch of the China trade, and generally with the details of the shipping business, his operations soon assumed such proportions that he began the construction of a great fleet of clippers, that "paved the way" between this port and those of the Far East: *Houqua, Montauk, Samuel Russell, Surprise, Oriental, N. B. Palmer, Contest, Jacob Bell, David Brown, Penguin, Benefactor* and *Maury* or *Benefactress*. Later he purchased several other vessels, among which were the *Golden State*, the *Yokohama, Sunda*, and the *Great Republic*—the wonder of the age—which he purchased from Captain N. B. Palmer, who bought her from the underwriters, after she was burnt, and then he had her rebuilt, putting her in the Liverpool trade, whence she was soon loading stores at Marseilles and carrying French troops in the Crimean War, after which she drifted into the California and other trades. Not until the *Alabama*, "that fatal barque, built in the eclipse and freighted with curses dark," began her depredations, did A. A. Low and Brothers lose a single vessel. Then in quick succession two were burned, one of which, the *Jacob Bell*, had a cargo of great value.

In 1845 he took his younger brother, Josiah O. Low, into partnership, and later his brother-in-law, Edward H. R. Lyman, but Abiel's leadership is reflected in the firm name of A. A. Low and Brothers. A third brother, Charles P. Low, commanded three of their ships, the *Houqua*, named after that celebrated Chinese merchant who proved himself a staunch friend of Americans; then the *Samuel Russell*, named for the eminent American merchant, founder of the house in China, with whom the brothers Low began their careers; and, lastly, the *N. B. Palmer*, which Captain Low took out, from the time she went down the ways until she was sold abroad in 1872. It was not long before the Lows had wrested the primacy in New York's China trade from the Griswolds. The counting house of the firm was for a long time on Burling Slip, and Mr. Low's residence was a fine house which he built on Brooklyn Heights, overlooking the East River, and from its windows he could see his ships come in or go out to sea, on their long, long voyages to China, California and other far distant places.

Abiel A. Low's association with the Chamber of Commerce of the State of New York covered nearly half a century. He was elected to membership in December 1846. At that period the institution, though always of great influence, was limited in numbers and in the scope of its work, yet it was the representative merchant body of the United States. By general accord, though by no charter limitation, its membership was confined to those who owned ships with occasional exceptions to those to whom cargoes were consigned. Every generation has the right of its own development and follows the line of its progress and growth, regardless of tradition; of this the generation which is now parting from the stage, is a fair example, and the broader scope and larger membership of the "Chamber" are a sequence of the changed nature of our business, in which commerce or the dealing with foreign countries has been relegated to a second place, and the interchange of our home industries has come to the front.

Abiel A. Low was the last of those great merchants who continued the traditions of the older school, the Howlands and Aspinwalls, Goodhues, Stevens, Griswolds, Minturns and Grinnells. They had succeeded the LeRoys, Bayards and Rays; the elder Lenoxes, in their turn, passed to their "final accounting," while Mr. Low was yet in his prime. Such he was, a Saul among the Prophets, in the full vigor of his admirable health, and at the height of his intellectual power, when summoned to the meeting of the Bank of Commerce to make provision for the payment of the interest on the debt of the United States due January 1861, and to save the distracted nation from default in the payment of a sum which our modern financiers would consider a "quantité negligeable." From this time forward, the Bank of Commerce, of which John Austin Stevens was President and Mr. Low from January 1854, a Director, led the way in the aid of the U. S. Treasury Department, in its colossal task of providing for the movement of the great armies which marched to sustain our national integrity.

The year 1858 was one of the greatest interest to New York; it was the year in which the Atlantic Cable was laid. Mr. Low had been active among those gentlemen who held up the hands of Cyrus Field and through good report and evil report had been steadily loyal to the great enterprise. The name of Abiel Abbott Low should be indissolubly connected with that of Mr. Field from the address which he made before the New York Chamber of Commerce, in August, 1858, on moving the resolutions of congratulation to the conceiver of the scheme. On this occasion, Mr. Low first disclosed that power of happy construction and of apposite illustration, which combined with a manner of mingled dignity and grace and a voice of winning melody, marked him as one of the best equipped and pleasing speakers of the day.

In 1860, our affairs with the eastern nations received a fresh impetus from the arrival of the Embassy from Japan to arrange for trade with that interesting country, which the peaceful triumph of Commodore Matthew C. Perry had opened to the outer world. A series of queries was arranged and presented to the Ambassadors. In their reply they stated that tea was an extensive product of their country, but that they doubted whether the quality of their growth would meet the American taste. But they were not only surprised, but delighted when Mr. Low informed them that he had already received samples and the quality was approved; and immediately after Mr. Low was the pioneer of this now important trade, which for some years he continued to the advantage of our own people and his own great profit.

At the annual meeting of 1863, Abiel Abbott Low was unanimously chosen President of the New York Chamber of Commerce, to succeed Pelatiah Perit, who had presided over the deliberations of the "Chamber" for eleven years; was now well advanced in age and no longer a resident of the City, having withdrawn from the old South Street mercantile house of Goodhue and Company.

Abiel Abbott Low has been called the last of our old style merchants. The diversion of the carrying trade had something to do with the disappearance of this great race, but Mr. Low ascribed the decline to quite another cause and that cause the very ocean telegraph which he helped to establish. When the petty trader who aspired to the honors of importation could at any time with a banker's credit send a cable dispatch and purchase his five chests of tea in Shanghai, the business of the merchant who bought whole "chops" and by his skill and enterprise placed whole cargoes on the market, was forever gone. What need now of those elegant clippers of polished wood, dainty with their snow white sheets and polished brass mountings? Their mission was gone. The improvements of science bringing the consumer into close relations with the producer enabled the petty trader to supply himself at first hand. It may be for the general benefit, but it destroyed the majesty of commerce. Mr. Low resigned his position as President of the Chamber of Commerce, on the twenty-fifth of November, 1866, and left for San Francisco the next day, for a journey around the world.

To the close of his long life Abiel Abbott Low preserved his personal vitality. The erectness of his carriage, the firmness of his step, as he would be seen wending his way from his counting house in Burling Slip to the regular meetings of the officers of the Bank of Commerce and of the Chamber of Commerce for which he had an almost parental regard, always drew attentive admiration. When Mr. Low died, his native city, Salem, Massachusetts, took full and official notice of his demise, half-masting the flags on its public buildings, and so forth, for he, who, in the full exuberance of youthful ardor, had left Salem's limited and depreciating commercial environment to seek a career elsewhere, had achieved wealth and world-wide fame as the most eminent merchant of the Metropolis of the Western World.

In 1850, the firm of N. L. and G. Griswold, prominent merchants of New York, decided to have a vessel built that would surpass anything at that time afloat as regards tonnage and speed, and to be in every respect a masterpiece in marine architecture. Mr. William H. Webb was commissioned to turn out a vessel meeting with the above requirements, the only stipulation being that she must be the best, if not the fastest, sailing vessel in the world. In order that the vessel might comply with the above specifications, every piece of timber was selected with the greatest care, the spars were the finest money could buy, and only the most skillful mechanics were employed in her construction. It is said there was no restriction placed on her cost, the owners only contracting for results, and relying upon the builder's experience and reputation for the success of the enterprise. The cost of her construction was about 120,000 dollars.

The vessel was launched on May 24th, 1851, and her name, the *Challenge*, embodied the idea actuating the minds of those responsible for the venture, expressive of the determination to occupy no secondary position on the seas, but to continue to demonstrate to the world that American ships and American shipbuilders were able to successfully meet and defy all competition.

Her initial trip was to be from New York to San Francisco and every effort was made to insure its success. Captain Robert H. Waterman, formerly of the *Sea Witch*, was secured as her commander. She sailed on July thirteenth, 1851, with a freight list of 60,000 dollars and a bonus of 10,000 dollars promised if she reached San Francisco in ninety days. Her manifest is said to have been twenty-eight feet long. Wind, weather and other conditions did not favor the vessel and she was 108 days reaching her destination, good time for the season of year, but hardly meeting expectations. There was a mutiny when the vessel was off Rio, and according to a letter said to have been written by Captain Waterman to a friend, fifty of the crew attacked the mate, with the intention, according to their confession, of killing him and afterwards the captain. The mate had been stabbed and badly beaten when Captain Waterman came to his rescue, striking three of them down, and quelling the mutiny, eight of the crew being flogged by the captain for their part in the affair. Seven of the crew died on the voyage, three as a result of falling from the mizzenmast, and four from dysentery.

On her arrival many wild statements were made reflecting on the captain and his officers, even to the extent of asserting that men at work aloft had been shot at and that they had been shaken from the rigging overboard. A mob, incited by irresponsible agitators, collected about the ship, and in the absence of Captain Waterman, who was uptown, seized the new master, Captain John Land, who had been sent out by the owners to take command, and threatened to shoot, hang or drown him unless Captain Waterman were turned over to them. At this stage of the proceedings the Vigilance Committee, which was then in charge of the police affairs of the city, interposed; the mob was dispersed; Captain Waterman and Mate Douglas were tried and honorably acquitted of all charges of brutal or unjust treatment.

Among other well known vessels of the Griswold fleet may be noted four different ships named *Panama*. All were the products of New York shipyards, Number One, of about 500 tons, being built by Isaac Webb about 1830; Number Two, of 612 tons, was built by William H. Webb in 1844; Number Three, of 1,139 tons, a clipper, came from the yard of Thomas Collyer in 1853, while Number Four, of 738 tons, was built by Ward and Bell in 1868. The operations of the four covered a long period of time, all being very successful and being

"George Griswold" Packet Ship—Receiving Supplies for the Relief of the Starving Poor of England, at Pier 9, East River, N. Y. — 1860. From an old print in the author's possession.

replaced as worn out. They made much money for the house of Griswold in the China trade, their tea cargoes being marked "Ship 'Panama'—N.L. & G.G.," after which they were diverted to other trades.

Singular as it may seem, both George and Nathaniel L. Griswold made a great deal more money outside of their business than in it. "Old Nat," as he was affectionately called on South Street, became interested in a dredging machine. He went up to Albany and secured a contract to dredge Albany Basin and also a bar in the river obstructing navigation, clearing up about 100,000 dollars on the contract. He used this dredger at various slips and other places in and around New York harbor. Then he built some of these dredging machines and sent them South to work. Mr. Griswold also made much money leasing docks from the City Corporation and then renting them out at a good profit.

George Griswold was of a very speculative turn of mind. He operated heavily in land speculations, and was in 1836-37 extensively interested in Brooklyn real estate. He was connected with Swartwout's gold mining operations in 1836. Gold was to be mined in North Carolina faster than it was afterwards in California. This speculative project went smash.

On June second, 1851, a Boston built clipper, of 1,782 tons, set sail from New York for California, practically unknown. She came back famous and electrified the nation with her performances.

There was great rejoicing in South Street when the *Flying Cloud* romped home, on April ninth, 1852, from China, after having dashed through the Heads of San Francisco in eighty-nine days, twenty-one hours from New York! It is the sailing ship record to this day, a second time bettered by herself eleven hours, and a third time in 1860 by the *Andrew Jackson*. It was regarded by the press not only as a personal victory for the owners, builder and captain of this bonny clipper, but as a triumph of the United States upon the sea! Her best day's run on the passage was 374 nautical miles, on which occasion eighteen knots of line were not sufficient, during squalls, to measure the rate of speed.

The owners of the *Flying Cloud,* Messrs. Grinnell, Minturn and Company, had her log printed in gold, upon white silk, for distribution among their friends.

It is said that the masts, spars and rigging of this vessel were fine examples of the skill of her sailors in clapping on fishings, lashings, stoppers, and seizings, while her topmast fids, crushed and broken, were taken to the Astor House and exhibited to the admiration of the town. Nearly all the clippers were rerigged in New York with stouter spars and rigging than they originally carried. The utmost skill and judgment were required to properly equip these heavily masted vessels with wooden spars and hemp rigging, and the sparmarkers and riggers of South Street, who had gained much valuable experience as to the requirements aloft of these large, powerful clippers, while their captains had at the same time become better acquainted with their peculiarities, were held in high esteem by shipbuilders, owners and masters.

Getting under way at noon, January twenty-first, 1854, the *Flying Cloud,* in tow of the tug *Achilles,* off the foot of Maiden Lane, commenced her famous record-breaking passage from New York to San Francisco. She arrived at the latter port April twentieth in eighty-nine days and eight hours, anchor to anchor, which is the record to this date.

From there she went to Hongkong, and when a few days out ran upon a coral reef in the China Sea and sprung a leak, despite which her commander, Captain Josiah P. Creesy, kept on going until he reached New York. This eventful homeward bound voyage is so well described by Walter R. Jones, President of both the Atlantic Mutual Insurance Company and the Board of Marine Underwriters at New York, in presenting Captain Creesy with a handsome set of silver, on February third, 1856, that we reproduce it:

"Sir:—On your late passage from China when in command of the celebrated ship 'Flying Cloud,' with a rich and costly cargo of delicate goods, the total value of which, probably, amounted to a sum of dollars, you encountered adverse currents, and stormy and foggy weather, which carried your ship upon a coral reef, on the 7th of August last, in the China Sea, striking with such severity that her bow was raised out of the water three or four feet, her shoe taken off her keel, and keel itself cut through to the bottom planking causing her to leak badly and to make a great quantity of water. With a skill that none but a first rate shipmaster possesses, you soon extricated her from her perilous situation, without cutting away her masts or making any other great sacrifice, which is often done, nominally for the benefit of whom it may concern, proving very frequently however, to the great detriment of all concerned. In a very short time you had her afloat ready to proceed, when the important question arose in your mind where you should go; on the settling of which much then depended. Again your good judgment manifested itself. The expensive and costly ports in the straits were near at hand, you determined to avoid them and no one can say how much you saved to those interested in your valuable ship and cargo, but it is reasonable to suppose that those concerned have been saved at least thirty thousand dollars and probably much more; in fact no one can possibly tell the extent of saving with much accuracy; all know it has been very large.

"At that time your qualifications as a skillful commander again became manifest and you seem also to have combined in yourself the talents of the merchant as well as the shipmaster. After relieving your ship your attention was directed to the next best movement, and in that you rendered us an important service; instead of running your ship into an expensive port before referred to where the positive and known charges would have amounted to a very large sum, you examined the condition of the vessel and the means at your command and although your crew was weak and insufficient you made up your mind to proceed homeward, and with a leaky ship you left the China seas and in a very short time thereafter, to the great relief of the Underwriters you reached this port in safety and with scarcely a damaged package on which a claim could be made upon the Underwriters. Taking into view the important services you have rendered to the Marine Insurance Companies of the city, by your energetic, prompt, skillful and successful conduct, they have caused a choice and weighty service of plate to be prepared, which I have now the honor, in their name, to present you, as a testimonial of their appreciation of your good conduct, so opportunely and satisfactorily rendered on the voyage referred to, and that you may long and successfully live to enjoy it is, I can assure you, the ardent wish of all the donors.

"We also desire to record our testimonial in your favor,

and to make known your example, that the timid may be encouraged and the energetic, sustained and strengthened in a similar course of conduct, should they meet with similar course of conduct, that, in avoiding an entry at a port in the Chinese Seas, and the necessity of discharging and reloading your cargo, you have saved the property from charges to a very large amount, your ship from a long detention, and your crew from the hazards of entering a sickly port, all of which it was most desirable for you to avoid, and in doing so you are entitled to our acknowledgments."

No masters of men deserved more credit than the commanders of the Cape Horn fleet. The crews of American ships sailing from the two Eastern ports, New York and Boston, which controlled the California trade, were largely composed of the rowdy and knavish class. Their baggage was on their backs, and their purse in every man's pocket. These vagabonds stepped—or were carried drunk or drugged, "shanghaied" oftentimes—on board an outgoing vessel, and "Hey, for California!" To maintain discipline and sail their ships, American shipmasters were often compelled to wage "belaying pin" and "knuckle duster" warfare, for this tough element shipped as sailors, which many were not, as a means of getting to the goldfields of California, when "off to the mines" they would go!

When Captain Josiah Perkins Creesy was appointed to command the *Flying Cloud*, he was well known in New York, as he had commanded the ship *Oneida* in the China and East India trade. He remained as commander of that vessel, with which his name shall ever be associated, until 1855, when he retired to his home in Salem. At the outbreak of the Civil War, he volunteered and was appointed a Commander in the United States Navy and assigned to the clipper ship *Ino*, a tiny, extreme clipper about half the size of the *Flying Cloud*, upon which a crew of eighty men from Marblehead was placed.

On her second cruise, in 1862, the *Ino* made the record run of twelve days, Boston to Cadiz, Spain. Had the fire of racing impelled Captain Creesy to push this little clipper to the extent which only he could, in defiance, perhaps, of orders? The record is not clear. At any rate, when the *Ino* was being repaired at Palermo, Commander Craven of the *Tuscarora* filed charges against the former skipper of the *Flying Cloud*, and the *Ino* was ordered to return from Cadiz to Boston. However, Captain Creesy had other commands during the war, and the *Ino* herself under other commanders, went in search of the *Alabama* and *Florida*, with guns screened and hull repainted like a merchantman.

Captain Creesy subsequently commanded the clipper *Archer*, and made two voyages to China. Eight years previously, in 1854, when the *Flying Cloud* made the fastest passage on record from any Eastern port to San Francisco, to the present time, he had beaten the *Archer* by seventeen days. American ships and shipping were on the decline, when Captain Creesy decided to retire to Salem once more, where he died in 1871, at the age of fifty-seven years. The names of Josiah Perkins Creesy and the *Flying Cloud* will be remembered with pride so long as the American clipper ships and their brilliant exploits hold a place in the memory of man.

Nautical history is rather vague about the final end of the *Flying Cloud*, and it may be news to many to learn that her hulk was lying within the last ten years in the deserted backwaters of the harbor of St. John, New Brunswick. It is claimed that the *Cloud* in a badly damaged condition was sold to a local merchant who used her in the timber trade for some years, and after she was dismantled again used her for a long time lightering deals in St. John harbor.

The extreme clipper ship *Comet* came out during the height of the controversy over the respective sailing abilities of New York and Boston built ships. Boston enthusiasts showed that out of the fourteen fastest passages made from Eastern ports to San Francisco eight claimed the honor of having their birthplace there against six representing the handicraft of New York shipbuilders, the averages being 109 and 112 days respectively. On the other hand, it was shown that all efforts to copy the New York models had met with failure; their bow, run, shear and general appearance seemed unobtainable in other yards. A Captain Stevens of Boston declared that the builders of that place could put as fine craft on the ocean as were ever launched from a New York yard. He ordered and superintended the construction of the *Martha Washington* on the best

New York model, and so determined was he to make her the equal of anything afloat that he even went to the expense of putting down the deck plugs with brass instead of yellow pine. She was finished, launched and taken to New York and was docked alongside the finest packet ships. The comparison proved victorious to the New York builders, and from that time on they held their reputation. The *Comet* was in all quarters conceded to be one of the most beautiful, fast and generally successful sailing ships ever launched from any shipyard. She slid down the ways in the yard of New York's most famous shipbuilder, William H. Webb, on July tenth, 1851. Her owners were Bucklin and Crane of New York, to whose order Webb had previously built the *Celestial*, the first clipper ship constructed for the California trade. This firm subsequently ordered from the same builder the medium clippers *Intrepid* and the celebrated *Black Hawk*. Captain E. C. Gardner, formerly of the *Celestial*, was appointed to the command of the *Comet*.

On her first voyage she left New York October first, 1851, and arrived at San Francisco on January twelfth, 1852; passage 103 days.

She made nine round voyages, New York to San Francisco, thence to Hongkong and return to New York, after her arrival home from this voyage until December 1862, and she was sold a few months afterward.

In March 1863, she crossed from New York to London and there the Stars and Stripes were hauled down and the Red Ensign hoisted. In a list of American ships sold by Messrs. George Crowshaw and Company at London during the year 1863, on account of the successful activities of the Confederate privateers, appears the *Comet*, with the sales price of 8,100 pounds sterling. Her name, quite appropriately, was changed to *Fiery Star* and she was put in the trade between England and Australia, being well adapted to carrying passengers. Her subsequent career, however, was short, for in the spring of 1865, when some three weeks out from Moreton Bay, Queensland, Australia, bound for London, she was discovered to be on fire. Captain Yule did everything possible to subdue the flames, battening everything down and pumping water into the lower hold, but all without avail. The flames burst through and about ninety persons, including all the passengers, embarked in the boats, leaving Mate Sergeant and seventeen members of the crew volunteers aboard the ship, there not being room enough for them in the boats. The ship when about burned through and ready to sink, was overtaken by the Dauntless, from London bound for Auckland, and the brave company rescued. On arrival at Auckland the populace subscribed a substantial sum in acknowledgement of their gallant conduct.

A young Swedish count came to this country in 1851 with some money and located at Portsmouth, New Hampshire, where he had a craft built to take passengers to the World's Fair in London. She was named in honor of Jenny Lind (known as the Swedish Nightingale), but when nearly completed the projector fell short of money, so the builders finished her, and she was taken to Boston and sold at auction. The prominent Boston shipping firm of Sampson and Tappan were soon thereafter reported as having become her owners.

The clipper ship *Nightingale* beyond question has a history more romantic and interesting than that of any other merchant ship of either American or foreign construction. Unique in the conception of her creation, in that the idea was artistic or esthetic rather than mercenary, she stands alone in the annals of shipbuilding. When circumstances forced her to become a mere merchantman, she at once came to the fore prominently as a racing clipper in the tea trade; her subsequent career as a slaver, though short, was exciting, and was followed by her service in the Federal Navy during the Civil War; later still, she was the flagship of the Collins Overland (or Western Union) Telegraph Company's fleet of ten sailing and steam vessels operating in the North Pacific; further along she was again a general trader and finally ended her days as a North Atlantic lumber drogher under a foreign flag. She sailed on every ocean: the Pacific (or Bering) Sea knew her as far north as sixty-five degrees; the Indian Ocean had her keel cleaving its waters at the rate of twelve, fourteen and even sixteen knots in the high latitudes of fifty, fifty-four and up to nearly fifty-six degrees south; in the Atlantic, she had been to fifty-eight off the Horn, while her last hailing-port, Krageroe,

Norway, is about the same latitude north. It is probable that no other merchant sailing ship has approached the record of the *Nightingale* in this respect. The elements were not always kind to her and many a heavy claim underwriters had to pay, but her career of forty-two years of strenuous service is sufficient proof of the excellence of the material and workmanship that went into her construction.

"You and I are out of a job!" exclaimed Captain Peter Peterson of the clippership *Nightingale,* to his first officer, "for the owners have sold the ship"; and so they had—for a slaver. Who had bought the *Nightingale?* Why was she sold for a slaver? Her late owners, Sampson and Tappan, of Boston, had steadfastly refused to sell any of their ships for use in that nefarious trade. The *Nightingale* having been sold to unknown parties, said to be in New York, for the next eight months her history is involved in mystery.

The loungers on the South Street piers wondered to themselves why a vessel bound to Acapulco and California needed so many water casks; for at the very last moment a barge load of "shakings," as staves and hoops for the manufacture of casks are called, was taken on board; and other remarks were made respecting the number of the crew; some may have said, jokingly, that the captain meant to fill the casks with gold dust—and one or two knowing fellows whispered that they had heard there was no insurance upon the vessel, which was so strange for so fine a ship; but the *Nightingale* was soon out in the stream, tripping down New York Bay at a rate of speed that soon brought her out on the broad reaches of the Atlantic, and the loungers and lookers-on returned home.

The *Nightingale* was known to have come out as a slaver on the African Coast, yet all her papers were so arranged that no U. S. Naval commander would assume the responsibility of seizing her without slaves being actually on board. Although the U. S. S. *Saratoga* had been watching her when she went into Kabinda, on April nineteenth, 1861, yet Captain Bowen coolly proceeded to make his arrangements to take slaves aboard. Upon a previous occasion he had been prevented from loading near the mouth of the river by being boarded by the *Saratoga* just when he had his human freight all ready to go aboard. Bowen then gave out that he was going to Benguela and had his slaves carried to Kabinda and there for a time he lay off the coast. If in the meantime his vessel was boarded, Bowen sent most of his crew to their hammocks to play sick. Having learned that all the United States Naval vessels had gone to Loango and that the *Saratoga* was bound there, and being short of provisions, Bowen ventured to run in, but again Captain Alfred Taylor of the *Saratoga* was on hand and boarded. He found men sick and the vessel all right. Next day another visit was made and still everything was found all right. The *Saratoga* weighed anchor soon afterward and bore away, apparently for Loango and Congo. As soon as it was dark, Captain Taylor tacked and ran down to Kabinda Bay, but, on approaching it, took in sail, and thus ran within a few miles of the *Nightingale* and anchored, and sent two boats under Lieutenant John J. Guthrie to surprise her and it was found that she had 961 slaves aboard and was expecting more.

When they boarded the *Nightingale* Captain Bowen was in the cabin smoking with friends from shore. He said, "Gentlemen, I have played a bold game and lost, as you have played better." The *Nightingale* would apparently have been away within an hour, and with such a start as to defy pursuit.

Lieutenant Guthrie was put in command of the prize and ordered to proceed to Monrovia, Liberia, and there deliver the African captives to the agent appointed to receive and provide for slaves recaptured by United States cruisers. Only about 800 were landed; nor did the prize crew escape the African fever that broke out soon after their departure from Kabinda. No provision had been made for these half-starved negroes, and the mortality among them, after landing, must have been appalling.

Captain Bowen and his mate escaped from the *Nightingale* the second night after the capture. As Bowen told the story, he was allowed to escape by Guthrie, who was, himself, a slaveholder. In fact all the officers of the prize *Nightingale* were Southerners. After the capture of the *Nightingale*, Bowen made his way to Boston in the disguise of a sailor, but a reward being out for his capture, he contrived to escape to Havana, where he had accounts to settle for "goods" previously delivered. There he remained until the excitement was over. In 1872 he commanded the American side-wheel steamer *Virginius*, which was suspected of being a Cuban filibuster. After that affair he returned to Colon and was for a time agent for the Pacific Mail Steamship Company. He subsequently left the isthmus and his old friends lost sight of him.

Captain Francis Bowen was the son of a New York merchant, but, ignoring his advantages of position and education, ran away to sea. He is described as a wiry little man, quiet, beardless, gray-haired, dressed like a clergyman, and in appearance as meek-looking and gentle as a dove—anything but the thorough sailor and reckless law-breaker that he was. He could speak French, Spanish and Portuguese; was well read and had been in every nook and corner of the globe. He possessed a keen and cultivated intelligence, was refined in his tastes, pleasant in address, blandly unconscious of depravity, cheerful in temper, fearless, cynical, witty if not wise, cool as the west wind and the last man on earth that a stranger would suspect of the crimes and misdemeanors he so freely confessed and appeared to regard with satisfaction.

Yachting next comes in for a share of our attention. In the year 1844 the New York Yacht Club was founded, and during the next decade, the Steers brothers, George and James R., achieved wonderful success in the construction of yachts and swift pilot-boats. The New York pilot-boat, rigged as a two-masted schooner, was probably the most seaworthy and speedy craft of her size in the world, and they were all capitally handled. And we had the fastest yacht afloat in the sloop *Maria*, a scientific racing machine, designed by Robert L. Stevens of Hoboken. This wonderful boat was the prototype of the racing yacht of the present day. But the *America* was an out and out pilot-boat, in construction and rig; she was sailed by "Old Dick Brown," a Sandy Hook pilot, and most of her crew belonged to the New York pilot fleet.

Commodore John C. Stevens, one of the owners of the *Maria* and also of the *America*, became acquainted with George Steers when he was serving his apprenticeship in the famous old shipbuilding yard of Smith and Dimon. Steers had built himself a tidy little catboat, with which he had won a prize

George Steers.   James R. Steers.

Interior of George Steers' "Model Room" as it Appeared at the Time of His Decease. — 1856.

offered by the Commodore. That is how they came to be lifelong friends and it led eventually to George Steers being commissioned to design the *America*.

The preaching of Paul at Ephesus scarcely produced a greater sensation among the idolatrous Ephesians, than did the yacht *America* among the sporting circles of the Old World, eighty-three years ago, on August twenty-second, 1851, when she turned everything topsy-turvy at Cowes. Americans whose crude notions of science in shipbuilding were regarded by a portion of the English press as little better than a contemptuous violation of Royal Mandates, would not have ventured to cross the threshold of the sporting circles of the New World, had not their unparalleled success in every branch of commercial art engendered the conviction that the genius developed by the institutions of their country were quite as favorable to excellence in yacht as shipbuilding.

The yacht squadrons of Europe viewed with contemptuous complacency the humble pretensions of an American shipbuilder (George Steers) at yacht building. The success of the *America* declared all the English yachts to be wrong from stem to stern, from keel to truck, and in the twinkling of a marlinspike every yacht owner formed a resolution to Americanize his vessel.

More than a yacht builder was George Steers. Before he designed the *America*, he had produced two great specimens of American enterprise in naval architecture and mechanical science, the steamships *Atlantic* and *Arctic*, at a cost of nearly 600,000 dollars each, for the Collins Line. Creator of a fleet of marvelous steamships, for he designed all the Collins Line vessels, and the warship *Niagara* of the United States Navy, yet he is remembered only for what may be termed "a racing machine!"

At the time of his death, September twenty-fifth, 1856, when only thirty-six years old, the magnificent Collins steamer *Adriatic*, had just been launched from Mr. Steers' yard, and was about to make her trial trip. She was the largest, finest and fastest steamship afloat and added much prestige to American shipbuilding.

The first American screw steamers to cross the Atlantic

were the *Pioneer* from New York to Liverpool in October 1851, and the *City of Pittsburgh* from Philadelphia to Liverpool in December 1851, under the management of the Philadelphia, New York and Liverpool Company, afterward known as the Inman Line. The *Pioneer* was 230 feet long, forty-two feet beam and thirty-one feet draft. The *City of Pittsburgh's* dimensions were: Length, 245 feet; beam, three feet; and draft, thirty-three feet. Engines in both cases were of the vertical, direct acting trunk type, with cylinders eighty-five inches by fifty-one inches and propellers ten feet in diameter.

In 1853 the *Ericsson* was built at New York to test the possibility of using hot air instead of steam as motive power. On her trial trip to Washington the following winter she averaged eight miles an hour on a consumption of five tons of coal in twenty-four hours. The speed, however, was not deemed sufficient for competition with the fast steamers and the backers withdrew their support, so the engines were removed and steam engines and boilers put in their place, after which the vessel was operated for a year by the Collins Line and later in the Bremen service.

When John Ericsson was an infant of four years, Fulton made his first trial trip of the steamboat *Clermont* running from New York to Albany and back at the average speed of five miles an hour; but it was not until thirty years after that time, that the problem of ocean steam navigation was finally solved by Ericsson, who had already won engineering distinction by the application of steam as a motor on land. Ericsson's claim to the practical introduction of the screw propeller has been disputed in some quarters, but there is no question whatever that by his introduction of the screw into the war steamer, the *Princeton*, 1842-44, he revolutionized naval construction and naval warfare. For the first time the machinery was carried below the water line out of the reach of hostile shot, and the well-founded objections of the old sailors that the use of steam imperiled the safety of vessels and added to their dangers was thoroughly removed. Yet Ericsson encountered active hostility, marine engineers and shipbuilders believing for years that paddle-wheels were more practical and powerful than propellers, so the screw propeller was slow in coming into use.

No one except an enthusiastic inventor and thoroughly trained engineer like Ericsson would have persisted against such discouragement as he received.

We regret that space does not allow us to follow the career of John Ericsson in detail until the day when the *Monitor* revolutionized naval warfare. From the launching of the *Princeton* up to his last brief illness, Ericsson's theories of naval warfare showed steady development. Never visionary and impracticable, single-minded in his pursuit of light, impatient of obstacles and yet unconquerable by them, unworldly after the fashion of self-seekers, generous, tender-hearted, terrible in his wrath, but gentle in his kindness, and unostentatious in his many charities, this great inventor's character and life present a most interesting study.

Shipbuilding in America went forward by leaps and bounds, not only in New York, but at Portsmouth, Damariscotta, East Boston, Newburyport, Medford, Stonington, Mystic, Philadelphia, and Baltimore, the hulls of the great American Merchant Marine began to take shape. Building ways appeared on the banks of every tidal inlet and backwater on the North Atlantic coast. The waterfront of every seaport rang with the sound of the broadax, adz, top maul and caulking mallet. With the sudden activity in American shipyards there came an endeavor to build better ships. Everywhere was a determined effort made to improve on existing models of ships and rigging, and scientific principles became a factor.

As the results of this intensive effort became apparent, the fame of American shipbuilders spread over the world. Then, as the United States came to be considered the shipbuilding center of the world, men came from foreign countries to work under American builders and familiarize themselves with our methods. There was no prejudice against foreigners then, and they were only asked if they were willing to work. New York from having taken the lead in building the first packet ships, came to be considered the principal shipbuilding place of the country.

From a coaster that sailed from Halifax, after a long, rather stormy voyage, there landed in New York about the year 1826, a lad of sixteen from Shelburne, Nova Scotia, who was destined to play a leading part in American shipbuilding annals, Donald McKay. At the most this young Nova Scotian could never have seen more than a few dozen small vessels lying at his home port at one time; but here were great ships by the hundreds—the entire waterfront was a forest of masts. There were ships from China, discharging aromatic chests of new teas; there stood a lordly Indiaman, unloading fragrant bales of mysterious content. There were ships from the Mediterranean, the Baltic, South America and Africa. Perhaps he saw a northwest coaster fur trader—at that time the aristocrat of the shipping world. He walked along South Street under an arcade that was formed by the bowsprits of ships. The street was crowded with drays laden with great bales and casks, going to and from the shipping, drawn by straining horses and driven by yelling teamsters.

But his chief interest lay in the great shipyards on the East River. They were his reason for coming to New York—he was going to learn to build those big ships. The sight of those yards, stretching along the shore for a mile or more, with building ways that held ships in every stage of completion, must have assured him that the reports he had heard in Shelburne, of the shipbuilding boom in the United States, were not exaggerated.

He first secured employment in the shipyard of Isaac Webb, to whom he soon became apprenticed, and where he first acquired a knowledge of the science and art of shipbuilding. We next hear of him in the yard of Brown and Bell, leading packet ship builders for the Western Ocean trade, where his marked ability and industry attracted the attention of Jacob Bell, who took an interest in him. It was through his kindly offices that Donald McKay went to New England, to superintend the construction of some ships for New York shipping houses at Wiscasset, Maine. His visit to the Eastern country opened up to his restless ambition a fertile field, so far behind the New York shipwrights were New England mechanics in their methods of construction, at that time.

Visiting Newburyport, he finished a ship for the noted builder, John Currier, Jr., who wished on the completion of the job, to bind him for five years more of service. This apparently advantageous offer was refused, and William Currier, offering him a partnership in his shipyard, he moved his family to Newburyport, and under the firm name of Currier and McKay, commenced his career as a shipbuilder. The little ship, *Courier*, built for Messers. Andrew Foster and Sons, of New York, was his first production. The firm of Currier and McKay was soon dissolved, models and molds being divided (with a saw) in two equal parts. McKay then connected himself with William Pickett, and, under the firm name of McKay and Pickett, the ships *St. George*, *John R. Skiddy*, and *Joshua Bates*, were built.

Previous to this, however, when finishing the ship *Delia Walker*, in the yard of John Currier, he had attracted the attention of her owner, Dennis Condry, by his superior mechanical ability, and this gentleman, and true friend, when traveling abroad afterwards, mentioned his acquirements to Enoch Train, of Boston, extracting, at the same time, a promise from Mr. Train that, before contracting for his contemplated line of packet ships, which were to sail in the European trade, he would, at least, visit this rising young shipbuilder. To fulfill the promise made, the eminent merchant visited Newburyport and the contract to build the ship *Joshua Bates* was made in an hour. It was "flint and steel" when these two master-minds—merchant and mechanic—struck together.

The *Joshua Bates* completed—a masterpiece of shipbuilding—Newburyport became too small for his restless ambition. "Come to Boston, I want you," was Enoch Train's invitation, and dissolving his pleasant and profitable partnership with Mr. Pickett, in 1845, McKay laid the keel of the *Washington Irving* in East Boston. She was the first of a fleet which contained many naval gems, all of which bore the unmistakable impress of his artistic taste in design and thorough honesty in carpentry. Excelsior! was his motto; the Best, and nothing but the Best for each and every craft for which he stood sponsor!

In the eight years from 1845 to 1853, Donald McKay built forty-nine large vessels, all famous for their beauty and speed. The eighteenth, *Stag-Hound*, his first real clipper, launched in a bitterly cold December afternoon in 1850, was a ship whose sharp bow, graceful sheer line, and long, narrow body made her the pioneer of her class.

Faster clippers and larger clippers were built by McKay, but for perfection and beauty of design, weatherliness and consistent speed under every condition, neither he nor any one else surpassed the *Flying Cloud*. She was the fastest vessel on long voyages that ever sailed under the American flag. Captain Josiah Perkins Creesy, of Marblehead, was her commander. On her maiden voyage, in the summer of 1851, the *Flying Cloud* made a day's run of 374 miles, logged 1,256 miles in four consecutive days, and arrived at San Francisco eighty-nine days out of New York. This run was only twice equaled—by herself in 1854 and by the *Andrew Jackson*, in 1860.

That same year, 1851, Donald McKay built two other clippers, the *Flying Fish*, almost as famous as the *Flying Cloud*, and the *Staffordshire*, and in 1852 the *Sovereign of the Seas*, the *Bald Eagle*, and the *Westward Ho*. In 1853 his yard turned out the clippers, *Empress of the Seas*, the *Romance of the Seas*, and the *Great Republic*, the latter the darling of Donald McKay's heart. She was the largest ship in the world, but unfortunately caught fire and burned to the water's edge before sailing on her maiden voyage, December twenty-seventh, 1853.

This was the last year of the McKay American clipper ships though he built in 1854 and 1855 six clippers for the English firm of James Baines and Company, engaged in the Australian trade.

In 1855, besides the ship *Donald McKay* built for the English firm, he launched for American owners the three medium clippers, *Defender*, *Amos Lawrence* and *Abbott Lawrence*. The following year there were built at his yard the four medium clippers, *Minnehaha*, *Baltic*, *Adriatic*, and *Mastiff*, and the bark *Henry Hill*.

Owing to financial depression during the four years prior to the Civil War, McKay built only one ship, *Alhambra*, in 1857. In the course of the war, McKay constructed for the navy the iron gun-boat *Ashuelot*, the iron-clad monitor *Nausett*, and, in 1874, the sloop of war *Adams*.

With the majority of the commerce of the world after the Civil War carried in British bottoms, there was very little

Donald McKay,
Master-Builder of Ships.

Josiah P. Creesy,
Commander of
The "Flying Cloud".

Clipper Ship "Flying Cloud",
from a painting by Charles R. Patterson, Courtesy of R. P. Stevens, Esq.

activity at Donald McKay's East Boston yard, though the *Helen Morris* and the second *Sovereign of the Seas* were launched in 1868, and the *Glory of the Seas* in 1869. In 1877, Donald McKay retired to his farm at Hamilton, where he died September twentieth, 1880, in the seventy-first year of his age.

Donald McKay built such ships as the world shall never see again; greatest of them all was the *Lightning*. Today we may look at pictures on the wall, but the breath of life is not in pictures. To see aright, we must behold the white-winged marine beauty riding before the gales like some archangel of the tempest. Four hundred and thirty-six miles in one day was the achievement of the *Lightning*, a sailing ship record for all time. Take notice, ye who boast of speed and progress, that this record was achieved in the year 1854! Only in our own day have we been able to surpass with steam and electricity that immortal record carved out in those roaring days by naked fists and manhood's hearts of oak.

The discovery of gold put a premium upon record-breaking sailing vessels for the run from New York or Boston round the Horn to San Francisco. Shipyards all along the Atlantic seaboard were continually striving for great sailing speed. The creation of such New York built ships as the *Sea Witch, Challenge, Comet, Gazelle, N. B. Palmer, Trade Wind, Contest, Sword-Fish, Messenger, Panama, Sweepstakes,* and *Young America*, among other splendid and beautiful craft, was the result. Thus the American Clipper Ship Era witnessed the highest development of the wooden sailing ship in construction, speed and beauty. More than a quarter of a century elapsed, devoted to discovery and invention in perfecting the marine engine and boiler, before the best clipper ship records for speed were broken by steam vessels.

The Astor House in New York and the Parker House in Boston hummed with excitement as partisans of the clippers drank their champagne, brandy and whisky neat, laying bets that represented fortunes in those days and would not be "sneezed at" today, while the wreaths of smoke from fragrant Havanas gracefully encircled the heads of the merchants, ship-builders and sea-captains who carried on well founded arguments concerning the merits of their favorite clippers and packets, also the men who commanded them, as well as their builders and owners, for some of the latter were known as being generous, not only in equipping their vessels, but in the treatment of crews—paying and feeding sailors well meant they often would continue on the same ship voyage after voyage, and that was conducive to good service afloat. There were shipowners who "skimped" on equipment, paid the smallest wages possible to crews, and some who sent unseaworthy vessels to sea; whilst others were known as so negligent of the conduct of their masters, that they made a practice of purloining a goodly portion of each sailor's wages, as well as furnishing bad or "rotten grub."

It was a day when ship-owners, merchants and clipper captains would bet, at places where they congregated, for stakes that were nothing less than the commercial supremacy of the world. Seated at one of the small marble-topped tables in the Astor House bar-room (we had not then imported *café*) were three men, deeply engrossed in conversation and oblivious to the murmur of small talk around them. Michael, the venerable bartender, was especially solicitous about them, as he passed to and fro, promptly serving them at only a nod towards the empty glasses from one of the trio. The national services of Daniel Webster, the interest which he always manifested in commercial affairs, and the debt of gratitude which the commercial men of the country owed to him, had been the subject of conversation by one of the men, who further alluded to the late Baltimore convention, and to his own efforts to secure the nomination of Mr. Webster as the Whig candidate for President. The speaker, Moses H. Grinnell, was senior member of New York's most influential shipping house, Grinnell, Minturn and Company. His companions were Donald McKay, then in the zenith of his fame as a builder-designer of ships, and his brother, Captain Lauchlan McKay, commanding the clipper *Sovereign of the Seas*, the latest addition to New York's celebrated Clipper Fleet, then lying "up for California," at Grinnell, Minturn's Wharf, on South Street near Pine, before embarking upon one of the most wonderful voyages ever made by an American ship.

The California clippers had no foreign competitors to sail against, and the racing among themselves was sufficiently keen to satisfy the most enthusiastic lover of sport. However, the China and Australia and other long sea voyages afforded opportunities for international rivalry.

Captain Arthur H. Clark, in his "Clipper Ship Era," writes entertainingly about some of these ocean contests:

"The first contest of clippers round Cape Horn took place in 1850, between the 'Houqua,' 'Sea Witch,' 'Samuel Russell,' and 'Memnon,' old rivals on China voyages, and the new clippers 'Celestial,' 'Mandarin,' and 'Race Horse.' All of these vessels had their friends, and large sums of money were wagered on the result, the four older ships, especially the 'Sea Witch,' having established high reputations for speed. The 'Samuel Russell' was commanded by Captain Charles Low, previously of the 'Houqua,' while the 'Houqua' was now commanded by Captain McKenzie; Captain Gordon was again in the 'Memnon,' and Captain George Fraser, who had sailed with Captain Waterman as chief mate, commanded the 'Sea Witch.'

"The 'Samuel Russell' arrived at San Francisco May 6, 1850, after a passage of 109 days from New York, thus knocking 11 days off the record, and her friends and backers felt confident that this passage could not be surpassed, at all events not by any of the clippers of that year. This opinion was in a measure confirmed when the 'Houqua' arrived on July 23rd, 120 days from New York, but on the following day the 'Sea Witch' came romping up the bay, 97 days from Sandy Hook, reducing the record by another 12 days. This passage astonished every one, even her warmest admirers, and well it might, for it has never been equalled by a ship of her tonnage and not often excelled even by larger vessels. This performance of the 'Sea Witch' was the more remarkable as she had rounded Cape Horn during the Antarctic midwinter.

"The remainder of the fleet arrived in the following order: 'Memnon,' September 27th, 123 days; 'Celestial,' November 1st, 104 days; 'Race Horse,' from Boston, November 24th, 109 days; and the 'Mandarin,' November 29th, 126 days from New York. These were all fine passages, especially when we consider that none of the vessels was over 1,100 tons register.

"One of the best ocean races of 1851 was that between the 'Raven,' Captain Henry; the 'Typhoon,' Captain Salter, and the 'Sea Witch,' Captain Frazer. These clippers sailed for San Francisco nearly together: the 'Sea Witch' passed out by Sandy Hook on August 1st, followed by the 'Typhoon' on August 4th, while the 'Raven' passed Boston Light on August 6th. All had able commanders, who carried Maury's wind and current charts to assist them. In this month of light and baffling breezes a quick run to the equator was hardly to be expected, but these clippers threaded their way across the calm belt of Cancer, ran down the northeast trades, and drifted through the doldrums, with surprising speed. The 'Sea Witch' still kept her lead at the equator, crossing on August 30th, closely followed by the 'Raven' and the 'Typhoon,' which crossed together on the 31st, so that the 'Raven' had gained four and the 'Typhoon' two days on their swift competitor. They all weathered Cape St. Roque and stood away to the southward for a splendid dash of over three thousand miles through the southeast trades and the strong westerly winds further south, all crossing the parallel of 50° S. in the same longitude, 64° W. The 'Raven' had gained another day on the 'Sea Witch' and these two clippers were now side by side, with the 'Typhoon' only two days astern.

"Here began one of the keenest races ever sailed upon the ocean. They all stood to the southward with studdingsail booms and skysail yards sent down from aloft, with extra lashings on the boats, spare spars, and skylights, while all hands hardened their hearts for a thrash to windward round Cape Horn. On this desolate ocean the clippers raced from horizon to horizon in heavy westerly gales and a long, fierce, sweeping head sea. For fourteen exciting days and nights, with single-reefed, double-reefed, close-reefed topsails, reefs in and reefs out, their keen, watchful captains made use of every lull and slant to drive their ships to the westward of Cape Horn, across the great, broad-backed, white-crested seas. The 'Sea Witch' and 'Raven' were having it out tack for tack, sometimes one and then the other gaining an advantage, both carrying sail to the utmost limit of prudence, lifting their long, sharp bows to the wild, surging seas, the cold spray flying across their decks and blue water swirling along their lee waists, each handled with consummate skill, and not a spar carried away or rope parted. The 'Typhoon' in hot pursuit, was pressing the two leaders and slowly closing upon them, for her greater length and power helped her here. Finally the 'Sea Witch' and 'Raven' emerged from this desperate contest side by side, as they had entered it, both crossing latitude 50° S. in the Pacific in fourteen days from the same parallel in the Atlantic. The 'Typhoon' had now gained another day, and was within twenty-four hours' sail of each.

"Clear of Cape Horn they all went away fast to the northward, rushing through the southeast trades with studding-sails, skysails, water-sails, and ring-tails—every yard of canvas set that would draw. On this stretch to the equator, the 'Sea Witch' fairly flew through the water, and crossed in 22 days from 50° S., leading the 'Raven' 2 and the 'Typhoon' 4 days. They now stood to the northward, close-hauled on the starboard tack, for their final struggle. Here again length and power counted in favor of the 'Typhoon,' and she came up with the 'Sea Witch' and 'Raven,' leading them both into port; the 'Raven,' too, for the first time fairly headed the 'Sea Witch.' The 'Typhoon' glided through the Golden Gate, November 18th, 106 days from Sandy Hook; the 'Raven,' November 19th, 105 days from Boston Light, and the 'Sea Witch,' November 20th, 110 days from Sandy Hook.

"This was a great victory for the 'Raven,' the only ship of her tonnage that ever outsailed the 'Sea Witch,' to say nothing of vanquishing the large and famous 'Typhoon,' a ship more than double her size. It should, however, be remembered with regard to the 'Sea Witch,' that she was at that time over five years old, and had led a pretty wild life under Waterman, while she had known no peace with Frazer in command, and had been strained and weakened by hard driving. Moreover, a wooden ship, after five or six years, begins to lose her speed through absorbing water, and becomes sluggish in light airs. In her prime and at her best with Waterman in command, the 'Sea Witch' was probably the fastest sailing-ship of her inches ever built.

"The California clippers were, of course, racing all the time, against each other and against the record and the strain upon their captains in driving their ships against competitors whose relative positions were unknown, was terrific. It became a confirmed habit with them to keep their ships going night and day in all weathers and at their utmost speed."

During the boom period of the clipper ship there was considerable rivalry between the builders of this type of vessel at New York and Boston, Massachusetts, and so keen became the competition to produce vessels of the highest speed and beauty of form, that all the skill of our best naval architects was brought into use. This subsequently led to challenges that were offered to test the respective speed of some of each city's clipper ships of prominence.

History has handed down to us that the *Flying Cloud* was far in advance of all clipper ships of her day in making record time. She was undoubtedly a vessel having fine lines for speed, and was most ably handled in all her voyages, but there was one other American ship of the same period that has been shown to be her equal, and this vessel was the *Comet*, a New York built vessel whose record for high speed over a long period of time is equal to any vessel of her class.

The one case that excited most interest was that just after the *Sovereign of the Seas* made her fast voyage from Honolulu to New York, arriving on May sixth, 1853, the *Comet*, arriving the next day from San Francisco, having made the quickest voyage between California and New York to that date: and as if to still further add fuel to the flame, the *Flying Dutchman* arrived the next day, the eighth of May, in eighty-five days from San Francisco. There was the *Sovereign of the Seas* adding to the fame of her builder-owner, that credit for fast clipper ships already acquired by the high speed of the *Flying Cloud*. They had not got over their shouting for what seemed to be the better model of the Boston built clipper ships, before there arrived the two New York built clippers in phenomenal time, to upset all opinions of the knowing ones on fast sailing vessels. It was now about even with the Boston and New York built ships, and this brought on a fever of speculation and banter from the opposing interests which in a few days warmed up the sporting blood in marine circles at New York and at Boston, and soon it was "handed out" that 50,000 dollars was ready to be placed on the Boston built vessel in a race from New York to San Francisco in ballast or otherwise, and to sail within thirty days

Fair Weather on the Deck of a Clipper Ship Carrying Gold-Seekers to California.

of each other, or together. This "chip on the shoulder" was recognized in a few days, when George Daniels, the owner, and William H. Webb, the builder, of the *Young America*, just completed, accepted the challenge from the owners of the *Sovereign of the Seas* for the sum of 20,000 dollars, 10,000 dollars for each, both vessels to be loaded, and to sail together or within thirty days of each other. This acceptance of the challenge was recognized by the owners of the Boston built vessel, "but the condition of the California freight market did not then offer any advantage to send the vessel to the Pacific coast, but hoped at a later date a better feeling would prevail that would enable them to place her in the San Francisco trade, and then to sail her for the stipulated amount against any ship Mr. Webb was willing to match against her." The Boston built vessel never entered the New York and San Francisco trade again.

The *Sovereign of the Seas* was registered at the Boston Custom House June nineteenth, 1852, Donald McKay, managing owner. This register was surrendered at the New York Custom House, June eighteenth, 1853, with Andrew F. Meincke of New York as sole owner. Funck and Meincke were ship brokers at the time at Ninety-three Wall Street, New York. The next day the vessel sailed from New York for Liverpool and was engaged in the Liverpool and London, and Melbourne and China trade for some years. In May 1854, the vessel passed into the possession of J. C. Godeffroy and Son of Hamburg, Germany, who purchased her from Donald McKay, her builder.

It was some time later than the *Sovereign of the Seas* and *Young America* excitement when those interested in the *Sweepstakes* offered to race that vessel against any of the widely-known Eastern built clippers for a distance of 1,000 miles to sea, vessel for vessel. This failed to bring forth any recognition of the challenger. These two cases show how deep seated was the rivalry between some of the builders of the two cities, and what sporting blood was in the veins of our shipping interests of that period. It must be remembered we had clipper ships of the highest speed at the time, the world over.

The great race to San Francisco in 1852 was between the *Sword-Fish* of New York and the *Flying Fish* of Boston, both extreme clippers and built respectively by William H. Webb and Donald McKay. The *Flying Fish* sailed from Boston November eleventh, 1851, and on the same day the *Sword-Fish* passed Sandy Hook. Large sums were wagered upon the result. Captain Nickels of the *Flying Fish* and Captain Babcock of the *Sword-Fish* were both young and skillful commanders, and it was believed by their friends that each would send his ship along at her utmost speed. The *Flying Fish* made an excellent run of nineteen days to the equator, leading the *Sword-Fish* by four days. From the equator to fifty degrees South, the *Flying Fish* was twenty-six and the *Sword-Fish* twenty-two days, so that they passed that parallel on the same day. They raced round Cape Horn, part of the time side by side, the *Flying Fish* making the run from fifty degrees South in the Atlantic to fifty degrees South in the Pacific in seven days and the *Sword-Fish* in eight days. From this point the *Sword-Fish* came up and steadily drew away. She made the run to the equator in nineteen days, leading the *Flying Fish* by three days, and from the equator to San Francisco in twenty days, gaining on this stretch another three days, and arrived at San Francisco February tenth, 1852, after a splendid passage of ninety days sixteen hours from New York. The *Flying Fish* arrived on the seventeenth, or ninety-eight days from Boston.

The keen rivalry between our clippers led to races over thousands of miles of seas; and upon the result large sums were often wagered. *It is said that Boston's waterfront contingent went broke when the "Swordfish" won this race.* Her passage of ninety days, the second best ever made from New York to San Francisco, together with many other fast passages, certainly places her very near the head of the American Clipper Fleet.

"His energy and skill, with that of his brother, Donald McKay, brought the two oceans (the Atlantic and Pacific) more closely together perhaps than did the work of any other two individuals following like professions in the world."

U. S. Senator George F. Hoar.

The Third Period

Captain Lauchlan McKay was born in Shelburne, Nova Scotia, December sixteenth, 1811, and it is safe to say that he was one of the brightest men who ever trod the deck of a ship. He was not only an accomplished shipmaster, but a capable shipbuilder and an expert master-mechanic, as well as an ingenious inventor.

Previous to 1839, when he published "THE PRACTICAL SHIPBUILDER," which was a text-book for every shipyard in the United States and used in the drafting lofts for hundreds of ships, Lauchlan McKay served an apprenticeship in the New York shipyard of Isaac Webb, an eminent shipbuilder of that day and known as "The Father of Shipbuilders." With his brother, Donald, who acquired fame as America's Foremost Designer and Builder of Ships, he swung the ax, shoved the plane and performed all the other functions of an apprentice, working hard and long every day "to learn the art, trade, and mystery of a ship-carpenter," as was stated in his "indenture" papers. His apprenticeship fulfilled, he became a full-fledged mechanic, and worked several years in various New York shipyards until he became a master shipwright. He was afterwards appointed carpenter in the United States Navy, serving on the frigate *Constellation*, with Admiral Farragut, who was a lieutenant at the time.

Soon after publishing "THE PRACTICAL SHIPBUILDER," in company with his brother Hugh he opened a shipyard at East Boston. Here they did repairing, and in 1846 built the barque *Odd Fellow*, in which Lauchlan sailed as master. In 1849 he commanded the ship *Jenny Lind*, built by Donald McKay, and made some excellent trans-Atlantic passages in her.

The clipper hull, like many other milestones of progress, was an evolution to which a number of persons contributed. In 1852 Donald McKay gave to the waters the *Sovereign of the Seas*, measuring 2,421 tons, a new record in size, with the longest and sharpest ends of any vessel then built. She was sent out to San Francisco in command of Lauchlan McKay and electrified the nation with her performances, and he made a record unparalleled in the history of a shipmaster.

Off the coast of Chile, the *Sovereign* was dismasted in a

storm, but Captain McKay re-rigged her at sea and kept his vessel on her course, despite her disabled condition, eventually making a record passage from Sandy Hook to the Golden Gate. The following extract from a letter written by one of the crew will be read with interest:

"On board ship 'Sovereign of the Seas,'
San Francisco, November 16th, 1852.
"On the night of October 12th, during a heavy gale, but carrying, as usual, a press of canvas, the maintopmast trestle-trees settled, which slackened the topmast stays, and away went the main topmast over the side, taking with it the fore topmast, foreyard and mizzen topgallant mast, and every stitch of canvas off the foremast. Here was a disaster to make the boldest heart beat quick, and even palsy the tongue. Yet the Captain quailed not. The hands were called, the ship hove to; and 'now,' said he to the mate, 'you take the mainmast, and I will take the foremast, and let us clear the wreck. Remember everything must be saved—nothing must be cut.'

"And to work they went in earnest. The members of the crew vied with each other in going overboard to clear the wreck—not a murmur was heard fore or aft, and before sunset the next day everything was on board; and the ship under her mainsail, cross-jack course and mizzen-topsail, was balling off 12 knots." (Note: Seventy feet of her foremast and mainmast were gone, and also four sails on each mast.) "Our decks were lumbered up to the leading blocks. The captain was everywhere: now setting a sailmaker's gang to work and repairing sails, next a carpenter's gang to making and fitting masts and yards, and the sailors generally to clearing the rigging, getting down the stumps of the topmasts, etc. Every man was employed and worked with a will, but at night the watch was regularly set, though the captain himself slept not. The watch on deck worked during the night, and all hands during the day. In a week both topmasts, topsail yards and foreyard were aloft and the sails bent, and in 12 days the ship was once more a-tanto, and as complete aloft as if nothing had happened. If the ship at the time of distaster, with the wreck of spars alongside could have been placed in the harbor of San Francisco, I have no hesitancy in asserting, that the damages could not have been repaired there, as we repaired them, for less than $25,000. During the whole of the disaster, such was Captain McKay's deliberate coolness and judgment, not a man suffered the slightest injury."

We next see the *Sovereign of the Seas* loading sperm oil at Honolulu—the pioneer vessel in transporting our whalers' catch in the Pacific to Atlantic home ports. With a crew numbering about one-third of what she had on the outward passage, she sailed for New York, February twelfth, 1853, with a cargo of 8,000 barrels of whale oil and a small amount of bone. Captain McKay had occasion to display his ability as a carpenter on this passage also. On the twentieth day at sea she sprung her fore-topmast; it was "fished" in a couple of days, but that mast, with the main topmast tender, were a source of anxiety for the remainder of the passage. Captain McKay arrived off Sandy Hook in eighty-two days out from Honolulu, a record at that time. On this run the *Sovereign* logged 374 knots or 433 statute miles in twenty-four hours, and sailed 5,391 nautical miles or 6,245 statute miles in twenty-two days, averaging 283 statute miles a day. Certainly this eventful voyage deserves to rank among the most notable in sailing ship annals.

The *Sovereign* sailed again on June eighteenth, 1853, for Liverpool, crossing from pier to anchorage in thirteen days, twenty-two hours. Upon arrival at Liverpool she was chartered by James Baines for his Australian "Black Ball Line." Thenceforth Captain McKay knew her no more.

Returning to Boston, he superintended the outfit of Donald McKay's ship o' ships, the *Great Republic*, the largest and most magnificent sailing vessel in the world, which he was to command in recognition of his splendid services as master of the *Sovereign of the Seas*. One of the many innovations introduced on the *Republic* was a capstan for purchasing the anchors instead of a windlass, which could be worked on both decks, the invention of Captain McKay.

But Lauchlan McKay was never to take the *Great Republic* out to sea. When laden at New York and nearly ready to sail for Liverpool, she was burnt, then scuttled and sunk. She had to be practically rebuilt and entirely re-rigged before she finally went to sea, more than a year afterward. She was still the largest sailing ship afloat and made speed records which caused every one to assume that she would have been the fastest, had her original lines and sail plan been kept.

When the *Lightning* on her maiden crossing from Boston to Liverpool made the phenomenal run of 436 nautical miles in twenty-four hours, her commander, James Nicol Forbes, had, as companion and adviser, Captain Lauchlan McKay, who also went on her as builder's representative. In the hands of these two experienced and skillful seamen, it is easy to understand how the *Lightning* developed her finest speed and made one of the shortest, as well as most remarkable, trans-Atlantic passages ever recorded; and it was not until 1885, thirty-one years afterward, that an ocean steamship exceeded her day's work.

While in England Captain McKay was offered command of the British ship *Nagasaki*, and he took her on a voyage from Liverpool to Australia. While at Sydney, New South Wales, he raised a large ship which had been sunk and given up as a wreck. Other parties had tried for a month and failed. He raised her in less than a week, showing that his knowledge of ship construction and mechanical skill enabled him to succeed where others had failed.

Subsequently, while still commanding the *Nagasaki*, he fell in with a ship in distress, the crew of which desired to be rescued. He had them and their effects transferred to his own ship, but suspecting something wrong, inspected the ship himself with his carpenter. Pulling around her, he discovered that she had been bored through in the run. When she pitched the splinters of the auger holes attracted his notice. It was evident that there had been foul play for the purpose of defrauding the underwriters. After considerable trouble the holes were plugged, the ship pumped out and Captain McKay placed his mate with men of his own crew in charge of her, who brought her safely to Bombay, where an investigation took place, but could not be completed because the ship's captain, officers and crew were on board the *Nagasaki*. Captain McKay was not only rewarded by the underwriters, but complimented by the British Board of Trade.

The Third Period

At the disappearance of the clipper ship, he, in connection with his brother-in-law, Captain Henry Warner, who had served as his mate many years and succeeded him in command of the *Sovereign of the Seas*, when he left her at Liverpool, started shipbuilding in Quebec, Canada, and continued there from 1864 until 1876. Afterwards he entered into partnership with Charles B. Dix, under the firm name of McKay and Dix, conducting a general shipping business and engaging extensively in the Greenland and Newfoundland trade. He retired in 1893, and removed to Roxbury, Massachusetts, where he lived with his nephew, William L. Kean, whose wife was also Captain McKay's niece.

He died April third, 1895, one of America's great men of action. The list is long and should ever remain memorable.

When once the captain of a ship loses his vessel, his prestige is gone and it is difficult for him to get another command. Granted there are often extenuating circumstances, yet the stigma, too often, remains and cannot be lived down. During the time of which we write, marine insurance underwriters were all powerful, especially men like Josiah L. Hale, who, despite the fact that he was President of the Atlantic Mutual Insurance Company, the largest and richest marine insurance corporation in this country, personally looked after all the ships, cargoes, and so forth, insured by his company in this City.

The illustration of the letter to Josiah L. Hale from Clayton T. Platt, the owner of the clipper ship *Messenger*, gives one a little insight as to the importance of a New York insurance underwriter, and indicates Captain Frank Smith had a staunch and appreciative friend in Mr. Platt. When the American bound tea ships were racing home from China, he brought the *Messenger* into port from Macao in ninety-three days, a passage noteworthy for the fact that she was only fifteen days from the line to Sandy Hook.

When Jacob Bell designed the *Messenger*, he laid down a ship as extreme in design and rig as any clipper ever produced in this country. She was so sharp that she could not carry her registered tonnage in dead weight, and very heavily sparred. This last may have accounted for her persistent ill-fortune, for she never completed any voyage in record time, although she has to her credit a number of very fast day's runs.

From the New York *Herald* of October twelfth, 1852, we extract the following:

"Yesterday the beautiful clipper ship 'Wild Pigeon,' Captain Putnam, hauled out of her birth, at the foot of Wall Street, and sailed for California. The bark 'Salem,' Captain Millet, also cleared yesterday for the same destination. Both vessels have large and valuable cargoes. The agent of the first named vessel had to refuse some one thousand barrels, for want of room. The 'Wild Pigeon' has only been in port twenty-nine days, and in the short space of twenty-eight working days discharged and received cargo, and is now again on her way to the Pacific.

"On the other side of the slip, just evacuated by the 'Wild Pigeon,' lies the Boston clipper ship 'Flying Fish,' Captain Nickels, also taking cargo for San Francisco. She arrived here some three weeks back, from Manila, and it is her first appearance in this port. She is of a similar model to the celebrated clipper ship 'Flying Cloud,' constructed by the same builder, Mr. Donald McKay, of East Boston, but has sharper ends, and is stated to be the sharpest vessel he ever launched. Like all clipper ships, she is filling fast, and will leave on or about the 23rd inst.

"Independent of the above, there are seventeen other vessels up for the same port. Among these are the following beautiful new clippers yet untried: The 'Flying Dutchman,' 'Contest,' 'John Gilpin,' and 'Tinqua.' The first two were built in this city—the 'Flying Dutchman' by Mr. W. H. Webb, the other by Messrs. Westervelt & Sons; the 'John Gilpin,' by Mr. Samuel Hall, of East Boston. The 'Tinqua' was constructed by Mr. George Raynes, of Portsmouth, N. H. She has not yet arrived here, but will make her appearance shortly, to commence loading in Mr. John Ogden's line of clippers, to which the 'Wild Pigeon' and 'Flying Fish' also belong.

"The other clippers loading here for San Francisco are the 'Game Cock,' 'Grey Feather' and 'Trade Wind,' all first class vessels. The freighting business for California is at present very active, several of the new clippers having had a portion of their cargo engaged before they appeared at their berths.

Private.

Philad'a May 15th 1852

Josiah L. Hale Esqr.
New York

My Dear Sir.

When I made insurance with you on Cargo p New Ship "Messenger" you asked me if there was not something against Capt Smith in the matter of the loss of a Steamboat, I knew nothing then, and on enquiry, I find no blame can or should attach to Capt Smith.

My reason for writing is in Consequence of a letter from the "Sun Mutual" informing us that in Case Capt Smith shall Command the "Messenger" they object to insure — they refer to Mr Henry Grinnell, or Grinnell Minturn &c, who has interested himself in the business very unwarrantably.

I am satisfied that Capt Smith is a Capable, upright & worthy man and do not think he deserves such treatment. Adversities overtake all men & if no misconduct can be justly attributed to the unfortunate I think they should be sustained.

Capt Smith was a large loser by the sinking of his Steamer — He Commanded our Ship "Susquehanna" on a 14 Months voyage, to our entire satisfaction, & that of our agents in San Francisco and Shanghai — Our Phoenix & Union Mutual offices insured Cargo by that vessel at as low rate as on a New Ship having such Confidence in the Captain —

There is much envy towards the masters of these fine Clipper Ships, and many false charges are frequently brought forward against them —

I feel a deep interest in sustaining an injured man, and cannot consent to Mr Grinnells interference,

May I ask you to give us your support if you shall be satisfied with Capt Smiths explanation & testimonials. —

very respectfully
Clayton F. Platt

"The clearances at this port for San Francisco, during the month of October, give one for every alternate day; and from the first of last month up to the present date, the number amounts to twenty, including the clipper 'Comet,' and other first class ships. The whole number from all our Atlantic ports during that period is thirty-six; which shows the great preponderating commercial enterprise of New York, over all the other commercial cities of the Union combined."

It was at a time when navigators were beginning fully to reap the benefit of Lieutenant Matthew Fontaine Maury's researches with regard to the winds and currents, and other elements connected with the physical geography of the sea, that four of these splendid clipper ships put to sea from New York bound for California's Golden Gate. And then began the most celebrated and famous ship race that has ever been run off upon this race course of the ocean, fifteen thousand miles in length.

They were ably commanded, and as they passed the bar at Sandy Hook, one by one, and at various intervals of time, they presented really a most magnificent spectacle. These ships and their masters were: the *Wild Pigeon*, Captain Putnam; the *John Gilpin*, Captain Doane; the *Flying Fish*, Captain Nickels; and the *Trade Wind*, Captain Webber. Like steeds that know their riders, they were handled with the most exquisite skill and judgment, and in such hands they bounded out upon the "glad waters" most gracefully. Each, being put upon her mettle from the start, was driven, under the seaman's whip and spur, at full speed over a course that it would take three long months to run.

It was the season for the best passages. Each one was provided with the Wind and Current Charts. Each one had evidently studied them attentively, and each one was resolved to make the most of them and do his best. All ran against time, but the *John Gilpin* and the *Flying Fish* for the whole course, and the *Wild Pigeon* for part of it, ran neck and neck, the one against the other and each against all. It was a sweepstake with these ships. The *Flying Fish* won.

In October 1852, there was a strike for wages among the

riggers, caulkers, stevedores and along-shore men, employed on the New York waterfront, to quell which the police and military were under arms. We extract the following from the New York *Times*, October thirteenth, regarding these "Shipping Riots":

"South and West streets were lined with men dressed in the garb of stevedores, having their cotton hooks and sheath knives in their belts. No disturbance was created on the North River side, the 'turn-outs' there contented themselves with walking up and down, and looking with a satisfied air upon the apparently deserted vessels. Several gangs of men were at work, and on being questioned by the men who were walking about, stated that their employers had agreed to give the price which they demanded. This was deemed a sufficient excuse, and the laborers were allowed to proceed.

"On the East side things wore a more disagreeable aspect. At quite an early hour the laborers gathered in crowds, and declared their determination to allow no work to be done on board the vessels.

"At Pier 14, several gangs of men were engaged discharging and taking in freight from the ships 'Roscius,' 'Arctic,' and 'Victoria.' The 'turnouts' seeing them employed made a descent there and insisted upon a suspension of work. Just then the Chief of Police arrived with a posse of officers and ordered the disturbers of the peace to leave the wharf. This they refused to do, and one of their number mounted upon a box and began to harangue his comrades, telling them not to leave till they had accomplished their object. The arrest of this orator was the commencement of quite a *mêlée*. The officers were resisted by the stevedores, who used their cottonhooks as weapons. When the officers found it necessary to go to work in earnest, they drew their 'short clubs,' and in a very few minutes cleared the pier, and the disturbance was completely quelled.

"At Pier 23 stevedores were at work loading the ship 'Great Western' when the 'turnouts' made their appearance and demanded that the work should cease. Mr. Charles H. Marshall, the owner of the 'Great Western,' asked what they demanded, and was told that they wanted the new scale of prices paid. Mr. Marshall said he had no objection to paying the price, and forthwith ordered his head workman to announce that the stevedores should have $2.00 per day and the riggers $1.75. But this did not satisfy them; they presented a paper for Mr. Marshall to sign, agreeing on his own part to pay these prices, and condemning all employers who would not pay them. This paper he refused to sign, saying that he had nothing to do with the business of his neighbors."

Prominent merchants and shipowners like Messers. Grinnell, Minturn and Company, C. H. Marshall, Robert Kermit and others made no objection to paying the prices asked, and only condemned the belligerent course pursued by the stevedores.

The military of the Third Brigade were under arms and it was understood that if their services were needed they would be summoned by the City Hall bell. Late in the afternoon they were informed their services would not be needed, so the men were dismissed.

Within a week this violent strike was over. One of the evils abolished was the levying of a shilling a day (twelve and one-half cents) by the "boss stevedores" on each man's pay. This had been done right along with the sanction of all concerned, the merchants, boss stevedores and workmen.

Captain Oliver R. Mumford arrived from San Francisco in November 1852 with the foremast of his ship, the clipper *Tornado*, very nearly prostrate, and the bowsprit broken off— the effect of a whirlwind in the Pacific a thousand miles west of Cape Horn. He had sailed her in this condition 8,000 miles in sixty-five days, with a crew that he describes as "the most worthless lot I ever saw on board a ship." The accident occurred at two o'clock A.M. on the eleventh of September, when the vessel was thirty-three days out, and about half-way home.

"The shock," says the captain's log book, "was instantaneous. The bowsprit was broken off close to the knightheads, and the whole of it carried inboard on the port side. The foremast instantly followed it close to the deck, being lifted from between the main-stays so that the heel of it grazed the house, and went over the side, tearing away the main and monkey rails. This immense weight of mast, yards, sails, and rigging lying across the main-stays, together with the surging of the ship, caused by the increasing sea, had to be cut adrift to save the mainmast, which on examination was found to be sprung."

The prospect of seeing New York again was not very bright, but the captain at once proceeded to business. In fourteen days, while the *Tornado* was at the mercy of the waves, he succeeded in completing a jury rig, and in fifty-one days thereafter sailed through the Narrows and into New York Harbor, without having once put into port for repairs. So much impressed were the officers of the New York, Atlantic, Astor, Sun, and Mercantile insurance companies with his brilliant skill and resolution that they presented him with a service of silverware.

"Blackbirders" were thick enough around South Street from say 1850 to 1860, and twenty-dollar slugs were "flying about like spoondrift off Hatteras in a nor'west squall" in certain slavers' rendezvous along the East River waterfront, but more especially was this apparent in a prominent bar-room —the South Street "Delmonico's"—just a few steps westward, on Fulton Street. It was come easy, go easy with those African traders, who were spendthrifts of the first class, and in the small backroom of this large well known bar-room, deals were made not only for sums that were appalling—but for human lives! "A voyage to the Coast! Blackbirds, Wool and Ivory in the Hold," were the predominating features that lay uppermost in the minds of a crowd of daring merchants, shipmasters and sailormen, who were well-ballasted with coin and anxious to prey upon the negro. Surely the negro in this country was better off by far, clothed and fed as he was down South, or in the West Indies, than when killing and eating his own flesh and blood as he did in Africa, was their matter-of-fact contention. And they were right—for certain African rulers would have killed thousands of their captives if the European slave-buyers had not purchased them and Americans taken them out of overcrowded barracoons on the West Coast of Africa.

There were several well known Spanish banking houses on Wall Street, where in a side room or "private" office, the owners, captain, and generally the supercargo of a slaver,

View of South Street about 1855.
From an old print in the author's possession.

could be found in earnest consultation. There were, it is true, certain New York merchants who looked askance upon this nefarious business, but they were not averse to embarking in it, "on the sly," for there was good, bright gold to be obtained. To stifle their consciences, if they had any, or for "camouflage," these same individuals were the loudest shouters at Sunday church services, and gave plentifully to all Abolitionist projects!

Bright and early, on the morning of February second, 1857, William Hall, first mate of the *Dorothea*, was on board that slaver-schooner, lying at Pier twelve, East River—a sailor once more. The crew and their dunnage soon came down, and the crew were all, for a wonder, sober. They were a fine lot, picked men, and Hall put them immediately at work—securing and lashing down things for sea about the deck and overhauling some of the running rigging. While the crew were busy, down came Captain "Frank" Bowen, and another man with their traps in a carriage. Both jumped over the rail and darted into the cabin. Beckoning Hall to come aft, Captain Bowen introduced him to Señor DeCastro, the supercargo. DeCastro was a Portuguese—a dark-skinned man with coal black whiskers up to his eyes, out of which he could not look straight.

"Get your lines ready, Mr. Hall, and soon as the tug gets here pull out; lose no time, or my friend here"—pointing to DeCastro—"will go in fits," was the Captain's order.

The tug by that time was alongside, and taking a line over the bow of the schooner she whipped her speedily out of the dock and down by Governor's Island. When outside the Narrows the sails were hoisted, the tug cast off, and with the strong westerly breeze and the ebb tide behind her the *Dorothea* skipped down Ship Channel and out by the Hook at a ten-knot clip.

Off the Sandy Hook lightship the steward called Hall into the cabin. He found Captain Bowen and DeCastro busy overhauling a mass of papers, accounts, and so forth.

"Now, Mr. Hall," said the Captain, "we have a good crew and I don't want them worked up on this run. Of course, there must be discipline, and sail must be taken care of, but anything like the treatment of sailors in the Atlantic trade won't do in this business. You understand, I think. We shall call first at Sierra Leone and we must get there soon as possible. I expect you to drive the vessel, and if she is not in her best trim take the men and shift the cargo till she is."

"Yes, yes, carry on to her, Mr. Hall; keep her going," said DeCastro, offering him a cigar; "days mean dollars to us in this run; thousands of them, perhaps. We have spent a great deal of money in fitting this vessel out, and you need not be afraid of her, I can assure you."

"Set your watches, Mr. Hall, and let her go east—southeast," said the Captain.

"Aye! aye! sir!" replied Hall, and went on deck.

The breeze was fresh from the northwest and the *Dorothea* slipped out to sea like a swallow on the wing.

Francis Bowen, the commander of the *Dorothea*, was an old African trader who knew all the ropes; but he took little interest in anything aboard excepting the navigation of the vessel. DeCastro had lived on the African coast and was, therefore, acclimated; and, besides, he was a good physician, particularly for the dreaded coast fever. The crew were Americans, and first class men all; the cook a Dutchman, was a good man; and the stores were of the best quality with all extras, such as wines, cigars, canned-goods, jellies, and so forth, in the cabin.

The *Dorothea* made a good run off shore and across the Gulf Stream, the westerly wind following her for ten days. Then she met a spell of light variable winds and calms as far as the Cape de Verde Islands, thence to the African coast were baffling and sometimes head winds. Thirty-five days out from New York the bonnie schooner, under the American flag, dropped her anchor and furled her sails in the harbor of Sierre Leone. She lay about one mile from the shore, and a quarter of a mile from a British man-of-war, a corvette.

"Johnny Bull takes some interest in us," said Hall to Captain Bowen after the sails were furled.

"Yes," replied the captain, "they will board us, no doubt, pretty soon."

The next morning, after breakfast, a boat from the man-of-war boarded the *Dorothea*, inspected her papers and searched her hold. The British officers were insulting in their behavior, and evidently disappointed in not finding some irregularity so that they might seize and condemn the schooner, which they felt sure was a slaver. But all was regular in her papers and cargo for a trading voyage on the coast, and Captain Bowen and DeCastro could not help chuckling at the discomfiture of Her Britannic Majesty's servants.

The morning after the search the *Dorothea* weighed her anchor to the chantey "Yankee John Storm Along," and topped her boom for the Congo River, passing close to the stern of the man-of-war and dipping her ensign as she sailed out of the harbor. The schooner's salute was not acknowledged by the corvette, but the Britisher's rail was crowded to get a look at the saucy Yankee. With a fresh breeze from the southwest, the *Dorothea* worked down the coast, and on the morning of the fourth day made Padrone Point. She had a fair wind about half way up the muddy Congo River, Captain Bowen acting as pilot. Thence to Port Leone, where she was to discharge her cargo, it was tedious work—mostly kedging. When in sight of the Portuguese Factory, her destination, a canoe-load of negroes, were sent out to pilot and assist her, and she was finally moored alongside the bank of the river. The day after she arrived at the factory a large gang of men were put at work discharging her cargo.

Waiting for the return cargo (negroes) to be ready was tedious, and the crew, idle as they were, would ramble about the shore despite the warnings of DeCastro, and all were taken down with the fever. DeCastro tended them assiduously and they got up again in a few days, but they were only ghosts of their former selves, and were as weak as rats.

The *Dorothea* then took aboard from lighters off the coast her cargo of men, women and children—"the finest lot of niggers that ever left the Congo River," said DeCastro, who superintended the embarkation. When all were aboard, the schooner filled her sails and started for the long run westward —to make the historical and revolting Middle Passage— standing well off shore out of the track of cruisers.

The crew had a relapse soon as they got out of the Congo, and ten sailors died in about as many days. Hall began to wonder what diabolical spirit of evil was hovering about the *Dorothea*, making the vessel a floating morgue, as she was gliding over a beautiful sea in the soft balmy weather of a marine paradise. Captain Bowen was too ill to attend his duties —the entire management of the vessel depended upon Hall.

The *Dorothea*, however, continued logging off the miles of her course to the westward in good style, and for a few days nothing unusual occurred except the death of three more men. Hall kept the deck now nearly all the time, so anxious he was to finish the disagreeable cruise. He felt at times as if he would like to drive the "hellish keel" and its freight of misery down to the bottom of the sea.

In about longitude forty west one day, "Sail Ho, to windward!" was cried by a man aloft. Hall immediately jumped upon the top of the house with his glass and made the stranger out, as well as he could, to be a large square-rigged craft. Every sail was pulling on the *Dorothea* except the jibs. The stranger nevertheless in a little while appeared to be drawing ahead. He was two points abaft the weather beam of the schooner, and Hall thought he looked like a man-of-war.

"Whoever he may be he'll be on top of us if we keep this course," thought Hall, so he hauled the schooner up a point-and-a-half to make the jibs draw, and in about two hours he could very well make out the hull of the strange ship.

"He will keep his course if he is a merchantman," said Hall to DeCastro, "and cross our wake." DeCastro began to get anxious and well he might. In an hour more the ship was in the wake of the schooner, when Captain Bowen, who had crawled on deck, asked Hall what he thought of the stranger astern.

"We'll know presently, Sir, but I think she is a man-of-war. A merchant vessel of that size would carry skysails; and she shows nothing above her royals. Ah! I thought so! Here she comes!" said Hall, when, like magic, her studding sails were set.

"Well, his size must tell against us, and if he gains now upon us what do you propose?" queried Captain Bowen anxiously.

"We'll wait and see if he does outsail us," replied Hall, "and if he does, I'll try him on the wind."

"Yes, that's the play. Have you noticed the barometer, Mr. Hall? It has dropped some two-tenths since morning. There is, too, some dirt around us; and we'll surely have a dark night and a good chance to give him the slip. I must lie down. I have no more strength than a cat," and the Captain went to his room.

The breeze was strengthening all the time, and Hall finally concluded that the man-of-war was gaining on the schooner and that no more time must be lost. "Call all hands," he ordered, and in a jiffy he took in the squaresail and lowered the yard on deck, hauled down the jib top-sail, luffed sharp and trimmed down all sheets, and then, close hauled, was dancing up to windward. As soon as the man-of-war noticed the schooner's maneuver down came his studding sails on a run and, bracing his yards up sharp, he stood in hot chase after the *Dorothea*. It was a "clinch" in earnest now. Hall took the wheel himself, and the schooner, as she felt the weight of the strong increasing breeze on her beam, began to send the heavy spray flying across her deck. She lay a good point higher than the man-of-war and nearly held her own in reaching along. Beckoning to DeCastro, Hall told him to get the negroes in the hold as close as possible up to the windward. The wind sails, of course, had been taken in, but all hatches were open as no heavy water was coming on board, and there was a good circulation of air in the hold. As night was coming on, and the breeze getting stronger all the while, supper was served to the crew early. The wind was howling at sunset, and Hall never quit the wheel.

He was a helmsman—a born helmsman—and he had steered no such trick as this since he was a boy sailing with his father in competitive tussles back of Cape Cod. It was soothing to his perturbed spirit to feel the gallant schooner under his feet as if she were alive with the strong press of the howling breeze that strained every rope, spar, and sail to the verge of rupture. Never since she had been launched had the *Dorothea* been driven so hard as by Hall's skillful manipulation of the wheel—now with touches light as a feather, and again exerting the strength of an athlete—she was eased and luffed from wave crest to wave crest, her lee rail buried at times, and the spray constantly flying over the weather rail and streaming across the deck like a mill sluice. Up to the windward she must climb! There were prison, disgrace and, perhaps, the rope if captured; and, with his eye constantly on the luff of the mainsail and the topmasts that were bending like coach whips, he kept the *Dorothea* a-going.

"Something will fetch away I fear," said Captain Bowen, who with blanched face was standing in the after door of the cabin.

"I hope not, Sir," replied Hall.

"But d———n it, you will drown us all, Hall!" exclaimed the Captain as the schooner heeled her lee deadeyes under and the water came rushing aft like a young Niagara.

"Better drown than hang," said Hall tersely, as he luffed the schooner out with a turn of the wheel.

DeCastro's swarthy face was nearly white, as he squatted under the weather bulwarks on the quarter, and scarcely a word could he speak while the *Dorothea* was forging along over and through the mad seas.

"Will they catch us?" he gasped with an appealing look in Hall's face.

"Not if things stand," said Hall, pointing aloft. "They won't catch us on top of water, Señor," and he smiled grimly as he whirled the wheel to meet a sharp sea that struck the weather side with a thud and nearly blinded all hands with its sheets of flying spray.

At eight bells Hall, satisfied with the weather gauge (position) the schooner had obtained, furled the topsails and extinguished all light on board preparatory to doubling on his course and giving the man-of-war the slip. It was very dark now and he tacked ship. Then he furled the flying-jib, double-reefed the mainsail, and hoisted it again. Next he lowered the foresail, put two reefs in it and tied it up with stops in case he should need it quickly.

"No use now to keep the negroes in the hold huddled together," said Hall, "as we are now under short sail." De-

Castro was pleased at this. "You may set the windsails too," said Hall; "give the poor devils down there all the air we can." Going aloft he could just make out in the darkness the man-of-war on the lee beam. But he had tacked—expecting, apparently, that the schooner would go about in the night and stand down to leeward on her original course.

A few days after the chase, the breeze had moderated considerably, and the next day it fell calm, with a heavy swell that made the schooner lurch and roll fearfully. Hall lowered the mainsail and secured everything about deck.

The captain managed to crawl on deck about noon and to Hall he said: "This calm will be short lived. The barometer is falling, and falling fast. The swell is abeam, and you see it is getting heavier. There certainly is wind behind it, although it is not the hurricane season."

Captain Bowen was an old West India and African trader and Hall felt that he was correct in his prognostications. The vessel now had no steerage way, and one could hardly stand on her deck she tumbled about so heavily. But Hall managed to put two reefs in the mainsail and foresail, then furled them again, and secured the booms with extra tackle.

By this time it began to look black and greasy, so to speak, on the starboard beam. Captain Bowen had gone into the cabin and lain down. No one but an able-bodied seaman was of any use on deck now. Hall went into the cabin and reported to the Captain the unusual "dirty" appearance.

"Make all your preparations, Mr. Hall, and expect the worst. You can see that the barometer is still falling." Hall immediately got the storm trysail up and bent it on the main, and also bent a small storm jib on the stay and saw that all the hatches, battens and tarpaulins were ready to make the hold tight at the last minute. In the afternoon watch it began to thunder heavily, with quick intermittent flashes of lightning out of the heavy dark clouds, and the negroes in the hold began to howl with fear.

"Poor devils," thought Hall, as he looked down the hatchway.

It was "feather white" to windward now, and black as midnight. Down came the squall in a smother of spray and rain.

It was lively work to get the storm jib set and sheeted home before the squall struck the *Dorothea*. Down she went—down, down, down,—lee rail under, and then down to her hatch-coamings, as if she never would come up again. All hands climbed up to windward.

"Hard up!" yelled Hall to the man at the wheel, as he made his way aft under the lee of the bulwarks to assist him. The gallant craft struggled to get up, and as the storm-jib filled she slowly fell off, righting herself as she swung around to the pressure of the jib and her helm. Hall and Frank (the best sailor in the *Dorothea's* crew) had all they could do at the helm when she righted to keep the vessel before the wind, which blowing so strong on their backs, fairly pinned them against the rim of the wheel. As it came down with a rush and a roar the blast cut the white crests off the top of the seas, sending the spoondrift down to the leeward like a snow storm, and breaking over the *Dorothea* in flying spray it stung the face like heavy hail. Speak—one could not! No sound uttered went beyond the lips until the first burst of the squall had passed.

The gallant craft felt now, to the men at the helm, like herself, and ran about seven knots under the storm jib, which was not much bigger than a table cloth. But she was going off her course about six points. This was bad, but it could not be helped; for until it moderated the schooner could not with safety be brought up and hove to.

About sunset Hall determined to risk it. He got the men aft and hoisted the main trysail partly up and sheeted it to the quarter. Then he hauled the storm jib into the mast, put his two best men at the wheel, and the remainder at the main trysail halyards, and waited for his chance. Catching, finally, a comparatively smooth time, he motioned to the men at the wheel—
"Hard down, and be quick about it."

"Hold on for your lives!" he yelled as the schooner came up in the wind, jumped her bowsprit out of sight under a big sea and threw a few tons of water over the quarter.

"Hoist away on the trysail!" and in less time than it can be told the *Dorothea* was lying to the wind and seas like a Mother Carey's chicken, buoyant and dry, as only an American clipper schooner can lie.

Hall breathed freer now, and to look about before night came on was his next business. The vessel was shipping no water to speak of, and to open the door and the windows of the forward house was imperative he thought. The stench that came up through the hatchway when it was uncovered was sickening.

"We must do something to help those miserable devils down there," said Hall, and he set a windsail through a quarter of the after hatch. In the strong gale prevailing the wind rushed down into the hold like the blast of a tornado carrying with it considerable of the spray that was flying over the vessel, but no heavy water.

One of the crew then reported to DeCastro that some of the negroes in the hold had been suffocated, or trampled to death, when they were all tumbled pell-mell down to leeward by the squall. Some sea biscuit was fed to the negroes now. They had had nothing to eat since the morning; and the crew got what they could from the cook for their supper.

The wind hauled to the south'ard during the night and by daylight the schooner was on her course and then Hall lowered the trysail and set the foresail. It was blowing a fresh gale now that was backed by the southeast trade wind, and the *Dorothea* jumped along on her course from sea to sea, shipping considerable water. The hatches forward were kept battened down, and the negroes could get nothing to eat in the morning but some hard bread. A wind sail in the after hatch, however, gave them good air in the hold. At five P.M. the seas were running more regular and the deck was drier, though the breeze had not abated much.

"Get those dead niggers up," said DeCastro to some of the crew who were comfortably resting themselves for'ard, and they passed up the after hatch twenty-six bodies. All were examined by DeCastro and pronounced dead before the crew tossed them over the rail.

"Too bad," said DeCastro lugubriously; "there go the doubloons."

And the black corpses floated past the side and out in the white foam of the wake where they bobbed mockingly, as it seemed, at the receding vessel.

"Horrible! Horrible! Sir," said Hall as he turned away and walked forward.

"Yes, I suppose it is," said DeCastro, nonchalantly puffing at his cigar, "but, you know, the niggers don't mind it, and it pleases the sharks."

Hall had no appetite for his supper that evening, but lay down instead to try and catch a nap. But he could not sleep, and at four bells he went on deck again, feeling ugly. The schooner was driving before it in grand style with her foresail wide off to port, and fairly leaping from sea to sea. Overhead it was pleasant; for, now and then, the moon shone through the clouds.

"I never sailed with such a freight before. I wonder how much this infernal craft will stand? So far I have not parted a rope-yarn," he said to himself, and calling the crew, to their surprise he ordered the square sail set on the staggering schooner.

"It is a fair wind, boys, and I'll be d——d if I want to see those dead niggers climbing over the taffrail," said Hall as they pulled the tack down. Under the additional press of sail, and before the following seas, the *Dorothea* now tore along like mad, at times burying her cat-heads and throwing the water in cascades high over her bows. It lulled a little at daylight, and then he piled on the fore topsail and a "raffee" set over the square-sailyard—leaving the halyards aft to serve as a backstay to the over-strained topmast. She fairly smoked along now, but ran as steady and true on her course as if she were in a groove.

Though the breeze next day was strong, the weather was pleasant and the decks comparatively dry. The negroes were bathed and fed as usual.

"We're making a good run, Mr. Hall," said DeCastro.

"We would make a better one if I could crowd more sail on her," replied Hall. Two days more of this hard press and early in the morning it was—"Land Ho" from the crosstrees. At high noon the *Dorothea* sailed through the passage between Martinique and Dominica into the Caribbean Sea. Hauling her wind a point or more, she then set the mainsail and the main topsail, and with the breeze still strong, but in smoother water, she stood up for the south side of Cuba.

"Keep your eye skinned for cruisers," said Captain Bowen who began now to stay more on deck.

Hall was perched in the cross-trees nearly all the time, but no suspicious sail could he see. Every one on board seemed to be happy now at the prospect of landing, and the childlike delight of the poor negroes, who were soon to view the "Promised Land," was pitiable. The wind veered till it was nearly abeam and the *Dorothea*, with the strong current setting her to the westward, ran like a locomotive along the south side of Porto Rico and Santo Domingo.

A crisis of the voyage was now at hand. The cargo must be landed in defiance of the cruisers that patrolled the Cuban coast. Captain Bowen and DeCastro began to get anxious. DeCastro particularly could not conceal his uneasiness. To fail now—to be captured, or be compelled to lose vessel and cargo in prevention of capture and, thereby, have the expense, trouble and misery of the cruise come to naught! The thought was harrowing. All went well, however, and on the evening of the thirtieth day from the Congo River, with Captain Bowen as the pilot, the *Dorothea*, skirting the bunch of keys close to the coast, furled her topsails and stood boldly in for the Cuban shore between Trinidad and Cienfuegos. When a few miles off—Captain Bowen hove to for the night. All hands were called at daybreak and coffee served.

"Take your glasses and go aloft, Mr. Hall," said Captain Bowen as the night began to lift. Look sharp in the offing, sir."

After a long and careful search Hall reported nothing in sight.

"Let her run in shore now," said DeCastro and, filling away, the schooner stood in to within a mile of the beach. Many boats—fishermen and pilot boats—were flitting about between the schooner and the shore, and one of them began now to wave a large white flag.

"Run down aboard of that fellow, Captain," said DeCastro, and in a few minutes the boat was alongside the schooner and a man climbing over her rail. He was a Cuban fisherman. As he doffed his cap he inquired in Spanish, for Señor DeCastro, and taking a letter from his bosom handed it to him. Walking aft as he read, DeCastro said to the Captain:

"It is all right now, sir. There are no cruisers about. We were not expected so soon. I must send a reply ashore." And hastily writing a note in pencil he handed it to the man in the boat, who immediately put off from the schooner.

"Let her run down the shore now," said DeCastro smilingly, "this man," pointing to the fisherman who had brought off the note, "will pilot us."

The Spanish stranger went to the knight-heads and directed Captain Bowen, who had taken the wheel. The negroes were now given their breakfast. All this business was novel to Hall, but he said nothing. Under her lower sails the schooner traveled down the shore. In about an hour, Hall saw that they were getting into shoal water. Walking aft to the Captain, who was steering as directed by signs from the man in the knight-heads, he said:

"There is white water close ahead of us, sir. Do you see it?"

"Yes, I see," said the Captain with a laugh. "It does look like it."

A few minutes more and with a shock and a grinding noise, the *Dorothea* fetched up "all standing."

"Lower away everything, Mr. Hall," and down came the sails on a run. "You may get your dunnage ready as soon as you like now, Sir," said the Captain to Hall.

Scarcely an hour passed before a large lighter having some men and a lot of clothing to cover the nakedness of the blacks was alongside. One of the men brought off some bags of specie, and saluting DeCastro went with him into the cabin. The crew were now called aft, and each man received one thousand dollars in doubloons and silver.

"Now, boys," said DeCastro, "help us get these niggers ashore." All hands turned to and assisted bundling the poor devils into the lighter and into their clothes.

"Strip the schooner," said DeCastro as he went ashore with the negroes in the lighter. "In an hour or two I'll be off again."

Under the direction of Captain Bowen the sails were

unbent, the running rigging unrove, some of the lumber below torn up, and everything of value on board made ready to send ashore. About five P.M., the lighter returned with DeCastro and a few more men and some combustibles—light, resinous pine stuff. Everything was tumbled immediately into the lighter. Then the dunnage of the officers and crew was taken out and the old bedding, rags, and so forth, together with the combustibles that were brought from the shore, were scattered throughout the schooner and saturated with kerosene.

"Is everybody ready for shore now?" asked DeCastro, as all hands gathered at the rail next to the lighter. "All ready," was the response. "But hold on," said Captain Bowen, "some one must start the fire."

"I'll be damned if I do," said Hall as he jumped over the rail and aboard the lighter.

"DeCastro and Captain Bowen laughed, and one of the sailors went back in the hold and lighted the piles that were there. The lighter had scarcely time to get clear of the old craft before she was in a blaze.

"It was as good a lot of negroes as ever landed in Cuba," DeCastro said, and Don Pedro Blanco, the millionaire Cuban slave dealer, had taken them all, three hundred and seventy. Of 420 that had left the Congo river, fifty had died—a very small percentage.

After making themselves as comfortable as they could for the night, in one of the outbuildings, DeCastro, Hall and Captain Bowen started early in the morning for Cienfuegos to settle up their business. They arrived there about noon, got something to eat, and then went to the office of a sugar merchant who was interested in the *Dorothea's* voyage.

Hall went aboard a coaster that night, lived on fish and garlic for three days, and, finally, arrived at Havana. There he had to wait a week for the mail steamer to sail. Before the steamer sailed DeCastro called on him at his hotel, and over a bottle of wine the *Dorothea's* voyage was sailed again.

"Mr. Hall," said DeCastro as he was about to leave him, "I shall make one more trip to the African coast, and in a larger vessel than the 'Dorothea.' I and my partners want you to go as Master. Of course, we will furnish all the money;

and we will give you as large an advance as you want, the regular captain's wages and one-eighth interest in the profits. You may purchase and fit out the vessel to your own liking. What do you say to my offer, sir?"

It was a little while before Hall could reply. Finally he spoke:—"Your confidence in me is flattering, I can assure you, but, DeCastro, if you were to give me the weight of every nigger in Africa, in gold, I would not engage in the business again," and as he looked in DeCastro's face, the Portuguese "Nigger Stealer" saw that the Yankee sailor meant what he said.

Captain Francis Bowen, who was celebrated as the "Prince of Slavers," returned to New York. Some time afterward he purchased the clipper barque *Sultana*, which had been built by Donald McKay in 1850, and used her in the African slave trade, most successfully. Landing a cargo of human freight at an unknown port about the Spring of 1860, Captain Bowen burnt her, and with the huge profits he had made in "Blackbirding," purchased the famous clipper *Nightingale*.

There is a good story told of Doctor Charles Cuthbert Cox, a leading divine of Brooklyn, who, when the slavery agitation was at its height, was appointed a delegate to the meeting of the British and Foreign Bible Society in London. Arriving late when the meeting was in session, he heard, as he entered, the voice of Doctor Hamilton of Leeds, England, denouncing America for her slaveholding propensities. This attack on his country aroused the doctor's fierce indignation, and when called upon to speak he commenced his address as follows:

"My Lord Bexley, Ladies and Gentlemen, I have just landed from America. Thirty days ago, I came down New York Bay in the steam-tug 'Hercules' and was put on the good packet ship 'Samson'—thus going on from strength to strength, from mythology to scripture—I do not yield to my British brother in righteous abhorrence of the institution of negro slavery; I abhor it all the more because it was our disastrous inheritance from our English forefathers and came down to us from the times when we were colonies of Great Britain. And now, if my brother Hamilton will enact the part of Shem, I will take the part of Japhet and we will walk backward, and cover with the mantle of charity the shame of our common ancestry."

This extemporaneous retort is regarded by many eminent authorities as one of the finest in the annals of oratory.

While the discovery of gold in California was a tonic to the shipbuilding industry, yet there was some fear in New York's trade circles that the West Coast was endangering the city's commercial supremacy.

Privately some merchants here attempted to throw cold water on the idea of fitting out so many ships for the California trade and an editor or two openly sought to discourage shipyard owners and accused them of disloyalty to the East. These comments reached California and one newspaper on the West Coast said in 1852:

"If our merchants on the Atlantic coast may complain that they have been injured by sending out to California the useless trash, that they could sell nowhere else, they may well be proud that the discovery of golden sands has done more in four years toward improvement in the style of shipbuilding than would have occurred from other general causes in half a century. The antiquated hulks which, like huge washing tubs, have been floating about the seas, sailing about as fast sideways as in any other direction, have been forced by the rapid spirit of trade with California to give place to entirely new models, graceful in their motions as swans on a summer lake and fleet as a cloud that is blown before the gale."

Such comments were hailed as tributes by the New York shipbuilders, who regarded them as distinctly complimentary and there was keen rivalry among them, and they were constantly spurred in their efforts to turn out faster and better ships "which would cut through the water like a knife and ride out storms like a buoy."

"Take good care of her, Mister, because after she's gone there will be no more like her," said William H. Webb, New York's famous ship-builder to the mate of *Young America*, before the departure of his wonderful maritime creation, upon her maiden voyage from New York to San Francisco. This occurred in the spring of 1853, and within our own time England's poet laureate, John Masefield, voices the same sentiment:

> "Those splendid ships, each with her grace, her glory,
>   Her memory of old song or comrade's story
> They mark our passage as a race of men,
>   Earth will not see such ships as those again."

Built expressly for the California and East India trade in 1853, the *Young America* was a most beautiful and successful ship and made many rapid passages under different commanders. Among others from New York to San Francisco, 103, 107, 110, 112, 117 and 116 days; San Francisco to New York, ninety-two, ninety-seven, eighty-five, 101, 103 and eighty-three days; the latter being the shortest record for loaded ship; San Francisco to Liverpool, 103 and 106 days; Liverpool to San Francisco, 117, 111 and ninety-nine days; the latter being the shortest on record; New York to Portland, Oregon, 127 days; Portland to San Francisco, seven days; San Francisco to Antwerp, 118 days; New York to Liverpool, eighteen days; Liverpool to Melbourne, eighty-one days; Callao to Queenstown, seventy-four days; Glasgow to Ottago, New Zealand, eighty-eight days; Ottago to Callao, thirty-six days; San Francisco to Hongkong, forty-seven days; Manila to New York, ninety-eight days.

The *Young America* for many years proved a veritable mint to her owners. Her original cost was 140,000 dollars but the freight list on her maiden passage, New York to San Francisco, was 86,400 dollars. She was also a money maker for friends and admirers, as her passages were the subject of more and larger wagers than was the case with any dozen other ships and she never disappointed her backers. Her lofty spars, beautiful lines and general handsome appearance always excited admiration and her name was a household word. Well-fitted-up cabins accommodated passengers, of which, for many years, she always carried a number.

This ship after thirty years' continuous service with only

The Famous New York Clipper "Young America", Built by William H. Webb in 1853. From a painting by Charles R. Patterson.

slight repairs was sold to Austrian parties, who changed her name to *Miroslav*. No other sailing ship has made such a record.

In this modern era, when some of the largest, strongest and most beautiful aerial creatures ever fashioned and flown by man takes one to California "overnight," this announcement of April twenty-third, 1853, reminds us how our grandfathers "flew" to San Francisco in the days when wind-propelled watercraft, not motors on an "air liner," was the mode of traveling:

"*Flying Craft for San Francisco, Now Up,*—The sylph-like clipper, 'Windward,' Capt. Comfort Whitney, one of the most gallant seaman of this port, is loading on the East River side (Pier No. 15) for the above-named port. She was built at Bath, by Trufant & Drummond, a most lovely craft, an honor to her owners and builders. She belongs to the Empire Line.

"The 'Texas' and 'Sandusky' are taking on freight and passengers, too, at Pier 17 for Australia. The former is fitted up in good style, with double berths fore and aft between decks for passengers.

"The noble 'Constellation' fell under our view, and we must pay our respect to her. She lay quiet, in all her majesty, at Pier 18, up for Liverpool, by H. P. Tapscott, 86 South Street. She is as noble a Roman as the noblest among her fraternity. Capt. William H. Allen is her commander than whom there is none more gallant.

"At Pier 19, reposed the noble, rightly-named packet ship, 'Queen of the West,' 1500 tons, nearly ready for sea, her day for sailing is the 25th instant. On that day she will depart under her highly gifted Commander, Capt. Hallett, one of nature's favorites, of the highest qualifications as a commander. Exactly opposite lies quietly snoring the 'New World,' awaiting the coming of the 6th of May, 1404 tons. Meantime her chivalrous 'Knight' is engaging himself among the élite and gaiety of the town. Capt. Hale Knight stands at the head of his profession. He wields a ship with consummate ability, in the most trying gales, and endears himself to his passengers and merchants.

"The 'Queen of Clippers,' a magnificent clipper of 2361 tons, Capt. Reuben Snow at the upper side of Peck Slip—a most attractive object. She has just been brought around from Boston, where she was recently launched, is in light ballast, and looms exceedingly lofty. The joiners are still on board, the staging at the main hatch was last Monday ready for taking in. She is a most magnificent ship of her class, 265 feet long by our estimation, but she must be longer, overall, an honor to all who have been interested in her construction. She is put up by F. D. Fowler, 60 Pearl Street, and Wm. S. Dayton, 45 Front. She bears most proudly a figure of a queen, with superb robes of beautiful workmanship, highly creditable. The ship is an honor to the mercantile marine of the nation, and an honor to her builders, her captain, and her merchants. Prosperity to all interested in her.

"At Pier 23, we contemplated the beautiful half clipper, 'Anglo-Saxon,' loading for the same port, up by Sutton & Co., 84 Wall Street, and Nivens, 18 Broad Street, but had not time to go on board—intending to return on board, but could not.

"The 'Flying Cloud' came next under our view. 'Just notice her yonder, at Pier 20, where Grinnell, Minturn & Company's California fleet are berthed,' you might exclaim! See her jaunty masts, high up in the air, squared so accurately by lifts and braces, with standing skysail yards even and royal studding sail booms! The spars are as delicate as lady-fingers and still they are strong enough to do the severest work, for severe work her gallant commander will get out of them before his voyage is over. How exquisitely she sits upon the water, like a duck for buoyancy, like a fawn for delicate symmetry. As the 'Flying Cloud' thus comes under our view, a perfect picture, we think how this matchless craft has made the voyage around the Horn in 89 days and 21 hours, (establishing a record which she herself beat some three years afterwards by about 13 hours). The 'Queen of Clippers' will have to handle her fins with amazing celerity to beat her. This fleet courser is commanded by a most competent navigator and bold, yet safe, sailor, Captain Josiah Perkins Creesy, who takes with him as he always has done on his China voyages, Mrs. Creesy."

"There is another new ship," was an expression to be punctuated with a period instead of an exclamation point and the big ships were moored three and four abreast in the East River docks awaiting turns at the wharves.

Here is an account of one of the most remarkable voyages ever made by a sailing ship. The reported day's run of 449 miles was often questioned and has never been proven to this day. The passage of eighty days, New York to Melbourne, Australia, was a record breaker.

The clipper ship *Flying Scud*, Captain W. H. Bearse, one of R. W. Cameron's celebrated Pioneer Line of Australia Packets, sailed from New York with one hundred and forty passengers, on Thursday, September twenty-eighth, 1853, crossing the Gulf Stream with a strong northerly breeze on the thirtieth of September. At eight P.M., the ship was struck with lightning. The first flash struck the ship forward, knocking down several men; one man was brought into the cabin incapable of standing from the shock, from which, however, he recovered in a short time. All felt their legs go from under them, and their nerves were greatly influenced by the electricity. The second flash struck the ship abaft the main and mizzenmast; this also knocked down most of the hands on deck, and, curious to observe, it had a great effect upon the compass. When first observed, the needle revolved with great velocity, and this continued for some time; when it ceased, the compasses were found to be considerably changed, and it was afterwards discovered that they varied five points to the eastward of their true bearing, which, after a lapse of five or six days, diminished to three points. These facts were clearly proved by the position of the sun and the bearing of the North Star.

In consequence of this derangement of the compasses (five in number), it was necessary to lay the ship to under close-reefed topsails for eighteen hours, although the wind was perfectly fair, and the ship might have run one hundred and fifty miles at least. It would appear that the lightning struck the mizzenmast and descended by the lightning-rod to the channels. The wind appeared to blow the copper wire of the rod against the chains, and here it was conducted through the bolt into the interior of the ship, where it magnetized a large quantity of iron and steel implements which were in the afterhold. To prove that these were the seat of attraction, Captain Bearse placed a compass in all parts of the ship. The influence varied in different places. On the topgallant-forecastle, the compass seemed somewhat to return to its proper bearing; abaft the mainmast, the influence was much stronger; and in the after part of the ship it was most potent. Placed upon the cabin floor, the compass still revolved with considerable velocity. On a board placed ten feet out upon the larboard side of the ship, the compass was found to become nearly correct; by this means the true course of the ship was found. The influence above mentioned prevailed during most of the passage, until the seventh December, in latitude forty-three degrees forty-five minutes south and longitude 110 degrees fifteen minutes east, where the compasses seemed to become more correct, being found to vary but three-quarters of a point to the eastward. It is also worthy of notice, that in this region several claps of thunder and lightning were observed, and that these were followed by thick foggy weather, which precluded the possibility of any observation for four days. When this was obtained, the *Scud* was found to be 150 miles to the southward of her true course in consequence of steering by the compass, supposing it to possess the same variation which has just been mentioned; but, when observation was obtained, the compass was found to have returned to its true bearing, and thus was the course of the ship deranged, and her voyage unnecessarily protracted.

On the first of October, after the true bearing of the compasses had been discovered, sail was made with a northerly wind, and the ship reached the region of the northeast trades on the twelfth of October, but found only light airs and baffling winds from southward and eastward. The southeast trades, however, were reached on the twenty-third of October in latitude five degrees eighteen minutes north and longitude thirty degrees twenty-seven minutes west; there found strong whole-sail breezes and kept with the ship until Sunday, November fifth, in latitude twenty-seven degrees forty-one minutes south and longitude twenty-nine degrees thirty minutes west. The *Scud* was then steered eastward with strong northerly and westerly breezes, the ship often going fifteen or sixteen knots in the hour. On Monday, the sixth of November, the ship ran the very large amount of 449 nautical miles in the twenty-four hours. After some calms and occasional gales from the eastward, which continued until the ship arrived on the twelfth of November in latitude forty-three degrees forty-eight minutes south, longitude five degrees three minutes east, she again obtained strong gales from the westward (this was evidently the westerly passage wind laid down in Lieutenant Maury's Sailing Directions), which continued with the ship, with but slight intermissions, until she arrived in latitude forty-three degrees three minutes south, longitude 139 degrees east, on the tenth of December. On the twenty-fourth of November, the *Scud* was in latitude forty-five degrees forty-seven minutes south, and longitude thirty-two degrees six minutes east, and arrived, as before stated, on the tenth of December, in longitude 139 degrees east, running the immense amount of 6,420 nautical miles in sixteen continuous days, thus averaging upwards of 400 miles per day. Taken as a whole, this voyage of the *Flying Scud* appears to have been one of the most successful attempts at speedy navigation accomplished by any vessel out of New York going eastward, since a due appreciation has been had of circular sailing, so beautifully and elaborately detailed by Lieutenant Maury, United States Hydrographer. It was accomplished by the *Flying Scud* under very considerable disadvantages, namely, she being two feet out of trim, having a very heavy deck load, and being extremely crank upon a side wind, which precluded the possibility of carrying the amount of sail that she was otherwise able to do.

Passage, eighty days.

He had been the friend and legal adviser of more than one generation of Minturns, Howlands, Aspinwalls, Kingslands and other prominent New York families, whose fortunes were made in Ships and Shipping during the Packet and Clipper Ship Eras; afterwards, and at the time of which we write, serving as the executor of many of their wills and a trustee of their estates.

"South Street in the days of sail represented larger and far more important financial and commercial interests than any place in America. Where in the thirties, forties and fifties, Americans, especially New Yorkers, bought shares in ships,—

today they come down to Wall Street and purchase stocks and bonds," narrated this fine old Knickerbocker gentleman, who had dwelt in Bowling Green when his grandfather and father, Andrew Foster, and Andrew Foster, Jr., were leading merchants on South Street.

"Here is how many ship-owning transactions were conducted," he continued reminiscently: "My father would buy an interest* in a sailing vessel, uncles, aunts and other relatives, also friends and neighbors would invest in the same ship. Americans have for many years, lost their interest in shipping largely because they have invested their money otherwise. And that constitutes a prime factor why we have lost our pre-eminence as a maritime power!"

As thus he interestingly commented upon a glorious past in New York's maritime history, the courtly old gentleman continued, pointing to a handsome picture of the famous clipper *Dreadnought* which hung upon the wall of his office:

"She was owned by representative New Yorkers, Gov. E. D. Morgan, Francis B. Cutting, my father, Andrew Foster Jr., and oldest brother, Frederic Giraud Foster; David Ogden, my uncle, and many of our friends were among those who originally subscribed to her construction. She sailed in David Ogden's line of packet ships—New York to Liverpool,—known also as the 'Red Cross Line.' Well do I remember her commander, doughty 'Sam' Samuels,—the most popular skipper ever engaged in trans-Atlantic service. Captain Samuels was an international hero; he and his ship were so well liked, that 'song birds' of those days endeavored to immortalize him in a song that found popularity on both sides of the Atlantic:

'There's a saucy wild packet, and a packet of fame,
She belongs to New York, and the "Dreadnought's" her name.
She is bound to the eastward, where stormy winds blow;
Bound away in the "Dreadnought" to eastward we go.

'Oh, the "Dreadnought's" a-howling down the Long Island shore;
Captain Samuels will drive her, as he's oft done before,
With every stitch drawing aloft and alow;
She's a Liverpool packet, Lord God, see her go!'"

---
* An "interest" or share in a sailing vessel represented a fractional part, ownership being divided into eighths, sixteenths, thirty-seconds or sixty-fourths.

So celebrated did the *Dreadnought* become, with her gallant commander,—the popular sea hero and the ideal tar—that this English version of the same chantey, was sung, when she was "bound to the westward"; first verse being the same as above, with this additional variation, among others:

"The time of her sailing is now drawing nigh,
Farewell, pretty maids, I must wish you good-by.
Farewell, to old England and all we hold dear;
Bound away in the 'Dreadnought' to the westward we'll steer.

"Oh, the 'Dreadnought' is hauling out of Waterloo dock,
Where the boys and girls on the pierhead do flock,
They will give us three cheers, while the tears freely flow,
Saying, 'God bless the "Dreadnought" where'er she may go.'"

There were five or six more stanzas, but we will refrain from giving them here.

The *Dreadnought*, the pride of her time, was built at Newburyport, in 1853, under the watchful eye of her skipper-to-be Captain Samuel Samuels, the beau ideal commander to nautical men of his day. It is said the owners sent a representative to England to get the right spelling of the name, which they found to be "Dreadnought" and not "Dreadnaught" after the famous vessel in Admiral Nelson's fleet.

We will not dwell upon her much-discussed "fastest passage from New York to Liverpool," because as Captain Arthur H. Clark told the writer, "It never came up until after 'Sam' Samuels was dead." Good luck always traveled with her, while she remained under his command, but hark to the tale of misfortunes that overtook all her sister ships in the Red Cross Line to which she belonged. We take the narrative from Captain Samuels' book, "From the Forecastle to the Cabin":

"The first ship lost was the 'St. George,' which was buried in the Chops of the British Channel. The second was the 'St. Patrick,' wrecked on the Jersey coast, but no lives lost. The third was the 'Highflyer.' She was never heard from. The fourth was the 'Driver,' lost on a voyage from Liverpool to New York. The crew and six hundred emigrants perished. The fifth was the 'Racer,' lost in the Irish Channel—no lives lost. The sixth was the 'Andrew Foster,' lost by collision in the Irish Channel, two lives lost."

Truly they that went down to the sea in ships in those days took their lives in their hands.

For more than a dozen years the *Dreadnought* (she was not an out-and-out clipper but what may be classed as a "medium" or half-clipper) was known as the "Wild Ship of the Atlantic," because of her rapid trans-Atlantic voyages. In all the years that Captain "Sam" Samuels commanded her, nothing ever surpassed her in anything above a four-knot breeze, and, it was claimed, her gallant commander had a "secret ocean path 'tween New York and Liverpool."

Even in our day when we talk flippantly about ocean liners of 50,000 tons, the story of the *Great Republic*, largest of all clipper ships, is of interest to seamen and landlubbers who love the deep blue sea. Like that other craft, also a forerunner of vessels of gigantic size, namely, the *Great Eastern*, her career was rather tragic. In spite of this she made records that added not a little to the fame of Donald McKay, who not only designed and built her but who was also the first owner.

The launching of this colossal wooden ship was a gala day for Boston. It took place on October fourth, 1853, and a public holiday was declared. The schools were closed and business came to a standstill. The conventional bottle of champagne, which by the way could be of strictly American manufacture as a type of the patriotism both of her owner and constructor, should have been gracefully broken over her bows, as she was christened *Great Republic*, a name selected as a tribute to the United States of America, but because of the temperance movement which was quite strong at that time, the great four-master was christened with a bottle of Cochituate water.

A few figures give an idea of dimensions of the *Great Republic*. Her foremast was 130 feet, her main 131, her mizzen 122, and her jigger 110 feet. She was 325 feet long, had a beam of fifty-three feet, was thirty-three feet deep, and of 4555 tons burden. Wire rope being unknown at that time, her standing rigging was made of hemp. Imagine the size of her main rigging, twelve and one-half inches in circumference. She carried 15,653 yards of sail. In the building of the hull 1,500,000 feet of hard pine, 986,000 feet of white oak, 336 tons of iron bolts and fifty-six tons of copper were used, not including the sheathing.

Ill luck followed the *Great Republic* from the beginning. The *Great Republic's* builder, unable to find a buyer for so large a ship, staked his faith on her and undertook to operate her. It was his hope that her maiden voyage would capture the blue ribbon for the fastest passage to Europe. Her ends were very long and sharp and her lines slightly concave, forward and aft. She carried a crew of one hundred men and thirty boys to enable her captain, Lauchlan McKay, a brother of her builder and owner, to shift sail quickly. She went from Boston to New York to load for Liverpool and she was nearly ready for sea when the disaster took place, which destroyed this mammoth clipper, also the ships *Joseph Walker* and *White Squall*.

About half past one o'clock on the morning of December twenty-seventh, 1853, the rigging of this stupendous new ship took fire, as a result of sparks carried from a burning building on Front Street; owing to the immense height of her masts, it was impossible for the engines to play upon the flames and the consequence was that the falling spars soon set her deck in a blaze. Some of the sails on the vessel were bent, and when they once became ignited no human power could save her. It was melancholy to see the noble ship almost instinct with life, the work of months, destroyed in a few brief hours. But a few days before, she had been regarded by admiring thousands, and the Governor, Members of the Legislature, and other prominent citizens. The sight presented by the burning vessel was really sublime and it was so intensely cold that the firemen were handicapped in their work and suffered considerably.

The ship *Joseph Walker* was built at New York in 1850. She was 1326 tons, owned by Samuel Thompson and his nephew and others and belonged to their line of New York and Liverpool Packets. She was valued at 90,000 dollars and was insured for near that amount. The *Joseph Walker* was bound out, and was to sail as soon as her cargo was completed. The clipper ship *White Squall* was built at this port in 1850. She was also valued at 90,000 dollars, and was owned by W. Platt and Sons of Philadelphia, and Booth and Edgar of New York. It was said she was fully insured, partly in Wall Street, and partly in Philadelphia. The *White Squall* arrived here from San Francisco on the twentieth of December and had no cargo of consequence on board. The hull of the *Joseph Walker* sank in her dock and furnished litigation with the city for many years.

An enterprising ship owner, Captain N. B. Palmer, bought the hull of the *Great Republic*, and she eventually became the property of A. A. Low and Brothers, who had her rebuilt. Her masts were shortened, she was cut down to three decks instead of four, and her yards were also shortened considerably. Instead of the original crew of one hundred and thirty she was manned by fifty men. But she was still the largest sailing vessel afloat and drew twenty-five feet of water on her maiden voyage to Liverpool.

The history of this greyhound of the days of sail was a checkered one, yet not without romance. Despite her reduced sail plan, she was very fast. Because of this the French government chartered her to carry troops during the Crimean War. She was able to carry sixteen hundred British troops from Liverpool to Marseilles on their way to the Crimea in infinitely more comfort than the other ships of the transport fleet. In 1857 she made her wonderful passage of ninety-two days from New York to San Francisco, racing the clipper *Westward Ho* and established a new record of sixteen days from Sandy Hook to the Equator. Soon after this she logged 413 miles in a day, and established herself as one of the fastest ships afloat. When the American Civil War broke out, as the majority of her owners were Southerners, she was seized as rebel property in New York and sold by auction, being immediately afterwards chartered to the Federal Government to assist the transport of General Butler's troops to Ship Island. Off Port Royal, the troops mutinied, but the outbreak was put down and they reached their destination. She was then sent down with coal to the Southern Squadron, and while bunkering two steam gunboats she broke adrift and drove ashore in the Mississippi, but was salved with very little difficulty.

In 1859 she was sold to the Merchant Trading Company of Liverpool for the low price of 25,000 dollars and renamed *Denmark*, but three years later, when on a passage from Rio to the United States, she was caught in a hurricane off Bermuda and foundered.

The packet ships slowly increased in tonnage, but did not much exceed 1000 tons until 1846 when the *New World*, of 1404 tons, was built by Donald McKay, followed by the *Guy Mannering*, of 1419 tons, and the *Albert Gallatin*, of 1435 tons, built by William H. Webb in 1849, these three vessels being the largest merchant ships afloat at that period.

The tonnage kept increasing until the appearance, in 1854, of the *Palestine* and *Amazon*, the last ships of the Morgan line to London, each of about 1800 tons, the *Palestine*, under Captain Josiah M. Lord, making the quickest passage of the line, having landed her passengers at Portsmouth on the fourteenth day out, enabling them to do business in London on a Saturday, while the passengers of the steamer that left New York next after she did reached London on the Monday following that Saturday. The passage of fourteen days to Liverpool in a packet-ship was of rare occurrence, although it was made several times by the *Independence*, 734 tons, built in 1834 by Smith and Dimon; by the *Montezuma*, of 1070 tons, built in 1835 by Brown and Bell; by the *Patrick Henry*, 997 tons, built in 1839 by the same firm; and by the *Southampton*, 1273 tons, built in 1849 by Westervelt and Mackay.

There were 306,279 emigrants who left English seaports, in 1852, for America, 217,459 of whom sailed from Liverpool, a large percentage being bound for New York. During the month of April, 1853, it is recorded that 27,000 embarked at Liverpool bound for America and kept steadily on, with slight changes, till the next year.

The prevailing fashion in naming ships in the days of sail was quite an expression of the general spirit of the time in which they were built. In the earlier periods of our mercantile history the taste was for names which indicated the more useful and burdensome properties; such as, the *Aid, Endeavor, Industry, Hopewell, Perseverance, Tryall, Ladies Delight, Fair Play, Trusty, Matchless, Farmers Fancy* and the like. *Blessing, Brother's Adventure, Happy Return, Only Daughter, Unity* and *Friendship* were popular titles repeated many times in vessels owned along the Atlantic Coast. Household names were also given to a great extent.

Merchants soon became richer and smarter, and sent their sons to colleges and their daughters to fashionable schools, who could not bear such homespun stuff; and all sorts of antique names were raked out of mythological dictionaries and silly ones out of novels. This was a sort of classic epoch; and was all very well for landsmen, perhaps, but sailors made sad havoc with the hard words, too often of foreign origin. The funniest of all possible speculations went the round of the forecastle, and right good luck was it to have among the crew one with "book larning" enough to put the matter straight.

Symptoms of an abatement of this classic fever soon made its appearance, and some daring owners dashed out with such names as the *Challenge, Eclipse, Mercury, Eureka, Raven, Invincible, Antelope, Stag Hound, Gazelle* and *Courser;* building their ships on models in a very respectable degree worthy of such fast names. This was quite an innovation, however, and was not submitted to with tolerable grace; and when A. A. Low and Brother brought out their *Houqua,* named after that well known Chinese Hong merchant; Howland and Aspinwall, the *Sea Witch,* with a Chinese dragon as her figurehead; and our ships bore names such as *Celestial, Mandarin, Oriental,* and *Celestial Empire,* it was quite clear that the elements of a large commerce existed between China and ourselves. To show that the old conventional ties had gone by the board, we find ships being named for prominent New York merchants, shipbuilders, shipmasters and statesmen: *Cornelius Grinnell* and *George Griswold, Jacob Bell* and *David Brown, Isaac Webb, N. B. Palmer* and *John Land, Patrick Henry, David Crockett, Daniel Webster* and *Ashburton.*

As they were the noblest ships of their day, the packets

Ship Cards — Pertaining to New York Shipping in Late Fifties.
Courtesy of the "Sperryscope" Magazine and Mr. Alfred T. Lawrence.

had the most dignified names: *President, Vanguard, Yorktown, Ivanhoe, Guy Mannering, London, New York, Sovereign, Courier, Orbit, Napoleon, Manhattan, Hercules, Independence, Albert Gallatin* and *United States* were the class of titles given them.

The London Packet Lines named their vessels in honor of well known English cities and counties like *London* and *Southampton, Devonshire* and *Northumberland;* while the Havre Line vessels bore such names as *Zurich, Bavaria, La Suisse, Duchess d'Orleans,* and so forth.

When E. K. Collins, Jr., established a new line of packets to Liverpool, called the Dramatic Line, nicknamed the "Theatrical Line," he called them after such famous actors and playwrights as *Garrick, Siddons, Shakespeare, Sheridan* and *Roscius.*

During the glorious Clipper Ship Era, the naming of ships was no slight expression of the mercantile spirit of the age and every possible name denoting speed found its way into ship nomenclature. The *Alert, Rapid, Comet, Wild Pigeon, Queen of Clippers, Flying Fish, Tornado, Eagle, Trade Wind, Typhoon, Hurricane, Winged Racer, Sweepstakes* and the *Flying Dutchman,* and such like fancies, were all the fashion.

As the California business inaugurated a new epoch in shipbuilding, we will just glance at the names of some of those handsome ships, which the laws then required under a penalty, as it does today, should be legibly painted thereon, to see how ship nomenclature does honor to the "Eldorado of the West" as is evidenced by *Westward Ho, Golden City, Golden State* and *Golden West.*

Under steam and canvas, there is the magnificent new S.S. *Golden Age,* which is desirous of taking Americans to Australia's gold fields and is, therefore, well-named. Patriotism and love of country now comes to the fore, with the "Independent Opposition Line for California" naming their fastest steamer *Uncle Sam* and the New York and San Francisco Line's new side-wheeler being called *Union.* Now comes Commodore Vanderbilt's Nicaraguan S.S. *Star of the West,* augmented by the *Prometheus,* inspiringly named for that mythical demigod, who was reputed to have made men from clay and endowed them with life by means of fire stolen from heaven.

The shortest time made up to 1855 between San Francisco and New York was by the S.S. *Golden Gate*, on the Pacific side, and the *George Law*, on the Atlantic side, of nineteen days, two hours of running time; eleven days, four hours on the Pacific side, and seven days, twenty-two hours on the Atlantic side. There was a very spirited race between the steamers *North Star* and *Atlantic* from New York to Aspinwall, in December 1859. They were driven with all the power of their engines to the end of the contest, but the *North Star* arrived at Aspinwall fifteen minutes before her competitor. Time from New York, seven days, three hours, twenty minutes.

On January eleventh, 1854, the fine new clipper ship *Red Jacket*, Captain Asa Eldridge, uncoppered and manned by a very indifferent crew, left her dock on South Street bound for Liverpool, to try out her adaptability for the booming passenger and freight business between England and Australia. She arrived at Liverpool on the twenty-third, the elapsed time from dock to dock being thirteen days, one hour, twenty-five minutes, establishing a record that stands to the present day. The passage was made without the loss of a rope yarn, although much stormy weather was experienced, with snow, hail and rain.

Captain Eldridge was well known in Liverpool, having, together with his brothers, John and Oliver, commanded some of the finest New York and Liverpool packet ships of their day; he had also commanded Commodore Vanderbilt's steam yacht *North Star* during her cruise in European waters in 1853. He was afterwards lost in command of the steamship *Pacific* of the Collins Line.

The *Red Jacket* attracted a great deal of attention at Liverpool being an extremely handsome ship. She made her first voyage from Liverpool to Melbourne in 1854 under command of Captain Samuel Reed in sixty-nine days, and as she received very quick despatch, made the passage to Liverpool in seventy-three days. The voyage round the globe, including detention in port, was made in five months and four days, though she lost considerable time through being among bergs and field ice off Cape Horn. She sailed this voyage under the American flag. Upon her arrival at Liverpool the *Red Jacket* was sold to Pilkington and Wilson, of that port, then agents of the White Star Line, for 30,000 pounds, and continued in the Australian trade for several years, becoming one of the most famous of the American built clippers.

On March fourteenth, 1854, the clipper *Comet* arrived at New York from San Francisco, from which port she had departed December twenty-seventh, 1853; passage, seventy-six days seven hours, anchor to anchor, the record over this route to this day. This passage stands as a classic in the annals of commercial navigation.

In the spring of 1854, freight rates to California were low with not much offering; in fact, the San Francisco market was so glutted with certain kinds of Eastern merchandise that much was being returned by clipper to the original shippers. On this account many first-class ships which had been in the Cape Horn run were diverted to the trans-Atlantic trade, and among those which loaded foodstuffs at New York for Great Britain was the *Comet*.

There was now a great change from the palmy days in San Francisco, when a dollar was paid for a pill, and the same for an egg; a hundred dollars for a pair of boots, and twice that amount for a decent suit of clothes; a single rough brick cost a dime, and a plank, some twenty feet long, was cheap at ten dollars. At one period of those wondrous times, common iron tacks of the smallest size sold for their weight in gold; and for a long time were in demand at from five to ten dollars an ounce. There happened to be no plaster walls in 'forty-nine, and small tacks were in extreme demand for fastening the usual muslin coverings to the wooden partitions of houses. Everything that was useful and really needed in those earlier days commanded the most astonishing prices. But in 1853, the stock of all kinds of goods was greatly overproportioned to the natural demand of the place, and prices fell. In this connection it must be taken into account that the commercial people of San Francisco generally acted as agents on commission for others, and did not often import as merchants on their own account. The losses therefore on merchandise did not so very much affect them, but had to be borne by merchants in New York, Boston or some other port on the Atlantic coast.

When nautical matters interested a greater ratio in the population of the metropolis than now, and New York was one of the most picturesque seaports of the world, her waterfront being lined with majestic clippers, and noble packet ships, their American ensigns and well-known house flags floating in the breeze, men and boys, too—for Young America was then pre-eminently shipminded—going along South Street readily recognized those ships by their figureheads. Bowsprits ran in over the wagons and traffic of the street, and beyond these lofty masts and intricate rigging predominated; the vessels all pressing close to the city, seemed almost human in their confident intimacy, for you could almost put your hand on their anchors, their figureheads, and their shapely bows.

As the fastest vessels built in the United States directly after the War of 1812 were from French models, which were attractively ornamented with figureheads and carvings on the quarters and stern, the time-honored plain head and stern were doomed. Keeping pace with our growth as a maritime power, the ornamental features on American ships continued, until it reached its highest degree of perfection in the 'fifties, when American clippers were unsurpassed in beauty as well as speed, and many of their figureheads were of considerable artistic excellence, being designed by skillful artists.

With shipbuilders, the forward part of a ship or "head" includes the figurehead, and John Willis Griffiths, in a "Treatise on Marine and Naval Architecture," thus delineates it:

"There is a certain fitness about the head of a ship that at once stamps an impression on the mind in relation to the entire ship, and why? We say that the head of a ship is like a portrait, we look at the physiognomy of a man, and judge of his intellectual endowments—of his internal and external qualities; so with the ship, it is the builder's portrait."

There was always some kind of a figurehead or ornamental decoration on the stem of the early New York packets, and it reached a high state of artistic merit when the Liverpool packet *Roscoe* was launched, September seventh, 1832. A good likeness of the distinguished man after whom this ship was named—the man to whom the city of Liverpool was indebted for its most valuable literary institutions—adorned her bow. Its workmanship was said to be of superior excellence; so from that time on there was a decided improvement in the artistic merit, also interest shown, not only in the figureheads of these bluff-bowed, straight-sided, square-sterned craft, but in the profuse decorative carvings that distinguished every ship, forward and aft, during the next decade or more, for their decorations astern were oftentimes the more attractive.

Let us hark back to the history of a few interesting and apropos figureheads and artistic trailboards, also stern decoration and other ornamental features, adorning American clipper ships whose coming and going into New York harbor, or any port in the world, were marked events.

The *Sea Witch*, one of the first clipper ships that cleaved blue water with her sharp bow, a product of New York's shipyards, had for a figurehead a Chinese black dragon, with open mouth and partly coiled tail, ending in a dart. She was built for the China trade and this was the symbol of the Chinese Empire. Your real sailorman, however, knew that it belonged to "Bully" Waterman's ship, so he shunned her as he would a leper—service aboard her was akin to "Hell Afloat."

The first flyer to be sent along the course of fifteen thousand miles between Sandy Hook and the Golden Gate was the *Memnon* of New York. She cut the time of the passage, which had previously taken six to eight months, to one hundred and twenty days! A statue of Memnon, the King of Ethiopia, who was killed by Achilles, contended, at the ship's bow, against the god of storms. The dew by the ancients was supposed to be the tears of Memnon's mother, who wept every morning over the loss of her son, so the student of mythology may see a simile as, bounding over the heaving blue wave-locks, the figurehead is bedewed with spray that eventually reaches the quarter-deck.

Two years previous to the advent of the *Dreadnought*, famed for her rapid passages across the Atlantic, under popular "Sam" Samuels, her owners, the Red Cross Line of New York and Liverpool packets, had the clipper *Racer* built. This was in

1851, when horse racing was a most popular sport, so a beautiful gilded head of a race horse ornamented her stem, while a large spread eagle embellished her particularly neatly molded stern.

The *Surprise* was the first clipper designed ship ever launched at Boston, or in New England for the matter of that, was built to the order of A. A. Low and Brother, of New York, and carried their house flag for many years. A finely carved eagle ornamented her bow, while her neatly formed elliptical stern was ornamented with the arms of New York.

Beautifully modeled and the largest and longest ship built to the date of her launching, May twenty-fourth, 1851, the *Challenge*, constructed at Webb's shipyard in New York, regardless of cost, carried as a figurehead a gilded eagle on the wing and each of her catheads bore the representation of an eye looking forwards.

To show how much importance was attached to a ship's figurehead in the days when Americans were shipminded—here's a case in point: When the clipper *Gazelle* was launched from the yard of William H. Webb, her owners, Messrs. Taylor and Merrill of New York, were very emphatic in their condemnation of the inartistic figurehead originally attached. It was removed and a billet substituted.

This controversy may have been why the same builder placed neither figurehead nor trailboards upon his next ship, the *Invincible*. Her bow rose nobly on the crest of the waves, with a liberty cap as a billet head, backed by the American coat-of-arms. The handsome round stern bore a carved eagle in relief, surrounded by scroll work.

The *Gamecock*, Boston's marine pride, whose shapely hull often won the admiration of the solons of South Street, carried a fighting bird, with outstretched neck and head, apparently eager for combat, or as if to crow over the whole fleet on the wide seas. She belonged to Daniel C. Bacon, one of Boston's most successful merchants and ex-sea captains. As President of the American Navigation Club, he once challenged the shipbuilders and owners of Great Britain to a ship race, from England to China, for 10,000 pounds a side. This challenge not having been taken up at the end of thirty days, the stake was increased to 20,000 pounds, or a higher sum if agreeable. But in spite of all, the challenge was not accepted, and that was never satisfactorily explained by the English.

The *Sea Serpent* carried a long slender serpent, whose lifelike, slimy-looking body, picked out in shades of green and gold, suggested his recent escape from the waters of one of the summer resorts along the Atlantic coast. The *Nightingale's* figurehead was a beautiful bust of Jenny Lind, the famous singer, known as the Swedish Nightingale, and for whom this ship was named.

With an angel holding trumpet to mouth, the *Flying Cloud* dashed through the heads of San Francisco, eighty-nine days out from New York! We are chronicling here no imaginary run of a "Flying Dutchman," but the actual performance of a first-class square-rigged and copper-fastened ship—the swiftest of the fast Yankee Clipper Fleet. There is a quiet exultation, after all, in bounding o'er the heaving blue wavecrests, with no impelling power but the swift breath of the God of Winds, which steam-driven decks can never give.

For a figurehead the clipper *Reporter* carried a full-length representation of a reporter taking notes, but it was not considered very artistic and one critic wrote: "It looks like Col. Green of the Boston Post before he lost his hair and got religion." On her maiden voyage she went over the "Triangular Route," Boston to New Orleans, from that port to Liverpool, then home, and lost on the passage a portion of the carved work on her head and her captain expressed the belief (perhaps hope) that the rest would follow before he reached Boston. Evidently he considered the "press representative" a "Jonah," after having a rough and slow voyage with one of those cotton cargoes that necessitated putting fifty bales on deck and about a dozen in his ship's cabin.

A short distance below Pike Slip, at 236 South Street, one would find a little shop, with "J. S. Anderson and John Fraser, Carvers," over the door; here a figurehead carver is making a woman for a new vessel. We had always been interested in the wooden sex. This man is their creator. He marks a center line on each side of the square block from which the figure is to be made: then he sketches the profile outline on two sides of the block and hews down to those lines. Then he sketches the front view on the hewed sides and cuts the block down. Afterward the corners are reduced to that plump roundness so characteristic of the figurehead. From four to six days sufficed for making the average specimen.

The fortress-like building which still stands at Seventy-one-Seventy-two South Street was built and owned by the well known China tea merchants, Messrs. N. L. and G. Griswold. Among the fleet owned by this house were four vessels, all named *Panama*, and the third ship so named carried at her bow a nude, full-length figure of a beautiful woman with arms extended, pure white and of great artistic merit. It was perhaps the most beautiful figurehead ever carried by a ship. An incident in her history is related that while at Hongkong, early in 1867, Chinese thieves one night stripped a large amount of her copper from one side and also badly damaged the figurehead in their efforts to steal it.

A noticeable feature of the *David Crockett* was a life-sized carved image of that eccentric backwoodsman-legislator. The coonskin cap and leggins, together with his long rifle, were in evidence, and the whole figure natural as life. It is stated that although this was carried on board the ship, it was never mounted in the usual position occupied by such ornaments. This image was presented to the San Francisco Chamber of Commerce by a prominent shipping merchant, and it reposes in their rooms, where it is a source of much interest and attention. Throughout her long career the *David Crockett* was a phenomenally successful ship. She proved a mint to her owners, Messrs. Handy and Everett, Lawrence Giles and Company and others of New York, and up to the time of her sale in 1883, at San Francisco, is said never to have cost the underwriters one dollar.

William H. Webb placed trailboards, handsomely decorated with carvings of national emblems, upon his ship *Young America*, one of the most popular vessels that ever sailed under the American flag, and which during thirty years' continuous service in the San Francisco trade, is said to have rounded the Horn fifty times.

Even after steam began to threaten their trade, the improvements in sailing ships went on, and reached a climax in the construction of the *Great Republic* by Donald McKay at East Boston. The figurehead on this—the largest vessel afloat December 1853—was a beautifully carved head of an eagle, covered with gold leaf. Before embarking upon her maiden voyage, this mammoth clipper was burnt and she sank alongside her pier at Peck Slip. She was later raised and sold by the underwriters to Captain N. B. Palmer, and he had this immense eagle head removed and taken to his home in Stonington, where it may now be seen in the Public Library.

In the golden days of South Street's maritime supremacy, the solons of that busy thoroughfare knew the characteristics of every vessel belonging to New York's great merchant fleet, from figurehead to each particular patch in the canvas. One of these men, "who seemed to be always basking in the sun," an ex-mate of the clipper *John Stuart,* in romantically describing how she steered like a pilot boat and carried sail, said that above the sky-sail she carried a main moonsail, and above that, consecutively, a cloud-cleaner, a star gazer, a skyscraper and an angel's foot-stool, the latter, however, being set only in dead calms, when the watch on deck were not allowed to sneeze for fear of carrying it away.

The good ship *Jacob Bell,* named for that well known New York shipbuilder and launched from his former yard, after his demise was described as being of faultless model. A notable feature was the helmsman's platform, which was of brass in the shape of a heart.

And now we come to the figurehead of the last of the clippers, built in 1869 by Donald McKay, the *Glory of the Seas*. She was consigned to flames for "junk" metal at a beach near Seattle, Washington, eleven years ago, but her figurehead was taken off some time before that regretful event. A full-sized classical female figure, in white, with flowing drapery, now stands like a monument at the head of the stairs in India House, Hanover Square, New York. It is the figurehead of the *Glory* which Mr. James A. Farrell presented to that organization some years ago; so that, right here in this city, we have one of the finest examples of the figurehead-maker's art extant.

There must have been more than art in those figureheads. Captains regarded them with pride, with sympathetic respect and even superstition; in this last, your real sailorman joined! "She was overhatted! Her spars were too long! But the chief reason she was cranky was, she with built without liquor," recites an old Jack Tar in his memoirs. Then he goes on to say, "She was built in a Maine shipyard without a drop of grog. So, to take the curse off, the steward carved a teak figurehead for her, in the shape of a dragon swallowing the moon. That was right in the middle of the California gold fury, mind you. Her Captain took a gold cargo for New York. He got to the Strait of Magellan with a cracked mainmast in splints, and then, off the Evangelists, the moon dropped out of the dragon's mouth. And the next thing was, a hornfish pierced her bottom. They sawed it off in the hold, and the water rushed into the ship a thousand strokes an hour. Then they lost an anchor trying to boxhaul her out of a narrow corner. It was a bad omen, the dragon not swallowing the moon!"

Woodcarving shops were still to be found along the East River waterfront during the 'eighties; and, with the precociousness of youth, we struck up an acquaintance with the owner. This artist-mechanic had been hewing away on a large block of wood, when he came to the point where drawing some outlines was necessary, after which one could discern the figure of an Indian. Stopping in his work to pull out of a capacious pocket a paper of "Honest Long Cut," meanwhile keeping up a running conversation, he spat out the contents of his previous "chaw." Then giving the wooden block upon which he was working a malignant look, with a growl he continued: "I have carved the figureheads for some of the finest clippers and packets turned out by 'Bill' Webb, 'Jake' Westervelt, 'Dave' Brown and other builders along the East River shore, and now I've come down to this—making wooden Indians for cigar stores!" Today even that inconsequential way of utilizing his skill would be denied him.

> "But his deft hands are dust,
> And his keen tools rust,
> And his soul is with the saints, I trust."

Ship Chandlery Shop on South Street.
From a pencil sketch in the author's possession.

"Among the Figureheads", A Figurehead Shop in New York with Carvers at Work, etc.
From a pencil sketch in the author's possession.

A passenger in his cabin on board one of Tileston and Spofford's Southern Packets bound from New York to Charleston, South Carolina, was informed that a ship sailing northward had been sighted from the mast-head, and was then approaching within speaking distance. He hastened on deck, and discovered the captain, with his speaking-trumpet in hand, ready to hail the stranger. But when the vessel came within call her commander had anticipated this, and in a very squeaking voice inquired the name of our traveler's ship. The proper answer was given, and then her captain inquired:

"What ship's that?"

The same squeaking voice responded, "*Ino.*"

Now the Southern packet skipper was not familiar with Greek mythology. He had neither heard nor read of *Ino*. So, thinking that he had misunderstood the reply, he again put the trumpet to his lips, and exclaimed:

"What name did you say?"

By this time, both vessels were fully abreast of each other, and there could be no mistaking the name that came over the waves, in the same peculiar tones: "*Ino.*"

The puzzled captain frowned, he turned towards the group of passengers on the deck, as if seeking an explanation. Two or three smiled, but no one volunteered to solve the puzzle. At length he said aloud: "It would be very strange if he didn't know the name of his own ship. Hang his impudence! Does he mean to insult me?"

Up again went the trumpet, and once more was heard the query, "What name did you say?"

The vessels were now so far apart that it seemed doubtful if the most stentorian voice could reach, but to the astonishment of all aboard the packet ship, quite distinctly came the answer for the third time, "*Ino.*"

Although a very polite man, and one who, as a rule, never swore before ladies, that packet master's anger overcame his sense of propriety, and once more lifting his trumpet to his mouth, he shouted, "Go to—Kamchatka!"

Whether the commander of the *Ino* heard the last words of the angry skipper we cannot say, but certain it is that he did not go to the place directed, for shortly afterward his safe arrival was reported at New York.

Said the New York *Daily Times* on September eleventh, 1855:

"The different shipyards along our rivers which, for some months past, have been almost deserted, are again in operation; the bands that were idle during the 'depression' are nearly all again employed. A great many more vessels are now on the stocks, many more have been ordered, and not a few have been launched within the past few days.

"Nearly all the ships now on the stocks are modelled with more reference to strength, capacity and safety than to show and speed. The day of clipper ships has gone by. The circumstances that called them forth—the desire to supply speedily the newly-opened market of California—has in a measure ceased to exist. A gain of a few days' time is not considered sufficient atonement for a small cargo, and that often more or less damaged."

At all of the New York shipyards one or more vessels were under way, and in this year the California fleet was increased by the building of such successful medium clippers as the *Andrew Jackson, Herald of the Morning, Mary Whitridge* and *Ocean Express*.

New York's commerce had not, like that of the mercantile classes of England, been aided by a direct trade with extensive colonial dependencies, but had been pushed to the very confines of the habitable globe, by the unaided energies of her own merchants. They had cast themselves on the ocean self-reliant and fearless, and entered into triumphant competition with the whole commercial world; by the beauty, speed and comfort of their ships they had left all rivals at an immeasurable distance behind, and vindicated the freedom of commerce from restriction.

Now we come to a turning-point in the history of the merchant marine of the United States. In the year 1857, Congress practically reversed its policy as to mail subsidies which it had adopted ten years earlier, and under which the New York Steamship Lines operating under the Stars and Stripes, for a decade had held their own very well in competition with the British subsidized lines, notwithstanding the advantage of a five years' start which the latter had enjoyed. This radical change of policy, which had the effect of cutting down materially the mail subsidy heretofore granted to the Collins Line and of reducing, though less seriously, that of the Pacific Mail Company, was mainly due to the jealousy which had developed in the South, partly owing to the agitation over the question of slavery, and in the agricultural West, toward the shipping interests of the northern seaboard.

The enormous total of 2,348,358 tons of American deep-sea shipping was registered in this same year, and so great was the demand for vessels that more than five hundred of different types, ships, barques, and brigs, all designed for the ocean-carrying trade, were launched from American yards. Only once later, in 1860, were these tonnage figures surpassed and then only slightly. The tonnage had more than doubled since 1846 when it was 943,307. And in the five years from 1851 to 1855, inclusive, 170,000 tons of American-built vessels were sold to English and other foreign buyers. Americans had made the mistake, however, of continuing to build sailing vessels after the era of steam and iron had arrived. In New York the rapid growth of shipbuilding was due less to the wooden-hull steamships built there than to the number of clippers, and packet-ships, too, launched in an endeavor to hold the ocean carrying trade and to increase it, even in competition with the lines of British steamships during the years 1850 to 1860.

The year 1857 was one of financial depression all over the United States. It was evident that shipbuilding had been overdone, for American vessels were idle, not only at the piers along the New York waterfront, but in Manila Bay, Hongkong, Foochow, Shanghai, Calcutta and many other foreign ports, where they lay tied-up for months. Freight rates which had been sixty dollars a ton to California tumbled down to ten dollars per ton. New York's East Side shipyards which had echoed to an endless chorus of topmauls were silent. On every hand great American shipping houses were failing. New York, being the commercial center of the country, was the first to feel the effects of the storm, and before the end of

December there were hundreds of failures among her merchants. Business practically came to a standstill, industries were paralyzed, and the working classes were thrown into a state of severe destitution, to which a long, severe winter added more horrors.

It was unfortunate, too, that at this period a powerful Southern political spirit had invaded Washington, and joined the agricultural element, in a demand for the reversal of the national policy toward our merchant marine. So, following congressional debates that lasted four years, all subsidy contracts were cancelled, and ruin stalked the wharves of New York's trans-Atlantic shipping and other foreign commerce. The ultimate result was devastating indeed, for this was a part of the uniform policy of the Southern statesmen, who hoped that crippling Northern enterprise and arresting the development of our commerce would insure a recognition by Great Britain of that Confederacy they already contemplated.

When the Collins line collapsed in 1858, the pessimistic theory had been gaining ground that ocean shipping was not a field in which American steamships could hope to prosper, or even pay their way. This unfortunate attitude would seem to have been justified by the course of events. The Bremen line had gone out with the Collins line. Commodore Vanderbilt himself disposed of his maritime interests in the earlier 1860's to take up railroading. His immediate competitor on the Atlantic, the older Havre line, which appears to have been perhaps the most ably managed of all those early American lines, succumbed at last in 1867; it had carried on for forty-five years, having started back in 1823 as a sailing packet service, turning to steam at the close of the 1840's when it acquired the Havre mail contract rights of the Bremen line. And the several attempts during the 1860's to establish new Atlantic lines of American nationality lasted no more than a year or two each.

The days were now over when Uncle Sam threatened to have old Johnny Bull swept off the sea—when the American secured double freights and would make five voyages to a British ship's four. England's Parliament had sense enough to repeal its foolish navigation laws that held their shipping back, and they then gave assistance to their merchant marine, so for many years after the Navigation Repeal Act, British shipping steadily advanced while our shipping and commerce, with unfavorable laws, continually went down.

There was a time when New York's wharves, ships and piers were "well enough" and perhaps were as ample and extensive as the demand for them justified; but times were changed in 1856, and those important works had to change with them. Ships were now constructed of huge dimensions, drawing great depth of water; and the kinds of conveyance by water, too, had been wonderfully altered and multiplied. The addition and general use of steamboats and towboats in various forms created a demand for a species of dock room in the port of New York and a sort of exclusive use thereof that had not been dreamt of by any one a few years before.

New York's indifference to commercial progress was evinced in nothing more than in her neglect to provide proper dockage, thus presenting a singular contrast to every other seaport of any magnitude known to ancient or modern commerce. The quays and docks of London, Liverpool, Cardiff, and indeed nearly all English ports, were first-class. While those extensively provided at Naples, Palermo, Bremen and Boston had attracted and perpetuated much of the business which gave them wealth and power, and would continue in their possession. At Saint Petersburg, in Russia, there was (in 1856) one granite pier four miles in extent. At Havre, France, the docks were the principal structures of importance, having cost immense sums, and were justly the pride of its citizens. In fact, there was not a city of Europe possessing navigation which did not surpass New York in the necessary provision for the proper convenience and protection of its shipping. Fernando Wood, Mayor in 1856, earnestly presented these facts to the Common Council, and urged that measures be taken at once to place New York on an equal footing with the great seaports of Europe, but a long time elapsed before docking facilities at this port could compare favorably with those in some European seaports, which enjoyed much less shipping than New York.

Romantic sentiments were freely expressed in the general

press on the occasion of any special performances, and such names as *Herald of the Morning, Young America, David Crockett,* and a host of others of the clipper fleet were frequently seen in print.

After reading of such and such a favorite ship's rapid passage or damage through storm or any other interesting incident, Mr. New York Citizen with his wife and family would stroll down to the waterfront to see the object of their enthusiasm tied up to her wharf; her hatches taken off, gear rove and all arrangements made for discharge; get the pungent odors of the cargoes, which to a landsman were delicious, particularly in those vessels from China, the East Indies, or the South Sea Islands. There were no fenced-in, closely guarded covered docks in those days; open wharves they were called, and commercialism and distrust were not paramount. Mr. Common People could even go aboard his favorite and, if he showed ordinary prudence in not getting in the way of the work then going on, could stroll all over the decks; watch at the hatches the stevedores in the hold and the freight hoisted to yard-arm before being swung to the wharf. From topgallant fo'castle a fine survey could be had of the symmetrical net work of masts, spars and rigging and the beautifully kept decks. Of course, some owners did have "No Admittance" signs at gangways: "Look out for the Dog" or "Keep Out—This Means You"; but to one properly conducting himself, observance of these drastic notices was not often insisted on.

In the first half of the nineteenth century, the word "merchant" usually described a "man with large capital who was an exporter of domestic and an importer of foreign goods, who owned his own ships, and usually their cargoes as well," and the ships of each house bore a distinguished flag.

In the Clipper Ship Era, America reached her zenith on the sea, so American house flags were known in every quarter of the globe. Then all the great fortunes of the United States were derived from maritime endeavor, hence the interest in ships was more than a sentiment. In those days New York was one of the most important and interesting seaports of the world; the waterfront was lined with majestic clippers, stately Indiamen, and noble packet ships, their American ensigns and well known house flags of many brilliant colors floating in the breeze. The following are some of these house flags: The crimson field and black ball, of Charles H. Marshall; the red, white and blue swallowtail, of Grinnell, Minturn and Company; the yellow, red and yellow horizontal bars with white "L" in center, of A. A. Low and Brother; the thirteen blue and twelve white squares, of N. L. and G. Griswold; the crimson field, white border, and white "D" in center, of George Daniels; the red, white and red vertical stripes with red "B" in center, of Vernon H. Brown; the blue and white half-diamonds, of Russell and Company; the crimson field and white diamond, of Augustine Heard and Company; the white swallowtail, red cross with white diamond in the center, of R. W. Cameron; the crimson swallowtail, blue cross, and white ball in the center, of Wells and Emanuel; the blue above white, white ball in blue and red ball in white, of D. and A. Kingsland; the white field and red cross in the center, of D. G. and W. B. Bacon; the white swallowtail and black "S." and "B.," of Snow and Burgess; the white field and black horse, of William F. Weld and Company. The flag of Howland and Aspinwall had a blue square in the upper corner of the luff and lower corner of the fly; the rest of the flag was white with narrow blue lines in the lower corner of the luff and upper corner of the fly, which formed squares, and also formed a white cross extending the full hoist and length of the flag. David Ogden's flag was a white field and red cross; Crocker and Warren's, blue above yellow with a yellow "C" in the blue and blue "W" in the yellow. Then there was the red swallowtail with white cross and black star in the center, of Samuel Thompson and Nephew; the blue field, white diamond, and black star, of Williams and Guion; the crimson field and black "X," of John Griswold. The Red Star or Saint Line carried a house ensign, originated by Byrnes Trimble and Company and later adopted by Robert Kermit, showing a red star in the center of a blue swallowtail, while Cornelius Comstock flew on the little clipper *Gaspee* and other vessels of his fleet a dark red swallowtail, with a white letter "C" occupying the inside half of the flag, while the outside was divided blue on the upper and white in the lower wedge-like parts of this flag.

These were the private signals of most of the leading New York shipowners, whose ships and commercial activities, more than half a century ago, enlivened the waterfront of New York.

It was the grave misfortune of the American steam marine at this critical period to be drawn into the maelstrom of sectional strife. The slavery controversy in the early 'fifties was becoming more and more the overmastering element in national politics. It so happened that the merchant shipping of the United States, and especially the steam shipping, was owned chiefly in New England and New York, where the anti-slavery agitation was most vehement. Moreover, the subsidized mail steamers all sailed from Northern ports, except a line from Charleston to the West Indies. It was a plausible argument that the entire country was contributing to the support of an interest by which only the northern seacoast directly profited. Besides—though this consideration did not come to count for much until secession was actively contemplated—these great, swift, strong mail steamers would be a formidable addition to the sea-power of the North, if the unhappy quarrel between the States should ever drift on to the arbitrament of war.

Gradually, therefore, the ocean mail system became more and more an issue of sectional politics, as the tariff system had become a few years earlier. The South never completely deserted the cause of the American steamship; some Southern statesmen remained its eager and consistent advocates, but in both Senate and House the alignment on the Ocean Mail appropriations as they came up year by year grew more and more sinister, and the friendly majorities steadily narrowed. The mere threat of adverse legislation checked at once the swift, steady growth of our steam tonnage. American steamships registered for deep-sea trade fell off from 115,045 tons in 1855 to 89,715 tons in 1856, to 86,873 tons in 1857, and to 78,027 tons in 1858. The spectacle of an almost solid South backed by much of the agricultural West assailing the mail subventions was an alarming omen, indeed, in those years when Southern influence was supreme in Washington.

Two deep-water sailormen, as most any landlubber could perceive "by the cut of their jib," Brocky Jones and his old shipmate, Jack Collins, were sauntering along South Street one day late in the Fall of 'Fifty-eight. Less than a week previously, they had "blew into port" from China on the clipper *Sword-Fish*. Then they had coin jingling in their pockets after a long Oriental run, fraught with danger and disaster; and now, without "a shot in the locker," it was either shipping at once aboard some "hooker" or getting into the clutches of those rapacious crimps or harpies who then so completely infested New York's waterfront.

There were three "outbounders" stranded on the beach at Hongkong, when Captain Crocker and his *Sword-Fish* reached that port from 'Frisco; Brocky Jones, Jack Collins and Bill Clark:

> "Old Bill Clark was six feet high
> With carroty locks, and a squinting eye,
> A billy-goat whisker, and a well-tanned cheek
> And a nose the shape of an eagle's beak.
> Brocky Jones, was squat and fat,
> A one-time famous packetship rat,
> As good a sailor, and as true a chum
> As ever swigged from a flask of rum."

As they wended their way among the shipping, hoping against hope to find a berth with an old shipmate or a master known to them, their thoughts were reminiscent of "decks awash, for'd and aft," bucking up against easterly gales in the Indian Ocean with big, heavy green seas coming on board, first on one side, then on the other, often breaking over the poop-deck, while the *Sword-Fish*, appropriately nicknamed by her sailors, the "Diving Bell," was running her westing down. Captain, officers and helmsmen were lashed at their posts and life lines spread fore and aft the deck. Large holes were made in the bulwarks to let the water run off, with marline spikes lashed across them to prevent the men being carried overboard by the suction.

While the ship was scudding under bare poles at the rate of fourteen knots, the only sail which had been carried, a close-reefed foretopsail, being blown out of the bolt ropes, a tremendous sea swept the *Sword-Fish's* decks, and clear over her rail went Old Bill Clark! Helpless, his fellow-shipmates and pals could only look on, he was so swiftly carried away!

> " 'Tis said the best of pals, at times, must part,
> And on that last voyage Old Bill did start.
> He 'croaked' and became an albatross,
> And went to dwell 'neath the Southern Cross.
> Brocky and Jack mourned for their chum,
> But could not drown their sorrow with rum."

In 1856, an American frigate and British warship met in mid-ocean, each carrying 1,000 miles of cable. The cables were spliced together and the two ships started slowly for opposite shores of the Atlantic, paying out the snaky coils behind them. Suddenly the cable snapped! It was futile to attempt to recapture it.

A second attempt was made with the *Niagara*, a vessel of 4,580 tons burden, which was built at the Brooklyn Navy Yard in 1854, after a model designed by Mr. George Steers, the builder of the celebrated yacht *America*, the symmetrical lines of which he carried out on the *Niagara*.

She was not put into commission until the spring of 1857, under command of Commodore William L. Hudson; and proceeded to England in April to undertake the work of laying the first Atlantic cable. One-half the cable (about 1250 miles) was put in the hold of the *Niagara* and the other half in H.M.S. *Agamemnon*, the two ships leaving Valencia, Ireland, August seventh, 1857, the *Niagara* paying out her part of the cable. The U.S.S. *Susquehanna* accompanied the expedition to lend assistance if needed. Four days after leaving Ireland the cable broke through defects in the paying-out machinery and the enterprise was abandoned for that year, the *Niagara* returning home.

In 1858, by direction of President Buchanan, the *Niagara*, still under command of Commodore William L. Hudson,

United States Navy, was placed at the service of the Atlantic Telegraph Company to coöperate with the vessels furnished by the British Government in another effort to lay the Atlantic cable, and she left New York, March ninth, and arrived in England the twenty-third.

With the *Agamemnon* she proceeded to the middle of the ocean, whence each vessel started homeward, each paying out her section of the cable. After a delay of about a month, occasioned by a break in the *Agamemnon's* sections three days after the work was begun, the ships had no further trouble and landed their ends of the cable successfully, the *Niagara* at Trinity Bay, Newfoundland, and the *Agamemnon* at Valencia, Ireland. Subsequently, as a fitting sequel to that enterprise of science, it was deemed best she should engage in some enterprise of distinguished philanthropy.

On the sixteenth day of August, 1858, the successful laying of the Atlantic cable was announced, and Queen Victoria transmitted a message to President Buchanan, receiving a response. New York City, where the idea had been conceived of uniting Europe and America "by a thin copper wire running along the bottom of the ocean," was hilarious with excitement. Bells rang, bonfires blazed, business ceased—and the press became jubilant over the news that the first Atlantic cable between America and England was working. The entire country praised Cyrus W. Field, whose vision, courage and determination had made this great accomplishment possible.

> "Twice did his bravest efforts fail,
> And yet his mind was stable,
> He wa'n't the man to break his heart
> Because he broke his cable!"

It may be of interest to recite an incident which is rarely alluded to. After a first successful operation, the messages of the Trans-Atlantic Cable were interrupted and belief in the enterprise flagged; doubts were even expressed of the good faith of the managers; but it was sufficient answer to recall the message which announced the signature of the Treaty of Peace with China, which, posted on the *Journal of Commerce* bulletin, put new life into the trade with the Orient—a number of vessels clearing at once in ballast, certain to outstrip the vessels of Great Britain in the ocean race for the first home freights of silks and teas.

But alarming news from Newfoundland! "Cable out of order. Impossible to understand messages from England." Less than two months after the "Cable Carnival," the great cable lay silent in the depths of the sea. The public was stunned! Field was ridiculed...shunned by his friends...dubbed a "dreamer." Those who helped finance the venture accused him of wasting their money. The whole scheme was called wild and foolish.

Field's task was rendered all the more difficult through its momentary success. But he refused to admit defeat; and in 1866, this time with the *Great Eastern*, the great electric link was laid—telegraphic communication was established between the Old World and the New!

The American ship was commencing to chant her "Lorelei," in November 1859, when the House of Griswold were negotiating the sale of their ship *Thomas H. Perkins*, as according to the accompanying fac-simile letter, with the bold signature "N. L. and G. Griswold," known and honored in commercial and financial circles throughout the world. Irrational and unjust statutes were driving the American flag from the ocean. While England, with favoring laws, was continually coming up, America, with unfavorable laws, steadily went down.

The *Perkins*, built at Medford, Massachusetts, in 1845, of 670 tons register, was square sterned like a Dutchman's *frow* and with a billet head like a chicken, so her two actual owners, G. Winthrop Gray and John N. A. Griswold, partners in the Griswold firm, were especially desirous of selling this old hooker in a foreign port, because the market here for such packets was practically nil. There were too many fine clippers and more modern craft being offered for sale at this time.

She had seen some hard usage in the China trade out of Boston and undoubtedly needed overhauling. The *Perkins*, we note, "would require coppering," and so forth, which certainly meant an outlay of 1000 dollars at least upon her

New York November 21st 1859

Capt. Jos. T. Stevens
    Sydney

      Dear Sir

          Your note of 2d inst, requesting us to supply your wife with money during your absence, was duly recd. We shall be happy to do as you desire.

          In our letter to you of 2d inst you were authorized to sell the Perkins for such sum in Stg as would nett here Twenty thousand dollars. We desire to modify this, by saying that, if on your arrival at Sydney you learn that Guano freights are $20 at Callao and you have good and reliable assurances that you can obtain $15 p. ton Homeward you will not sell the ship for less than $25000 payable in Sydney or its equivalent in London. If on the other hand Freights in the East are low and you are not certain of obtaining more than $10 p. ton from Callao. We would wish the Ship to be sold for $20000 Dollars if possible.

We send you herewith Power of atty to execute Bill of Sale if required, but we would prefer to have the price of the Ship remitted to London to be paid over to Messrs Baring Brothers & Co upon delivery of the Bill of Sale by them. If you give Bill of Sale at Sydney. You will see that the sum of
£ 4100 the equivalent of $ 20000 in Sydney, exge 10/e
or £ 5100 — — 25000 " , "
is remitted to Messrs Baring Brothers & Co London for our a/c' in <u>undoubted Bank Bills</u>.

On the other side we give you rough estimate of the result by sale of the Ship for $20000 Dollars and the apparent reduction in cost of the Ship if $15 is obtained for guano; all which you can revise and be governed accordingly.

Touching the adjustment of your a/c, in the event of sale of the vessel, we can only say that, it will be made up precisely as if you were 1/16th owner, you participating to that extent in the profit by the sale as you would in the profit derived from freights. If you do not continue in the Ship after she changes ownership (as we think you may) we will pay your passage and your wages until you reach the U. States.

With Respect
Your Sert
Nath. L & Geo Griswold

Over

return home. A foreign owner, too, would likely keep her in commission for a while without re-coppering. This and maybe more her shrewd, far-seeing Yankee owners duly considered.

Jack had his abode in New York as well as the aristocrat, although his location was somewhat different. Where the lanes were the darkest and filthiest, where the dens were the deepest and foulest, where the low bar-rooms, groggeries, and dance-houses were the most numerous, where the vilest women and men abided, in the black sea of drunkenness, lewdness, and sin, the sailor had his New York home.

Shaping a true course into Water or Cherry Street from South Street at Roosevelt, one finds little vestige of the days when those thoroughfares were noted as the port of the deep-water sailors' boarding houses. On Water Street, in the regions under the shadow of the Brooklyn Bridge, every corner had its bagnio. But most famous of all sailors' haunts was Cherry Street, where there were more than a hundred houses for seamen, and each one viler than in any other locality in New York. Jack's landlord kept him in debt. He was robbed in a few days of all his hard-earned wages—robbed boldly by daylight, and he had no redress. A walk along this single street revealed a sight not to be found in any other part of the city, not to be exceeded by any other vile locality in the world; a hundred houses, located on both sides of the street, the most infamous in the city, where brawls, rioting, robberies, and murders took place; a hundred dance houses, whose unblushing boldness threw open doors and windows, that all who will may look in on the motley group of boys and old women, girls and old men, seamen and landsmen, reeking with drunkenness, obscenity, and blasphemy; hundreds of low groggeries, each crowded with customers, black and white, old and young, foreign and native! All along the sidewalk women would sit, stand, or recline; women clean and women filthy; neatly dressed and in the vilest array; women at work, and modest, apparently, as could be found in any street, steadily at their employ, with children around them; women who loaded the air with vilest imprecations, and assaulted the passer-by with insolence, ribaldry, and profanity.

The dance houses kept by the Germans were very neat, tasty, and attractive. The bar which stood by the door was as elegant as that at the Saint Nicholas or Fifth Avenue Hotel. Polished counters, brass railings burnished like gold, huge looking-glasses reflecting back the elegant decanters and bottles in the rear, flowers, pictures, statuary, paintings, made the place equal to any gin palace in London. The decoy dancers were of the better class, but persons on the direct road to the lowest stratum. Pianos exquisitely played, with harp and viol and other instruments, made music of which Damrosch would not be ashamed. Captains, mates, longshoremen, and the higher order of seamen patronized these better class establishments, and commenced here their travels in the path that leads to death. By the side of these more genteel sailor dance houses could be seen dwellings of the lower grade. Some of them were in low, damp cellars, down rickety stairs, with white-washed walls and a fetid atmosphere, where a dozen of the most degraded creatures could be found, bloated, bold, blasphemous, dressed in short scarlet or fancy dresses and red boots, presenting a ghastly and sickening sight. The room dimly lighted by candles, a negro playing on a wheezing fiddle, a group of men in appearance and manners to match the women, made not a bad specimen of pandemonium. Here all night long the sound of revelry, the shouts of the drunken, and oaths of reeking blasphemy could be heard. The keeper of the den, the most desperate of his class, stood at the door. He welcomed all comers, and admission was free. All who came had a partner assigned them. The lewd and boisterous dance began; at its close all would go up to the bar to drink. The wife of the keeper—or the one who passed for his wife—presided over this department, which corresponded to the vile den in which it stood. The customers paid for the entertainment and the music by treating themselves and their companions. The drinks over, the dancing commenced again. After every round all present would go up and drink, and alternate drinking and dancing continued through the night. No one was allowed to remain unless he joined in the dance. If he refused to pay for the liquor, he would be hustled out of the cellar on to the sidewalk, and probably brutally assaulted. The landlord was usually able to do this himself. A bully, brutal and as rugged as an ox, he was aways able to defend himself; if not, he had companions within call. All the desperate women, at a signal from their keeper, like bloodhounds, would tear a man to pieces. Customers would come in, take a dance, treat the company, and depart. Some remained for an hour or two; some were carried off senseless, for the vile liquor was often drugged; some were removed to foul dens that surrounded the place, and were never heard of more. Stupefied and robbed, many were sent to sea and never returned; many were foully dealt with. Poor Jack's millennium was far in the future!

The term "land sharks" was applied to a class of men, rapacious, tyrannical, brutal, and degraded, who held the New York sailors in their grip, and never relinquished their hold till he was beyond Sandy Hook, and who grasped him before he landed on his return voyage. From necessity or choice, ship captains played into the hands of these desperadoes, made them of importance, and helped them to fleece the sailor, and to hold him in degrading tyranny. Their character and their business were well known to merchants and to commanders of vessels. Next to the pilot they boarded the vessel off Sandy Hook, fastened on the sailor, and secured him and his luggage. Some few captains would not allow these land sharks on board. But when resisted, so desperate were they that they had to be beaten off by clubs. A resolute captain often had to put his flag at half-mast, and call the police boat to his assistance. The police sometimes had to shoot these fellows before they could be driven back. The captain engaged a crew from these men. Owing to the system of advanced wages, sailors went to sea in debt, and so the land sharks received their wages from the captain, made the men drunk, and hustled them on board the vessels for a long voyage. On board the ship, the sailor awoke from his debauch and found himself without clothing, friendless and penniless. He did not know who shipped him, what ship he was on, or where he was going. When he came back he would find a long account run up against him, said to have been contracted while he was drunk. Again he would be robbed of his earnings, kept on shore as long as it was profitable to keep him, drugged, and sent again to sea. A few merchants once made an attempt to separate the sailors from these miscreants. The captains were ordered to find their men elsewhere, and to have no connection with the land sharks. Sailors could not be found. Vessels loaded and ready for sea remained at the wharves. The terrible power of the landlords was found in the fact that not a seaman could be found in New York to man the ships. For two weeks the merchants held out, and then yielded by a compromise. But that compromise established the power of this depraved class. Fraud, extortion, robbery and crime had a new lease of life. The vilest dens for boarding houses, the deadliest rum, the basest companions, gamblers and women, lodgings in cellars where no human being ought to have been kept, bad literature, bad songs and corrupting music, held as in chains of steel the New York sailor.

With the passage of the sailors' boarding-houses went that sinister parlance of the old windjammer days—crimps, blood money, bone-money, shanghaing, "put the bully to sleep!" These quaint retreats of deepwater men, which years ago made New York's waterfront dangerous and mysterious, picturesque, too, have gone to the last port, together with their "big-hearted" masters, rollicking accordions, clogging tars, tall schooners of "steam," blazing rum, fat girls and bossy parrots swearing at the gay flamingoes and scratching marmosets, perched in the sunlight at the swinging doors. There the principal jargon heard behind constantly swinging doors was that of the Liverpool quays and Scandinavian fjords, interspersed with the nasal twang of "Down Easters," the braggadocio of "Blue Noses" and the carefree bluster of lads from the Emerald Isle.

Farewell, the old deepwater sailors' boarding-houses and those dens of iniquity whence the strains of the accordions floated from behind the swinging doors, with the sailors "home" from the seas! What tales of humor and pathos the barred entrances of these remaining gloomy relics could relate, if they could but speak, as the sou'easter yammers along the waterfront in the late watches of the night, which once had no ending!

About 1858 or '59, it was estimated that there were a

The Third Period 417

hundred and fifty thousand sailors belonging to the port of New York; and from these stews and dens the men were taken on whose fidelity the lives of thousands depended, and who represented, in foreign lands, the intelligence, culture, and religion of America. They furnished the means by which men rolled in wealth, sat in their crimson pews, and lived in lordly dwellings. But few thought of the sailor to whom the metropolis was indebted for its high place among the nations of the earth, or attempted his elevation. A few chapels along the East and North Rivers, known as Bethels, contained on Sunday a handful of the sons of the sea. A few Homes had been erected, but the charges of extortion and cruelty, and the bad repute that hung around them, turned even moral sailors to the common boarding-houses for seamen. The sailor could always be found among the most neglected of the population of New York.

Popular interest was excited in July 1860 by the arrival of the enormous steamer *Great Eastern*, which lay for a time on exhibition at the foot of Hammond Street, where she was visited by thousands who wondered at the proportions which justified her earlier name of *Leviathan*.

A few particulars of this, the largest vessel ever built up to this time, will form a suitable subject to this sketch of shipping in general. She was designed by the celebrated marine architect and engineer, Isambard K. Brunel, and built by John Scott Russell, at Blackwall, on the "wave line" principle. He also made the paddle engines, while the screw engines were built by James Watt and Company of Birmingham, Brunel having decided to use two means of propulsion. The dimensions of the *Great Eastern* were,—length on upper deck, 692 feet; breadth, eighty-three feet; depth extreme, fifty-eight feet; nominal power of paddle-engines, 1,000 horse; of screw-engines, 1,600 horse power; tonnage, 22,500; number of plates in hull, 30,000; rivets for fastening same, 3,000,000; and weight of iron used in the construction, about 10,000 tons. She was not only given a double bottom, but also a tubular upper deck, and with other similar features of her construction, was one of the strongest ships ever built. The double hull and water-tight compartment system was the great advantage derived in having iron ships, as it gave the greatest strength with the least possible weight of material, also producing the safest vessel afloat. She was partially square-rigged and could spread 6,500 square yards of canvas; carried twenty anchors, which, with cables, totaled 253 tons. Her launching, broadside on, into the Thames took place actually three months after the first attempt.

The *Great Eastern* was the first vessel fitted with a steam-steering gear, by means of which one man, located between the paddle-boxes, could steer this huge craft more effectually than did twenty to thirty men before with the old arrangement.

She was an unlucky ship, for from the very first she had a number of accidents and lost several lives before she started on her maiden voyage across the Atlantic in June 1860. Her original owners became bankrupt, so her new purchasers put her on the New York service; but as a passenger and cargo steamer, she could not be made to pay. She was a triumph for engineering, however; her successful laying of the Atlantic cable fully justifying the assertion that there was no other vessel which could have so successfully laid the long submarine telegraph cables, which linked together distant nations.

The idea in building such an immense vessel was, that she should be able to carry sufficient coal for a voyage to Australia and back, besides a large cargo, and a great number of passengers; her proposed accommodation for the latter being 4,000, and, on an emergency, for 10,000 soldiers. The *Great Eastern* was a fine ship in many ways, and her design contained some very valuable features in addition to its faults. Had she been allowed to run on the long distance trades, for which she was designed, she might have been a great success, instead of which she proved a great financial failure. It was not until 1899 that her dimensions were exceeded. In 1887 she was sold to ship-breakers and was broken up in the Mersey. When the sealed double bottom was opened the skeleton of a man (a riveter who was reported missing during her building) was found in one of the compartments, and superstitious sailor-men explained her bad luck by recalling that it was always unlucky to carry a corpse on board ship.

In those years when its ships were on the crest of the

wave of prosperity, the chief sources of the export wealth of the United States were agricultural. From 1851 to 1860 the products of American farms and plantations—wheat, flour, rice, hops, apples, corn and cornmeal, tobacco, cotton, potatoes, sugar raw and refined, cheese, cattle and beef and pork products —constituted about eighty-two per cent of all the exports from the United States. The value of these agricultural exports increased from nearly 147,000,000 dollars in 1851 to more than 261,000,000 dollars in 1860. American exports to Europe grew in value from about 36,000,000 dollars in 1821 to nearly 250,000,000 dollars in 1860, and those to all other parts of the world from 19,000,000 dollars to 84,000,000 dollars in the same interval. These exports were, of course, paid for by the imports of hardware, silks, oils, wines, teas, coffees, spices, and so forth, to the United States. At the outset, in 1821, the figures balanced almost evenly, but in 1860, the imports exceeded the exports in value by about 20,000,000 dollars.

During the early years of the nation's life and for a brief period after 1815, discriminating duties favoring American vessels were in force. These duties were laid, however, in retaliation for similar duties exacted by other nations and were justifiable for this purpose. Discrimination, however, as a means of building up a merchant marine is an acknowledged failure and has everywhere been abandoned in favor of reciprocity.

Every phase of national progress, every forge ahead in economic development, every click of advance in commerce and industry, was put in motion through the activity of sailing ships and sailormen. This bold statement will not even quiver when one looks into the retrospect of exploration, colonization and legitimate trading abroad, as distinguished from crude barter.

It can be truly said that the square-rigged sailing ships "held on" as "cargo-carriers," for a long time against the more modern steam vessel, and they disappeared so suddenly as to make their passing almost imperceptible as compared with their long period of usefulness and activity. Like the brilliantly colored autumn leaves they were most beautiful in their dying moments, and as they passed away they had reached the acme of their perfection. They had lived their life, but up to the last these thoroughbreds of the sea were ever ready to go. Their race was run, their sun was setting, and like the American Indians in their picturesqueness, they seemed to hinder progress—progress for which they had done so much in shaping the world's destiny. The old sailors in their superstition believed their ships to be human and sensitive, and today they would say they "died hard" and were unappreciated in their fight for existence. They are gone, but they have left behind them a halo of sentiment and record of achievement.

The port of New York drew its adolescent strength from the marvelous feats in voyaging which were common in the days of sail. Yet how little do we appreciate the pioneering which was done in maritime affairs in the United States. Are we not too apt to follow the academic view, and lay all the laurels in distant Tyre and Carthage, where the Phœnicians developed sea sense and sagacity?

Let us remember the American shipbuilders who built ships, that for swiftness, were objects of pride to ourselves, and of envy to other maritime powers. Those fairy-footed argosies were only outrivaled by the advent of iron construction. Think also of the captains and mates who thrashed those white-winged beauties around the Cape of Good Hope and the Horn. Try to realize what American seafarers were up against in the days when vessels, cargoes, and lives depended on the skillful manipulation of ropes and sails. Wireless signaling was unknown, coastal life saving stations were few, uncharted dangers frequently proved their location by seizing a vessel in their cruel fangs!

Even to begin to understand the evolutionary steps which this writing touches on, the reader must be reminded of a progressive principle, which could be termed the root of marine logic. It can be expressed thus: Broadly speaking, industry means manufacturing things, but sea commerce means the sale and world wide distribution of those commodities. Exporting and importing are the arteries and veins of a nation or country. It is the traffic which ebbs and flows in those channels that

East River Waterfront in the Clipper Era.

makes, and measures, much of the wealth of these United States.

The percentage of American merchandise carried in the foreign trade of American ships fell off somewhat, it is true, in the years from 1831 to 1860. The benefits of the policy of reciprocity, and of the activity and energy of American shipping interests, was to be found in the constantly increasing tonnage of ocean-going vessels flying the United States flag, a large percentage of which was engaged in the carrying trade between foreign countries, and rarely entered or cleared from an American port. Thus in the forty years from 1820 to 1860 the tonnage of the United States shipping registered for the foreign trade increased fourfold, while that of the entire British Empire only doubled.

The following table illustrates the growth of foreign shipping at the Port of New York from 1821 to 1882, and is especially interesting on account of the light it throws on the transition from sail to steam navigation:

Foreign Arrivals

Years	Steamers	Ships	Barks	Brigs	Schooners	Total
1821	..	260	4	315	331	912
1844	3	471	351	929	451	2,208
1855	163	767	715	1,148	597	3,391
1859	268	713	872	1,269	885	4,007
1865	455	625	1,420	1,184	1,042	4,706
1877	1,074	389	2,234	1,076	1,451	6,244
1879	1,591	681	3,234	1,028	1,548	8,077
1882	1,945	407	1,857	896	1,371	6,476

The whole question of the survival of our steam fleet in the deep-sea trade between 1846 and 1860 was a question of national protection or the lack of it. One of the greatest New York merchants and shipowners of his time, Abiel Abbott Low, has left this authoritative statement of the cause that ruined the American merchant marine, and of the remedy that would have saved it:

"My own belief is that the policy of England in subsidizing lines of steamers to the various ports of the world, had given her a prestige which is almost insuperable.... My own impression is that large subsidies, while they would cost the government something in the beginning, would cost the government nothing in the end.

"I only know the English have always, in peace and war, manifested a determination to hold the supremacy on the ocean, and the supremacy which they acquired by arms in war they have in peace acquired by subsidies. They have deliberately and intentionally driven the Americans from the ocean by paying subsidies which they knew our Congress would not pay. I believe it has been the deliberate purpose on the part of England to maintain her supremacy upon the ocean by paying larger subsidies than any other nation, as long as subsidies were necessary to preserve their control.

"I believe that when the Collins line was running, the subsidy to the Cunard line was renewed for the express purpose to enable it to run off the Collins line. It was renewed several years before the expiration of the subsidy granted, so that the Cunard line might enter upon contracts for new ships, and a committee of the English Parliament, similar to this committee, was employed to make the most minute investigation into the matter. It was after the most careful inquiry by that committee that the contract with the Cunard was renewed for the express purpose of enabling that line to run the American steamers from the ocean; and they have driven us from the ocean by that policy just as effectually as they ever did drive an enemy from the ocean by their guns."

In December, 1860, the parade of Southern States out of the Union began, with South Carolina in the fore; other slave-holding States followed in rapid succession. Business was arrested, and the winter was one of apprehension and distress.

During the late forties and until the outbreak of our Civil War, the most interesting and important period in the history of the United States merchant service, New York merchants and shipping men saw our deep sea tonnage mount to its highest figure, and they witnessed with dismay the melancholy decline. It was a period which opened with the promise of renewed and absolute American mastery of ocean-carrying, and it closed beneath the shadows of actual or impending defeat. While it is a hasty and superficial judgment, which dates the shrinkage of the American Merchant Marine

The Third Period

from the war of 1861-65, yet that was one of the powerful contributive causes. But several years before the first shots were fired against the S.S. *Star of the West*, when she was hastening to the relief of Fort Sumter, the decline in shipbuilding and ship-owning had set in. The decay of our sea-borne commerce would have gone on if the Civil War had never been fought, but the proportions it assumed would never have been reached, if the war had never been contemplated.

When the war became a certainty the wharves of New York were worth seeing. There was a busy expectation and more haste than discretion, especially in the dispatching of South-bound vessels. The schooners which were regular as clockwork in their appearance on the East River were hurried away to their home ports, not to return. They were wanted in the Confederacy, and their captains were generally willing to take chances on the "other side." Bermuda, Cuba and foreign ports were havens of safety and profit, when the light craft, laden with cotton or naval stores, could be run out through the narrowing lines of the blockading squadron. Many vessels which were owned jointly by Northern and Southern owners were chartered for use in the quartermaster's department, or sold at an appraised value to the government. New York tug boats were taken under charters, with the accruing clause, and when there was little to do in New York harbor found ready employment elsewhere, from Washington and Baltimore, down to Virginia and North Carolina waters.

The American people are not less tenacious than the British people, or less enterprising, or less patriotic. Our merchant marine in that critical period of transition from sail to steam was as truly and directly the victim of the feud between the States as was that fair region of Virginia meadow, hill, and forest between the Potomac and Richmond, the scene of the death-grapple of the two mighty armies from 1861 to 1865.

The Civil War caused a halt in American overseas steamship operation, as the vessels were commandeered for transport service and it was not until 1866 that American trans-Atlantic steamship operation was resumed by the North American Lloyds, organized by Ruger Brothers, William H. Webb, E. W. Barstow and others, which purchased the steamers

Atlantic, Baltic and *Western Metropolis,* supplemented by the chartered steamers *Ericsson, Merrimac, Mississippi* and *Northern Light* for operation between New York and Bremen, calling at Southampton.

Mistaken measures, bad administration, unfortunate sectional strife, civil war, and party spirit set at naught the work of the fathers under the Constitution, so our ocean navigation and active commerce soon stood far below the proportions complained of by the patriots of 1789, when the retaking of our equitable share of international trade and transportation was the redeeming work of America's early statesmen.

PART IX

THE AFTERMATH

1861—1914

(FROM THE COMMENCEMENT OF THE CIVIL WAR TILL OUTBREAK OF THE WORLD WAR, AUGUST 1914)

IX

MELANCHOLY SILENCE AND INACTIVITY ALONG NEW YORK'S WATERFRONT—AFTER THE CIVIL WAR EVERYTHING CHANGED—THE WAR AND LEGISLATION WHICH FOLLOWED GAVE OUR MERCHANT MARINE ENTERPRISE HARD BLOWS—WHY THE AMERICAN LOST HIS LEADERSHIP UPON THE SEA—THE DECADENCE OF AMERICAN SHIPBUILDING TRACEABLE TO A VARIETY OF CAUSES—STRUGGLE BETWEEN AMERICAN SAILING PACKET LINES AND STEAMSHIPS WAS AN ANIMATED ONE—WILLIAMS AND GUION LINE—A SAILING VESSEL'S FAST VOYAGE ACROSS THE ATLANTIC JUST BEFORE WOODEN SHIPS WERE WITHDRAWN—STEAMSHIPS *ALASKA* AND *OREGON*—CONGRESS REFUSES A PATRIOTIC AMERICAN SHIPOWNER PERMISSION TO SAIL HIS FLEET UNDER THE AMERICAN FLAG—OUR CIVIL WAR PRACTICALLY CLOSED THE TRANSITION FROM SAIL TO STEAM; WHAT THE FORCE OF COMMERCIAL CIRCUMSTANCES HAD NEARLY CONSUMMATED, CONFEDERATE CRUISERS FINISHED—FACTORS THAT CONTRIBUTED TO THE STRIKING OF THE AMERICAN FLAG ON DEEP WATER—THE GREAT WAR FOUND US WITHOUT A MERCHANT MARINE—WE BUILD ONE AT GREAT COST—SHORTLY AFTER WAR IS ENDED, WE SCATTER, DESTROY OR GIVE AWAY OUR SHIPS—TO SUCCESSFULLY MAINTAIN A MERCHANT MARINE, ALL AMERICANS MUST BE SHIP-MINDED!

IF ONE did not wander through the neighborhood of the docks, one would never suspect that the old town of New York had ever suffered reverses. Where formerly the broad wharves swarmed with "lumpers" or longshoremen, busily unloading the cargo of tea, nankeens, silks and china goods, or heaping the docks with rum, sugar, molasses and coffee, there arise pyramids of dilapidated hogsheads and boxes, rusty and old stevedore gear, and so forth. The hoarse orders of the landing have given place to a silence, broken only by the distant hum of the great metropolis to the north and westward, punctuated by the tremolo of a paddle-wheel steamboat treading its way up or down the East River, and filling the air, once redolent with foreign spices, with the stench of steam from its exhaust and bilge water, as she maneuvers alongside one of the piers along South Street.

After the war everything changed! Reconstruction elsewhere led to reconstruction of the shipping. The fast-sailing clippers had been wearing themselves out by hard-pressed voyages; many had fallen prey to the Confederate cruisers, and were destined to be the basis of claims growing out of the Geneva Award, and many had for safety changed ownership while in foreign countries, and found a living in far-off waters under another flag. Steamers which had survived the arduous requirements of the government service were to be had cheap. Vessel owners who were early on hand when the war broke out had grown rich by the sale or charter of their craft, and were willing to take second-hand boats at auction prices when the government offered bargains. Many of the Southern trade houses were extinct; others were crippled financially beyond resuscitation. The trade at home ports for Southern productions had fallen into new hands. The schooners gave way to small, moderately fast steamers. Fernandina, Charleston, Savannah, Galveston, Wilmington, Newbern, Norfolk found these steamers entering their waters instead of the "fore-and-afters," and the schooner became the exception, not the rule. Nearly ten years of inattention gave American shipping a chance to die out. The war and the legislation which followed it gave our merchant marine enterprise hard blows. There was little encouragement, and certainty was dimmed by constant additions to the fleet of ocean wanderers from foreign ports.

Why did the American lose his leadership upon the sea? Because of the passing of the sailing ship, is commonly given as the reason, but this is superficial. The same men who gained renown in sail could gain renown in steam.

The decadence of American shipbuilding is undoubtedly traceable to a variety of causes. Just as America had the "boom" in building wooden ships between eighty and ninety years ago, so Great Britain during the decade 1870-80 virtually enjoyed a monopoly in building iron steamships. The Clyde was supreme. It was somewhat less than ninety years ago when steamers began with anything like regularity to enter into competition with sailing packets for the foreign trade. For a number of years the latter held out stoutly for supremacy, and it was not until well along in the fifties that they acknowledged themselves beaten. When the change from sail to steam became inevitable, America made at least one determined effort to meet the issue in the establishment of the Collins Line of home built steamships. These craft were models in their day, stout and fast, but the line failed to perpetuate itself, and then England carried all before her. The struggle between the American packet lines and the continually growing steamship lines for a number of years was an animated one.

The Williams and Guion Black Star Line of packets, for example, was not withdrawn until about 1866 to give place to the Black Star Line of Steamships, including such magnificent specimens of capacity and speed as the *Alaska* and *Arizona*. And it may be noted here that just before the wooden ships were withdrawn one of the Black Star Line, the *Adelaide*, Captain Robert Cutting, made the voyage from New York to Liverpool in twelve days and eight hours, the fastest on record for a sailing vessel. The *Adelaide*, of course, was a New York built ship; a medium clipper launched in 1854, by A. C. Bell, son of Jacob Bell.

That the *Adelaide* was a fast ship is unquestioned, but the published statement respecting this unusual run cannot be substantiated.

In a few months the *Oregon* was added to the list, a monster of 8,000 tons' burden, and it was fondly anticipated by the Williams and Guion people that she would be able to improve on the *Alaska's* time, of six days eighteen hours and thirty-seven minutes from New York to Queenstown, and seven days one hour and fifty minutes from Queenstown to New York. Some time after the close of the war Mr. Williams, in the fervor of a white-heat patriotism, went before the bar of Congress and asked permission to sail the fleet of his company under the American flag, but, under the fear of establishing a "dangerous precedent," the request was politely refused, so they went and added glory to the British ensign for several years.

The Civil War practically closed the transition from sail to steam for freight and passenger traffic between Europe and America. And what the force of commercial circumstances had nearly consummated, the Confederate cruisers practically finished, for they dealt American shipping a blow from which it never fully recovered.

Then, again, the change from wood to iron and later to steel and the unpreparedness of this country for that change, sounded the deathknell of the sailing ship. Big units of capital that had been derived from maritime interests, realizing that the day of iron and steam had come, were won away from the sea. Our navigation laws forbade building abroad, and in 1866, the United States was actually attempting to compete in the North Atlantic with wooden paddlers! Railroad construction, the development of iron, coal and oil lands and manufacturing, proved that the shore was competing with the ocean; the land was robbing the sea of its labor and Americans were compelled to realize there was no hope of regaining that supremacy of the seas which the Yankee ship and its Yankee crew had held for many years. Furthermore, the restrictive laws upon American ocean-going passenger trade proved such a warping influence that it is really remarkable how well the American ships were able to adapt themselves to these adverse conditions.

When every sea knew our flag, American vessels were the fleetest and the best, with iron men to command and man them. Our interest in shipping then kept pace with our growth in population and territory; and so long as wooden vessels were the only vehicles of commerce, and other nations refrained from heavily subsidizing their shipping, our merchant marine continued to be prosperous. The United States, with its extended coast lines on both the Atlantic and Pacific Ocean, and the outlook of its Gulf States upon the southern seas, is clearly destined for all time to be akin to the sea. And yet, as a people, we have been wayward and inconstant in the presence of this manifest destiny.

When the Great War found us without a merchant marine

deserving the name and we were obliged to turn our energies and our resources, without reckoning the cost, into a frenzied and intensive program of shipbuilding, to repair the reckless neglect of the years that had passed, we realized how short-sighted had been our persistent refusal to maintain our merchant marine upon a respectable footing. But this stern lesson was only partly learned. No sooner had the war ended than the fatal indifference began once more to manifest itself. The great fleet of merchant vessels we owned at the close of the war, we proceeded to scatter, destroy and give away. Somehow, the opinion became prevalent that the Government should get out of business; that we could shift the responsibility for maintraining a permanent merchant marine to private enterprise exclusively. We overlooked the fact that neither private capital, nor the American people generally, had yet been educated to an appreciation of the true value of the merchant marine as an adjunct to our commerce and a vital element in our national defense; and in conclusion we would add, that to maintain a foremost position as a sea power, Americans, east, west, north and south, must be shipminded, incurably maritime!

COMPLETE LIST OF MERCHANTS AND COMMERCIAL HOUSES, ETC., LOCATED ON SOUTH STREET IN THE YEAR 1852

(Taken from Doggett's New York City Directory for 1852. The only issue arranged by Streets and House Numbers—not Names.)

No.	Name	Business
1	Nehemiah Mason and Foote Solomon Foote	Liquor
	M. H. Mead	Clothing
	Samuel Noyes	Grindstone
	W. W. Townsend	Accountant
	Asa Blake	Refectory
2-3	Robert F. Sage	Commission Merchant
4	J. S. Whitney and Company J. F. Whitney	Commission Merchant
	Smith and Boynton Life Smith John Boynton	Commission Merchant
5	A. D. Baker	Cider
	A. M. Keeler	Measurer
	E. W. Dunham and Son Edward Dunham	Merchants
6	Sturges and Company J. J. Sturges J. S. Sturges	Commission Merchant
7	P. P. Demorest	Provisions
	J. J. Schoonmaker	Ship Agent
	William Schuyler	Ship Agent
	Durant, Lathrop and Company J. C. Durant	Ship Agent
	James McDonnell	Agent
	J. W. Burnham	Agent

Here Moore Street intersects

8	Alva Whedon	Agent
	H. J. Holmes	Agent
	Henry Arppen	Liquors
	Thomas Kimball	Agent
	C. C. Newkerck	Agent

No.	Name	Business
9	Lefferts and Benson } R. B. Lefferts Robert Benson, Jr.	Commission Merchant
	J. B. Wright and Company	Commission Merchant
	D. Ryder and Company } J. J. Ryder	Cider
10	C. V. Spencer	Commission Merchant
	Cowing and Company } J. A. Cowing	Commission Merchant
11	P. J. Nevins and Sons } J. R. Nevins P. J. Nevins, Jr.	Commission Merchant
	E. Fish and Company	Commission Merchant
12	B. Hook	Liquors
	Thomas Birdsall	Bowling
13	S. and D. S. Bloomfield	Ship Chandlers
	A. VanOrden	Harbormaster
14	I. H. Graft	Liquors

Here Broad Street intersects

15	William Parker and Son } Wallis Parker	Liquors
	Alanson Cash	
	L. W. Brainard	Agent
	Grain Measurers' Office W. M. Cahoone William Osborn J. G. Ketcham R. Cahoone W. Beach O. J. Smith R. Vaughan	
	M. Gray	Agent
	J. S. Conklin	Agent
	Flour Inspectors' Office C. P. Tappan Thomas Hadden John Marshall J. B. Oakley Daniel Brinkerhoff Henry Shields W. W. Vardley P. J. Chamberlin	
16	Wicks and Douglass } F. J. Wicks R. J. Douglass	Flour
	J. H. Redfield and Company	Agents of Swiftsure line
	N. VanSantvoord	Agents

No.	Name	Business
17	N. H. Wolfe	Commission Merchant
	I. H. Reed	Commission Merchant
18	Adams and Sturges ⎫ J. L. Adams ⎬ W. Sturges ⎭	Commission Merchant
	Clark and Coleman ⎫ S. M. Clark ⎬ E. W. Coleman ⎭	Commission Merchant
19	J. M. Fisk and Company ⎫ Josiah Fisk ⎬ Elijah Fisk ⎭	Commission Merchant
	Dwight Johnson	Commission Merchant
20	Dows and Cary ⎫ David Dows ⎬ I. B. Cary ⎭	Commission Merchant
	Edward Bill	Broker
	Charles Powers	Broker
	E. L. Bill	
21	Allen and Whittelsey ⎫ Joseph Allen ⎬ Elisha Whittelsey ⎭	Commission Merchant
	C. W. Wolfe	
	J. M. Williams	Broker
	W. L. Boyd	Commission Merchant
	J. D. Viall	Commission Merchant
	J. N. Coff	
	H. Beeckman	
22	Samuel J. Rogers	Commission Merchant
	W. S. Griffith	Agent

Here Coenties Slip intersects

23	Dominguez and Avezzana ⎫ Gregory Dominguez ⎬ Joseph Avezzana ⎭	Commission Merchant
	E. and W. Herrick	Commission Merchant
	Thompson and Hunter ⎫ A. K. Thompson ⎬ Marcus Hunter ⎭	Commission Merchant
	Josiah Jex	Commission Merchant
	W. A. Crolins	Sailmaker
24	S. W. Lewis	Commission Merchant
	I. B. Lewis	Commission Merchant
	Ezra Lewis	Agent
25	Gorham, Basset and Company ⎫ Ezekiel Gorham ⎬ Z. D. Basset, Jr. ⎬ W. J. Russell ⎭	Ship Chandlers

No.	Name	Business
	Foster and Nickerson	
	A. K. Foster	
	Joshua Nickerson, Jr.	Commission Merchant
	Lorenzo Nickerson	
26	Howes and Company	
	Mulford Howes	Commission Merchant
	Amos Howes	
27	J. O. Ward and Company	Ship Chandlers
	Oliver Bryan, Jr.	
	George Godfrey	Commission Merchant
	Nesmith and Sons	
	Henry Nesmith	
	James Nesmith	Commission Merchant
	J. J. Nesmith	
	S. M. Megie	Sailmaker
28	Merritt and Trask	
	W. H. Merritt	Ship Chandlers
	B. I. H. Trask	
	Brett, Vose and Company	
	M. W. Brett	
	C. L. Vose	Commission Merchant
	J. E. Brett	
	Edwin Coffin	Commission Merchant
	Francis Alexander	Commission Merchant

Here Cuyler's Alley intersects

No.	Name	Business
29	Smith, Wade and Company	
	C. W. Smith	
	William Wade	Ship Chandlers
	C. F. Brumer, Jr.	
	R. P. Buck and Company	Commission Merchant
	B. P. Sherman	
	W. J. Chapman	Blockmaker
30	Walsh, Carver and Company	
	Lewis Walsh	
	Benjamin Carver	Ship Chandlers
	J. H. Walsh	
	Eli Hoppock	Commission Merchant
	Tobias Lord	Commission Merchant
31	Scudder Hawkins	Clothing
	R. C. Read	Commission Merchant
32	Saltus and Company	
	Francis Saltus	
	A. N. Saltus	Iron
	Theodore Saltus	
33	Hargous Brothers	
	P. A. Hargous	Commission Merchant
	L. E. Hargous	
34–35	Aymar and Company	Commission Merchant

No.	Name	Business
36	F. C. Berte and Company / J. A. Pendleton	Commission Merchant
	E. C. Dean	Medicines
	Underwood and Wiley / Horatio Underwood / Edward Wiley	Commission Merchant
	N. L. McCready and Company / J. W. Mott	Commission Merchant
37	H. D. Brookman	Commission Merchant
	J. T. Martin	Towboat
	Merchants Pilots / Francis Perkins, Secretary	Pilots Association
38	Joshua Atkins and Company / Joshua Atkins, Jr. / Edwin Atkins	Ship Chandlers
	Ralph Post	Commission Merchant
39	Patrick Ford	Clothing
	Perkins and Delano / Joseph Perkins / J. W. Delano	Ship Chandlers
	A. G. Benson and Company / John Benson	Commission Merchant
	J. C. Connor and Company	Sailmakers
	Pillsbury and Sanford / N. O. Pillsbury / J. H. Sanford	Commission Merchant

Here Old Slip intersects

No.	Name	Business
39	Franklin Market	
	Police Station, 1st district	
	Robert Silvey, Captain	
	Samuel Gage, Jr.	Refectory
40	John M. Michael	Grocer
	Eagle and Hazard / Horatio Eagle / W. H. Hazard	Commission Merchant
	Jeremiah and Nathaniel Briggs	Commission Merchant
	A. W. Weldon	Commission Merchant
	William Hartman	Towboat
	N. B. Carney	Commission Merchant
	G. W. Blackstock	Gauger
	Timothy Kellog	Broker
41	J. J. Taylor and Company / P. V. King / N. W. Chater	Commission Merchant
	Youngs, Hawkins and Company / H. I. Youngs / R. H. Hawkins / J. F. Youngs	Commission Merchant

No.	Name	Business
42	Alsop and Chauncey } J. W. Alsop Henry Chauncey	Commission Merchant
	W. J. S. Ryer	Weigher
	Henry Coit	Commission Merchant
	Richard Sterling	Weigher
44	Moses Taylor and Company } P. R. Pyne	Commission Merchant
	H. A. Coit	Commission Merchant
45	J. H. Brower and Company	Commission Merchant
	B. B. Blydenburgh	Commission Merchant
	C. A. Heckscher	Merchant
46	Benjamin Richards	Commission Merchant
	William Whitlock, Jr.	Commission Merchant
47	Augustin Averill and Company } J. F. Joy	Commission Merchant
	Jonathan Thompson	Commission Merchant
	J. C. Lord	Commission Merchant
	I. C. Whitmore	Merchant
48	Daniel Curtis and Company	Commission Merchant
	Spofford, Tileston and Company } Paul N. Spofford Paul N. Spofford, Jr. Thomas Tileston E. S. Howard	Commission Merchant
	Joseph Foulke and Sons } P. L. Foulke Joseph Foulke, Jr. William Foulke	Commission Merchant

Here Gouverneur Lane intersects

49	Schermerhorn, Banker and Company } J. J. Schermerhorn Edward Banker E. H. Schermerhorn	Ship Chandlers
	G. S. Stephenson	Commission Merchant
50	William Aymar and Company } Samuel Aymar G. A. Degraw	Ship Chandlers
	John H. Talman	Commission Merchant
	W. H. Talman	Commission Merchant
	Manley and Embury } R. F. Manley August Embury	Distillers
	W. S. Root and Son } William Root	Weighers
51	Adams and Hawthorn } William Adams R. H. Hawthorn	Commission Merchant

No.	Name	Business
52	Crosby, Crocker and Company	Ship Chandlers
	E. Richardson and Company } F. S. Richardson	Commission Merchant
	J. W. Phillips	Merchant

Here Jones Lane intersects

53	Storer and Stephenson } Albert Storer E. S. Stephenson	Ship Chandlers
	M'Gaw, Foster and Company } J. M'Gaw J. R. Foster C. F. Stephenson	Commission Merchant
54–55	Howland and Aspinwall } H. E. Howland J. A. Aspinwall S. W. Comstock	Commission Merchant
56	Russell and Copland } Henry Russell James Copland	Grocers
	James Henry	Commission Merchant
	B. and J. H. Wood	Weighers
	J. P. Stanton	Commission Merchant
	M. M. Freeman and Company } H. C. Freeman	Brokers
57	Augustus Whitlock and Company } W. S. Whitlock	Ship Chandlers
	J. W. Elwell	Commission Merchant
	John P. Elwell	Broker
	Smyth and Clarkson	Commission Merchant
58	Merritt and Company } J. T. Merritt Benjamin Merritt M. F. Merritt	Ship Chandlers
	Hemmenway and Beveredge } W. J. Hemmenway James Beveredge	Sailmakers
	C. H. Church and Company	Commission Merchant
	J. B. Sardy	Commission Merchant
	Henry Glover	Chronometers

Here Wall Street intersects

60	Charles Felch	Grocer
	Badger, Peck and Company } Jacob Badger W. M. Peck	Commission Merchant
	Francis Church J. F. Goodridge	Sailmaker

No.	Name	Business
	John Rodman	Lighterage
	John Robinson	Painter
	J. B. Gager	Commission Merchant
61	Joseph Murphy	Grocer
	Stevens and Mott } S. G. Stevens } C. D. Mott	Commission Merchant
	Olney and Sessions } George Olney } G. W. Sessions	Commission Merchant
	Edwin Henry	Coal
	C. H. Pierson	Commission Merchant
	William Pierson	Commission Merchant
62	Hussey and Murray } G. F. Hussey } D. C. Murray	Commission Merchant
	Abraham Herder	Hardware
63–64	Goodhue and Company } R. C. Goodhue } C. C. Goodhue } Pelatiah Perit } R. W. Weston } H. Gray, Jr.	Commission Merchant
65	Foster, Elliot and Company } Andrew Foster } G. J. Elliot } F. G. Foster	Merchants
66	Olyphant and Son } D. W. C. Olyphant } J. D. Taylor } R. M. Olyphant } David Olyphant	Commission Merchant
67	Dunham and Dimon } Thomas Dunham } Frederick Dimon	Commission Merchant
	G. A. Johnson	Liquors
	W. R. Bertram	Ballast
68	Frost and Hicks	Commission Merchant
	W. J. Frost } Elias Hicks } Everett and Brown } S. K. Everett } E. B. Brown	Commission Merchant
	J. M. Hicks and Company } George Bell	Ship Chandlers

Here Pine Street intersects

| 69 | R. L. Lane | Sailmaker |
| | John M'Murray | Commission Merchant |

South Street

No.	Name	Business
	Alfred Ladd	Commission Merchant
	H. M. Nichols	Gauger
	Martin Brown	Merchant
70	Tucker, Cooper and Company R. S. Tucker W. B. Cooper W. H. Carter	Commission Merchant
	John Griswold	Merchant
	Alexander Wiley	Shipping Merchant

Here Depeyster Street intersects

No.	Name	Business
71–72	Nathaniel L. and George Griswold	Merchants
	J. Dowley	Merchant
73–74	Wetmore and Cryder W. S. Wetmore Samuel Wetmore, Jr. John Cryder J. L. Roberts	Merchants
	H. K. Corning	Merchants
	Collins Vose and Company Frederick Vose	Merchants
	C. L. Perkins	
75	Timothy Coleman	Clothing
	T. M. Dougherty	Liquors
	Harnden and Company	Commission Merchant
	Van Brunt and Slaight J. A. Van Brunt H. L. Slaight	Commission Merchant

Here Maiden Lane intersects

No.	Name	Business
76	Robert Kermit	Merchant
	A. Weld	Grocer
77	Antonio Aranguren	Importer
	Calvin Durand	Commission Merchant
	J. T. B. Maxwell	Ship Chandlers

Here Fletcher Street intersects

No.	Name	Business
78	Grinnell, Minturn and Company M. H. Grinnell R. B. Minturn Cornelius Grinnell	Merchants
80	Hicks and Company J. H. Hicks H. W. Hicks W. W. Howland	Merchants
82	W. W. DeForest and Company G. F. Thomas R. W. Rodman J. G. DeForest	Commission Merchant

441

No.	Name	Business
83	R. B. VanZandt	Broker
	W. T. Plummer	
	P. W. Byrnes and Company	Commission Merchant
	Edward Saul	Commission Merchant
	John Wendall	Ship Chandler
84	E. D. Hurlbut and Company } J. D. Hurlbut	Commission Merchant
	Lyman Allyn	Commission Merchant
85	H. L. Sill	Ship Chandler
	William Nelson	Commission Merchant
	Laytin and Sneden } William Laytin } Samuel Sneden	Sailmakers
86	W. and J. T. Tapscott and Company } Robert Lethbridge	Shipping Merchants, Emigration and Foreign Exchange Offices
	James T. Tapscott	Camphene, Alcohol and Turpentine Distillers and Dealers in Naval Stores
	Robert Lethbridge and Company	Ship and Cabin Stores
	Zerega and Company } Augustus Zerega	Merchants
	F. Bernier	Commission Merchant
87	A. Woodhull	Commission Merchant
	W. H. Furman	Commission Merchant
	Abrm. Fardon and Son } Abrm. Fardon, Jr. } William Fardon	Sailduck

Here Burling Slip intersects

88	Flanders and Geran } Benjamin Flanders } G. W. Geran	Sailmakers
	George Bulkley	Agent
89	Woodward, Ryberg and Fentz } Joseph Woodward } Charles Ryberg } John Fentz	Notaries
	H. A. Walton and Company	Hotel
	A. H. Stevens	
	H. L. Gilson	
90	Clark and Company } J. M. Clark } J. N. Clark	Notaries
	Morris Reynolds	Clothing
91	Charles Farrar	Hotel

South Street

No.	Name	Business
92	Meacham and Stow } G. L. Meacham } John Stow	Fruits
93	R. S. Williams and Company } Thomas Williams, Jr. } E. S. Potter	Grocer

Here Fulton Street intersects

| 94–103 | Fulton Market | |

Here Beekman Street intersects

104	E. Y. Foote	Liquors
	Brain and Mountain } John Brain } John Mountain	Agents
	Curtis Akerly	Fruit
105	Ashley, Fish and Company } S. B. Ashley } J. D. Fish	Grocer
	Sidney Green	Merchant
	New Jersey Pilot Office	
106	C. M. Terry and Company } N. M. Terry } J. Della Torre	Ship Chandlers
	William Cartwright	Sailmaker
107	Patrick O'Brien	Hats
	C. H. Rogers	Commission Merchant
	W. D. Murphy	Sailmaker
	George Bell and Company } Samuel Bell, Jr.	Grocer
108	Jacob Wilson	Ship Chandlers
	John Murphy	Cotton
109	D. M. Messerole	Ship Chandler
	Bromley and Wilson } William Bromly } James Wilson	Sailmakers
110	C. J. Sturke and Daniel Dornman	Grocers
	Cornelius Murphy	Cotton
111	Adam Hoyt	Ship Chandler
112	Saxton and Webb } John Saxton } C. B. Webb	Commission Merchant
	J. B. Haskins	Sailmaker
	Thomas Lockyer	Forwarding
113	John Fay	Liquors
	Isaac Vanclief	Commission Merchant
	Parisen and Janbrin } R. F. Parisen } G. L. Janbrin	Agents

443

No.	Name	Business
114–115	Burr, Waterman and Company J. S. Burr Stephen Waterman J. A. Burr	Blockmaker
	Slate, Gardiner and Company Oliver Slate, Jr. William Gardiner	Commission Merchant
	J. H. Lyles	
116	Silas Wright	Storage
	E. M. Hemingway and Company Horace Hemingway	Commission Merchant
	J. L. Houghton	Gauger
117	John Munson	Agent
	W. A. Tooker	Clothing
118	Winslow Ames	Hotel
	G. I. Seixas	Exchange

Here Peck Slip intersects

151	Peter Hoeft	Liquor
	Randall and Harris L. G. Randall Charles Harris	Agents
	James Swan	Exchange
152	W. A. Crooker	Grocer
153	E. Goodwin and Brother W. H. Goodwin	Tobacconist
154	J. L. Sanford and Company C. T. Goodwin	Bakers
155	J. H. Hobby	Liquors
	Patrick Draddy	Junk
156	Thos. Owen and Son T. J. Owen	Commission Merchant
157	W. J. Steward	Grocer
	O'Reilly's and Company J. A. O'Reilly Thomas O'Reilly	Distillers
	J. L. Norwood	Upholsterer
	John Josephs	Sailmaker
158	Lawrence Waterbury	Cordage
	S. S. Goodwin	Ballast
158–159	Gaunt and Derrickson James Gaunt J. T. Derrickson	Papermakers
160	S. and J. G. Lucas	Commission Merchant
	Charles Rose and Company	Commission Merchant
161	John and D. F. Meyer	Liquors
	Gerry and Horton T. A. Gerry Edmund Horton	Sailmakers

South Street

Here Dover Street intersects

No.	Name	Business
162	John Baker	Lawyer
	J. Wintringham	Grocer
163	James Lindsay	Grocer
	Edward Boylen	Liquors
	Armour and Bakewell }	
	John Armour }	Sailmakers
	Thomas Bakewell }	
164	Peter Hall	Liquors
	Morris and Ostrom }	
	Henry Morris }	Stevedores
	W. B. Ostrom }	
	J. C. Church	Notary
	E. P. Chaffee	Notary
166	Egleston and Battell }	
	Thomas Egleston }	Iron
	Joseph Battell }	
167	Johnson, Stanley and Company }	
	J. H. Johnson }	Commission Merchant
	E. L. Stanley }	
	M. B. Francis	
168	W. S. Babbidge	Grocer
	Edward Dayton	Gauger
	B. S. Van Tuyl	Weigher
	John Daniels	Sheet Iron
	John Davidson	Blockmaker
	W. P. Holland	Gauger
169	Williams and Hinman }	
	J. S. Williams }	Ship Chandlers
	W. K. Hinman }	
	Macy and Rich }	
	F. H. Macy }	Sailmakers
	J. H. Rich }	
170	Donovan O'Conor and Company }	
	T. Donovan }	
	M. O'Conor }	Junk
	James Hikey }	
171	Henry Dougherty	Sailduck
172	J. M. Reilly and Company }	Liquors
	Miles O'Reilly }	
173	R. F. Aitken	Porterhouse
174	T. J. Berry	Sailmaker
	Michael Glinnen	Junk
175	Collis and Mitchell }	
	W. E. Collis }	Ship Chandlers
	W. L. Mitchell }	

Here Roosevelt Street intersects

No.	Name	Business
176	N. T. Swezey and Company C. B. Prindle	Commission Merchant
176½	W. B. Sparrow	Grocer
177	W. A. Brown and Company D. S. Brown	Grocer
178	Jessup and Fox R. M. Jessup Charles Fox	Grocer
179	Harry R. Miller	Grocer
180	James Cleland	Flour
181	Underhill and Bool Thomas Underhill C. A. Bool	Grocer
	William Mallory	Grocer
182	T. P. Cooper	Grocer
	W. A. Walker	Commission Merchant
	Henry Camerden	Sailmaker
	Benjamin Fuller	Rigger
183	R. Jennings	Bowling
184	Medad Platt and Company J. L. Davis	Grocer
185	G. B. DeForest and Company Philander Hanford	Commission Merchant
186	A. B. and S. Davis	Flour
186½	R. I. Folger	Cooper
187	Hollenbeck and Steward C. H. Hollenbeck J. J. Steward	Liquors
	Smith and Beach —. Smith A. Beach	Pyrotechnists (fire works mfrs.)
	Henry Meyer	Liquors

Here James Slip intersects

No.	Name	Business
188	James Scott	Grocer
	N. F. Wilson	Sailmaker
189	John Smith	Junk
190	J. H. Abeel and Company G. A. Dunscomb	Iron
191	A. H. Badger	Grocer
	John Chrystal	Sailmaker
192	J. D. Cocks	Grocer
193	C. E. Thorn	Ship Chandler
194	J. and D. Westfall	Importers of brandy and wine

Here Oliver Street intersects

No.	Name	Business
195	G. M. K. Underhill	Grocer
196	N. H. Baylis	Ship Chandler
197	G. M. Smith	Commission Merchant
	J. L. Cooper	Boarding
198	W. H. Slocum	Refectory
199	A. H. Burrell	Sailmaker
	Dennis Hanly	Hats
200	John Hicks	Bowling
201	John Reed and Company	Liquors
	Daniel Comstock	
202	Nathaniel Bunce } N. R. Bunce	Hotel

Here Catharine Slip intersects

Catharine Market

Here Catharine Slip intersects

203	Jacob Duryee	Liquors
204	Joseph Munson	Liquors
	William Dalton	Grindstones
205	G. A. Kirkland	Grocer
206–209	J. J. Hicks	Storage
210	C. F. Codwise	Iron
	John Hadwick	Grocer
211	George Marinor	Blacksmith
212	John Bacon and Son } J. E. Bacon	Iron
213	George Turner	Shipjoiner
	Hermann Meyer and Company	Liquors
	Aaron Drucker	
214–221	Bonded Warehouse	
	H. P. Husted	Storage

Here Market Slip intersects

222	James Wilkins	Liquors
	J. L. Cromwell	Carver
223	O. C. Craney	Liquors
	John Neil	Painter
224	John Mitchell	Blockmaker
	C. and R. Poillon } Richard Poillon, Jr.	Shipwrights
225	John Carroll	Blacksmith
226	Leland and Beach } J. A. Leland E. P. Beach	Candles
	White and Lander	Riggers

No.	Name	Business
227	W. H. Bush	Liquors
	J. H. Elliott	Painter
228	Pettee and Mann D. L. Pettee Moses Mann	Iron
230	J. D. Westlake	Iron
231	T. J. Burns	Blacksmith
232	Wright and Roberts John Wright E. J. Roberts	Dealers in copper and Ship Chandlers
233	Westlake and Coger C. J. Westlake John Coger, Jr.	Iron
234	Peter M'Namara	Shipwright
235	James Harkness and Son Peter Harkness	Blockmakers
	Conklin, Hoyt and Son Daniel Hoyt	Blacksmiths
	W. A. VanNostrand	Blacksmith
236	J. S. Anderson	Carver
	John Fraser	Carver
	M. G. Hagadorn	Painter
	A. H. Doughty	Tinsmith
237	Judson and Burr W. W. Judson R. J. Burr	Blockmakers
	John Van Blarcom	Blacksmith
238–239	J. B. Hobby	Storage Warehouse
240	Thomas and Branch Robert Thomas William Branch	Grocers

Here Pike Slip intersects

No.	Name	Business
241	R. Lewis	Liquors
	J. J. Connolly	Painter
	D. A. Tooker	Weigher
242	Elijah Wilson	Shipjoiner
	Richard Thum	Blacksmith
	Westcott and Ferguson W. B. Westcott W. B. Ferguson	Blockmakers
243	J. E. Jennings	Shipjoiner
	F. Rogers	Waterproofing
	McPherson, Gray and Company Peter McPherson William Gray L. McKay	Shipwrights
244	Fletcher and Mount William Fletcher G. W. Mount	Boats

No.	Name	Business
	King and Smith ⎫ T. H. King ⎬ S. S. Smith ⎭	Shipjoiners
	Lane and Church ⎫ A. R. Lane ⎬ A. B. Church ⎭	Blacksmiths
245	E. Buckman and Company	Shipwrights
246	William Holland	Porterhouse
247	D. and W. Morrow	Boats
	I. Hall and Company ⎬ W. S. Phelps	Blacksmiths
248	John Weeden	Carver
	W. H. Wright	Blacksmith
249	Otto Kohler	Liquors
250	C. L. Ingersoll	Boats
251	Charles and R. S. Roberts	Lime
	Phillips and Cabre ⎫ —. Phillips ⎬ Alexander Cabre ⎭	Riggers
252	Edsall and Bryan ⎫ James Edsall ⎬ W. J. Bryan ⎭	Shipwrights
253	R. S. Place	Blacksmith
	C. J. Dodge	Carver
	Cornelius Van Stratton	Rigger
	John Verhoff and Company	Sailmakers
254	W. A. Freeborn and Company ⎬ J. F. Freeborn	Ship Chandlers
	Sectional Drydock Company	
	Hatcher and Dixon ⎫ Thomas Hatcher ⎬ Henry Dixon ⎭	Riggers
255	G. E. Bussey	Liquors
256	Storage	
257	Henry Jones and Son ⎬ H. H. Jones	Blacksmiths
258–260	J. L. Dannat	Lumber
260	Nelson Wolcott	Refectory

Here Rutgers Slip intersects

260	T. V. Brooks	Carver
	J. D. and Frederick Meyer	Porterhouse
	W. H. Barnes	Inspector
	James Gorham	Sailmaker
261	J. P. Brunjes	Ship Chandler
262–263	Bellows, Thompson and Company ⎫ D. Y. Bellows ⎬ George Thompson ⎬ C. N. Bellows ⎭	Oil

No.	Name	Business
	Lyles and Polhamus ⎫	
	Henry Lyles, Jr. ⎬	Oil
	H. A. Polhamus ⎭	
266	J. G. Macy	Storage
	Josiah Macy and Sons	Oil
269–270	New York Rice Mill	
	McMahon and Company ⎫	
	Michael McMahon ⎬	Coopers
	Edward McMahon ⎭	

Here Jefferson Street intersects

271	G. B. McCoy	Liquors
	William and Nicholas Sheil	Painters
	Z. S. Burrill	Sailmaker
272	Tiebout and Parker ⎫	
	John Tiebout ⎬	Ship Chandlers
	T. L. Parker, Jr. ⎭	
	Hendershott and Whitmill ⎫	
	George Hendershott ⎬	Shipwrights
	Francis Whitmill ⎭	
	Robinson and Adams ⎫	
	William Robinson ⎬	Riggers
	Samuel Adams ⎭	
	Sheldon and Young ⎫	
	W. H. Sheldon ⎬	Sailmakers
	James Young ⎭	
	C. Hartnedy	Junk
275	C. H. Carver	Blacksmith
276	William Dennistoun	Stoves
	Townsend Hendrickson	Grocer

Here Clinton Street intersects

	U. S. Public Stores ⎫	Storekeeper
	Seixas Nathan ⎭	
	William Alexander	Clerk
	Tobacco Inspection Warehouse	Storage
1–4	Jacob Duryee	
	Woolsey and Company	Sugar Refiners

Here Montgomery Street intersects

277	Pritchard, Wing and Company ⎫	
	John Pritchard ⎬	Grocer
	L. B. Wing ⎭	
	A. W. Barnard	Wood
	J. T. Barnard	
	J. B. and John Smith	Weigher
	John Parsons	Sparmaker

No.	Name	Business
278	Michael McManus	Liquors
	John Clark	Shipwright
279	John Tilton	Liquors
	M. T. Ruyon	Ship Chandler
280	Robert Benson, Jr.	Oil
281	G. S. Messerve	Liquors

Here Gouverneur Street intersects

    Richard Squires   Liquors

Here Jackson Street intersects

James Wilson	Liquors
—. Henderson	Stevedore
Nathaniel Reeder	Boatman
E. and J. F. Broderick	Lumber

LIST OF PIERS IN NEW YORK

December, 1817

East River

No.
1. South Side of the Battery—west side of Whitehall Slip
2. East side of Whitehall Slip
3. Moore Street Wharf
4. Broad Street Wharf, Exchange Slip
5. Delafield's Wharf
6. West side of Coenties Slip
7. Middle Pier of Coenties Slip
8. East side of Coenties Slip
9. Dustan's Wharf
10. Saltus's Wharf
11. West side of Old Slip
12. East side of Old Slip
13. Gouverneur's Wharf
14. Jones' Wharf, west side Coffee House Slip
15. Murray's Wharf, east side of Coffee House Slip
16. Pine Street Wharf
17. West side of Fly Market Slip
18. East side of Fly Market Slip
19. West side of Burling Slip
20. East side of Burling Slip
21. Fulton Street Wharf, east side of Brooklyn Ferry
22. Stevens' Wharf
23. West side of Peck Slip
24. East side of Peck Slip
25. Dover St. Wharf
26. Jones Wharf
27. Agnew's Wharf
28. Minturn and Champlin's Wharf
29. West side of New Slip
30. East side of New Slip
31. West side Newmarket Street Ferry
32. East side Newmarket Street Ferry
33. Pearsall's Wharf
34. Townsend's Wharf
35. West side Market Slip
36. East side Market Slip
37. Barnes' Wharf
38. Dunlap and Grant's Wharf
39. West side Pike Street Slip
40. East side Pike Street Slip
41. Clason's Wharf
42. Ackerly's Wharf
43. West side Rutger's Slip
44. East side Rutger's Slip
45. Rutger's Wharf
46. Gouverneur's Market Slip—Haymarket

(Numbers extending to Eckford's Wharf Manhattan Island to No. 56.)

CITY WHARVES ON THE EAST RIVER IN 1853

No.

1–2	Foot of Whitehall Street	28	Elephant Wharf, Foot of Dover Street
3	Foot of Moore Street		
4–5	Foot of Broad Street	29	India Wharf, West Side Roosevelt Street
6	West Side Coenties Slip		
7	Middle Pier Coenties Slip	30	Central Wharf, East Side Roosevelt Street
8	East Side Coenties Slip		
9	Foot of Cuyler's Alley	31	West Side James Street
10	West Side Old Slip	32	Foot of James Street
11	Old Slip	33	Foot of Oliver Street
12	East Side Old Slip	34	Foot of Catherine Street
13	Foot of Gouverneur Lane	35	East Side Catherine Street
14	Foot of Jones Lane	36	Judd's Wharf, West Side Market Street
15	Orleans Wharf, West Side Wall Street		
		37	Foot of Market Street
16	East Side Wall Street	38	East Side Market Street
17	Foot of Pine Street	39	West Side Pike Street
18	West Side Maiden Lane	40	East Side Pike Street
19	Foot of Fletcher Street	41	Between Pike and Rutgers Streets
20	West Side Burling Slip		
21	East Side Burling Slip	42	West Side Rutgers Street
22	Foot of Fulton Street	43	East Side Rutgers Street
23	Foot of Beekman Street	44	Foot of Jefferson Street
24	Stevens' Wharf, East Side Beekman Street	45	Foot of Clinton Street
		46	Foot of Tobacco Inspection
25	West Side Peck Slip	47	Foot of Montgomery Street
26	East Side Peck Slip	48	Foot of Gouverneur Street
27	Foot of Dover Street	49	West Side Walnut Street
		50	East Side Walnut Street

INDEX

Ackerley, Samuel, shipbuilder, 18, 39
Adriatic, Collins Line steamship, 299, 304
Advertising methods of old merchants, 148
Alabama, Confederate cruiser, 324, 333
Albion, first New York packet ship, lost 1822, 142, 143, 216, 217
Alexandria, Georgetown and Washington City packets, 146
America, ship (brought first elephant into this country), 18
America, yacht, 338, 339
American Merchant Marine, given a magical impetus by First Congress, 15, 133, 134, 131, 132, 150, 151, 153, 154, 159, 255, 256, 257, 341, 419; A. A. Low states causes that ruined, 420, 421, 422, 423, 424, 428, 429; causes of decline, 430, 431
American merchant traders, how they obtained insurance on cargoes, 59-60
American shipping, 5, 15, 49, 403, 404, 405, 418, 419, 420, 421, 422, 423, 424
American vessels were carrying over ninety per cent of American exports and imports, 1821 to 1830, 150-151
Ann McKim, Baltimore clipper, 209, 210
Arctic, Collins Line steamship, 201; launched, 298-9, 303; is sunk off Cape Race, 304
Arrow, New York privateer, story of, 81, 82
Antarctic, Collins Line steamship, 299
Aspinwall, Gilbert, merchant, 31
Aspinwall, John, master mariner and merchant, 31
Aspinwall, William H., 112, 240-2, 258-9, 284
Astor House, scenes at in the clipper era, 345, 346
Astor, John Jacob, 40, 49, 50, 51, 52, 53, 99, 165, 166
Atlantic, Collins Line steamship, 299, 303
Atlantic Cable, 325; laying of, 410, 411, 412
Atlantic, crossing in 1797, 20, 21, 22
Atlantic Mutual Insurance Co., 246-7; letter to commander of *Flying Cloud*, 330-2, 357
Auctioneers and auction or "vendue" sales, 150, 205, 206, 207, 316
Aymar & Co., merchants, 120, 121, 189

Aymar, Benjamin, 120, 121, 124, 125

Bache, Theophilat, 103
Baker's City Tavern, 138
Baltic, Collins Line steamship, launched, 299-300, 303
Baltimore packets, 146
Bank of America, 96
Bank of the United States, 106
Barker, Jacob, merchant, capitalist, biography of, 45-47
Barrett, Walter ("Old Merchants of New York"), 140-1
Battery boatmen, 124
Battery, when it was a fashionable promenade, 121-5, 295-6
Bayard, William, merchant, 30, 125, 138, 167
Beaver, John Jacob Astor's ship, 40, 49-52
Bell, Jacob, master shipbuilder, 175-7, 294; launches Collins steamship *Baltic* with ship *St. Louis* same day, 299-300, 342, 357, 358
Belvedere Club, The, 22, 23, 24, 25
Beneficial effect to American shipping of legislation by First U. S. Congress in 1789, 15, 18, 19
Bennett, James Gordon (New York *Herald*), 200, 216-7, 317-8
Bergh, Christian, master shipbuilder, 39, 42, 69, 70, 72, 163, 172-73, 179
Betsey, first vessel to carry American flag around the world, 1797, 20
Betsy, first vessel to sail from New York to Great Britain after Revolution, 4
Black Ball or "Old" line of sailing packets, 127, 128, 129, 130, 131, 137, 138; statement of passages, 153, 164, 183, 196, 197, 313
Bonaparte, Napoleon, 25, 49, 79, 80
Boorman, Johnston & Co., merchants, 193-4
Boston, British frigate which fought French ship *L'Ambuscade* off Sandy Hook, 16, 17
Boston packets, 147
Boston ships, 315-7
Bottomry Bonds, the earliest form of insurance, 60
Boulton & Watts, builders of the engines for Fulton's *Clermont*, 46

453

454 Index

Bowen, Captain Francis, called "Prince of the Slavers," 336-8, 362-76
Boyd, John J., shipping merchant, 167-8
Boyd and Hincken, 165, 166
British navigation laws, 10
British Queen, steamship, 214-15
British West Indies, slaves perishing in from 1780 to 1787, 10
Broome, John, merchant, biography of, 28, 29
Brown, Adam & Noah, 38, 39, 43, 69, 70, 173
Brown and Bell, shipbuilders, 175, 176, 177, 179, 259, 389
Brown, David, master shipbuilder, 175, 176, 177
Brown, Noah, master shipbuilder, 38, 39, 67, 69, 70, 71, 74-78, 176, 247
Brown, William H., master shipbuilder, 176; launches steamships *New World, Arctic, Boston* same day, 298-9; steamships *Pacific* and *Independence*, with steam up, 299
Brownne, Charles, shipbuilder, 37, 38, 174
Byrnes, Trimble & Co., 139, 407

Cadmus (Havre packet), 165, 169-70; first ship to hoist the Bethel flag, 254
California gold rush of '49, 241, 268-70, 272, 295, 312, 345, 377
California (first steamer to enter the Golden Gate), 278, 279, 312
Cameron, R. W., pioneer line of Australian packets, 381; houseflag, 407
Canal boats, 247-8
Canton, pioneer voyages to, 5, 6, 7, 8, 9, 10
Carnes, F. and N. G., merchants, 202, 203, 204, 205
Carpenter, Stephen, builder of frigate *New York*, 37
Celestial, clipper ship, 313, 314, 317-8, 334
Challenge, clipper ship, 311, 313, 327-8, 345, 396
Chamber of Commerce of the State of N. Y., 83, 242, 319, 320-23, 324-5, 326, 327
Champlin, John T., merchant, 112, 113
Chanties, 225-6, 295-6
Charleston packets, 146, 401
Chauncey, Isaac, Commodore U. S. N., 56, 67, 68, 69, 70, 73, 111
Cheese, exporting to England, 260
Cheeseman, Forman, shipbuilder, 36, 37
Cheeseman, Thomas, shipbuilder, 36
Cherry Street, sailors' boarding houses, etc., on, 413, 414, 415, 416, 417
China trade, 5, 7, 28, 94, 98, 201-5, 218, 235; "Hong" merchants, 263-5, 295, 312
Citizens' steamboat line for Philadelphia, Baltimore and Norfolk, 147
Clark, Arthur H. ("Clipper Ship Era"), quoted, 295; ocean contests, quoted, 347-9, 385
Clermont, Fulton's first steamboat, 46, 58

Clinton, De Witt, Mayor of New York, 44, 66, 67, 115, 127
Clipper epoch, 309, 310, 311; naming ships, 391
Clipper ships, American, 256-7, 289; sailing for California, 295-6; 315-18, 346; racing to California, 347-9, 350, 391
Coal, shipping to England, 259
Coastwise trade, 133-4, 145-7, 242-3
Coffee House slip fire, 25
"Coffin Brigs," British, 3
Collins, Edward K., shipowner, 168, 176, 197-201, 290
Collins, S. S. Line, 197-201, 303-4, 339; naming ships, 391, 403, 404, 422, 429
Colon, Gilbert the Poet of, Poem, 268
Columbia Insurance Company, 96, 97
Comet (afterwards *Fiery Star*), 311, 313, 333-5, 345, 393
Commerce at New York, 3, 4, 56, 218, 318; comments on, 377, 403, 404, 405
Commercial Advertiser (New York), 51, 52, 163, 184
Common Council grants relief to Irish immigrants, 19, 20
Congressional Acts, U. S., 15, 16, 90, 290, 291; March 3rd, 1847, 303, 402, 403, 408, 409
Constable, James, merchant, 24
Comstock, Cornelius, shipping merchant, houseflag, 407
Corp, Samuel, merchant, 23
Cotton, a deal in, 140, 141
Courier and Enquirer, 168
Courtenay, Capt. George W., commander of British frigate *Boston*, 16, 17
Crassous and Boyd, 150, 165, 167
Creesy, Captain Josiah Perkins, 330-3, 380
Crossing the Atlantic in 1797, 20, 21, 22
Cumshaw, Chinese customs duty, 9
Cunard S. S. Line and Samuel Cunard, 218-9, 276-8, 422
Cutler, Carl ("Greyhounds of the Sea"), quoted, 19; quoted, 296, 297, 298

David Crockett, clipper ship, 141; figurehead of, 398
Day's run, *Sovereign of the Seas*, 355; *Lightning*, 356
Dean, Capt. Stewart, 8, 9, 10
Decline in shipping, 408, 409, 427, 428, 429
de Forest, Emily Johnston, quoted, 106, 107; quoted, 194
Delafield's wharf, first dock along East River waterfront, 1799, 25
Depau, Francis, founder of Havre Packet Line, 165, 166, 169
DePeyster, Captain Augustus, 165, 166
DePeyster, Captain Frederick A., 209, 211-13
DeRham, Henry C., merchant, 165
Description of ship offered for sale in 1799, 24

Index

"*Devonshire*, Ode to the," 231
Dramatic line of sailing packets, 176, 197
Dreadnought, famous trans-Atlantic packet, 384, 385, 386, 395
Drew, Daniel, 282, 284, 289
Dry docks, history of, 180-2
Dunderberg, U. S. Government steam-ram, 314
Dunham, David, 136-7

Eagle creates sensation on South Street, 260
East India merchants, 91, 92, 201-205
East Indian trade, 91, 92, 312
East River, city wharves, in 1853, on, 453, 454
East River piers, December 1817, 451, 452
Eckford, Henry, master shipbuilder, 38, 39-42, 47, 67, 69, 70, 72, 73, 136, 173
Elephant, first ever seen in America, 18
Embargoes on American shipping, 17, 44, 106
Empress of China, first American vessel ever sent from United States to China, 5; sea letter for, 6
Ericsson, John, inventor, 340-1
Erie Canal, 61, 127, 144, 159, 182, 205-6
Experiment, pioneer vessel in China trade, 7, 8, 9, 10
Exports, early, of New York, 83
Extending our foreign trade, 16, 24, 153-4

Far Eastern voyages, early, 5, 6, 7, 8, 9, 10, 19
Field, Cyrus W., 325, 410, 411, 412
Figureheads, story about, 394, 395, 396, 397, 398, 399, 400
Financial panic, of 1837, 219; of 1857, 403, 404
Fire Club and when they were "stumped," 99-102
Fire epidemic in New York (1796-7), 25, 26
Fire insurance in Japan, how conducted in the eighteenth century, 26
Fireproof stores, introduction in New York of, 25
First American screw steamers to cross the Atlantic, 339-40
First Collector of Customs at New York under Continental Congress, 7
First legislation by U. S. Congress, 15, 16
First marine insurance company, organized in New York after Revolution, 59
Fish and Grinnell 113, 115, 117, 138, 139, 149, 236
Fish, Preserved, merchant, 113, 116, 138, 236, 237, 238
Flying Cloud, 239, 272, 329-33, 344, 350, 380, 397
"Flying Craft for San Francisco," up April 23rd, 1853, 379, 380
Flying Dutchman, clipper ship, 313, 350
Flying Fish, Boston clipper ship, 352

Flying Scud, account of one of the most remarkable voyages, 381-3
Foreign commerce, relative to, 15, 19, 90, 153-4, 266, 318, 319, 402, 403, 404, 405, 418, 419
Foreign shipping at New York, table illustrating growth of, 421
Foreign trade, exports, etc., 10, 16, 24, 150, 151, 403, 418, 419, 420, 421
Foster, Andrew, merchant, 194, 195, 384
Foster and Giraud, merchants, 194-6
Fox and Livingston, owners of Havre Packet Line, 166
France, preparations for war with (1798), 21, 22
Franco-British naval combat off Sandy Hook, 16; scenes after battle, 16, 17
Franklin, John, merchant and shipowner, 18
Franklin, steamship, 166, 280
"French Claims," 108, 109
French depredations, 80, 97
French packet service between New York and Lorient, 4, 5
Fulton (Havre Line steamer), 166
Fulton Market ("The American Billingsgate"), 251-3
Fulton, Robert, 44, 46, 71, 72
"Fulton the First" or "Demologos," 38

Galloway, ship launched in 1807, 42
Gamecock, Boston-built clipper, 396, 397
Garrick, Dramatic Line packet, 176, 219
Gazelle, clipper ship, 311, 313, 317-8, 345
General Armstrong, New York privateer, 80, 82, 83, 124, 144-5
Glory of the Seas, figurehead now in New York, 399
Goodhue and Company, 104, 105, 137, 148, 164, 196, 207
Goodhue, Jonathan, 103, 105, 119
Gouverneur & Kemble, merchants, 18, 23, 24
Gouverneur, Joseph, merchant, 23, 25
Gracie, Archibald, 32, 103, 108, 109, 119
Gray, William, Salem merchant, 103, 108
Great Britain's navigation laws, causes great suffering upon her West Indian colonies, 10
Great Eastern, steamship, 412, 417; why an unlucky ship, 418
Great Republic, largest clipper in the world, 323-4, 344, 355, 386, 387, 388, 389, 399
Great Western, British steamship, 214, 215
Greek frigate scandal, 31
Griffiths, John Willis, 175, 257, 259; re tonnage laws, 301, 302; delineates "head" of a ship, 394
Grinnell, Cornelius, 114
Grinnell, Henry, merchant, 238-9
Grinnell, Joseph, merchant, 115, 117, 138, 139, 237, 238
Grinnell, Moses H., merchant and shipowner, 235-8, 260, 346

456 Index

Grinnell, Minturn and Co., 113, 115, 117, 138-40, 207, 236-240, 259, 265-6, 329, 361, 380; houseflags, 407
Griswold, George, East India merchant, 92, 95, 96, 329
Griswold, John, shipping merchant, 137, 143, 163; houseflags, 407
Griswold, Nathaniel, East India merchant, 92, 96, 329
Griswold, N. L. and G., East India merchants, 92, 93, 94, 207, 312, 327; houseflag, 407, 412, 413

Havre packets, 149, 150, 165-8; second line, 166, 167, 172, 177
Henry Clay, Swallow Tail packet, 176, 253; wrecked on Jersey coast, 265-6
Herman, steamship, 274, 279
Hicks, Isaac, 32, 45, 46
Hoffman, Josiah Ogden, first in a line of great lawyers, 23, 24
Hone, Philip, celebrated New York diarist, 42, 259-60
"Hong Merchants," 263-5
Hope, pioneer ship in China trade, 6
Houqua (clipper ship), 177, 209, 259, 323
Houqua, letter to celebrated Chinese "Hong Merchant," 112, 113
House flags of New York merchants, 406, 407, 408
Howland, Gardner G., 111, 240
Howland, G. G. and S., 110, 111
Howland, Samuel S., 111, 240
Howland, William Edgar, 111, 112
Howland & Aspinwall, 112, 189, 207, 240-2, 257-9, 261-3; houseflags, 407
Hoyt & Tom, merchants, 106
Hudson River sloops, 125-127
Humboldt, steamship, 166, 280

Immigrants, 253; value of, 254, 389
Independence (packet), 389
Ino, clipper ship, 332-3, 401, 402
Insurance, origin of, 59
Invincible, clipper ship, 311, 313, 396
Irish immigrants, 19, 20, 118
Isaac Bell, Havre packet ship, 166, 300
Isaac Webb, Black Ball liner, 313

Jacob Bell, clipper ship, 323, 324, 399
Jacob Bell, pioneer New York tugboat, 184-6
Jefferson, President Thomas, 49
John Gilpin, loss of the ship, 94, 95
Johnson's Doctor, delineation of a ship, 4
Johnston, John, merchant, 194
Jones' wharf, 24, 214
Joseph Walker, clipper ship, 387; hull furnished litigation with City, 388

Kermit, Robert (Red Star Line of packets), 139, 140, 141, 361; houseflag, 407

King, James G., 119
Kingsland, D. and A., houseflag of, 407

Lafayette, General Marquis de, 169, 170
Lake Champlain, New York shipbuilders build warships on, 70, 71
Lake Erie, warship building at, 70, 71, 74, 77
Lambert, John, description of New York, 1807-8, 54, 55
L'Ambuscade, French frigate, 16, 17
Launches of ships, 18, 179-80; three steamers same day, 298-9; double launching, 299-300
Law, George ("Live Oak George"), 284-86, 288-90
Law, William, supercargo, 112
"Leave Her, Johnny, Leave Her," Chanty, 225-6
Lenox, Robert, member of Common Council and New York merchant, 20, 42, 138
Le Roy, Bayard & Co., 30, 31, 106, 111, 240
Le Roy, Bayard & McEvers, merchants, 23, 24, 25, 30, 31, 111, 167
Lightning, fastest ship that ever sailed the seas, 345, 356
Liquor, advertising imports of, 30
Liverpool packet lines, 138-40, 141-3; advertisements, 149, 174
Liverpool (packet ship), 176
Livingston, Schuyler, 192-3
Loeber, L. Elsa, librarian, Chamber of Commerce, quoted, 320-3
London *Illustrated News*, 294-5
London packet lines, 143; advertisements, 149, 172, 177, 230-5; naming ships, 391
London *Times* sounds an alarm, May, 1827, 150-1
Low, Abiel Abbott, merchant, biography, 323-7
Low, A. A., and brothers, 259, 294, 312, 323, 324, 325, 326, 327, 388, 396; houseflag, 407; makes statement of causes that ruined American merchant marine, 421, 422
Ludlow, Gulian, merchant-banker, 23, 25
Lydig, David, flour merchant, 126, 127

McEvers, Charles, merchant; one of the founders of the New York Stock Exchange, 23, 24, 25
McKay, Captain Lauchlan, 173, 346; biography, 352-7, 387
McKay, Donald, master shipbuilder, 173, 177, 195, 316; biography, 341-5, 346, 351, 352, 353, 355, 376, 386, 387, 389, 399
Manhattan Island—not Island of Manhattan, 37, 38, 43
Marine Insurance Company, first company that confined itself wholly to sea risks, 59, 119

Index

Marshall, Benjamin, founder of the Black Ball Line, 128, 129, 130
Marshall, Captain Charles H., principal owner of Black Ball Line, 196-7, 274, 360, 361; houseflag, 407
Marshall, John, Chief Justice of the U. S. Supreme Court, 286-7
Maury, Matthew F. ("The Pathfinder of the Seas"), 270-3, 383
Medium clippers, advent of, 402
Memnon, clipper ship, 395
Memorial of Sundry Mechanics of the City of New York, 43, 44
Memorial to President Jefferson and Congress, addressed by the merchants of New York, 48, 49
Merchants' exchange, 145, 150
Merchants of New York, 22, 23, 24, 25, 28, 29, 30, 31, 32, 95, 97, 123, 137, 138, 145, 189, 190, 319, 320, 326, 377, 406, 422, 423
Messenger, clipper ship, 357, 358
Minthorne, Mangle, member of Common Council, 20
Minturn & Champlin, 32, 42, 112, 113
Minturn, Robert B., merchant and philanthropist, 237, 239-40
Mobile packets, 146
Monteiro, Joaquim, merchant, 32
Montezuma, Black Ball packet, 312, 389
Morgan, Captain E. E., 143, 163-4, 229-35
Morgan, Charles, steamship and railroad owner, 290; biography, 291-4
Morris, Robert, 5
Morse, Samuel F. B., invention of telegraph, 162-3
Mumford, Gurdon S., 96, 97
Mumford, John I., merchant and editor, 190-2
Mumford, John P. & Co., 96
Murray, Mumford and Bowen, 96
Murray wharf, 25, 26
Mutiny on Black Ball packet *Columbus*, 211-13
Mutual Insurance Company, 119

Naming ships in days of sail, 389, 390, 391, 392
Narrows, the, 66, 84, 123, 124
Natchez, sailing records of, 261
National treasury, money collected for, in 1806 and 1808, at New York, 56
Neilson, William, 117, 118, 119, 120, 125
Neilson, William, Jr., 119, 120
New Orleans packets, 145, 146
New World, California steamship, novel launching of, 298-9
New York, advantages of its site, 28
New York against Boston ships controversy, 333-4, 350, 351, 352
New York and Boston Steamboat Line, via Hartford, 147

New York Argonaut's song of the days of 'forty-nine, 281
New York City in 1793, 16, 17; in 1812, 65, 66
New York, commercial growth of, 19, 90, 143-4, 309-10
New York Dry Dock Co., history of, 180-2
New York, great fire of 1835, description of, 186, 187, 188, 189
New York *Herald*, 200-1, 275, 358, 359
New York Insurance Company established 1797, 119
New York marine dry dock, 176
New York, mercantile conditions in, 10, 11
New York merchants dispatch ship *Betsy* to London, 1784, 4
New York, privateering, 35, 69, 78, 79, 80-83
New York, recovery after the Revolution, 7, 36
New York sends first vessel from this country to China, 5
New York shipbuilding, 19, 36, 37, 38, 39, 40, 41, 42, 43, 69, 171-2, 173-80, 199, 275, 278, 294-5, 298-300, 309, 315
New York shipping, 19, 56, 219, 420, 421, 422, 423, 424
New York shipyards, 171-2; observations of a stroller, 275, 309-11, 402, 403
New York waterfront conditions, 405, 406; when war became a certainty, 423; melancholy silence along, 427, 428
New York, U. S. frigate, donated by New York merchants, 37
New York's population in 1702, 7
New York's tonnage in 1812, 65
New World, steamship launched, 298; novel features, 299
Nexsen, Elias, owner of *Experiment*, 7, 8
Nightingale, the most romantic and interesting Yankee clipper, 335-338, 376, 397
Non-intercourse act, 61
Norfolk, regular line (packets), 146
North River Insurance Co. scandal, 47
North River Steamboat Company, 38
North River, steamboat (ex-*Clermont*), 46, 71
Norway and "Full Reciprocity," 151-2
Novelty Iron Works, 298, 299

Ogden, David, shipping agent, 195, 384; houseflag, 407
Ogden, Jonathan, 119, 125
Ohio, U. S. naval vessel, 40
Old City Dock, 7
"Old Line" (see "Black Ball Packet Ship Line")
Old New York, when the solid men of, gathered, 22, 23, 24, 25
Old Ship Line advertising in 1827, 148-50
One of the most remarkable passages ever made by a sailing ship, 381, 382, 383

Oneida, brig, the only war vessel constructed on Lake Ontario before War of 1812, 42, 70
Onrust or *Restless*, first ship built in New York, 18
Oratory, one of the finest extemporaneous retorts, 376-7
"Orders in Council" issued by British government, 17, 80
Oriental, clipper ship, 294, 295, 323

Pacific, Collins Line steamship, 299; lost at sea, 304
Pacific, first trans-Atlantic passenger ship (Black Ball Line), 128
Pacific Mail Steamship Co., 241-2, 278-80, 289-90, 319, 403
Packet captains, 226-8
Packet ships, 128-131, 133, 138-40, 141-43, 161-2, 163-5, 171-2; races, 208, 225-6, 259, 260, 273
Paddle-wheels, descriptive of, 287-8
Palmer, Captain Nathaniel B., 323, 388, 399
Panama (Isthmus) and Panama Railroad, 268-70, 284, 285-6, 289-90, 315
Panama, ships, Numbers One, Two, Three and Four, 94, 95, 328-9, 398
Paragon, Hudson River steamboat, 71, 72, 73
Paulding, James K. (U. S. naval agent), 167, 168
Peabody, Joseph, 103, 108
Peck Brothers, steamboat owners, 184
"Peep O'Day Boys," 123
Perit, Pelatiah, merchant, 104, 131, 326
Perry, Oliver H., commodore U. S. N., 71, 74, 76
Petersburgh packets, 146
Phelps, Thaddeus, merchant, 138, 139
Philadelphia and New York packets, 146, 147
Philadelphia, London "X" Line packet, 163-4
Phoenix, pioneer steamboat, 58, 135
Platt, Clayton T., ship owner, 357, 358; owner of clipper *White Squall*, 388
"Polizza" (policy of insurance), 60
Post and Minturn, 116, 117
Post and Russell, 116
Post, Henry, Jr., 116, 117
Post, Joel & Gotham, 32
Postage, rate of, between 1784-1792, 5
President Polk's message relating to discovery of gold in California, 267-8
President, U. S. frigate, 37
Prime, Nathaniel, financier, 119, 140
Privateering, history of, 78, 79
Privateers, 78, 79, 80
Prize fight and camp meeting, apropos a, 185-6
Progress and cosmopolitanism of the New York merchant, 91, 92, 319, 320

Queen of the West (packet), 176

Racer, clipper ship, 141; lost in English Channel, 386; figurehead, 395, 396
Races, ship; trans-Atlantic packets, 208-9; contests around Cape Horn, 347-9, 350, 351, 352; challenge by American Navigation Club, 396, 397
Rainbow, pioneer clipper ship, 175, 209, 257-9
Reciprocity, pros and cons of, 151, 152, 153
Record sailing passages: Trans-Atlantic, 14, 355, 385, 389, 392, 429; Canton to New York, 296-8; New York to California, 344; Australian, 383, 392; California to New York, 350, 393; Honolulu to New York, 355; Sandy Hook to Equator, 388
"Redemptioners" or white slaves, 26, 27, 28
Red Jacket, clipper ship, 392, 393
Reid, Capt. Samuel C., 82, 83, 124, 144-5
Reporter, figurehead of ship, 397
Resolute, blowing up of the tugboat, 186
Respondentia Bonds, 60
Riker, Captain Andrew, 80, 81
Robert Fulton (first vessel designed for ocean service), 136-7, 139
Roscoe (packet), 174
Roscius (packet), 176
Russell, John W. and Gilbert, 116, 117, 137
Rufus W. King, New York's pioneer towboat, 182-4
Rutgers, Colonel Henry, 69, 71

Safety barges between New York and Albany, 148
Sailors, 255, 256; sing chanties, 295-6; two deep-water sailormen look for a berth, 409, 410; where they lived in New York, 413, 414, 415, 416, 417, 420
Saint Line of packets organized, 140
Samuels, Captain "Sam" of the *Dreadnought*, 385, 386, 387
San Francisco glutted with merchandise, so ships diverted to trans-Atlantic trade, 393, 394
Saratoga, New York privateer, 80, 81
Savannah, pioneer steamship, 134-6, 273-4
Scourge, New York privateer, 82
Sea Witch, 259; record China passage, 296-8, 327, 345, 395
Senator, Bonanza steamboat, story of the, 281-4
Shaw, John, New York merchant, 23, 25
Shaw, Major Samuel, 5, 6
Shedden, Patrick & Co., 29, 120, 121
Shipbuilders, relative to, 172, 173-80, 256-7, 309, 310, 311, 420
Shipbuilding at New York, 17, 18, 19, 35-42, 66, 90, 159, 160-1, 257, 275, 309-15, 341
Shipmasters, American, 22, 132-3, 266
Signal stations, notifying arrival of ships, 123-4, 144-5, 168
Sirius, pioneer British steamer, 214, 215

Index

Slavery, re (white slaves or indenturers, Negroes), 26, 27
Slave trade (Africa), 56, 57; cruise of *Nightingale*, 336, 337, 338; voyage to Africa, "Blackbirds, Wool and Ivory in the Hold," 362-76
Smith & Dimon, 174-5, 176, 257-8, 278, 338, 389
Smith, Captain Frank, 357, 358
Smith, Thomas H., China tea merchant, 98, 99-102, 103, 138
Smith, Thomas H. and Sons, greatest tea merchants in U. S., 98, 99, 102, 103
South Street, merchants and commercial houses, etc., in 1852, complete list of, 432 to 450 inclusive
South Street, New York's street o' ships, 3; filling-in causes sickness, 19, 90, 92; topographical description, 150; scenes on, 247-50, 254-5; story long current on, 261-3, 295, 329; clippers loading, October twelfth, 1852, 358, 359, 379, 380, 383, 384, 394; inactivity after war, 427, 428
Sovereign of the Seas, Boston ship, 344, 346, 350, 351, 353, 354, 355
Splendid, Havre packet, too large for China trade, 174
Spofford, Tileston & Co., 137, 243-6
Stag Hound, Boston-built clipper ship, 315-7, 343
State Street and its former residents, 121-125
Steamboat Case, the famous (Gibbons vs. Ogden), 286-7
Steamboat race on Hudson River, between *Oregon* and *Cornelius Vanderbilt*, 288-9
Steamboats, early efforts of American inventors to attain success in building, 57
Steamboats, early, on Hudson River, 71, 72, 73, 126
Steam navigation, 57, 218-9, 319
Steers, George, shipbuilder, 181, 304-5
Steers, Henry, 180-181
Steers, James R., shipbuilder, 181, 304
Stevedores and longshoremen, 249, 250
Stevens, Colonel John, of Hoboken, 58, 135
Stevens, Commodore John C., owner of yacht *America*, 338-9
Stevens, Ebenezer, General, 29, 30, 42
Stevens, Robert L., inventor, 58, 135, 162, 338
Stoddard, Captain Henry, 139-40
Strikes, labor, along New York waterfront, 207, 208, 360, 361
Subsidies, U. S. Government, 290, 291, 303, 402, 403, 408, 409
Sun, old steamboat, 184
Supercargoes, 22, 97
Superior, packet ship, 173, 174
Swallow Tail Line of Liverpool packets, 113, 138-40, 197, 237, 249

Swallow Tail Line of London packets, 197, 237, 249
Sweepstakes, clipper ship, 351
Swiftsure and Towboats (barges running between New York and Albany), 148
Swordfish, clipper ship, 311, 313, 345, 352, 409, 410
Sylphe, first vessel in French packet service, 5

Talbot, Olyphant and Company, 97
Talcott, Noah, 48, 137, 148
"Taylor, John—A Scottish Merchant of Glasgow and New York," 106, 107
Tea, duty on, 93, 98, 99
Thomas H. Perkins, ship, offered for sale, 412, 413
Thompson, Francis, founder of Black Ball Line, 128, 129, 131, 164
Thompson, Jeremiah, founder of Black Ball Line, 128, 129, 130, 131
Thompson, Jonathan, Collector of the Port of New York, 102, 170
Tompkins, Governor Daniel D., the great war governor, 66, 67, 68, 69, 72, 73, 97, 247
Tonnage laws detrimental to American commerce, 300-2, 408, 409
Tontine Coffee House, New York's first insurance office, 59
Tornado, struck by whirlwind, 361, 362
Towing, history of early, at New York, 182, 183, 184, 185, 186
"T" rails, first shipment brought over by packet ship *Charlemagne*, 162
Trans-Atlantic steamship service, 303-4, 423, 424
Trans-Atlantic voyages, dangerous conditions existing in, 164
Trask, Captain Benjamin I. H., 228-9
Trials and tribulations of a marine reporter in 1840, 217-8
Two Brothers, Voyage of the snow, 20, 21

United States Government stops "White Slavery," 28
United States Hydrographic Department founded, 271-2

Vail, Thomas, shipbuilder, 39, 43
Van Rensselaer, General Stephen, 73
Vanderbilt, Commodore Cornelius, 287-91, 404
Varick, Richard, Mayor of New York, 19, 20
Victoria, "X" Line packet, 232
Voyage across the Atlantic, story of a, in 1797, 20, 21, 22

"Wandering Heir, The" (Charles Reade), 27
War of 1812, 49, 62
Washington, General George, funeral honors paid to, 32

Washington, George, President of the United States, 3, 10
Washington, steamship, 168, 274, 279
Waterman, Captain Robert H. ("Bully"), 261-3, 296-8, 327-8, 395
Water Street, sailors' boarding houses, etc., on, 413, 414, 415, 416, 417
Webb, Isaac, master shipbuilder, 173, 174, 176, 311, 342, 353
Webb, William H., 176, 179, 274, 278, 280; launches ship *Celestial* and steamship *Alabama* same day, 300; makes triple launch, *Golden Gate, Isaac Bell* and *Gazelle*, 300, 310-15, 317-8, 327, 328, 334, 351, 352, 377, 389, 396, 398, 423, 424
Webster Daniel, 286-7, 346
Westervelt and Mackay, shipbuilders, 274, 280, 389
Westervelt, Jacob A., shipbuilder and Mayor of New York, 177-8

Wetmore & Co. (William S. Wetmore), 235
Whetten, Captain John, 9, 166
"White Slaves" or "Indenturers," 26, 27, 28
White Squall, clipper ship, 177, 387, 388
Whitlock, William, Jr., merchant and shipowner, 137, 168-71
Williams & Guion (Black Star Line), 407, 429, 430
Wright, Isaac, founder of Black Ball Packet Line, 128, 129, 130, 164
Wright, Isaac & Son, 128, 145

Yachting, 338, 339
Yankee traders who did much for New York's prosperity, 44-48
Yellow fever epidemic of 1822, 137-8
Yorkshire, New York to Liverpool packet ship, 312
Young America, clipper ship, 312, 313, 314, 345, 350, 351, 377, 378; name changed to *Miraslav*, 379, 398